BUSINESS LAW

BUSINESS LAW

J. Scott Slorach MA (Oxon), Solicitor
Principal Lecturer in Law and Head of Corporate Training Design,
Nottingham Law School, Visiting Professor, Strathclyde University

Jason G. Ellis MA (Oxon), Solicitor
Principal Lecturer in Law and Head of Corporate Programmes on the Legal Practice Course, Nottingham Law School

Blackstone Press

Published by
Blackstone Press Limited
Aldine Place
London
W12 8AA
United Kingdom

Sales enquiries and orders
Telephone: +44-(0)-20-8740-2277
Facsimile: +44-(0)-20-8743-2292
e-mail: sales@blackstone.demon.co.uk
website: www.blackstonepress.com

ISBN 1-84174-237-6
© J S Barlow and A G King, 1993
First published 1993
Second edition 1994
© J S Slorach, J G Ellis, J S Barlow and A G King, 1995
Third edition 1995
Fourth edition 1996
Fifth edition 1997
© J S Slorach, J G Ellis, 2001
Sixth edition 1998
Seventh edition 1999
Eighth edition 2000
Ninth edition 2001

British Library Cataloguing in Publication Data
A catalogue record for this book is available from the British Library

This publication is protected by international copyright law. All rights reserved. No part of this publication may be reproduced, stored in a retrieval system, or transmitted in any form or by any means, electronic or mechanical, photocopying, recording or otherwise, without the prior permission of the publisher.

Typeset in 10/12 Palatino by Montage Studios Ltd, Tonbridge, Kent
Printed and bound in Great Britain by Antony Rowe Limited, Chippenham and Reading

CONTENTS

Preface	xi
Acknowledgments	xiii
Table of Cases	xv
Table of Statutes	xix
Table of Regulations	xxiii

PARTNERSHIPS — 1

1 Characteristics of Partnerships — 3

1.1 Introduction — 1.2 Relevant law — 1.3 Definition of partnership — 1.4 Nature of partnership and terminology — 1.5 Number of partners — 1.6 Capacity — 1.7 Duration of partnership — 1.8 Partnership name and publicity of information

2 Partnership Management and Finance — 7

2.1 Introduction — 2.2 The legal relationship between the partners (s. 24) — 2.3 The duty of good faith — 2.4 The partnership's finances — 2.5 The distinction between a partner and a lender — 2.6 Division of profits and sharing of losses between partners — 2.7 Payment of interest — 2.8 Partnership property

3 Liability of Partners to Outsiders — 17

3.1 Introduction — 3.2 Nature of liability — 3.3 Partnership and agency — 3.4 Persons held out as partners — 3.5 Liability of new partners — 3.6 Partners' liability in tort — 3.7 Suing or being sued

4 Partnership Disputes — 23

4.1 Introduction — 4.2 Dissolution by the court — 4.3 Appointment of a receiver — 4.4 Arbitration — 4.5 Expulsion of a partner

5 Termination of and Retirement from a Partnership — 27

5.1 Introduction — 5.2 Dissolution of partnership — 5.3 Retirement of a partner — 5.4 Death

CONTENTS

COMPANIES — 37

6 Limited Companies — 39

6.1 Introduction — 6.2 Corporations — 6.3 Sources of company law — 6.4 Registration — 6.5 Types of registered company — 6.6 Public and private companies — 6.7 Separate legal personality — 6.8 'Lifting the veil of incorporation'

7 Formation of a Limited Company — 47

7.1 Introduction — 7.2 Promoters — 7.3 Pre-incorporation contracts — 7.4 Methods of providing the client with a company — 7.5 Steps leading to incorporation — 7.6 The certificate of incorporation — 7.7 Steps necessary after incorporation — 7.8 Comparison of tailor-made with shelf company — 7.9 Change of name — 7.10 Change of objects — 7.11 Change of accounting reference date

8 Directors and Secretary — 61

8.1 Division of powers within a company — 8.2 Appointment of directors — 8.3 Retirement of directors — 8.4 Removal of directors from office — 8.5 Powers of directors — 8.6 Directors' duties — 8.7 Statutory provisions concerning directors — 8.8 Managing directors — 8.9 Alternate directors — 8.10 Shadow directors — 8.11 The directors and protection of outsiders — 8.12 The company secretary

9 Shareholders — 79

9.1 Introduction — 9.2 Registration of membership — 9.3 Powers and duties of shareholders — 9.4 Internal disputes – introduction — 9.5 Section 14, Companies Act 1985 — 9.6 *Foss* v *Harbottle* — 9.7 Actions by shareholders – procedure — 9.8 Section 459, Companies Act 1985 — 9.9 Just and equitable winding up — 9.10 Shareholders and profits — 9.11 Declaration and payment of dividends — 9.12 Restrictions on sources of dividends

10 Company Finance — 95

10.1 Introduction — 10.2 Issue of shares — 10.3 Share capital — 10.4 Financial assistance by company for purchase of shares — 10.5 Classes of shares — 10.6 The power to borrow — 10.7 Secured loans — 10.8 Registration of charges — 10.9 Priority of charges — 10.10 Remedies of debenture-holders — 10.11 Receivers — 10.12 Position of debenture-holders — 10.13 Steps to be taken by a lender to a company — 10.14 Alteration to the capital clause

11 Disposal of Shares — 115

11.1 Introduction — 11.2 Transfer of shares — 11.3 Transmission by operation of law — 11.4 Buy-back and redemption by a company — 11.5 Financial assistance

12 Company Meetings and Resolutions — 123

12.1 Types of general meeting — 12.2 Resolutions — 12.3 Calling a general meeting — 12.4 Notice of meetings — 12.5 Proceedings at meetings — 12.6 Written resolution — 12.7 Minutes and returns

TAXATION — 131

13 The Taxation of the Income Profits and Losses of Sole Traders and Partnerships — 133

13.1 Introduction — 13.2 Income profits — 13.3 The basis of assessment for income tax — 13.4 Losses under the income tax system — 13.5 Income tax liability of partnerships

14 Capital Gains Tax and Inheritance Tax on Business Assets — 143

14.1 Introduction — 14.2 Capital gains tax — 14.3 Partnerships — 14.4 Shareholdings — 14.5 Business assets owned by an investor — 14.6 Inheritance tax — 14.7 The purchase by a company of its own shares

15 The Corporation Tax System — 165

15.1 Introduction — 15.2 Calculation of profits – corporation tax — 15.3 Assessment – corporation tax — 15.4 Loss relief under the corporation tax system — 15.5 Close companies

16 Taxation of Retained Profits, Dividends, Directors' Fees and Debenture Interest — 175

16.1 Introduction — 16.2 Retained profits — 16.3 Taxation of distributions — 16.4 Directors' fees — 16.5 Interest on debentures — 16.6 Conclusion

17 Capital Allowances — 191

17.1 Introduction — 17.2 Plant and machinery — 17.3 Industrial buildings — 17.4 Other expenditure which attracts capital allowances

18 The Tax Consequences of Leaving and Joining a Partnership — 197

18.1 Introduction — 18.2 The tax consequences of the dissolution of a partnership — 18.3 The tax consequences of the retirement of a partner — 18.4 The tax consequences of death — 18.5 The tax consequences of expulsion from a partnership — 18.6 The tax consequences of admission of a new partner

19 Value Added Tax — 207

19.1 Introduction — 19.2 Registration — 19.3 Taxable supplies and the charge to VAT — 19.4 Accounting for VAT

THE EUROPEAN COMMUNITY — 211

20 The Right of Establishment, the Right to Provide Services and the Free Movement of Goods — 213

20.1 Introduction — 20.2 Establishment and services — 20.3 Limitations on the rights of establishment and provision of services — 20.4 The free movement of goods

21 Treaty of Rome, Articles 81 and 82 — 219

21.1 Introduction — 21.2 Article 81 — 21.3 Article 82 — 21.4 Enforcement of competition policy — 21.5 The Competition Act 1998

INSOLVENCY — 225

22 Bankruptcy — 227

22.1 Introduction — 22.2 The bankruptcy procedure — 22.3 The trustee in bankruptcy — 22.4 Effect of the bankruptcy order on the bankrupt personally — 22.5 Assets in the bankrupt's estate — 22.6 Distribution of the bankrupt's assets — 22.7 Duration of the bankruptcy and discharge of the bankrupt — 22.8 Individual voluntary arrangements

CONTENTS

23 Company Insolvency Proceedings — 241

23.1 Introduction — 23.2 Administration orders — 23.3 Voluntary arrangements (sections 1 to 7) — 23.4 Receivership — 23.5 Liquidation or winding up — 23.6 Liquidators — 23.7 Collection and distribution of assets in liquidation — 23.8 Order of entitlement to assets — 23.9 Dissolution — 23.10 Application to partnerships

24 Liabilities Arising from Insolvency — 259

24.1 Wrongful trading — 24.2 Transactions at an undervalue and preferences — 24.3 Transactions defrauding creditors — 24.4 Floating charges

SPECIAL TOPICS — 263

25 The Partnership Agreement — 265

25.1 Introduction — 25.2 Is a written partnership agreement necessary? — 25.3 The clauses of the partnership agreement — 25.4 Issues for an incoming partner

26 The Articles of a Private Company — 271

26.1 Table A — 26.2 Provisions concerning shares and membership — 26.3 Provisions concerning meetings of shareholders — 26.4 Provisions concerning directors — 26.5 Alteration of articles

27 A Debenture Document — 279

27.1 Introduction — 27.2 Terms relating to repayment and interest — 27.3 Terms relating to security — 27.4 Clauses designed to give the lender further protection

28 Shareholders' Agreements — 283

28.1 Introduction — 28.2 The advantages of a shareholders' agreement — 28.3 Drafting a shareholders' agreement — 28.4 Legal limits on the use of shareholders' agreements — 28.5 Enforcing the agreement

29 Company Searches and Company Accounts — 289

29.1 Introduction — 29.2 Official notification — 29.3 Company searches — 29.4 The duty to submit accounts — 29.5 Small and medium sized companies — 29.6 Profit and loss account — 29.7 Balance sheet — 29.8 Format of accounts — 29.9 Interpretation of accounts — 29.10 Solvency — 29.11 Profitability

30 Sale of a Business to a Company — 301

30.1 Introduction — 30.2 Income tax — 30.3 Capital gains tax — 30.4 VAT — 30.5 Stamp duty — 30.6 Subsidiary matters

31 Choice of Business Medium — 311

31.1 Introduction — 31.2 Risk of capital — 31.3 Expense — 31.4 Management — 31.5 Publicity — 31.6 Taxation – trading profits — 31.7 Interest relief — 31.8 Capital gains — 31.9 Inheritance tax — 31.10 Pensions and social security — 31.11 Raising finance — 31.12 Conclusion

32 Public Companies — 321

32.1 Introduction — 32.2 The distinguishing features of a public company — 32.3 Seeking and maintaining a listing

33 Business Contracts — Agency or Distributorship Agreements — 331

33.1 Introduction — 33.2 An agent or a distributor? — 33.3 Agency agreements — 33.4 Distributorship agreements — 33.5 The Competition Act 1998

34 Limited Liability Partnerships — 355

34.1 Introduction — 34.2 Key elements of LLPs — 34.3 Factors influencing choice — 34.4 The prospects for LLPs

Index — 363

PREFACE

Another edition; another preface. We sometimes let it slip that we 'write a book'. This conjures up images of sales on a par with J. K. Rowling, six figure advances and trips to Hollywood to negotiate with all the major studios about the film rights.

Ah well, virtue is its own reward.

Jason G. Ellis
J. Scott Slorach
Grand Cayman, July 2001

ACKNOWLEDGMENTS

Chapter 33 is based on the following articles:

'Distributorships — Low Risk Expansion into New Markets' by Michael Arnold (a partner in Evershed Wells & Hind) (*PLC Magazine*, Volume IV, Number 2, March 1993).

'Agency Agreements — New Protection for Commercial Agents' by Jeremy Scholes and Nick Blane (*PLC Magazine*, Volume IV, Number 10, November 1993, pp. 31–46).

'Agency Agreements — EC Competition Law, Drafting and Termination', by Jeremy Scholes and Nick Blane (*PLC Magazine*, Volume IV, Number 11, December 1993, pp. 39–48).

'Commercial Agents Regulations: Postscript — DTI's Last Minute Amendments' by Jeremy Scholes and Nick Blane (*PLC Magazine*, Volume V, Number 2, March 1994, pp. 39–44).

The authors would like to thank Michael Arnold, Jeremy Scholes, Nick Blane and *PLC Magazine* for their help with this chapter.

TABLE OF CASES

A Company, re (No. 004377 of 1986) [1987] 1 WLR 102	87
Aas v Benham [1891] 2 Ch 244	10
Allen v Gold Reefs of West Africa Ltd [1900] 1 Ch 656	276
Aluminium Industrie Vaasen BV v Romalpa Aluminium [1976] 2 All ER 552	254
AMB Imballaggi Plastici v Pacflex [1999] 2 All ER (Comm) 249	335
Associated Portland Cement v Kerr (1945) 27 TC 108	180
Australian Fixed Trust Proprietary Ltd v Clyde Industries Ltd (1959) SR (NSW) 33	276
B&Q Ltd v Shrewsbury & Atcham Borough Council [1990] 3 CMLR 535	216
Baillie v Oriental Telephone Co. Ltd [1915] 1 Ch 503	85
Beattie v E. and F. Beattie Ltd [1938] Ch 708	83
Bell Houses Ltd v City Wall Properties Ltd [1966] 2 QB 656	52
Bennett v Ogston (1930) 15 TC 374	186
Blisset v Daniel (1853) 10 Hare 493	8, 25
Bratton Seymour Service Co. v Oxborough [1992] BCC 471	83
Brown v Abrasive Wheel Company [1919] 1 Ch 290	276, 277
Browne v La Trinidad (1887) 37 ChD 1	75
Bushell v Faith [1970] AC 1099	64
Boston Deep Sea Fishing Co. v Ansell (1888) 39 ChD 339	68
Bushell v Faith [1970] AC 1099	64, 275, 284, 314
Clemens v Clemens Brothers Ltd [1976] 2 All ER 268	84
Const v Harris (1824) T & R 496	8
Cook v Deeks [1916] 1 AC 554	67, 82, 85
Copeman v William J. Flood and Sons Ltd [1941] 1 KB 202	180
Cotman v Brougham [1918] AC 514	52
Creasey v Breachwood Motors Ltd [1992] BCC 638	45
Dale v De Soissons [1950] 2 All ER 460	184
Davies v Braithwaite [1931] 2 KB 628	181
Deutsche Grammophon GmbH v Metro-SB-Grossmärkte GmbH [1971] CMLR 631	217
Duffen v FRA BO SpA [1998] TLR 379	339
Edwards v Clinch [1981] 3 All ER 543	181
El Ajou v Dollar Land Holdings [1993] 3 All ER 717	45
Eley v Positive Government Security Life Assurance Co. (1876) 1 ExD 88	83
Elgindata, re [1991] BCLC 959	87
English and Scottish Mercantile Investment Co. v Brunton [1892] 2 QB 700	111
Fairway Magazines, re [1993] BCLC 643	260
Fall v Hitchen [1973] 1 All ER 368	181
Ferranti [1994] BCC 658	249
First Energy (UK) v Hungarian International Bank, The Times, 4 March 1993	76
Floydd v Cheney [1970] 2 WLR 314	24
Foley v Hill (1848) 2 HL 28	306
Foss v Harbottle (1843) 2 Hare 461	40, 84, 87, 276
Garner v Murray [1904] 1 Ch 57	32
Glassington v Thwaites (1823) 1 Sim & St 124	10
Great Western Railway Co. v Bater [1920] 3 KB 266	181

xv

TABLE OF CASES

Case	Page
Griffith v Paget (1877) 5 ChD 894	83
Heintz van Landewyck Sàrl v Commission [1981] 3 CMLR 134	220
Hochstrasser v Mayes [1959] Ch 22	184
Hogg v Cramphorn Ltd [1967] Ch 254	68, 85
Jones v Lipman [1962] 1 WLR 832	45
Kayford Ltd, re [1975] 1 All ER 604	254
Keck and Mithuard [1993] ECR I-6097	216
Kontogeorgas v Kartonpak [1997] 1 CMLR 1083	336
Law v Law [1905] 1 Ch 140	9
Leyland DAF	249
MacConnell v E. Prill and Co. Ltd [1916] 2 Ch 57	114
Mahony v East Holyford Mining Co. (1875) LR 7 HL 869	75
Mairs v Haughey [1993] 3 All ER 801	185
Mercantile Credit Co. Ltd v Garrod [1962] 3 All ER 1103	19
Micro Leisure Ltd v County Properties and Developments [2000] TLR 12	71
Miles v Clarke [1953] 1 All ER 779	15
Ministère Publique v Willy van Waesemael [1979] ECR 35	214
Mitchell v B. W. Noble Ltd [1927] KB 719	180
Monolithic Building Co., re [1915] 1 Ch 643	109
Moore v Piretta PTA [1998] TLR 379	339
National Provincial and Union Bank of England v Charnley [1924] 1 KB 431	109
New Bullas Trading, re [1994] BCC 36	281
Nicholl v Austin (1935) 19 TC 531	182
Niemann v Niemann (1890) 43 ChD 198	19
Noble (R.A.) (Clothing) Ltd, re [1983] BCLC 273	86
Norman v Theodore Goddard [1992] BCC 14	67
O'Neill and another v Phillips and others [1999] TLR 391	87
Page v Combined Shipping & Trading [1997] 3 All ER 565	339
Panorama (Developments) Guildford Ltd v Fidelis Furnishing Fabrics Ltd [1971] 2 QB 711	76
Paramount Airways [1994] BCC 172	249
Pedley v Inland Waterways Association [1977] 1 All ER 209	63
Pender v Lushington (1877) 6 ChD 70	83
Piercy v S. Mills & Co. Ltd [1920] 1 Ch 77	68
Popat v Schonchhatra [1997] 3 All ER 800	358
Postgate and Denby, re [1987] BCLC 8	86
Powell v Brodhurst [1901] 2 Ch 160	19
Procurer du Roi v Dassonville [1974] ECR 837	215
R v Registrar of Companies, ex parte Esal (Commodities) Ltd [1985] 2 All ER 79	108
R v Royal Pharmaceutical Society of Greater Britain [1989] 2 All ER 758	215
Regal (Hastings) Ltd v Gulliver [1967] 2 AC 134	67, 82
Read v Astoria Garage (Streatham) Ltd [1952] Ch 637	84
Rewe-Zentral AG v Bundesmonopolverwaltung für Branntwein [1979] 3 CMLR 494	216
Royal British Bank v Turquand (1856) E and B 327, 119 ER 886	75
Russell v Northern Bank Development Corporation [1992] 1 WLR 588	275, 286
Salomon v A. Salomon and Co. Ltd [1897] AC 22	44, 301
Samuel Tak Lee v Chou Wen Hsien [1984] 1 WLR 1202	65
Sanderson v Durbridge (1955) 36 TC 239	182
Shuttleworth v Cox Brothers and Co. (Maidenhead) Ltd [1927] 2 KB 9	276, 277
Sidebottom v Kershaw, Leese and Co. Ltd [1920] 1 Ch 154	276
Stekel v Ellice [1973] 1 WLR 191	14
Tower Cabinet Co. Ltd v Ingram [1949] 2 KB 397	34, 35
Trego v Hunt [1896] AC 7	30
Trevor v Whitworth (1887) 12 App Cas 409	99
United Brands Co. v Commission (Case 27/76) [1978] 1 CMLR 429	222

TABLE OF CASES

Vacuum Interrupters Ltd, Re [1977] 1 CMLR D67	352
Williams v Simmonds [1981] STC 715	184
Wood v Odessa Waterworks Co. (1889) 42 ChD 636	83
Yarmouth v France (1887) 19 QBD 647	191
Yorkshire Woolcombers' Association Ltd, Re [1903] 2 Ch 284	107

TABLE OF STATUTES

Business Names Act 1985   5, 6, 8, 35, 58
   s. 1   5, 6
   ss. 2–3   6
   s. 4   6
   s. 4(1)(a)–(b)   6
   s. 4(2)   6

Capital Allowances Act 1990   191, 193, 194, 195
   Part II   193
   Sch. AA1   192
Capital Allowances Act 2001   191
Civil Liability (Contribution) Act 1978   17
Companies Act   41, 49, 76, 79, 81, 92, 96, 124
Companies Act 1948   53
Companies Act 1980   43, 117, 118
Companies Act 1985   39, 40, 43, 44, 54, 55, 56, 58, 60, 61, 72, 73, 90, 109, 110, 118, 120, 273, 276, 313, 314, 326, 359, 360
   s. 1   42, 49, 322
   s. 1(2)   321
   s. 3A   52
   s. 4   52, 60
   ss. 5–6   60
   s. 7   53
   s. 9   54, 58, 275
   s. 10(2)   54
   s. 13(3)   40, 55
   s. 14   82–4, 85, 86, 265
   s. 16   275
   s. 19   275
   s. 22(2)   80
   ss. 25–26   50
   s. 28   51, 59
   s. 28(2)–(3)   51
   s. 28(6)–(7)   59
   s. 29   50
   s. 32   51
   s. 35   52, 74, 105, 315
   s. 35A   73-4, 75
   s. 35A(1)   74
   s. 35A(2)(a)   74
   s. 35A(2)(c)   74
   s. 35A(4)–(5)   74
   s. 35B   74, 75
   s. 36C   48
   s. 42   59, 325
   ss. 43–47   325
   ss. 49–52   53
   s. 80   97, 129, 272, 291, 324
   s. 80(10)   97
   s. 80A   97
   s. 81   98, 323
   s. 88   98

Companies Act 1985 — *continued*
   s. 89   97, 324
   s. 90   324
   s. 91   97, 324
   ss. 92–94   324
   s. 95   97, 129, 324
   s. 96   324
   s. 100   98
   s. 101   42
   s. 117   42
   s. 121   97, 113, 124, 129
   s. 121(4)   113
   s. 123   114
   s. 125   104, 114, 277
   ss. 126–129   277
   s. 130   99
   s. 135   99, 114
   ss. 136–141   114
   s. 142   324
   s. 151   104, 120, 324
   s. 151(1)–(2)   120
   s. 152   120
   s. 152(1)(a)(ii)   120
   s. 153(1)   120
   s. 155   120, 121, 129, 324
   s. 155(2)   121
   s. 155(4)–(6)   121
   s. 156   324
   s. 157   121, 324
   s. 158   324
   s. 159   99, 162
   ss. 160–161   162
   s. 162   99, 162
   s. 163   162
   ss. 164–167   129, 162
   s. 168   162
   s. 169   162
   s. 170   100, 101, 162
   s. 171   162
   s. 171(3)   102
   s. 171(4)–(5)   102, 103
   s. 172   162
   s. 173   129, 162
   ss. 174–181   162
   s. 183(5)–(6)   117
   s. 185   116, 273
   s. 219   162, 163
   s. 226   92
   s. 227   45
   s. 239   70
   s. 241   292
   s. 241(3)   293
   ss. 246–249E   43

TABLE OF STATUTES

Companies Act 1985 — *continued*
  s. 263   91, 92
  s. 263(1)–(3)   90
  s. 264   114
  s. 266   292
  s. 270   92
  s. 275   92
  s. 277   93
  s. 282   42, 322
  s. 283   76
  s. 285   74–5
  s. 288   69, 73, 77
  s. 292   43
  s. 293   43, 325
  s. 303   63, 64, 72, 89, 128, 129, 275
  s. 303(5)   64
  s. 305   56, 70, 308
  s. 309   69
  s. 312   64
  s. 317   70, 72
  s. 318   70, 73
  s. 319   72, 129
  s. 320   71, 308
  s. 322A   74
  s. 324   56, 70, 73
  ss. 325–328   56
  s. 330   71, 173, 324
  ss. 331–336   71
  s. 337   71, 129
  ss. 338–347   71
  s. 348   55, 59, 308
  s. 349   55, 59
  s. 351   56, 308
  ss. 352–353   80
  s. 354   56, 81
  s. 359   81, 84
  s. 360   81
  s. 363   291
  s. 367   126
  s. 368   63, 125, 126
  s. 368(3)   126
  s. 369(3)   127
  s. 370   126
  s. 370(2)   126
  s. 370(4)   128
  s. 371   126
  s. 372   43, 128
  s. 373   128
  s. 379(1)   63
  s. 379A   125
  s. 380   129
  s. 381   128, 129
  s. 381A   325
  s. 381C   129
  s. 391   129
  s. 395   108–9, 110, 254
  s. 395(1)   109
  s. 399   108
  s. 400   110
  s. 401   108
  ss. 406–408   110
  s. 425   243
  s. 458   45
  s. 459   84, 86–8, 277
  s. 459(1)   86
  s. 461(1)–(2)   87
  s. 652   292

Companies Act 1985 — *continued*
  s. 711   55, 59, 290
  s. 713   292
  s. 716   5
  s. 716(2)   5
  s. 741(2)   72
  s. 744   106
  Sch. 1   54
  Sch. 4   297
  Sch. 15A   129
Companies Act 1989   40, 43, 110, 125
  s. 4   92
Companies Acts   39, 40, 327
Company Directors Disqualification Act 1986
  64–5, 73, 257, 359
Competition Act 1980   350
Competition Act 1998   223, 345, 350–3
  Sch. 1   352
  Sch. 3   352

Deeds of Arrangement Act 1914   237

European Communities Act 1972   223

Finance Act 1958
  s. 34(4)   306
Finance Act 1989   183
Finance Act 1991
  s. 72   139
Finance Act 1994   192
Finance Act 1996   166, 186
  s. 81   186
  s. 82   187
Finance Act 1997   193
Finance Act 1998   151
Finance Acts   40, 136, 170
Financial Services Act 1986   42, 44, 328, 329
  Part IV   323

Income and Corporation Taxes Act 1988
  40, 133, 134, 179, 183
  s. 6(4)(a)   165
  s. 9   165
  s. 12   167
  s. 13   168
  s. 19   181
  s. 63   301
  s. 63A   138
  s. 74   134, 180
  s. 74(b)–(q)   135
  s. 113   198, 199, 268
  s. 113(1)–(2)   199
  s. 131   181
  s. 141   183
  s. 145   182
  s. 146   183
  s. 148   184, 185
  s. 153   183
  s. 160   184
  ss. 167–168   183
  s. 188   185
  s. 188(1)(b)   185
  s. 188(4)   185
  s. 209(2)   188
  s. 209(2)(a)–(b)   176
  s. 209(2)(d)(iii)   176
  s. 249   176

TABLE OF STATUTES

Income and Corporation Taxes Act 1988 — *continued*
    s. 313   185, 186
    s. 349(2)   187
    s. 380   139, 140, 142, 198, 302
    s. 380(1)(a)   138, 139
    s. 380(1)(b)   139
    s. 381   140, 171
    s. 382   198
    s. 385   139, 140, 142
    s. 386   302
    s. 388   140, 198, 302
    s. 389   140, 198
    s. 393   170, 171
    s. 393A   171
    s. 402   172
    s. 414   172
    s. 419   172
    s. 577   135
    s. 579   180
    s. 590   180
    s. 596A   185
    s. 832(1)   165
    s. 837   183
    Sch. A   133
    Sch. C   133
    Sch. D   134, 181
        case I   133, 134, 141, 179, 180, 186, 198
        case II   133, 134, 141, 179, 180, 186, 198
        case III   133, 187
        case IV   134
        case V   134
        case VI   134, 192, 302
    Sch. E   134, 141, 181, 182, 184
    Sch. F   134, 176, 178
Inheritance Tax Act 1984   156, 158
    s. 4(1)   204
    s. 10   202
    s. 94   173, 318
    ss. 95–102   173
    ss. 103–111   204
    s. 112   160, 204
    ss. 113–114   204
    s. 163   202
    s. 163(1)   202
    s. 202   173
    ss. 227–228   204
Insolvency Act 1986   40, 44, 125, 228, 230, 231, 233, 235, 237, 241, 246, 248, 256, 257, 359
    Part VIII   237
    ss. 1–7   246
    s. 14(1)(a)   244
    s. 15(1)   244
    s. 15(2)   245
    ss. 22–23   245
    s. 25   245
    s. 29(2)   248
    ss. 43–44   249
    s. 84   251
    s. 84(1)(c)   125
    s. 86   107
    s. 122   323
    s. 122(1)(g)   24, 88
    s. 123   250
    s. 126   253
    s. 129(2)   107
    s. 130   253
    s. 165   253

Insolvency Act 1986 — *continued*
    s. 167   253
    s. 178   254
    s. 213   45
    s. 214   45, 73, 259
    ss. 238–239   243, 260
    s. 245   243, 261
    s. 249   260
    s. 251   72
    s. 339   234
    s. 340   234
    s. 423   233, 234, 261
    ss. 424–425   233, 261
    Sch. 1   244, 248
Insolvency Act 2000   65, 247

Judgments Act 1838
    s. 17   236

Law of Property Act 1925   248
    Part III   106
    s. 30   235
    s. 85   106
    s. 101   111
Limited Liability Partnerships Act 2000   355, 356, 357, 358
    s. 1(2)–(4)   356
    s. 1(5)   356, 358
    ss. 2–3   356
    s. 6(1)   357
    s. 6(4)   357
    s. 8   357
    ss. 14–16   355, 359
    s. 17   355
Limited Partnership Act 1907   3

Mental Health Act 1983   29, 65
    s. 96   29

Partnership Act 1890   4, 18, 27, 33, 203, 265, 266, 314, 355
    s. 1(1)   4, 13
    s. 1(2)   4
    s. 2   4
    s. 2(1)–(2)   4
    s. 2(3)   4, 11
    s. 5   19–20, 357
    s. 6   18
    s. 8   20
    s. 9   17, 36, 43
    s. 10   21
    s. 14   21, 34, 35
    s. 14(1)   34, 35
    s. 17(1)   21
    s. 17(2)   33
    s. 19   8
    s. 20(1)   14
    s. 21   14
    s. 23(1)–(2)   22
    s. 24   7, 9, 11, 12
    s. 24(1)   12, 358
    s. 24(2)   9
    s. 24(3)   13
    s. 24(4)   12
    s. 24(5)   8, 24
    s. 24(6)   13
    s. 24(7)   8, 268

TABLE OF STATUTES

Partnership Act 1890 — *continued*
  s. 24(8)　8, 266
  s. 24(9)　9
  s. 25　9, 25, 204
  s. 26　28, 33
  s. 26(1)　5
  s. 27　29
  s. 28　9
  s. 29　9
  s. 29(1)　9, 10
  s. 29(2)　9
  s. 30　9, 10
  s. 32(a)–(b)　28
  s. 32(c)　5, 28
  s. 33(1)　28
  s. 33(2)　22, 25, 28
  s. 34　28
  s. 35　29
  s. 35(a)–(b)　29
  s. 35(c)–(d)　23, 24, 29
  s. 35(e)　29–30
  s. 35(f)　23, 24, 29, 30
  s. 36　34
  s. 36(1)　31, 34, 35
  s. 36(2)　34
  s. 36(3)　34, 36
  s. 37　31
  s. 38　30, 31
  s. 39　31
  s. 42(1)　36
  s. 43　36
  s. 44　12, 31, 32, 33
  s. 44(a)　32
  ss. 45–46　4
Powers of Criminal Courts Act 1973　230

Resale Prices Act 1976　350
Restrictive Trade Practices Act 1876　350

Sale of Goods Act 1979　350
Stamp Act 1891
  s. 54　306
  s. 57　306
  s. 59　306
  s. 59(1)　306

Stock Transfer Act 1963
  s. 1　116
Stock Transfer Act 1982　96

Taxation of Chargeable Gains Act 1992
    40, 143, 144, 147, 302
  s. 3　148
  s. 21(1)　143
  s. 24(2)　201
  s. 45　147
  s. 58　149
  s. 152　150, 154, 166, 305
  ss. 153–160　154, 166
  s. 162　303, 304, 305
  s. 162(4)　303
  ss. 163–164　148
  s. 164BA　152
  s. 165　148, 149, 304, 305
  s. 222　147
  s. 262　147
  Sch. 6　148
Taxes Management Act 1970
  s. 8(8)　134

Value Added Tax Act 1983
  s. 33　305
Value Added Tax Act 1994　207, 208
  Sch. 1　207
  Sch. 8　208
  Sch. 9　208

European legislation
Treaty of Rome　219
  art. 28　213, 215, 216, 217
  art. 30　213, 216–17
  art. 43　213
  art. 48　213
  art. 49　214
  art. 55　213
  art. 81　219–22, 223, 340, 341, 342, 346, 348,
    350, 352
  art. 81(1)　219, 220, 221, 222, 341,
    346, 352
  art. 81(3)　220, 221, 346
  art. 82　219, 222, 223, 340, 346, 350

TABLE OF REGULATIONS

Civil Procedure Rules
  Sch. 1, RSC
    Ord. 15
      r. 12(1) 85
    Ord. 81 21
Commercial Agents (Council Directive) Regulations
  1993 (SI 1993/3053) 333, 334–40, 342,
  343, 344
  regs 3–4 336
  reg. 7 336, 337
  reg. 8 336
  reg. 10 337
  reg. 12 337
  reg. 13 337, 342
  reg. 14 337
  reg. 15 337
  reg. 15(3) 337
  reg. 17 337, 338, 339
  reg. 17(3) 338
  reg. 17(4) 340
  reg. 17(6) 338
  reg. 18 339, 342
  reg. 19 340
  reg. 20 340
Commercial Agents (Council Directive) (Amendment)
  Regulations 1998 335
Companies (Summary Financial Statement)
  Regulations 1992 (SI 1992/3075) 293, 324
Companies (Tables A to F) Regulations 1985
  (SI 1985/805) 53, 63, 271, 322
  Table A 40, 49, 50, 53, 54, 58, 62, 65, 80, 81, 89, 92,
    99, 105, 113, 114, 118, 125, 126, 127, 128, 266, 271,
    272, 273, 274
    arts 2–3 272
    art. 23 272
    art. 24 117, 272
    art. 24(a)-(c) 117
    arts 25–28 272
    art. 30 119
    art. 32 113, 114
    art. 35 99, 101
    art. 37 125
    art. 38 126, 127, 274
    art. 39 126
    art. 46 128
    art. 50 124, 274
    art. 64 62
    art. 65 72
    art. 66 66

Companies (Tables A to F) Regulations 1985
  (SI 1985/805) — *continued*
    art. 70 65, 66, 105
    art. 72 72
    art. 73 63, 274
    arts 74–75 63
    art. 76 274, 275
    art. 77 275
    arts 78–79 62, 275
    art. 81 65
    art. 84 63, 72
    art. 88 66
    art. 91 66
    art. 93 66
    art. 94 66, 70, 274, 275
    art. 95 274
    art. 96 66
    art. 99 76
    art. 102 89
    arts 111–116 126
    art. 122 127
  Table F 322
Competition Act 1998 (Land and Vertical Agreements
  Exclusion) Order 2000 351, 352

Insolvency Rules 1986 241
  r. 6. 1 229
Insolvent Partnerships Order 1986 33
Insolvent Partnerships Order 1994 33, 256, 257

Limited Liability Partnerships Regulations 2001
  355, 358, 359
  reg. 7 358
  reg. 7(1) 358

Public Offers of Securities Regulations 1995
  (SI 1995/1537) 323

Transfer of Undertakings (Protection of Employment)
  Regulations 1981 (SI 1981/1794) 307
  reg. 3(1) 308
  reg. 5 308

European secondary legislation
2nd Company Law Directive 90
Directive 86/653 334, 337, 338
Regulation 17/62 223
Regulation 1983/83 347
Regulation 2790/1999 221, 222, 352

PARTNERSHIPS

ONE

CHARACTERISTICS OF PARTNERSHIPS

This chapter covers the following topics:

1.1 Introduction
1.2 Relevant law
1.3 Definition of partnership
1.4 Nature of partnership and terminology
1.5 Number of partners
1.6 Capacity
1.7 Duration of partnership
1.8 Partnership name and publicity of information.

1.1 Introduction

1.1.1 TYPES OF BUSINESS MEDIUM

The established business media in the United Kingdom are sole traders, partnerships and companies. Sole traders by definition tend to be relatively small concerns, as do partnerships, although a number of professional partnerships overturn this assumption. Companies cover the full spectrum of business sizes.

Chapters 1 to 5 of this Guide cover partnerships; **Chapters 6** to **12** cover companies. Since 6 April 2001, a new business medium has been in existence, known as the 'limited liability partnership'. This is discussed in **Chapter 34**. As limited liability partnerships are a hybrid of company and partnership law concepts, it is recommended that they are not studied until partnerships and companies have been covered.

In this chapter, we will look at the rules for determining whether a partnership has come into existence as well as the formalities with which businesses which will be run through partnerships must comply. (This Guide will not consider the rules relating to limited partnerships created under the Limited Partnership Act 1907.)

We will not look separately in this chapter, or in the ones which follow, at sole proprietorships. However, many of the formalities to which partnerships are subject (for example, in relation to the choice of a business name) apply equally to sole proprietors.

1.2 Relevant Law

Much of the law relating to partnership is to be found in the Partnership Act (PA) 1890. The Act was mainly declaratory of the law of partnership as it had developed up to 1890. The Act does not provide a complete code of partnership law, and indeed s. 46 specifically provides that: 'The rules of equity and of common law applicable to partnership shall continue in force except so far as they are inconsistent with the express provisions of this Act'.

1.3 Definition of Partnership

The definition of a partnership is to be found in s. 1(1) PA 1890 which states: 'Partnership is the relation which subsists between persons carrying on a business in common with a view of profit.' (A registered company is specifically excluded from the definition by s. 1(2).) To satisfy the definition two or more persons must be carrying on a business. It follows from this that an agreement to run a business in the future does not constitute an immediate partnership, nor does the taking of preliminary steps to enable a business to be run. 'Business' is defined by s. 45 PA 1890 as including 'every trade, occupation or profession'.

Section 2 PA 1890 lays down certain 'rules for determining the existence of a partnership'. These provide that:

(a) Joint or common ownership of property 'does not of itself create a partnership' even where profits from the property are shared (s. 2(1)).

(b) The sharing of *gross* returns does not of itself create a partnership (s. 2(2)). A person is not, therefore, a partner in a business merely because he receives commission on sales which he has introduced.

(c) The receipt of a share of *profits* is prima facie evidence of partnership (s. 2(3)). This topic is dealt with in **2.6**.

It should be noted that a written partnership agreement is *not* a prerequisite for the existence of a partnership. The existence of a partnership is *always* a question of fact.

1.4 Nature of Partnership and Terminology

A partnership is, in law, a very different type of institution from a company. The most significant difference is that partners have unlimited liability for the debts of the partnership, whereas the liability of shareholders for company's debts is limited. (The liability of partners to creditors is considered in **Chapter 3**.) Partnerships, unlike companies, are not required to go through any registration process when they are formed and, again unlike companies, they are under no obligation to make their accounts public.

A partnership is not a separate legal entity from its partners (in contrast to companies which are legally distinct from their shareholders). However, to a limited extent in relation to litigation (see **Chapter 3**) and taxation (see **Chapter 13**), the existence of the partnership is recognised as being independent of the individual members.

As a means of recognising the differences which exist between a partnership and a company, the former is commonly referred to as a *firm*.

1.5 Number of Partners

The maximum number of persons who may be members of a particular partnership is usually 20 (s. 716 Companies Act (CA) 1985). However, under s. 716(2) certain professions, including those of solicitors and accountants, are exempt from this limit.

1.6 Capacity

Generally speaking, any person including a minor (person under 18) is legally capable of forming a partnership with any other person. Companies as well as individuals can, provided their objects clause gives them the power to do so, enter into a partnership with other companies or with individuals. (This Guide will not consider any rules applicable where one or more companies are members of a partnership.)

1.7 Duration of Partnership

Most partnerships are partnerships 'at will'. This means that no particular period is agreed upon as being the time during which the partnership is to last. A partnership at will can be dissolved by notice by any partner unless there is an agreement to the contrary (see ss. 26(1) and 32(c) PA 1890).

A partnership for a fixed term or for a term defined by reference to some event (e.g., the completion of some particular job) is also possible. Such a partnership cannot generally be dissolved by notice.

There may sometimes be difficulty in deciding when a partnership begins. Because of the way partnership is defined, this is essentially a question of fact. The terms of a partnership agreement as to commencement may be evidence (though not conclusive) of when a partnership begins.

1.8 Partnership Name and Publicity of Information

A partnership is entitled (subject to what is said below) to choose any name which it wishes. There is nothing in partnership law corresponding with the requirement that a company should have a corporate name which is registered with the Registrar of Companies (see **7.5.1.1**).

The law relating to partnership names is now contained in the Business Names Act (BNA) 1985. The Act permits the free use of certain names and requires approval for others. In addition it contains rules requiring publicity as to the membership of partnerships in certain circumstances.

1.8.1 AUTOMATICALLY PERMITTED NAMES

If the business of a partnership is carried on under a name which consists of the surnames of all the partners, no restrictions apply (s. 1 BNA 1985). This is also the case where the name consists of the partners' surnames together with 'permitted additions' and nothing else. The permitted additions are:

(a) the forenames or initials of the partners;

(b) the addition of an 's' to a surname to signify that there is more than one partner with that name; and/or

CHARACTERISTICS OF PARTNERSHIPS

(c) a statement that the business is being carried on in succession to the business of a former owner.

Where the name of the partnership does not consist solely of the surnames of the partners, or of the surnames of the partners together with permitted additions, then the disclosure requirements of s. 4 BNA 1985 will apply and in some cases approval of the name is required under ss. 2 and 3.

1.8.2 DISCLOSURE REQUIREMENTS OF s. 4 BNA 1985

Any partnership which uses a business name (other than one permitted under s. 1 BNA 1985) is required to state the name of each partner (together with an address for service in Great Britain) on:

(a) every business letter;

(b) order for goods or services;

(c) invoice;

(d) receipt; and

(e) written demand for payment of a debt (s. 4(1)(a) BNA 1985).

The same information must also be given by a notice in a prominent position at each place of business of the partnership (s. 4(1)(b) BNA 1985). The same information must also be given (in writing) to anyone with whom the partnership has had dealings or negotiations and who asks for the information (s. 4(2) BNA 1985).

The requirement of including names and addresses in letters, etc., does not apply to a partnership with more than 20 members provided that, instead of the partners' names, the letter states the address of the principal place of business and that the names and addresses of the partners can be inspected there.

1.8.3 APPROVAL UNDER ss. 2 AND 3 BNA 1985

Section 2 BNA 1985 makes it an offence to carry on business (without the approval of the Secretary of State) under a name which suggests a connection with the government or a local authority, or which includes a word specified in regulations made under the Act. Section 3 gives the Secretary of State power to make such regulations. Regulations have been made under the Act which specify scores of words for which approval is required.

Partners who are starting a business and who wish to use a business name should consult the regulations. If they find that their name includes a word covered by the regulations they should first write to the government department or other body (if any) which is to be consulted in relation to that word asking it whether it objects. They should then apply to the Secretary of State for approval stating that they have made such a request and enclosing a copy of any reply that they have received from the government department or other body that they have consulted.

TWO

PARTNERSHIP MANAGEMENT AND FINANCE

This chapter covers the following topics:

2.1 Introduction
2.2 The legal relationship between the partners (s. 24)
2.3 The duty of good faith
2.4 The partnership's finances
2.5 The distinction between a partner and a lender
2.6 Division of profits and sharing of losses between partners
2.7 Payment of interest
2.8 Partnership property.

2.1 Introduction

In this chapter we will look at:

(a) the ways a partnership can be managed;

(b) the relationship of the partners to each other and the obligations which partners owe to each other; and

(c) how the finances of a partnership can be handled, both in terms of raising capital to finance the business and distribution of profits the business makes.

2.2 The Legal Relationship Between the Partners (s. 24)

Section 24 PA 1890 lays down a number of rules which regulate the relationship between partners and the management of their business. These rules '... may be varied by the consent of all the partners, and such consent may be express or inferred from a course of conduct'. The most common way in which the rules in s. 24 are varied is where the partners enter into a partnership agreement (see **Chapter 25**).

If partners do not wish specific provisions of s. 24 to apply to their business then, for certainty, contrary provisions should be incorporated in their partnership agreement.

Several of the subsections of s. 24 deal with the relationship of the partners in respect of the distribution of profits and losses made by the partnership; these subsections are dealt with in **2.6**.

PARTNERSHIP MANAGEMENT AND FINANCE

2.2.1 MANAGEMENT OF THE BUSINESS

Section 24(5) PA 1890 provides that (subject to contrary agreement, express or implied):

Every partner may take part in the management of the partnership business.

If the management structure of a particular partnership is to be different from the equality of partners presumed by s. 24(5), then express agreement should be made. For example, a large partnership may have different grades of partners, major decisions being taken only by the senior grade. Similarly, some partners may be 'sleeping partners', that is, partners who have contributed capital but who do not take an active part in management or decision-making.

2.2.2 DECISIONS OF THE PARTNERS

Section 24(8) says that (subject to contrary agreement, express or implied):

Any differences arising as to ordinary matters connected with the partnership business may be decided by a majority of the partners, but no change may be made in the nature of the partnership business without the consent of all the partners.

In most circumstances, therefore, a simple majority of the partners is required to take a decision. If there is an equality of votes a decision has not been taken and the status quo is preserved.

2.2.3 RESTRICTIONS ON MAJORITY RULE

There are three main limitations imposed on the ability of the majority of the partners to bind the whole firm. First, partners are under a fiduciary duty to each other and so must exercise their powers for the benefit of the firm as a whole. For example, in *Blisset* v *Daniel* (1853) 10 Hare 493, a power was given (by the partnership agreement) to the majority of the partners permitting them to expel a partner. The majority exercised this power with a view to obtaining cheaply the expelled partner's shares in the partnership. This was held to be an illegal use of the power to expel as it amounted to a breach of the duty of good faith required of a fiduciary.

Secondly, the majority may not impose their views on the minority without first consulting them (*Const* v *Harris* (1824) T & R 496). However, there is no requirement that consultation should take the form of a meeting (unless the partnership agreement so provides).

Thirdly, the following provisions of the Partnership Act limit majority rule:

(a) Section 24(8) requires unanimity for a change in the partnership business. This is so that a partner who has decided to invest in one particular type of business will not be forced to invest in something else against his wishes.

(b) Section 24(7) provides that: 'No person may be introduced as a partner without the consent of all the existing partners.' Such a rule is vital to the running of a small partnership where each partner will wish to ensure that his fellow partners cannot force him to go into partnership with someone of whom he disapproves. In a large partnership it may be considered appropriate that s. 24(7) should not apply (so that, for example, the senior partners may be given power to decide who to take on as junior partners and who to promote to senior partnership), in which case the partnership agreement must exclude the requirement of unanimity in this respect.

(c) Unanimity is required by s. 19 for an alteration to the partnership agreement. The agreement of the partners to an alteration can be inferred from a course of dealings.

(d) Section 25 prevents expulsion of a partner by a majority of the partners unless all the partners have *expressly* agreed to such a power being conferred.

2.2.4 OTHER PROVISIONS

Other provisions of s. 24 which affect the relationship between the partners are as follows:

(a) Section 24(2) gives a partner a right to be indemnified by the firm in respect of payments made and personal liabilities incurred 'in the ordinary and proper conduct of the business of the firm or in or about anything necessarily done for the preservation of the business or property of the firm'.

(b) Section 24(9) gives all the partners a right to inspect and copy the partnership accounts.

2.3 The Duty of Good Faith

2.3.1 EQUITABLE PROVISIONS

The contract of partnership is a contract *uberrimae fidei* (of the utmost good faith), so that a partner is required to disclose all relevant information in his possession to his partners. If he fails to do so his partners may set aside transactions which they have entered into with him as a result of the non-disclosure.

Similarly, a partner owes a fiduciary duty to his fellow partners; that is, he owes the duty of good faith to his partners in his dealings with them which a trustee owes to a beneficiary.

2.3.2 STATUTORY PROVISIONS

The requirement of good faith in dealings between partners is of general application, but three particular aspects of the duty are dealt with in ss. 28–30 PA 1890.

2.3.2.1 Duty to disclose information

Section 28 provides that: 'Partners are bound to render true accounts and full information of all things affecting the partnership to any partner or his legal representative.' This is really just a formulation in statutory language of the duty of disclosure imposed by equity. A good illustration of the working of the rule is given by *Law* v *Law* [1905] 1 Ch 140. In that case one partner offered to buy the share of another at a price which seemed fair to the vendor who was not actively engaged in running the business. The purchaser, however, knew of facts which made the vendor's share more valuable than the vendor realised. When the vendor discovered this it was held that he was entitled to rescind the contract of sale on the ground of non-disclosure.

2.3.2.2 Duty to account for secret profits

Section 29 states that:

(1) Every partner must account to the firm for any benefit derived by him without the consent of the other partners from any transaction concerning the partnership, or from any use by him of the partnership property, name or business connection.

(2) This section applies also to transactions undertaken after a partnership has been dissolved by the death of a partner, and before the affairs thereof have been completely wound up, either by any surviving partner or by the representative of the deceased partner.

This section imposes similar restrictions and duties on partners as apply to company directors (see **8.6**). Any profit made in breach of the section is held on trust for the benefit of the partnership as a whole. The rule applies to transactions entered into by a partner where the opportunity came to him as a result of the partnership, to commissions received on contracts introduced to the partnership, to sales of property to the partnership by a partner and to profits derived from sales of partnership property. A partner may retain any such profit if his partners consent following full disclosure of the circumstances.

2.3.2.3 Duty to account for profits from competing business

Section 30 PA 1890 provides that:

> If a partner, without the consent of the other partners, carries on any business of the same nature as and competing with that of the firm, he must account for and pay over to the firm all profits made by him in that business.

The provisions of s. 30 are quite narrow. In order to succeed under this section the partners must show that the businesses are of the same nature and that they are in fact competing for the same customers. Thus in *Aas* v *Benham* [1891] 2 Ch 244, a partner in a firm of shipbrokers was held not to be accountable for profits he had made from shipbuilding. However, in *Glassington* v *Thwaites* (1823) 1 Sim & St 124, a partner in a morning newspaper who set up an evening newspaper was held to be accountable. It should be noted that there is overlap between s. 30 and s. 29(1) (see **2.3.2.2** above) — a partner may be held accountable because he is competing with his partners or because he is using 'the partnership property name or business connection'; often a partner who sets up a new business will be doing both these things.

2.3.2.4 Preventing a partner from setting up a non-competing business

A partner who sets up a non-competing business and who does not use the partnership property, name or business connection is not liable to his partners in any way under the Act. Many partnership agreements, therefore, provide that the partners are to devote their whole time to the partnership and specify that the partners are not to start any other businesses. With such an agreement the partners may be able to obtain an injunction, damages or dissolution of the partnership against the partner who sets up a new business, even though it does not compete with the firm's business. They will not, however, have any right to make him contribute his profits in the other business to the partnership.

2.4 The Partnership's Finances

2.4.1 SOURCES OF FINANCE

The sources of finance for a partnership are basically the same as those available to any business. A partnership will need assets and cash in order to run its business. Money (or in some cases assets) may be contributed in the form of a permanent investment by the partners or it may be borrowed from either the partners or outside sources. Once the business of the partnership has started further finance may also be provided by retention of profits.

2.4.2 PARTNERS' CAPITAL

The permanent investment of a partner is described as his 'capital'. The capital of a partner may be contributed by him in the form of cash or property (including, for example, business premises or the goodwill of an existing business). The term 'capital' is somewhat ambiguous. It refers to the actual cash or other assets contributed to the partnership by a partner and the indebtedness of the partnership as a whole to the partner resulting from this investment. A partner's capital in this latter sense should be contrasted with other debts which the firm owes to the partner, as repayment of the capital cannot normally be claimed from the firm until dissolution (see **5.2.2.3**). Other indebtedness to a partner (for example, a loan) may be repaid before dissolution.

2.5 The Distinction between a Partner and a Lender

As we saw in **Chapter 1** the essential nature of a partnership is that two or more people are sharing profits of a business. A person who merely lends to a partnership is not a partner. The distinction between a partner and a lender is extremely important as a partner bears unlimited liability for the debts of the partnership whereas the lender only stands to lose the money invested if the business fails (if he has taken security for his loan, his risk of losing even that much may be small). However, if a business is successful a partner stands to earn a great deal of profit whereas a lender will receive only interest on his loan.

Many investors would like to have the best of both worlds, i.e., limited liability and a share of profits. This can be achieved by investing in a company. However, in the case of partnerships s. 2(3) PA 1890 effectively restricts this type of investment. Section 2(3) provides that: 'The receipt by a person of a share of profits ... is prima facie evidence that he is a partner ... but does not of itself make him a partner ...'. The subsection then sets out some particular rules which provide that:

(a) A person does not become a partner merely because a debt or other liquidated sum is paid to him by instalments out of profits.

(b) A servant or agent does not become a partner merely because his remuneration varies with profits.

(c) A widow or child of a partner is not a partner merely because a proportion of profits is paid to that person as an annuity.

(d) A lender whose interest varies with profits is not automatically a partner if the contract is in writing and signed by all the parties.

(e) A vendor who receives payment for his business in the form of an annuity varying with profits is not automatically a partner.

Sharing of profits is only prima facie evidence of partnership and particular types of contract are covered by the five rules mentioned above. However, there remains a risk that anyone who receives a share of profits *may* be held to be a partner and therefore personally liable for debts. Anyone entering into such an arrangement who does not wish to take on the risk of unlimited liability should take steps to ensure that he or she does not become a partner, e.g., by avoiding any suggestion that he has a right to take part in management and by having a written agreement setting out the terms of his involvement with the firm.

2.6 Division of Profits and Sharing of Losses between Partners

Section 24 PA 1890 lays down a number of rules as to division of profits. These rules may be varied by an express or implied agreement of the partners and for the avoidance of doubt it is preferable to state in a partnership agreement how both profits and losses are to be shared even if the agreement follows some or all of the statutory presumptions. Section 24 deals with the division of both income and capital profits.

PARTNERSHIP MANAGEMENT AND FINANCE

2.6.1 SHARE OF PROFITS AND LOSSES (s. 24(1))

Section 24(1) states:

> All the partners are entitled to share equally in the capital and profits of the business, and must contribute equally towards the losses whether of capital or otherwise sustained by the firm.

This rule may be broken down into three parts which will be examined in turn.

2.6.1.1 Sharing of capital

The first part of the rule states that 'all the partners are entitled to share equally in the capital'. On the face of it this means that when a partner leaves the firm or when the firm is dissolved he is entitled to take out a part of the capital corresponding with the total amount of capital divided by the number of partners. However, in practice this is unlikely to be so. All the rules in s. 24 are subject to contrary agreement express or implied. Where the partners have contributed unequally to the capital, there is an *implied* agreement that they are entitled to withdraw capital unequally. For example, if A contributes £10,000, B £20,000 and C £30,000, those are the sums which each can withdraw on leaving in the absence of any express agreement to the contrary.

2.6.1.2 Sharing of profits

The second part of the rule in s. 24(1) states that 'all the partners are entitled to share equally in the profits of the business'. The provision of capital in unequal shares *does not* give rise to the implication that this part of the rule has been displaced. Thus in the example given above if the profits of the firm were £9,000, A, B, and C would each be entitled to £3,000. If a partner is to receive more than an equal share of profits because of his capital contribution or the work he does, this must be specifically agreed to and should be expressly stated in the partnership agreement.

The rule as to share of profits applies to capital as well as income profits. 'Capital profits' is the term for amounts remaining following the payment of all creditors and repayment of capital contributions to partners on the dissolution of a partnership. When the firm in our example is dissolved, any capital profit will be shared equally even though the capital was not contributed equally. Thus after A has received £10,000, B £20,000 and C £30,000, any surplus will be divided equally. The partners are, of course, free to agree to the contrary. It may well be decided that capital profits should be divided in the same ratio as capital was provided. The ratio in which capital profits are divided (sometimes called the 'asset surplus ratio') is often different from the income profit sharing ratio.

2.6.1.3 Sharing of losses

The third part of the rule in s. 24(1) states that losses of capital and income are prima facie to be shared equally. However, if the partners share profits unequally (because of an express or implied agreement to do so), then s. 44 PA 1890 says that losses will also be shared unequally unless there is an agreement to the contrary.

2.6.2 INTEREST ON CAPITAL

Section 24(4) provides that: 'A partner is not entitled ... to interest on capital.' Where capital is contributed unequally it may be considered appropriate to make provision in the partnership agreement for interest on capital to compensate the partner who has contributed more. The agreement should specify the rate of interest or the method by which the rate is to be determined. Interest on capital is *not* a deductible expense of the business in determining its net profits (see **13.5.2**). It is merely a preferential appropriation of profits. This means that once the net profit of the partnership has been ascertained the partners' first entitlement will be to interest and then the remaining net profit will be allocated in accordance with the agreed profit-sharing ratio.

2.6.3 INTEREST ON LOANS

In the absence of contrary agreement a loan by a partner to the partnership carries only 5% interest (s. 24(3) PA 1890). It should be noted that this rate of interest is paid only on 'actual payments or advances'. Interest is not payable under s. 24(3) on a share of profits which is simply left in the business. The partners are, of course, free to agree that interest will be paid on undrawn profits if they wish.

2.6.4 REMUNERATION OF PARTNERS

Section 24(6) provides that: 'No partner shall be entitled to remuneration for acting in the partnership business.' In many partnerships the division of work between the partners is unequal, and therefore it will have to be expressly agreed that some of the partners be paid a salary to compensate them for the extra work which they have done. As with interest on capital, a salary payable to a partner is *not* a deductible expense but is merely a preferential appropriation of profit.

Example In a partnership with three members it might be agreed that:

(a) the profit-sharing ratio will be D 20%, E 40%, F 40%;

(b) that interest on capital will be paid at a rate of 10% p.a. (D's capital is £10,000, E's £20,000 and F's £30,000); and

(c) that D is to have a salary of £20,000 p.a.

If profits of £100,000 are made they will be divided as follows:

		£	£
Profit			100,000
Interest:	D	1,000	
	E	2,000	
	F	3,000	
			6,000
Salary:	D		20,000
Share of profits:	D (20%)	14,800	
	E (40%)	29,600	
	F (40%)	29,600	
			74,000
			100,000

In some partnerships (particularly professional partnerships) there may be relatively junior partners who are entitled to a salary to the exclusion of any other share of profits. At first sight it is hard to see how such 'salaried partners' can be regarded as partners at all, as partnership requires that the partners are 'carrying on business in common with a view of profit' (s. 1(1)

PA 1890). Nevertheless, in *Stekel* v *Ellice* [1973] 1 WLR 191, it was held that a salaried partner could be, in law, a full partner with all the rights and duties which that entails.

2.6.5 DRAWINGS

The amount to which a partner is entitled from the profits in a firm (as salary and interest, if agreed to, and share of profits) will not be known until the profit and loss account has been drawn up after the end of the partnership's financial year. The partnership agreement will, therefore, usually provide that a partner is to have the right to take a specified amount of money on account of his expected profits during the course of the year. Sums taken on account in this way are called 'drawings'. If at the end of the year the partner has taken less than he was entitled to he can draw the balance; if he has taken more than it turns out he was entitled to then the partnership agreement will probably require him to pay back the excess and/or pay interest on it. The partnership agreement may provide that each partner is to leave undrawn in the business a proportion of his entitlement to profit. This is because businesses normally need to retain funds to meet increased costs of trading and to fund any future expansion.

2.7 Payment of Interest

A payment of interest by a partnership to a creditor will usually be a business expense. This is because the interest payment will satisfy the test for deduction of expenses, that is, that the payment is incurred 'wholly and exclusively for the purposes of the trade'. (As mentioned above, payment of interest on capital to a partner is *not* a business expense, it is an allocation of profits to the partner.)

Where a partnership *receives* interest this is treated as income of the partners.

2.8 Partnership Property

2.8.1 INTRODUCTION

There is a major reason why it may be important to decide what property is and what is not partnership property. When the firm is dissolved each partner is entitled to retain any property which is his own personal property; property which is partnership property is used first to pay creditors of the firm and then any surplus is distributed among the partners in accordance with the terms of the partnership agreement (equally in the absence of contrary agreement). This is so, once it is decided that an asset is partnership property, even though the asset was introduced by one particular partner and the asset has risen in value thus creating a capital profit for the partnership.

2.8.2 DEFINITION

Partnership property is partly defined by s. 20(1) PA 1890 as:

> All property and rights and interests in property originally brought into the partnership stock or acquired, whether by purchase or otherwise, on account of the firm, or for the purposes and in the course of the partnership business . . .

Section 21 deals with a slightly different situation and states:

> Unless the contrary intention appears, property bought with money belonging to the firm is deemed to have been bought on account of the firm.

2.8.3 THE TEST

Whether property is partnership property or remains the separate property of a partner depends on the intention of the partners, express or implied. Property is not partnership property merely because it is used by the firm. The court does not readily assume, therefore, that property introduced by a partner thereby becomes partnership property.

This is illustrated by the leading case of *Miles* v *Clarke* [1953] 1 All ER 779. Clarke carried on a photographic business in premises of which he owned the lease. He and Miles went into partnership and for a time the business was successful. However, eventually a petition for dissolution was presented as the partners were unable to agree. The question arose as to which assets were partnership property and which belonged to the partners individually. Harman J held that in the absence of express agreement he would hold property to be partnership property to the extent necessary to give business efficacy to the agreement. Therefore, the lease of the business premises belonged on dissolution to Clarke alone, each partner was entitled to his own business connections which he had brought into the firm and only the stock in trade (unused films, chemicals, etc.) could be regarded as partnership property.

THREE

LIABILITY OF PARTNERS TO OUTSIDERS

This chapter covers the following topics:

3.1 Introduction
3.2 Nature of liability
3.3 Partnership and agency
3.4 Persons held out as partners
3.5 Liability of new partners
3.6 Partners' liability in tort
3.7 Suing or being sued.

3.1 Introduction

In the course of carrying on the partnership's business, the partners will incur debts and other obligations. In this chapter, we look at the nature of the partners' liabilities in these circumstances as well as the extent to which an individual partner can bind the partnership as a whole. We will then go on to look at whether it is possible for individuals who are not partners at the time the debt or obligation was incurred (whether because they have been held out as partners or because they are admitted to the partnership subsequently) to be liable for that debt or obligation.

3.2 Nature of Liability

Partners are liable for the debts and obligations of the partnership without limit (s. 9 PA 1890). Their liability is joint in the case of contractual obligations and joint and several in the case of tortious obligations (see **3.6**). The significance of this distinction was much reduced by the Civil Liability (Contribution) Act 1978 which allows proceedings to be brought successively against persons jointly liable despite an earlier judgment against others.

Where a partnership is unable to pay its debts out of partnership property, the creditor is entitled to obtain payment from the private estates of the partners. Special rules apply in such cases, so as to attempt to do justice both to the creditors of the firm and to the creditors of the individual partners. It is not our intention to deal with these rules in detail. However, they may be summarised as follows:

(a) in the first instance, the partnership property is used to pay partnership creditors in priority to private creditors and the private property of each partner is used to pay his private creditors in priority to partnership creditors;

LIABILITY OF PARTNERS TO OUTSIDERS

(b) if the private creditors of a particular partner are paid in full from private property, then partnership creditors may resort to the balance of that partner's private property; and

(c) if the partnership creditors are paid in full from partnership property then the private creditors of a partner may resort to the balance of his share of the partnership assets.

3.3 Partnership and Agency

3.3.1 INTRODUCTION

The relationship between partnership law and agency is very close. Indeed, most of the rules regulating the relationship between a partnership and the outside world can be explained purely in terms of particular applications of agency principles.

3.3.2 TYPES OF AUTHORITY OF A PARTNER

The partnership as a whole is bound by a partner acting within the scope of his authority. The authority of a partner may arise in three ways:

(a) First, the authority of the partners (or of a particular partner) may be specifically agreed upon by the partners — authority of this type is called 'express actual' authority.

(b) Secondly, authority may be implied either from a course of dealings between the partners (which amounts to an actual agreement) or because the authority is a natural consequence of an authority actually given to the partner — this is normally called 'implied actual' authority.

(c) Thirdly, authority may arise from the fact that a person dealing with a partner is, in certain circumstances, entitled to assume that the partner has authority to bind the firm — this type of authority is generally called 'apparent' or 'ostensible' authority, although terminology in agency law is far from consistent.

3.3.3 EXPRESS AND IMPLIED ACTUAL AUTHORITY

The scope of express and implied actual authority depends on the agreement between the parties. The partnership agreement may specify what powers the partners individually are to have and may specify that some are to have greater powers than others. The extent of actual authority, whether express or implied, is not, in practical terms, of great significance to a person dealing with a partner. This is because, whether or not there is actual authority, he will be able to rely on apparent authority in most circumstances in relation to most normal types of transaction. The outsider need only rely on actual authority where the partner has done something which the law does not consider to be within the apparent authority of a partner.

A partnership is bound by decisions and actions of its employees acting within the scope of their authority. An outsider seeking to rely on a decision or action of an employee would have to show that the employee had actual authority, had been held out (by the partners) as having actual authority or had been held out (by the partners) to be a partner. An individual partner cannot delegate authority to the employees (this is an application of the well known maxim of agency law *delegatus non potest delegare*).

The Partnership Act 1890 has little to say about a partner's actual authority. However, s. 6 recognises that the firm is bound by 'the acts or instruments' entered into with the authority of the firm.

LIABILITY OF PARTNERS TO OUTSIDERS

3.3.4 APPARENT AUTHORITY

3.3.4.1 General principles

The scope of apparent (or ostensible) authority is not always easy to establish or describe. Such authority is sometimes said to result from a type of estoppel whereby the principal (in this case the partnership as a whole) represents, by words or conduct, that the agent (that is the partner who is negotiating with the outsider) has authority to bind the firm. Once such a representation is made and acted upon by the outsider the partnership cannot deny the authority of the individual partner to bind the firm. Alternatively, apparent authority may be said to arise simply from the fact that the partner who is negotiating *appears* to have authority to bind the firm and it is, therefore, reasonable for the outsider to assume such authority. In fact nothing really turns on this distinction, since application of either test is likely to produce the same result in most circumstances.

3.3.4.2 Section 5, PA 1890

It is clear that the liability of the firm may result from the actual holding out of an agent (not necessarily a partner) as having a particular authority. However, in most cases the outsider seeks to rely on an apparent authority resulting from the fact that a person is known to be a partner in a firm. The outsider is then entitled to assume that the partner has the usual authority of a partner to bind his firm. This principle is laid down in s. 5 PA 1890 which says:

> Every partner is an agent for the firm and his other partners for the purpose of the business of the partnership; and the acts of every partner who does any act for carrying on in the usual way the business of the kind carried on by the firm of which he is a member bind the firm and his partners, unless the partner so acting has in fact no authority to act for the firm in the particular matter, and the person with whom he is dealing either knows that he has no authority, or does not know or believe him to be a partner.

The easiest way to understand the scope of the section (and thus of that part of the partner's authority which derives from the usual authority given to partners generally), is to examine ach of the qualifications on a partner's authority which the section recognises.

(a) *Partner can only bind the firm 'for the purposes of the business of the partnership'*

The first qualification is that the partner can only bind the firm 'for the purposes of the business of the partnership'. The section does not say, therefore, that *anything* which a partner does binds the firm. The partnership agreement may be of some assistance in deciding what is the scope of the partnership business. However, it is not conclusive. In *Mercantile Credit Co. Ltd* v *Garrod* [1962] 3 All ER 1103, Mocatta J held that the test as to whether a type of business is within the scope of the partnership depends on what is apparent to the outside world in general. Consequently a sleeping partner in a garage business whose agreement specifically excluded dealing in cars was held liable on a contract for the sale of a car as this was within the scope of what outsiders would expect the business to include.

(b) *Partner must do act 'for carrying on in the usual way the business of the firm'*

The second qualification in s. 5 is that the partnership is only bound if a partner does an act 'for carrying on in the usual way the business of the firm'. This restriction excludes the liability of the firm where the transaction is for the purposes of the business but is itself of an unusual type. For example, in *Niemann* v *Niemann* (1890) 43 ChD 198, a debt was owed to a partnership; one of the partners intended to accept payment of the debt in the form of shares in a company. This was held not to be binding on the other partner in the absence of a specific agreement. Similarly, *Powell* v *Brodhurst* [1901] 2 Ch 160 decided that a partner does

LIABILITY OF PARTNERS TO OUTSIDERS

not have ostensible authority to accept payment of a debt due to another partner personally rather than to the firm.

(c) No actual authority and outsider knows this or does not know or believe that person is a partner

The third qualification to s. 5 is that the firm is not bound if the partner has no actual authority and the outsider either knows this or does not know or believe the person with whom he is dealing to be a partner. Clearly in such cases the firm is not bound whether one takes the view that apparent authority depends on estoppel or on appearance of authority. The outsider cannot say that he has relied on any misrepresentation nor can he claim that there appeared to be authority when he knows this to be untrue or does not think he is dealing with an agent at all.

A partner who makes a contract with an outsider without authority will be personally liable to the outsider for breach of warranty of authority where the partnership as a whole is not made liable on the contract. However, where a contract made without authority is ratified by the partnership, it becomes binding on them as well as on the outsider.

Section 8 PA 1890 provides that an outsider is not prejudiced by any restriction placed on the powers of a partner unless he has notice of it.

3.3.5 EXAMPLES OF APPARENT AUTHORITY

The question of what apparent authority a partner has in a particular case is determined by the application of s. 5 to that particular case. This is at least in part a question of fact. However, over the years the courts have decided upon examples of powers which will be assumed to be covered by apparent authority in the case of all partners in the absence of some special circumstance. The court has also recognised certain powers which it will be assumed all partners in a trading partnership have in the absence of some special circumstance. The powers of partners in a trading partnership are more extensive than the powers of partners in general. This is because the court recognises the need of the partners and the persons dealing with them to rely on normal trading practices.

Examples of powers assumed to be available to partners generally include:

(a) power to buy and sell goods (not just stock) used in the business;

(b) power to hire employees;

(c) power to receive payment of debts due to the partnership;

(d) power to pay debts owed by the partnership including a power to draw cheques for this purpose;

(e) power to engage a solicitor to represent the firm.

A partner in a trading partnership will be assumed to have all the above powers and also:

(a) power to grant security for borrowings (this does not, however, include a power to create a legal mortgage);

(b) a wider power than is given to a non-trading partner to deal with cheques and bills of exchange.

3.4 Persons Held Out as Partners

So far we have only considered the liability of actual partners to outsiders. A person who holds himself out as a partner or who 'suffers himself to be represented as a partner' is liable to anyone who 'on the faith of such representation' gives credit to the firm as if he were a partner (s. 14 PA 1890). The commonest example of the application of this rule is where a person allows his name to be used by the partnership (e.g., on notepaper) after he has ceased to be a partner (as to which, see **5.3.3.3(b)**).

A person cannot be held liable under s. 14 unless he has in some way contributed to the mistake made by the person giving credit to the firm, for example by allowing his name to be given as a partner. It is not, however, necessary that he himself should have done anything to inform the person giving credit.

Section 14 only applies where credit is given to the firm. This is construed widely so that, for example, the apparent partner is liable where goods are delivered, as well as where cash is lent, to the firm.

3.5 Liability of New Partners

Section 17(1) PA 1890 provides that 'a person who is admitted as a partner into an existing firm does not thereby become liable to the creditors of the firm for anything done before he became a partner'. This provision ensures that an incoming partner is not liable to the existing creditors of the firm merely because he has become a partner.

As between himself and the existing partners the incoming partner may agree to pay a share of debts owed to existing creditors. This does not make him liable to the existing creditors as they are not privy to the contract. The new partner may become liable to existing creditors by a novation (that is, a tripartite contract between the old partners, the new partner and an outsider whereby the existing contract between the old partners and the outsider is discharged and replaced by a contract between the new firm, including the new partner, and the outsider). However, this will not be a regular occurrence.

3.6 Partners' Liability in Tort

A partner who himself commits a tort is liable according to general principles of the law of tort. The liability of the firm as a whole is governed by s. 10 PA 1890:

Where, by any wrongful act or omission of any partner acting in the ordinary course of the business of the firm, or with the authority of his co-partners, loss or injury is caused to any person ... the firm is liable ... to the same extent as the partner so acting or omitting to act.

It should be noted that the firm (as opposed to the actual tortfeasor) is only liable if either the commission of the tort was authorised by the partners or was committed 'in the ordinary course of business'. A partnership is also liable to the same extent as other employers (under common-law principles of vicarious liability) for torts committed by its employees.

3.7 Suing or Being Sued

A partnership is not a separate legal entity. Nevertheless, the partners may sue or be sued in the firm's name under Ord. 81 of the Rules of the Supreme Court (now contained in Sch. 1 of the Civil Procedure Rules). All the partners at the date when the cause of action accrued are

LIABILITY OF PARTNERS TO OUTSIDERS

then parties to the action. Where an action is brought against a partnership in the firm's name the writ may be served on any partner, on any person having control or management of the business at the principal place of business or by post to the principal place of business.

A person who has a judgment against a partner for the partner's personal liability may enforce that judgment against the partner's share of partnership property by means of a charging order (s. 23(2) PA 1890). He may not enforce such a judgment against the partnership property by means of execution or garnishee proceedings (s. 23(1)). Where a charging order is made the other partners may discharge it by paying off the judgment debt; if a sale of the property is ordered, they may purchase it. A charging order gives the other partners a right to dissolve the partnership if they wish (s. 33(2)).

FOUR

PARTNERSHIP DISPUTES

This chapter covers the following topics:

4.1 Introduction
4.2 Dissolution by the court
4.3 Appointment of a receiver
4.4 Arbitration
4.5 Expulsion of a partner.

4.1 Introduction

We saw in **Chapter 2** that a decision of the majority of the partners on an 'ordinary matter' is binding on the minority. The wishes of the majority prevail over those of the minority who object. However, partnership law provides some machinery for protecting the partner who is aggrieved by what the other partners have done.

In this chapter we will look at the remedies available to a partner, which include dissolution of the partnership, appointment of a receiver and remedies available under the terms of the partnership agreement itself.

4.2 Dissolution by the Court

Dissolution of a partnership may occur automatically (e.g., on the death of a partner) by notice (e.g., any partner can give notice dissolving a partnership at will) or by court order (e.g., in the case of permanent incapacity of a partner). The various circumstances in which dissolution takes place will be considered in **Chapter 5**. In this chapter we intend to consider only those types of dissolution which provide a remedy to a partner against his co-partners under s. 35(c), (d) or (f), PA 1890.

4.2.1 SECTION 35(c): CONDUCT PREJUDICIAL TO THE BUSINESS

Section 35(c) provides that a partner may apply to the court for dissolution 'when a partner, other than the partner suing, has been guilty of such conduct as, in the opinion of the court, regard being had to the nature of the business, is calculated to prejudicially affect the carrying on of the business'. This paragraph may be relied upon even though the prejudicial conduct has nothing directly to do with the partnership. A conviction for dishonesty, for example, would be likely to be regarded as prejudicial conduct in the case of many professional partnerships even though the dishonesty did not relate to the practice as such. The test is an objective one so that it need not be shown that the guilty partner *intended* to affect the business (this is so despite the use of the word 'calculated' in s. 35(c)).

4.2.2 SECTION 35(d): BREACH OF PARTNERSHIP AGREEMENT

Section 35(d) provides that a partner may apply to the court for dissolution 'when a partner, other than the partner suing, wilfully or persistently commits a breach of the partnership agreement, or otherwise so conducts himself in matters relating to the partnership business that it is not reasonably practicable for the other partner or partners to carry on business in partnership with him'. This paragraph contemplates that the trust between partners has broken down. If this breakdown results from persistent breaches of the partnership agreement or conduct in relation to the business (although not conduct in relation to other matters), then the court can order dissolution. Many of the cases under this paragraph have revolved around financial irregularities (such as failure to account for money received on behalf of the partnership or payment of private debts from partnership money).

4.2.3 SECTION 35(f): JUST AND EQUITABLE DISSOLUTION

Section 35(f) provides that a partner may apply to the court for dissolution 'whenever in any case circumstances have arisen which in the opinion of the court render it just and equitable that the partnership be dissolved'. This provision is the equivalent of s. 122(1)(g), Insolvency Act 1986, which is in essentially similar terms but applies only to companies. The cases decided under s. 122(1)(g) (and its predecessors) are relevant also to s. 35(f), especially where the company which was the subject of the petition was intended to be run as if it were a partnership. Deadlock or other irreconcilable differences between partners are the most likely grounds on which a successful petition could be based. Exclusion of a partner from management (contrary to s. 24(5)) would also be grounds for petition, although this case would also probably be covered by s. 35(d).

4.3 Appointment of a Receiver

The court has power to appoint a receiver to run the business of a partnership for the protection of the partners. The receiver's duty is to carry on the business of the partnership for the benefit of the partners generally, not to realise a security, so that his position is quite different from that of a company receiver appointed by a debenture-holder. There is comparatively little authority as to when a receiver will be appointed but it does seem to be an exceptional step and the court is particularly reluctant to make an appointment in the case of a professional partnership (*Floydd* v *Cheney* [1970] 2 WLR 314).

4.4 Arbitration

Disputes may be solved by arbitration if the partners agree to this. It is common to make provision for arbitration in the partnership agreement. As in other types of contract an arbitration clause cannot effectively oust the jurisdiction of the court altogether. A clause drawn widely in an attempt to oust the jurisdiction of the court entirely will be held to be void. If an action is commenced despite the presence of an arbitration clause the court has a discretion to stay the proceedings to enable the arbitration to take place.

The court action can continue without there being any question of a stay when, as a matter of construction, the court decides that the dispute which has arisen is not covered by the arbitration clause in the partnership agreement. The clause should expressly state that disputes arising during dissolution may be referred to arbitration and that the clause is binding on assignees of partners.

4.5 Expulsion of a Partner

4.5.1 INTRODUCTION

We have seen in this chapter that it is possible for a partnership to be dissolved by the court as a way of giving the plaintiff partner a remedy against his co-partners. However, the circumstances of the dispute within the partnership may be such that some partners would prefer to get rid of one or more of their co-partners without fully dissolving the partnership.

4.5.2 REQUIREMENT FOR PROVISION IN PARTNERSHIP AGREEMENT

This is only possible if an appropriate provision is included in the partnership agreement, as s. 25 PA 1890 provides that:

> No majority of the partners can expel any partner unless a power to do so has been confirmed by express agreement between the partners.

The question as to whether expulsion should be provided for, and if so by what majority, is one of the issues which must be considered when a partnership agreement is being drafted (see **Chapter 25**).

4.5.3 CONTENT OF EXPULSION CLAUSE

Where an expulsion clause is included in the agreement it will normally state that specific activities (such as fraud) or breaches of certain terms of the partnership agreement (such as that requiring a partner not to compete with the partnership or to devote the whole of his time to the business) will justify expulsion. Bankruptcy of a partner is a ground for the automatic dissolution of the whole partnership (s. 33(2) PA 1890) but in order to avoid the consequences of dissolution it is common for the partnership agreement to provide that a bankruptcy will not cause dissolution, rather that it will justify expulsion.

An expulsion clause will generally deal with the manner in which the expulsion is to be effected. It is normal to provide that written notice must be given to the offending partner and that it is to have immediate effect. The partnership agreement will normally distinguish expulsion and retirement in respect of financial arrangements. Thus, if annuities are to be paid the agreement would normally provide that an expelled partner should forfeit his rights.

4.5.4 EXERCISE OF EXPULSION CLAUSE

If an expulsion clause is included in the partnership agreement, then the power must be exercised strictly in accordance with the agreement and in a bona fide manner and for the benefit of the partnership as a whole (*Blisset* v *Daniel* (1853) 10 Hare 493).

FIVE

TERMINATION OF AND RETIREMENT FROM A PARTNERSHIP

This chapter covers the following topics:

5.1 Introduction
5.2 Dissolution of partnership
5.3 Retirement of a partner
5.4 Death.

5.1 Introduction

An individual may cease to be a partner on the happening of one of the following events:

(a) the dissolution of the partnership;

(b) his retirement; or

(c) expulsion from the partnership.

If the partnership is dissolved, the *partnership* will come to an end and its assets and business dealt with accordingly. The situation is different on the retirement or expulsion of a partner. Here, the former partners can carry on the *business*, albeit through the medium of a newly constituted partnership.

In this chapter we will consider the legal consequences of the occurrence of these events.

The taxation consequences of the events covered in this chapter will be considered in **Chapter 14**.

5.2 Dissolution of Partnership

If an event occurs which causes a partnership to be dissolved, the partnership relationship ceases and any partner may demand that the assets of the business are realised. Under the Partnership Act 1890 certain events result in automatic dissolution unless the partnership agreement provides otherwise. Dissolution is such an extreme step that it is common for partners to provide expressly in their partnership agreement that dissolution is *not* to occur automatically on the occurrence of the events specified in the Partnership Act.

TERMINATION OF AND RETIREMENT FROM A PARTNERSHIP

5.2.1 THE METHODS OF DISSOLVING A PARTNERSHIP

5.2.1.1 Dissolution by notice

Under ss. 26 and 32(c) PA 1890 one or more partners can, at any time, give notice to their fellow partners to dissolve the partnership. This notice takes effect from the date specified in the notice but if the notice is silent on the point, it takes effect from the date when all partners received the notice. Dissolution under ss. 26 and 32(c) can result in an immediate dissolution of the partnership. This could have disastrous consequences for the business.

However, ss. 26 and 32(c) can be overridden if the partnership agreement contains provisions to the contrary. As a result many partnership agreements require a minimum period of notice to be given before the partnership is dissolved.

5.2.1.2 Dissolution by agreement

The partnership agreement can specify circumstances which cause the partnership to be dissolved, such as the occurrence of a particular event. The agreement can also specify the manner in which the partnership will be dissolved.

5.2.1.3 Automatic dissolution

A number of events cause partnerships to dissolve automatically:

(a) *Bankruptcy, death or charge*

The death or bankruptcy of a partner causes the partnership to be automatically dissolved, unless the partnership agreement contains provisions to the contrary (s. 33(1) PA 1890). Since dissolution is a serious matter for the other partners, many partnership agreements provide that, instead of causing automatic dissolution, the death of a partner shall give rise to the same consequences as a retirement (see **5.3**). A bankruptcy is often treated in the same way as an expulsion (see **4.5**). If a partner allows his share of the partnership property to be charged for his personal debts, the other partners have an *option* to dissolve the partnership (s. 33(2) PA 1890).

(b) *Illegality*

Partnerships formed to carry out an illegal activity or which are contrary to public policy are automatically dissolved. A change of circumstances (including a change in the law) can subsequently make illegal a partnership initially formed for a legal purpose. In these circumstances, s. 34 PA 1890 provides that the partnership is dissolved on the happening of the event which makes the business unlawful (for example, the date the change in the law takes effect). A provision to the contrary in the partnership agreement will not override s. 34.

(c) *By expiration*

Under s. 32(a) and (b) PA 1890, a partnership is dissolved:

(i) if it was entered into for a fixed term, upon the expiration of that term;

(ii) if it was entered into for a single adventure or undertaking, upon the completion of that adventure or undertaking.

A provision to the contrary in the partnership agreement overrides s. 32(a) and (b).

If the agreement is silent and the partnership continues despite the occurrence of the events set out above, s. 27 provides that a partnership at will, dissolvable by notice, is brought into existence. Such a partnership is subject to the terms of the original agreement to the extent that these do not conflict with the incidents of a partnership at will.

5.2.1.4 Dissolution by the court

Finally, a partner may apply to the court for dissolution of the partnership provided one of the statutory grounds for dissolution by the court exists. This is only really an option when an easier method of dissolution is not available, either under the Partnership Act or under any partnership agreement.

Under s. 96 of the Mental Health Act 1983, the court has power, if satisfied after considering medical evidence that a partner is a mental 'patient', to dissolve or give directions for the dissolution of any partnership of which a 'patient' is a member. A 'patient' is a person incapable, by reason of mental disorder, of managing his own property and affairs.

In addition to s. 96 MHA 1983, s. 35 PA 1890 sets out grounds for dissolution by the court. Those grounds which give the partners a remedy in the event of a dispute (that is to say, s. 35(c), (d) and (f)) have been considered in **4.2**. The full list of s. 35 grounds is as follows:

Section 35(a)

Repealed by the predecessor to the Mental Health Act 1983.

Section 35(b)

When a partner, other than the partner suing, becomes permanently incapable of performing his part of the partnership contract.

Whether or not a partner has become *permanently* incapable is a question of fact. Since there may be difficulties in proving either that the partner is incapable or that his incapacity is permanent, and since there will be difficulties in running a partnership where a partner has a long illness, it is common to include a term in the partnership agreement allowing expulsion or insisting on retirement once a partner has been absent through illness for more than a specified time.

Section 35(c)

When a partner, other than the partner suing, has been guilty of such conduct as, in the opinion of the court, regard being had to the nature of the business, is calculated to affect prejudicially the carrying on of the business (see **4.2**).

Section 35(d)

When a partner, other than the partner suing, wilfully or persistently commits a breach of the partnership agreement, or otherwise so conducts himself in matters relating to the partnership business that it is not reasonably practicable for the other partner or partners to carry on the business in partnership with him (see **4.2**).

Section 35(e)

When the business of the partnership can only be carried on at a loss.

This is arguably one of the most important grounds for dissolution. In order for s. 35(e) to be invoked, the circumstances must be such as to make it a practical impossibility for the

TERMINATION OF AND RETIREMENT FROM A PARTNERSHIP

partnership to make a profit. If the partners who find themselves in this position cannot agree to bring the partnership to an end, this may be a valuable right if a delay in terminating the partnership will increase the amount of the loss, for which all the partners will be personally liable. It is important to note that a partnership is not necessarily insolvent simply because it is making a loss. It may well have valuable assets which, when sold, will discharge all liabilities and provide a surplus for the partners.

Section 35(f)

Whenever, in the opinion of the court, it is just and equitable that the partnership be dissolved (see **4.2**).

5.2.2 THE LEGAL CONSEQUENCES OF DISSOLUTION

5.2.2.1 Continuing authority of partners for purposes of winding up (s. 38 PA 1890)

The occurrence of one of the events set out in **5.2.1** will cause the partnership to be dissolved but there may be various steps which need to be taken to wind up the affairs of the firm. Section 38 provides that, after the dissolution, the authority of each partner to bind the firm (as well as the other rights and obligations of the partners) continues despite the dissolution but only to the extent necessary to wind up the affairs of the partnership, and to complete transactions begun but unfinished at the time of the dissolution. However, where the dissolution is by order of the court, this authority can be terminated by the appointment of a receiver (who will simply wind up the business) or of a receiver and manager (who will continue running the business but only with a view to the beneficial realisation of the assets by means of, for example, a sale of the business as a going concern). Such appointments are likely to be made where there is a likelihood of dispute if the former partners try to wind up the affairs of the partnership.

5.2.2.2 Realisation of partnership property on dissolution

Once the firm has been dissolved, the value of the assets owned by the partnership will be ascertained, as will the extent of the debts and liabilities owed to creditors. In so far as it is necessary, the assets will be sold to raise the funds to discharge the debts. The partners may merely sell the assets used in the business or they may decide to sell the business as a going concern. If the partners decide to adopt the latter course of action, they may be able to sell the business for more than the aggregate market value of the assets used in the business because the sale price may take into account the 'goodwill' attaching to the business. (It should be borne in mind that the purchasers in this instance may well be some of the partners from the dissolved firm who wish to continue the business under a new guise.)

Goodwill has been defined as 'the whole advantage, whatever it may be, of the reputation and connection of the firm' (*Trego* v *Hunt* [1896] AC 7). This 'advantage' can arise as a result of various factors. If the partners have considerable expertise in their chosen field, their customers may return repeatedly. This 'goodwill' may, however, be largely personal to the partners with the result that it would disappear if they ceased their involvement in the business. Conversely, if the firm is situated in a prime location (such as the main shopping street in the town), the business may be very successful because of the convenience of access for its customers. In this latter case, the goodwill may attach to the premises rather than the partners, and so may be a very valuable asset of the partnership since it can be passed on to successors.

If the firm has saleable goodwill, a value will be attached to it. The valuation of goodwill is somewhat speculative and any formula for determining its value is inevitably rather artificial. A common formula is to ascertain the net profits of the business for a particular year and then for the parties to agree to multiply the period's profits by an agreed number, often two or three.

Where goodwill is sold, the purchasers will want to protect their investment against the loss of custom arising from the former owners setting up in competition in the same vicinity. Accordingly, the purchaser may wish to include a restrictive covenant in the sale agreement to guard against this possibility. If the purchasers are some of the partners of the dissolved partnership, they too should consider including restrictive covenants to protect their interests.

5.2.2.3 Application of the partnership property on dissolution (ss. 39 and 44 PA 1890)

Once the assets and liabilities have been ascertained, s. 39 entitles each partner to have the property of the partnership applied so that the debts and liabilities of the firm are discharged first. Once these liabilities have been met, any surplus is distributed to the partners (after deducting any sums for which each partner is liable to contribute to the firm, such as contributions to make up losses or deficiencies of capital). In order to ensure that the assets of the partnership are not distributed to the partners personally before the outside creditors are paid off, s. 39 goes on to give each partner the right to apply to the court to wind up the business and affairs of the firm in such a way as to ensure that the s. 39 order for application of assets is observed.

Section 44 provides that once the creditors of the firm have been paid, subject to any contrary agreement, the assets of the firm shall be applied in the following order:

(a) in repaying advances received from partners;

(b) in repaying the amounts shown as standing to the credit of each partner on his capital account; and

(c) any balance being divided between the partners in accordance with the profit sharing ratio.

If the partnership has made losses (including losses or deficiencies of capital), these shall be met in the following order:

(a) from profits;

(b) from capital;

(c) from contributions made by the partners in the proportion in which profits are divisible.

Both parts of s. 44 are subject to contrary agreement. In particular the partners may agree to share surplus assets and to contribute to capital losses in a ratio different from the normal profit sharing.

5.2.2.4 Notification of the dissolution

Section 38 gives partners continued authority to bind the firm after dissolution for the purpose of winding up the business (see **5.2.2.1**). If a partner exceeds this authority, under s. 36(1) PA 1890 outsiders dealing with the firm after a change in the constitution are entitled to treat all apparent members of the firm as still being members until the outsider has notice of the change (see **5.3.3.3**).

In order to protect themselves from liability for unauthorised debts incurred after the dissolution, the partners in the dissolved firm are entitled publicly to notify the fact of the dissolution (s. 37 PA 1890). To obtain protection from liability on unauthorised debts incurred with *existing* customers, the former partners should give notice personally to the customer.

TERMINATION OF AND RETIREMENT FROM A PARTNERSHIP

Notice in the *London Gazette* is sufficient to gain protection from liability on debts with *new* customers (this point is considered in more detail in relation to retirement in **5.3.3.3**).

5.2.3 PROBLEMS ON DISSOLUTION

5.2.3.1 Introduction

When the value of the partnership business is insufficient to pay back all monies owing, problems can arise on a dissolution. Such a shortfall can result in two main outcomes: either the outside creditors can be paid off but there is insufficient cash to pay back partners' capital contributions; or there is not even enough to pay back outside liabilities. Each of these will be looked at in turn.

5.2.3.2 Insufficient to pay back partners' capital

This is best explained by reference to a number of examples.

> **Example 1** A, B and C are in partnership sharing profits equally, each having contributed £50,000 to the partnership. If only £90,000 remains (after paying off creditors), then there is a shortfall (loss) of £60,000, which according to s. 44(a) should be borne equally.
>
> Technically, each partner should pay into the business £20,000 so that each can draw out his £50,000 in full. It is plainly impractical to do this, however, and each partner would simply draw out £30,000.
>
> **Example 2** Instead suppose that A, B and C are in partnership sharing profits equally, each having contributed £50,000, £40,000 and £10,000 respectively to the partnership. If only £40,000 remains to satisfy partners' contributions, then there is a shortfall (loss) of £60,000, which again should be borne equally. Here it is more crucial that each partner contribute to the loss because of their initial unequal contributions. Note, in particular, that C will have to pay in £20,000 to receive £10,000 back. In reality, however, A and B will pay nothing and C will contribute £10,000. (This figure is reached by setting-off C's capital entitlement against the £20,000 contribution). The resulting £50,000 will then be divided between A and B to give them £30,000 and £20,000 respectively, which amounts to their initial capital contributions less £20,000.
>
> **Example 3** Suppose in example 2 that C could not, in fact, contribute any further money. According to *Garner* v *Murray* [1904] 1 Ch 57, A and B would not have to make good this deficiency but simply pay in £20,000 each in the usual way. The resulting £80,000 would then be distributed between A and B according to their ratio of contribution, i.e., 5:4. A would receive £44,444.45 ($^5/_9$ × £80,000) and B £35,555.55 ($^4/_9$ × £80,000.)

It will be noted that there is a curious disparity between examples 2 and 3 in that in example 2, because he can contribute, C is worse off than in example 3. Because of this, it is crucial when advising potential partners in a business to consider whether or not they wish to avoid the effect of s. 44 and agree that the partner who contributes the most should bear the most loss.

5.2.3.3 Insufficiency to meet liability to creditors

In **5.2.3.2** it has been assumed that creditors' and partners' loans have been fully satisfied. If the assets of a partnership prove insufficient to meet these liabilities first, the situation is much the same; any deficiency must be made up by partners according to their profit-sharing ratios (subject to any contrary agreement). Again the problem comes when a partner is unable to contribute. Here the situation is more pressing because the overriding effect of s. 9 means that outside creditors are not concerned with the niceties of s. 44 and the partners who can pay must pay to satisfy these liabilities. If this is not done, then the outside creditors will look to enforce their entitlements by legal means.

The inability of partners to pay off their creditors is a topic in itself — such partners will face potential bankruptcy (see **Chapter 22**). However, since the Insolvent Partnerships Order 1994 (amending the previous Order of 1986), it is possible for creditors to apply to have a partnership wound up as if it were an unregistered company. This procedure is essentially the same as for a registered company. However, for the most part, such an application is unlikely to be of use to a creditor unless it is in conjunction with bankruptcy petitions against the partners in question (see **23.10**).

5.3 Retirement of a Partner

5.3.1 CIRCUMSTANCES WHEN 'RETIREMENT' OCCURS

The term 'retirement' is most frequently applied to mean a person retiring from full-time work having reached the statutory age of retirement. However, in the partnership context 'retirement' simply means leaving the partnership voluntarily irrespective of the age of the partner in question.

5.3.2 RETIREMENT UNDER THE PARTNERSHIP ACT 1890

Partnership agreements can, and should, contain provisions dealing with retirement by partners. This is because the Partnership Act 1890 does not specifically deal with retirement. Under the 1890 Act the only option available to a partner is to give notice under s. 26. If a s. 26 notice is given the partnership will be *dissolved* (see **5.2.1.1**); the section does not permit a partner to retire leaving the partnership otherwise unaffected. To avoid this, suitable provisions must be included in the agreement. One common form of wording provides that the partner wishing to retire should give written notice of a specified length (say, six months or one year). On expiry of the notice period, the retiring partner will leave and may be entitled to some financial settlement from his former partners but otherwise the partnership continues unaffected.

Partnership agreements frequently provide that a deceased person is to be treated as having retired. Additional problems relating specifically to death are considered in **5.4**.

5.3.3 THE LEGAL CONSEQUENCES OF RETIREMENT

5.3.3.1 Debts incurred before retirement

The mere fact that a partner retires does not release him from his obligations in respect of debts incurred while he was a partner. Section 17(2) PA 1890 provides that 'a partner who retires from a firm does not thereby cease to be liable for partnership debts or obligations incurred before his retirement'.

To avoid the problems of having to meet such debts after retirement, the retiring partner should, if possible, ensure that the debts are paid before he leaves. Since this may be difficult in many cases, the partner will be concerned to gain protection in other ways. In some cases it may be agreed that he will be indemnified by his former partners or that he will be released from his obligations by the creditor.

TERMINATION OF AND RETIREMENT FROM A PARTNERSHIP

5.3.3.2 Debts incurred after retirement

The general rule is that only partners are liable for debts incurred by the partnership and so ceasing to be a partner prevents the *former* partner becoming liable on future debts as the retirement terminates the agency relationship. However, this general rule is subject to ss. 36 and 14 PA 1890. Under these sections a former partner becomes liable for debts incurred *after* he has left the partnership in certain circumstances.

5.3.3.3 Section 36

Section 36(3) provides that the estate of a partner '... who, *not having been known to the person dealing with the firm to be a partner*, retires is not liable for partnership debts contracted after the date of the ... retirement'.

The date at which knowledge is tested for the purposes of this subsection is the date of retirement. If a creditor does not know at that date of the retiring partner's connection with the firm, the former partner will not be liable; the fact that the creditor may subsequently discover the former membership cannot make the former partner liable.

The subsection was considered in *Tower Cabinet Co. Ltd* v *Ingram* [1949] 2 KB 397. A and B were in partnership. A retired and B continued the business under the old name. After A's retirement, the business ordered goods from a new supplier and failed to pay. The supplier sought to enforce judgment against A. The only knowledge the supplier had of A's connection with the firm was that A's name appeared on headed notepaper which, contrary to A's express instructions, had not been destroyed. The court found that, as the customer had no knowledge prior to A's retirement that A was a partner in the firm, A was completely protected by s. 36(3). (A further question arose of A's possible liability under s. 14(1) — see below.)

In cases where creditors know of the partner's connection with the firm before the former partner retires, s. 36(3) is of no assistance. Section 36(1) provides that 'where a person deals with a firm after a change in its constitution, he is entitled to treat all apparent members of the old firm as still being members of the firm until he has notice of the change'. It is necessary to consider what constitutes 'notice' for this purpose; and what makes a former partner an 'apparent' member of the continuing firm.

(a) *Notice*

Section 36(2) provides that in *respect of persons who had no dealings with the firm before the date of the dissolution or change* a notice in the *London Gazette* (where the firm has its principal place of business in England and Wales) will be sufficient notice.

Thus, to protect himself from liability to new customers who knew of his connection with the firm a retiring partner should ensure that a notice is published in the *London Gazette*.

Notice in the *London Gazette* will not be sufficient to relieve the former partner from liability in respect of customers who *did* have dealings with the firm prior to the dissolution or change. If the retiring partner wishes to be absolutely protected from liability for future debts he should give the customers formal notification.

(b) *Apparent membership*

Where persons dealing with the firm know that a person was a partner, that partner will be liable for new debts so long as he is an apparent member of the firm (and until he gives notice). Persons may be 'apparent members' either because a customer has had dealings with them before or because their names appear on the notepaper or on a sign on the door or because the customer has some indirect information about their being partners.

A retiring partner should ensure that his apparent membership of the firm is terminated. He should give actual notice to existing customers and should publish a notice in the *Gazette* to cover the situation where people have not had dealings with the firm but are aware of the partner's connection with the firm.

5.3.3.4 Section 14

Liability for subsequent debts may also arise under s. 14 PA 1890. It will be recalled from **3.4** that s. 14(1) provides that:

> Every one who by words spoken or written or by conduct represents himself, or who knowingly suffers himself to be represented, as a partner in a particular firm, is liable as a partner to any one who has on the faith of any such representation given credit to the firm, whether the representation has or has not been made or communicated to the person so giving credit by or with the knowledge of the apparent partner making the representation or suffering it to be made.

Therefore, even if no liability arises under s. 36, the former partner may be liable to any person (whether they had previous dealings with the firm or not) who has given 'credit' to the firm on the faith of a representation that he is still a partner which is made by the former partner or which he has 'knowingly' allowed to be made.

The word 'apparent' in s. 14(1) has the same meaning as in s. 36(1) so that the decision in the *Tower Cabinet* case (see above) is equally relevant in these circumstances. In the case, it was alleged that the former partner had allowed himself to be held out as a partner. However, since the former partner had not authorised the use of the old notepaper, he had not 'knowingly' allowed himself to be held out as an 'apparent' partner and so no liability under s. 14 arose.

A retiring partner should ensure that his name is removed from any signs and that any notepaper is destroyed in order to prevent an accusation that he knowingly allowed himself to be represented as a partner.

5.3.3.5 Compliance with Business Names Act 1985

After the change in the partnership, the notepaper will normally be changed and care should be taken to ensure that it complies with the requirements of the Business Names Act 1985 (which were considered in **1.8**).

5.3.3.6 Dealing with the finances

Once the partner has retired from the firm, the arrangements for severing, or changing the basis of, the financial connection with the firm will be of considerable importance. These matters are generally covered by the partnership agreement and usually relate to the provision for the partner (and for his dependants) of some form of pension (whether paid by the former partners, under an approved annuity contract, or under a consultancy arrangement). In addition, the arrangements will deal with the former partner's entitlement (if any) to payment for his share in the partnership assets (which may include goodwill).

If there is no agreement, the former partner has a right to receive the net value of his share in the partnership property from his former partners.

5.4 Death

5.4.1 INTRODUCTION

As we saw in **5.2.1.3** above, death causes the automatic dissolution of a partnership. In order to avoid inconvenience to the surviving partners it is common to provide in the partnership agreement that instead of causing an automatic dissolution of the partnership, a deceased partner shall be treated as if he had retired.

5.4.2 RIGHT OF ESTATE TO SHARE IN PROFITS AND OBTAIN AMOUNTS DUE

Subject to contrary agreement, s. 42(1) of PA 1890 provides for the situation where any member of a firm has died (or otherwise ceased to be a partner) and the surviving (or continuing) partners carry on the business of the firm without any final settlement of accounts as between the firm and the outgoing partner or his estate. The outgoing partner or his estate is entitled at the option of himself or his personal representatives to claim:

(a) such share of the profits made since the dissolution as the court may find to be attributable to the use of his share of the partnership assets; or

(b) interest at the rate of 5% p.a. on the amount of his share of the partnership assets.

Any amount due from the surviving partners to the deceased partner's personal representatives in respect of his share is a debt accruing at the date of the death (s. 43 PA 1890).

5.4.3 TREATMENT IN THE PARTNERSHIP AGREEMENT

Raising a large capital sum to pay to the estate of a deceased partner may strain the resources of a partnership which is continuing after the death of a partner. This issue is normally dealt with by the partners in the partnership agreement as follows:

(a) By taking out insurance cover.

(b) By providing that on death (and/or retirement) capital sums due should be paid by yearly instalments over a specified period — interest being payable on the amount outstanding.

(c) By providing for a method of calculating the amount due.

(d) By providing that the deceased (or retiring) partner is to be entitled to a fixed amount in lieu of a share of profits. This avoids the need to apportion profits to the date of death (or retirement).

5.4.4 LIABILITY FOR DEBTS

Every partner is jointly liable for debts and obligations of the firm incurred while he is a partner. In addition, s. 9 PA 1890 provides that the estate of a deceased person is severally liable for such debts and obligations so far as they remain unsatisfied *but* subject to the prior payment of the deceased partner's personal debts. A partnership creditor can, therefore, proceed against the estate of a deceased partner in respect of partnership debts (even after obtaining a judgment against the other partners) provided some part of the debt is unsatisfied. However, partnership creditors are postponed to the deceased partner's own creditors.

So far as subsequent debts are concerned, s. 36(3) PA 1890 provides that the deceased partner's estate is not liable for partnership debts contracted after the death. However, if the deceased partner's personal representatives take part in the management of the business they make themselves liable for debts incurred from the time their participation commences.

COMPANIES

SIX

LIMITED COMPANIES

This chapter covers the following topics:

6.1 Introduction
6.2 Corporations
6.3 Sources of company law
6.4 Registration
6.5 Types of registered company
6.6 Public and private companies
6.7 Separate legal personality
6.8 'Lifting the veil of incorporation'.

6.1 Introduction

In this chapter we shall begin to look at the legal position of limited companies. Many businesses are run by limited companies. These range from international conglomerates to companies owned by one person running a small business. Before turning to the detailed legal rules about companies we need to see how they fit into the complex pattern of institutions which the law has created. We shall also introduce the distinction between private and public companies. Further information about public companies will be found in **Chapter 32**.

6.2 Corporations

A 'company' is in law a corporation, that is, an artificial legal 'person' with rights and obligations distinct from those of its members. Business associations were occasionally made corporations by Royal Charter from about the sixteenth century (for example, the East India Company in 1600), but until the industrial revolution few businesses were incorporated. With the growth of the canal and railway systems, incorporations were permitted in increasing numbers under Acts of Parliament. The vast majority of corporations are now companies formed under the Companies Act 1985 or under earlier legislation superseded by that Act.

6.3 Sources of Company Law

6.3.1 COMPANY LEGISLATION

The Companies Act (CA) 1985 is the most important source of company law. It consolidates legislation contained in earlier Companies Acts and other pieces of legislation dealing with

LIMITED COMPANIES

company law. The 1985 Act has been amended in significant respects by the Insolvency Act 1986, the Companies Act 1989 and a number of statutory instruments made under the Act.

The 1985 Act applies throughout Great Britain although a number of provisions apply only to Scotland or only to England and Wales. Northern Ireland has its own legislation which is substantially the same as the British legislation.

6.3.2 JUDICIAL DECISIONS

Some of the basic rules concerning companies result from judicial decisions and do not appear in the Act. Of special importance are the rules of equity relating to fiduciary relationships (which play a major part in determining the legal position of company directors) and the rule in *Foss* v *Harbottle* (see **9.6**). There are also hundreds of reported cases in which Companies Acts have been interpreted by the courts. Most of these cases were decided before the 1985 Act came into force but continue to be authoritative interpretations of the consolidated legislation.

6.3.3 TAX LEGISLATION

The taxation of companies is largely dealt with in the Income and Corporation Taxes Act 1988 as amended by subsequent Finance Acts. Companies' capital gains are largely dealt with in accordance with the Taxation of Chargeable Gains Act 1992, as amended. Again, many decisions of the courts have interpreted the meaning of this legislation. The taxation of companies is examined in detail in **Chapter 15**.

6.3.4 THE GENERAL LAW

It is worth pointing out that the general law applies to companies as it applies to individuals, except to the extent that it has been modified by specific rules of company law. The general law of contract, for example, applies to companies with very few modifications, as does the law of tort, conveyancing and so on. This is really just a consequence of the fact that a company is a corporation and, therefore, in law a 'person' with legal rights and obligations.

6.3.5 THE COMPANY'S OWN REGULATIONS: ARTICLES OF ASSOCIATION

Despite the vast amount of law which applies to companies, a great deal of freedom of choice is given to each individual company as to how it will be administered. This is both desirable and inevitable because of the widely differing circumstances in which each company operates. To provide for its own internal administration each company must have a set of regulations known as *articles of association* (**Chapters 7** and **26**). These may be specially prepared for the company by the draftsman who assists with its formation; however, the Companies Act provides for a model form of articles (Table A) and most of the regulations adopted by a company will follow that model. The provisions of Table A are contained in a statutory instrument (SI 1985 No 805) which came into force with the 1985 Act. Companies formed before the 1985 Act usually have regulations based on earlier versions of Table A.

6.4 Registration

A company is formed under CA 1985 by a process called *registration*. This involves sending a number of documents and a fee to the Registrar of Companies, the official responsible for registering companies in England and Wales. A company comes into existence on the issue of a *certificate of incorporation* by the Registrar. At this time, '. . . the subscribers of the memorandum (see **7.5.1**), together with such other persons as may from time to time become members of the company, shall be a body corporate by the name contained in the memorandum' (s. 13(3) CA 1985).

The Registrar is also responsible for maintaining records relating to registered companies. These records contain information which companies are required by law to disclose in relation to a wide range of matters. Records are kept at the Companies' Registry, which is in Cardiff.

The process of registration is examined in more detail in **Chapter 7**. The making and interpretation of a search of a company's records at the Companies' Registry is considered in **Chapter 29**.

6.5 Types of Registered Company

6.5.1 COMPANIES LIMITED BY SHARES

Most registered companies are 'limited by shares'. This expression refers to the *liability* of the members (or shareholders — the terms are almost interchangeable) of the company for that company's debts on a liquidation. The effect of a company being limited by shares is that, on a liquidation, the liability of a member is limited to the amount, if any, which remains unpaid on his shares. This is described further below.

When a company issues shares, the person taking the shares must agree to pay for them. Usually payment will be made immediately but sometimes shares will be issued 'unpaid' (sometimes expressed as 'nil-paid') or 'partly-paid', in which case payment must be made later. If the company goes into liquidation and is insolvent, any member who has not fully paid for their shares is liable to pay the amount outstanding to the liquidator, who will apply such amount in paying the company's debts. That is the extent of that member's liability for the company's debts. In the case of a member who has paid in full for his shares, he will have no liability (in normal circumstances) for the company's debts.

6.5.1.1 Comparison with partnership

The position of a shareholder in a limited company is quite different from the position of a member of a partnership (see **3.2**). If a partnership business fails each of the partners stands to lose not only what he has invested but also any private wealth which he may have. Limited liability can be an enormous advantage to a businessman, although creditors (particularly those who have lent money to the company) may require personal guarantees of the company's debts from shareholders, thus reducing the advantage.

6.5.2 COMPANIES LIMITED BY GUARANTEE

A small number of companies are limited by guarantee rather than by shares. This means that each member undertakes to pay a specified amount if the company is wound up while he is a member or within a year after he ceases to be a member. Most companies limited by guarantee are charities or other non-trading companies.

6.5.3 UNLIMITED COMPANIES

An unlimited company is one which is registered under the Companies Act but without any limit on the liability of the members. If an unlimited company goes into liquidation the members are liable to contribute the whole of their private wealth (if so much is needed) to the payment of the company's debts. The creditors cannot sue the members direct but must claim in the liquidation. The liquidator then calls for contributions from the members.

LIMITED COMPANIES

6.6 Public and Private Companies (see also Chapter 32)

6.6.1 CLASSIFICATION

Nearly all company law rules apply equally to all companies. There are a small number of rules which distinguish between 'public companies' and 'private companies'. A public company is defined by s. 1 CA 1985 as 'a company limited by shares . . ., being a company:

(a) the memorandum of which states that the company is to be a public company; and

(b) in relation to which the provisions of [the Companies Act] as to the registration or re-registration of a company as a public company have been complied with . . .'.

The same section defines a private company as any company which is not a public company. On incorporation the promoters (that is, the people who form the company) will decide whether it is to be a public company or a private company and will draft the memorandum accordingly.

6.6.2 DIFFERENCES

The principal differences between public and private companies are as follows:

(a) *Authorised minimum share capital*

A public company cannot commence business until a certificate is issued by the Registrar showing that the authorised minimum share capital has been issued (s. 117 CA 1985). The authorised minimum is currently £50,000 but can be increased by statutory instrument. A private company can commence business as soon as it is incorporated.

(b) *Payment for shares*

A public company cannot issue shares unless each share is immediately paid for at least to the extent of 25% of the nominal value plus the whole of any premium (s. 101 CA 1985) (for the definitions of nominal value and premium see **Chapter 10**). A private company can issue shares without requiring immediate payment for them.

(c) *Issuing shares*

A public company can issue shares or debentures to the public (hence the description 'public company'); a private company is prohibited from doing so by the Financial Services Act 1986.

(d) *Name*

The name of a public company must end with the words 'Public Limited Company' or its equivalent (equivalents include PLC and, for Welsh companies, Cwmni Cyfyngedig Cyhoeddus or CCC). The names of private limited companies cannot end with these words and must end with 'Limited' or its equivalent (e.g., Ltd, Cyfyngedig or Cyf) unless the company has obtained permission to dispense with the use of the word 'Limited' in its name.

(e) *Directors*

A public company must have at least two directors, a private company need only have one (s. 282 CA 1985).

(f) *Miscellaneous*

There are a large number of smaller differences between the two types of company — for example, the directors of a private company need not retire at 70, those of a public company must (unless certain procedures are followed) (s. 293 CA 1985); a proxy can speak only at a meeting of a private company (s. 372 CA 1985); a single resolution at a meeting of a private company may validly elect two or more directors, in the case of a public company each appointment must be voted on separately (unless the meeting first unanimously approves the moving of a single resolution) (s. 292 CA 1985).

6.6.3 OTHER DEFINITIONS

All companies are public or private but there are a number of other categories of company to which special rules apply:

(a) *Quoted company*

A company is in this category if its shares are quoted on a stock exchange. A quoted company must keep a special register of those shareholders with 3% or more of the shares. Because of Stock Exchange rules only public companies can obtain a quotation.

(b) *Close company*

This category is relevant only for tax purposes; special tax rules apply to close companies (see **15.5**). Virtually all private companies are close and so are some public companies. A company which is not close is sometimes called an 'open company' but 'non-close company' is more correct.

(c) *Small and medium-sized companies*

These are companies which because of their relatively small size (in financial terms) are exempt from providing certain information in their accounts. In addition, certain categories of small companies are now exempt from the requirement to have an audit of their accounts. Definitions of small and medium-sized companies, and the various exemptions applicable to them, are given in ss. 246–249E CA 1985.

(d) *Partnership company*

This category will be introduced by regulations made under the Companies Act 1989. A partnership company will in most respects be an ordinary private company but with regulations suitable for a company which is owned by its own employees.

(e) *Elective regime company*

This category was introduced into CA 1985 by the Companies Act 1989. An 'elective regime company' is an ordinary private company which has opted out of certain provisions of the Companies Act. It will only be possible to opt out if the shareholders unanimously agree. Once they have done so the company need not hold an annual general meeting nor a shareholders' meeting to consider accounts. The procedure for calling meetings and issuing shares is also simpler than in the case of other companies.

6.6.4 PRE-CA 1985 PRIVATE COMPANIES PROVISION IN ARTICLES

As was explained above, a company is now public if its memorandum says so and it complies with certain other requirements; otherwise it is private. Until the Companies Act 1980 (now consolidated in CA 1985) came into force a company was public unless its *articles* made it private by including provisions which:

LIMITED COMPANIES

(a) restricted the right to transfer shares;

(b) restricted membership to 50;

(c) prevented public issue of shares.

For a considerable time to come many private companies will have articles doing these three things because they were formed at a time when they could not be private companies unless their articles contained such restrictions. It should be noted that modern private companies need not include any of these provisions in their articles, although many do restrict the right to transfer shares and the restriction on public issue is imposed independently of the articles by the Financial Services Act 1986.

6.7 Separate Legal Personality

As we have already seen, a company is a 'body corporate', that is, it is a legal person distinct from its members and officers (i.e., its directors and secretary). Even if a company is 100% owned and controlled by a shareholder, that company has a completely separate legal personality from that of the shareholder. This is clearly illustrated in the leading case of *Salomon* v *A. Salomon and Co. Ltd* [1897] AC 22.

A number of consequences flow from this separate legal personality, so that a company:

(a) is able to own property;

(b) is liable for its own debts;

(c) can sue its debtors;

(d) is liable to be sued by its creditors; and

(e) has 'perpetual succession' — this means that the company does not cease to exist just because a member (however many shares he may own) dies or otherwise ceases to be a member.

6.8 'Lifting the Veil of Incorporation'

There are a number of circumstances in which the court may be willing to ignore the fact that a company is a separate legal person. Legislation also sometimes ignores the distinction between a company and its members. These circumstances are rather fancifully described as 'lifting the veil of incorporation' because the law looks behind the legal 'veil' which separates the company from its members and officers.

The occasions when the veil of incorporation is lifted are hard to classify and it is probably open to the courts to extend the circumstances in the future. It is, of course, open to Parliament to do so by legislation.

6.8.1 COMPANY LEGISLATION

The Companies Act 1985 and the Insolvency Act 1986 contain a number of rules which depart from the general principle of separate corporate personality; for example:

(a) *Fraudulent trading*

Section 213 of the Insolvency Act 1986 provides that *any person* who is or was knowingly a party to fraudulent trading by a company whose business is being carried on with intent to defraud creditors or other persons, may be liable to pay the debts of the company. This liability arises only if the company is being wound up (although criminal penalties may be imposed for fraudulent trading under s. 458 CA 1985 even if the company is not being wound up).

(b) *Wrongful trading*

Section 214 of the Insolvency Act 1986 provides that *directors* of the company may be personally liable in cases of wrongful trading. This arises where a company becomes insolvent and the directors then fail to take steps to protect creditors. This type of liability only arises if the company is being wound up.

Sections 213 and 214 are discussed further in **Chapter 24**.

(c) *Group accounts*

Where companies are members of a group, group accounts must be produced to reflect that the financial transactions of the subsidiaries are in reality activities of the holding company (s. 227 CA 1985).

6.8.2 DECISIONS OF THE COURTS

6.8.2.1 Attempts to avoid legal obligations

The courts have occasionally lifted the veil of incorporation by making orders against companies where the proprietors have used a company as a means of avoiding a personal legal obligation. For example in *Jones* v *Lipman* [1962] 1 WLR 832, the defendant had contracted to sell land to the plaintiff and later conveyed it to a company in an attempt to avoid the possibility of an order of specific performance (an order of specific performance cannot normally be made once a third party has acquired rights in the subject-matter of the contract). The company was owned and controlled by the defendant and so an order of specific performance was made against the company as well as the vendor.

In *Creasey* v *Breachwood Motors Ltd* [1992] BCC 638 a company transferred all its assets to another company. That other company was substituted for the first company in pending litigation. However, in giving its judgment the court made it clear that this will not be done as a matter of course, the circumstances have to show that there is a good reason for the ruling (for example, to protect the interests of a creditor against an unfair attempt by the original defendant to obtain an advantage for its shareholders).

In *El Ajou* v *Dollar Land Holdings* [1993] 3 All ER 717 it was held that the knowledge of a director that assets were acquired as a result of fraud could be imputed to the company so that the assets acquired by the company could be recovered by the victim of the fraud. (The action failed, on its facts, as the plaintiff was not able to prove such knowledge.)

6.8.2.2 Agency and trusts

In a few cases the court has held that a company is either an agent for its shareholders or their trustee; however, the exact scope of these decisions is rather unclear and these cases ought to be regarded as providing exceptions rather than general rules. A company will *not* generally be regarded as either an agent for, or trustee of, its members.

LIMITED COMPANIES

6.8.3 TAX LEGISLATION

Tax legislation often imposes tax liability on shareholders to reflect the fact that transactions of their company are in reality transactions conducted on their behalf. It is not proposed to deal with all the rules involved but the following examples should be sufficient to indicate their scope:

(a) The companies in a 'group' of companies (i.e., broadly speaking, a holding company and its subsidiaries) are in many ways treated as one company for corporation tax purposes. Thus the rate of tax depends on the size of the group's profits rather than on the size of each company's profits, losses made by one member of a group can generally be set off against profits made by others, and dividend payments within the group may be ignored for tax purposes.

(b) Gifts made by a close company are treated as made by its members for the purpose of inheritance tax.

(c) The sale of a business to a company in return for shares can usually be ignored for capital gains tax purposes.

SEVEN

FORMATION OF A LIMITED COMPANY

This chapter covers the following topics:

7.1 Introduction
7.2 Promoters
7.3 Pre-incorporation contracts
7.4 Methods of providing the client with a company
7.5 Steps leading to incorporation
7.6 The certificate of incorporation
7.7 Steps necessary after incorporation
7.8 Comparison of 'tailor-made' with 'shelf' company
7.9 Change of name
7.10 Change of objects
7.11 Change of accounting reference date.

7.1 Introduction

In this chapter, we shall look at the process by which a limited company is formed and at the documentation required both for and following the formation. We shall also look at shelf companies, as alternative means of providing a company to a client.

A solicitor advising a client on the formation of a new business or on changing an existing business into a company, would first discuss the advisability of incorporation, compared to the alternatives of remaining a sole trader or forming a partnership. This requires a detailed knowledge of partnership law, company law and relevant tax considerations. We therefore leave the topic of choice of business medium until **Chapter 31**.

For the rest of this chapter, we shall assume that, following discussion, the client has decided that he wishes to form a company. Once this stage has been reached, the solicitor should discuss with the client the following:

(a) the effect of incorporation and the legal requirements of running a company;

(b) whether the company should be formed by the solicitor or whether a shelf company should be used (see **7.8**);

(c) the problems which may arise if contracts are made in the name of, or on behalf of, the company before incorporation; and

FORMATION OF A LIMITED COMPANY

(d) the steps to be taken after incorporation, as required by the Companies Act 1985.

Unless a shelf company is being used, the solicitor will then prepare the documents required for incorporation. If a shelf company is being used, this step will be unnecessary.

We shall now consider these matters. It should be borne in mind that especially in relation to the proposed company's constitution, circumstances will vary from case to case. This Guide is particularly concerned with the problems likely to be faced by a two-or three-man business.

7.2 Promoters

Those who wish to form a company are usually known as the 'promoters' of the company. There is no legal definition of a promoter; whether someone is a promoter is a question of fact. However, it is generally accepted that a promoter owes certain duties to the company which he seeks to create. These include duties of good faith and disclosure. It is important to advise promoters of their potential liability for any contracts which they might enter into on behalf of the proposed company prior to its incorporation (see 7.3).

For the purposes of this chapter, we have used the term 'promoters' to include those wishing either to form a tailor-made company or to purchase a shelf company, which company will be used as a vehicle for their business.

7.3 Pre-incorporation Contracts

Difficulties may arise in relation to contracts made by the promoters on behalf of a proposed company. They may wish to make contracts to acquire premises, machinery, stationery and so on, prior to the company becoming incorporated. This may be due to a desire to have things 'up and running', so that trading can commence immediately the company is incorporated. This creates a problem as the company cannot enter into contracts until it has been incorporated as, until such time, it is not a legal person. The promoters cannot act as its agents, since the principal does not exist.

Should the promoters purport to enter into a contract *on behalf of* the unformed company, s. 36C CA 1985 will apply. This provides that:

> A contract which purports to be made by or on behalf of a company at a time when the company has not been formed has effect, subject to any agreement to the contrary, as one made with the person purporting to act for the company or as agent for it, and he is personally liable on the contract accordingly.

The threat of personal liability means that the safest course is to enter into contracts only after incorporation, when they can be entered into by the company. If this is not possible, then the following may be considered:

(a) preparing a draft contract which will be entered into by the company following incorporation;

(b) entering into a binding contract under which the promoters are personally liable until incorporation, at which time the contract is *novated*, i.e., a new contract on the same terms is entered into between the company and the third party (note that the third party's consent to novation will be required); or

(c) entering into a binding contract under which the promoters are personally liable until incorporation, at which time the promoters transfer the benefit of the contract to the

FORMATION OF A LIMITED COMPANY

company in return for the company's agreement to *indemnify* them in respect of their liability to the third party.

7.4 Methods of Providing the Client with a Company

There are two main methods by which a client can be provided with a company. The solicitor may actually form a new company, using the procedure set out in **7.5**. In doing so, he can ensure that the company meets the client's particular requirements in every way: the company is effectively 'tailor-made' and brought into existence for the client.

Alternatively, the solicitor can arrange for the client to acquire a 'shelf' (or 'off-the-peg') company. This type of company *has already been incorporated*, either by law stationers or, sometimes, by the firm of solicitors. Since the company already exists, it must be *transferred* to the client.

These methods are compared later in **7.8**. For the moment, we shall look at the steps required for the incorporation of a tailor-made company.

7.5 Steps Leading to Incorporation

For a company to be registered under the Companies Act, the promoters or their solicitor must deliver to the Registrar of Companies the following:

(a) a memorandum of association;

(b) articles of association (but see **7.5.2**, for adoption of Table A by reference in the memorandum);

(c) Form 10, setting out details of the registered office, the directors and secretary of the company;

(d) Form 12, a statutory declaration of compliance with the requirements of the Companies Act;

(e) the Registrar's fee (currently £20).

In this chapter we will consider the formation of private limited companies only. Of the documents that have to be submitted to the Registrar the most important are the company's memorandum and articles; great care must be taken to ensure that they are suitable for the particular circumstances.

7.5.1 MEMORANDUM OF ASSOCIATION

Section 1 CA 1985 provides that every company must have a memorandum, which is sometimes described as the company's 'charter'. Its principal function is to set out the *raison d'être* of the company and to regulate its dealings with outsiders. Five compulsory clauses *must* be included in the memorandum. These relate to:

(a) the name of the company;

(b) the registered office;

(c) the objects of the company;

FORMATION OF A LIMITED COMPANY

(d) the liability of the members;

(e) the authorised share capital of the company.

The memorandum must also contain the 'association' and 'subscription' clauses. The former states that the persons who subscribe (i.e., sign) the memorandum wish to be formed into a company and that they each agree to take a specified number of shares in the new company. The latter sets out the names, addresses and descriptions of the subscribers and the number of shares each agrees to take. The memorandum must be signed by a minimum of one subscriber, who signs in the presence of at least one witness, and each subscriber must agree to take at least one share. (Two subscribers is the minimum for a public company.)

Further clauses may be included, covering anything which could be contained in the company's articles, however, this is rarely done in practice.

We shall now consider each of the required clauses in turn.

7.5.1.1 The name

Choice of name

Generally, the promoters have freedom of choice as far as the company's name is concerned. The purpose of a company's name is to differentiate the company from all other registered companies. Sections 25–26 CA 1985, therefore, prohibit the Registrar from registering a company with a name which:

(a) does not end with the word 'limited' (or its Welsh equivalent 'cyfyngedig' if appropriate — see below) if the company is a private limited company.

(Section 30 provides that a company limited by guarantee may apply for dispensation from using the word 'limited'. The objects of a company applying for this exemption must be the promotion of commerce, art, science, education, religion, charity or a profession and its memorandum or articles must prohibit the members from taking any profits out of the company.)

(b) is the same as that of an existing registered company; or

(c) in the opinion of the Secretary of State constitutes a criminal offence, or is offensive;

(d) includes the words limited, unlimited or public limited company (or the Welsh equivalents or abbreviations of these words) *other than at the end of the name;*

(e) includes words suggesting a connection with the Government or a local authority or particular words specified in regulations (made under s. 29 CA 1985). In such cases, however, the Registrar may give approval for registration of the name. In the case of words specified in the regulations, consultation with government departments or institutions specified in the regulations is sometimes required before the Registrar gives his approval.

If a name is rejected by the Registrar a certain amount of expense and delay is bound to occur, as the promoters or solicitor will have to submit a further set of documents applying for formation with a new name. The new memorandum will have to be printed (although 'printing' in this context includes most types of photocopying) and so will the new articles (unless Table A is adopted by reference in the memorandum). To minimise the risk of a name being rejected the promoters or solicitor should consult the index of company names kept by the Registrar of Companies shortly before the application for registration. If the name is already in use a new name should be chosen. If the name is not in use then the application should progress quickly as there is no procedure for reserving a name.

Power of Secretary of State to order change of name

The Secretary of State has power to direct a company to change its name in the following circumstances:

(a) within 12 months of registration, if the name is too like a name appearing in the index of names at the time of registration or is the same as a name which should have been in the index at that time (s. 28(2) CA 1985);

(b) within five years of registration, if misleading information was given at the time of registration (s. 28(3) CA 1985); and

(c) at any time, if the name gives 'so misleading an indication of the nature of [the company's] activities as to be likely to cause harm to the public' (s. 32 CA 1985).

Passing-off

Registration of a company with a particular name does not give the company any protection against a passing-off action if an existing business trades under a similar name and its business is likely to be affected by the similarity.

Trade marks

If a company registered a name which included a registered trade mark of another business, it would be open to an action for infringement of such trade mark. It may therefore be prudent for the promoters or their solicitor to inspect the trade marks register before applying for registration, should there be any concern in this regard.

Change of name by company

Section 28 CA 1985 provides that, after a company is formed, it is free to change its name by passing a special resolution subject to the same restrictions as apply to choice of name by a new company. The procedures required to be followed to change a company name are dealt with in more detail in **7.9**.

7.5.1.2 Registered office

The second compulsory clause in the memorandum sets out the *situation* of the company's registered office. It does not state the address of the company's registered office (this appears in Form 10 — see **7.5.3**), but only that the office is situated in England (which includes Wales for this purpose) or Wales (to the exclusion of England) or Scotland as appropriate. The function of this clause is to determine the company's domicile, and it can only be altered by Act of Parliament.

If the office is to be in Wales (to the exclusion of England), the company's name may end in the word 'cyfyngedig' rather than 'limited'. The memorandum and articles may, in such cases, be printed in Welsh but a certified translation into English is required.

7.5.1.3 The objects and the ultra vires doctrine

The third compulsory clause specifies the company's objects, or purposes, and the powers it is to have.

FORMATION OF A LIMITED COMPANY

Common law doctrine of ultra vires

The effect of this doctrine was that any contracts made, or acts done, by the company not within the objects clause or reasonably incidental thereto, used to be void. Because of this rule objects clauses have traditionally been drafted very widely. In particular it is usual to find many sub-clauses which seek to list all the businesses and activities which the company could conceivably wish to undertake in the future. These will be followed by a statement that each sub-clause should be construed as independent of each other. In *Cotman* v *Brougham* [1918] AC 514 it was held that this did in fact make each sub-clause an independent object. Without such a statement the later sub-clauses would be construed as being dependent on the 'main objects' stated in the first few sub-clauses.

In *Bell Houses Ltd* v *City Wall Properties Ltd* [1966] 2 QB 656 it was held that an objects clause saying that the company could carry on any business which the directors believed could be 'advantageously carried on by the company in connection with or ancillary to the company's other businesses' was valid.

Decisions such as these reduced the significance of the ultra vires rule for companies; however, it remained problematic and companies continued to draft wide, and very long, objects clauses.

Effect of legislation on the ultra vires doctrine

Section 35 of the Companies Act 1985 all but abolishes the rule in relation to transactions between *a company and an outsider*. However, the directors may be liable to the company if it suffers loss as a result of a breach of the objects clause — see **Chapter 8**. Despite this, most companies still submit a long form of objects clause when they register. An alternative is now available under s. 3A CA 1985 and this provides:

> Where the company's memorandum states that the object of the company is to carry on business as a general commercial company —
>
> (a) the object of the company is to carry on any trade or business whatsoever, and
>
> (b) the company has power to do all such things as are incidental or conducive to the carrying on of any trade or business by it.

Where a company adopts this simple form of objects clause the powers of the company will include power to carry on any trade or business.

The number of companies which have chosen to be incorporated with an objects clause in the new simple form is not known. It is thought that most new companies are adopting a 'belt and braces' approach and have both the new form of clause and a traditional long-form objects clause following it.

Alteration of objects

A company may alter its objects clause by special resolution (which requires 75% of the votes cast in order to be passed — see **Chapter 12**) under s. 4 CA 1985. This is dealt with in more detail in **7.10**.

7.5.1.4 The liability clause

This merely states whether the members' liability for the debts of the company is limited or unlimited but it does not specify *the manner* in which the members' liability is limited (e.g., by shares or by guarantee). The clause is unalterable but if a company wishes to change the nature of liability it may re-register under ss. 49-52 CA 1985. The detailed provisions are complex, and beyond the scope of this book; the main requirements are that the unanimous consent of all the members is needed to convert from limited to unlimited but only a special resolution — that is, a 75% majority — is necessary to change from unlimited to limited.

7.5.1.5 The capital clause

The final compulsory clause in the memorandum states the amount of the company's 'authorised share capital' and how it is divided into shares of a specified nominal value (sometimes called the 'par value'). It is possible to divide the shares into different classes enjoying different rights (such as preferential dividend or voting entitlements) but this is normally done, if at all, under provisions in the articles.

The company cannot issue shares in excess of its authorised share capital as stated in its memorandum. However, the shareholders can resolve to increase this limit and therefore the capital clause does not restrict the amount which can be invested in the company.

At this stage it may be useful to explain the terminology commonly applied to share capital:

(a) *Authorised capital* limits the maximum number of shares which the company can issue.

(b) *Issued capital* is the part of the authorised share capital which has been issued to the members. The issued capital is calculated by multiplying the number of shares issued by their nominal value.

(c) *Paid-up capital* is the amount received to date from the members for their shares, whether in cash or in the form of assets. Since the company may, if it wishes, call for only part payment at the time when shares are issued, the paid-up capital may be less than the issued capital.

7.5.2 THE ARTICLES OF ASSOCIATION

The second document which must be drafted before the company is incorporated is the articles of association (s. 7 CA 1985). These regulate the company's internal affairs and contain regulations dealing with such matters as directors' powers, proceedings at members' meetings, conduct at board meetings and so on. The promoters decide what form the articles take.

7.5.2.1 Choice of form of articles

There are no compulsory clauses but the Companies (Tables A to F) Regulations 1985 contain a standard set of articles which set out regulations (called Table A) intended to be suitable for an 'average' company. The company may:

(a) have prepared specially drafted articles;

(b) reprint Table A either with or without amendment; or

(c) adopt Table A by special reference in its memorandum (in which case it need not submit a printed copy of its articles when applying for registration).

If this last procedure is followed the adopted Table A will be in the form laid down in the Regulations in force at the date of incorporation. While later Regulations and/or Acts may change Table A from time to time this will not affect companies already registered. Therefore, for the purpose of reference, copies of Table A in the appropriate form should be kept. It should be noted that the present Table A was introduced on 1 July 1985. It is substantially different from its predecessor (contained in the Companies Act 1948 and amended on a number of occasions) which will form the basis of the articles of most companies incorporated before July 1985 for many years to come.

Unless Table A is adopted by reference in the memorandum, the articles submitted for registration must be 'printed' and must be signed by the subscribers to the memorandum in the presence of a witness.

When preparing to incorporate a company, one of the most important matters to discuss with the promoters is the contents of the articles and their effect. Because Table A is a standard form it may not be suitable for every company and should be altered to meet the circumstances. Other possible provisions are considered in **Chapter 26**.

7.5.2.2 Amendment of articles

Should the company be incorporated with unsuitable articles or should circumstances change, s. 9 CA 1985 allows amendments, provided a special resolution approving them is passed (see **Chapter 26**).

7.5.3 FORM 10

This is a statutory form which is a statement of the first directors and secretary and intended situation of the company's registered office. It is required by s. 10(2) and sch. 1 CA 1985. The form is supplied with notes explaining its completion. The following points should be noted:

(a) The *address* of the company's first registered office appears in this form, not in the memorandum; later it can be moved anywhere within the country specified in the 'office' clause in the memorandum. The registered office may be changed by giving notice to the Registrar, using a Form 287. The change is effective in relation to service of documents when registered by the Registrar although service of documents at the old registered office remains valid for a further 14 days after registration. A company is required to keep certain registers and documents at its registered office and to make them available for public inspection (see **7.7.3**).

(b) The company must have at least one director and if only one is appointed he must not also be the company secretary. This ensures that every company has at least two separate officers. (Note that a public company must have at least *two* directors — see **32.2.2.4**.)

(c) The information required in relation to the directors includes details of other directorships.

(d) The persons named as directors and secretary, and who sign the form to signify their consent, automatically become the first directors and secretary of the company even if the articles provide otherwise.

7.5.4 FORM 12

This is a statutory declaration of compliance with the registration requirements of the Act. It must be completed by the solicitor engaged in forming the company or one of the company's directors or secretary named in Form 10.

7.5.5 THE FEE

The documents must be sent to the Registrar of Companies together with the fee of £20. This will result in the application being processed within five to six days. If the new company is required urgently, it is possible to pay a fee of £100, which guarantees same-day incorporation.

7.6 The Certificate of Incorporation

The Registrar will examine the documents and, provided they are in order and the chosen name is still available, he will sign a certificate of incorporation stating that the company was incorporated under the Companies Act 1985 and that the company is limited (if appropriate). The Registrar specifies the company's registered number on the certificate and this must be quoted on all official documents and business letters.

Under s. 13(3), from the date of incorporation the company becomes a legal entity. At the same time as the Registrar issues the certificate, he must (under s. 711 CA 1985) 'officially notify' the fact of issue. This means he must place a notice to this effect in the Government's official newspaper (in England and Wales, the *London Gazette*).

7.7 Steps Necessary after Incorporation

Once the certificate of incorporation has been issued the company's existence begins. There are then certain procedural and statutory provisions to be complied with. In addition to matters such as the issue of shares and fixing the company's accounting reference date, which will be dealt with soon after incorporation, these steps relate to the following formal requirements:

(a) the company's seal (if there is to be one);

(b) the publication of the company's name;

(c) the keeping of certain statutory 'books'.

7.7.1 THE SEAL

There is no legal requirement for a company to have a seal. If the company does have one, the company's name must be engraved on it. Whether or not the company has a seal, documents signed by a director and the secretary and expressed (in whatever form of words) to be executed by the company will have the same effect as if they were under the company's seal.

7.7.2 PUBLICATION OF THE COMPANY'S NAME

The Companies Act 1985 contains a number of provisions concerning publication of a company's name. A company is required to:

(a) display its registered name outside every office or place of business in which its business is carried on, in a conspicuous position and in letters which are easily legible (s. 348 CA 1985);

(b) ensure that its name appears on all business letters, notices, cheques, orders for money or goods, invoices, etc. (s. 349 CA 1985).

7.7.2.1 Company name: liability of officers

An officer of the company who uses an incorrectly engraved seal or issues a letter, invoice, etc. or signs a cheque, order for money, etc. on which the correct name does not appear is liable to a fine. However, where the document in question is a cheque, bill of exchange, promissory note, order for money or goods, there is additional, more serious, liability, in that the signatory will be personally liable to the holder of the cheque, etc.

FORMATION OF A LIMITED COMPANY

7.7.2.2 Company stationery

A further practical point relating to the name and its publication is that the promoters will need to have stationery printed which complies with the statutory requirements. This cannot, however, be done until the certificate of incorporation has been issued, confirming that the chosen name was accepted and giving the company's number. Section 305 CA 1985 requires that if the name of *any* director appears on a business letter (other than in the text or as a signatory) on which the company's name appears, then the forenames (or initials) and surnames of *all* the directors who are individuals and the corporate names of all the corporate directors must appear in legible characters.

7.7.2.3 Letters and order forms

Section 351 CA 1985 requires the company's letters and order forms to specify:

(a) the place (i.e., country) of registration of the company and its registered number;

(b) the address of its registered office;

(c) that it is a limited company if it has been granted a licence to dispense with 'limited' as the last word of the name.

Failure to comply makes the company and every officer authorising the issue of a letter, etc. liable to a fine.

7.7.3 THE STATUTORY BOOKS

7.7.3.1 The books

The Companies Act 1985 requires companies to keep certain 'books' (i.e., records — they need not be bound volumes). The company can prepare its own books or buy them from law stationers. As far as a private limited company is concerned, the most important books it must keep at its registered office are:

(a) A *register of members*, containing each member's name, address, dates of entry on the register and cessation of membership together with details of the shares held. (Note that s. 354, CA 1985 requires an index of members to be kept if a company has more than 50 members and the register is not already kept in the form of an index.)

(b) A *register of directors* and a *register of secretaries* setting out their names, addresses, and, for directors only, details of any other directorships. It is advisable to include details of the period of holding office since problems may arise in the future as to whether a board decision was validly passed and enquiries of the directors holding office at the time may be necessary; similarly for secretaries. (See **8.7.1.1**.)

(c) A *register of the interests of directors*, their spouses and infant children in shares and debentures of the company, its holding and subsidiary companies as required by ss. 324-328 CA 1985. The purpose of this is to ensure that the extent of a director's direct or indirect control over the company is known.

(d) A *register of charges* which must be kept even if the company has not yet charged any of its assets. It sets out details of the property charged and the terms of the charge.

(e) Copies of the company's *memorandum and articles*.

7.7.3.2 Inspection of company books

All these books must be available for inspection by members, creditors and the general public for at least two hours daily during business hours. The Secretary of State has power to make regulations concerning the times when registers are to be available. Certain of the books may be kept at a place other than the registered office provided the Registrar is notified.

7.7.3.3 Other documents to be kept by a company

Other documents which should be kept at the registered office include:

(a) Copies of all instruments creating any charge over the company's property (whether or not registrable at the Companies Registry (see **10.8**)) and a register of brief particulars of the charges. The copies and register are available for inspection by members and creditors free of charge and by anyone else on payment of a fee prescribed by regulations.

(b) The directors' service contracts, which can only be inspected by members.

(c) The minute book of general meetings of the company, which can only be inspected by members.

7.8 Comparison of Tailor-made with Shelf Company

This section compares a company which is tailor-made to the promoters' particular requirements in every way to one which is bought from a stock of shelf or off-the-peg companies.

7.8.1 THE TAILOR-MADE COMPANY

This is a company formed following the procedure outlined above. The documentation will be tailored to the promoters' requirements, with the memorandum and articles including provisions appropriate to the particular circumstances of the case. The promoters will most likely be the subscribers to the memorandum (the company's first members) and may also be the company's first directors and secretary.

At first sight, this method appears more expensive due to the time involved in taking instructions on, and then drafting, the required documentation. In addition, there will be a delay between taking instructions and the company's incorporation (although Companies House currently offers an expedited, same-day, incorporation service for £100).

7.8.2 THE SHELF OR OFF-THE-PEG COMPANY

This is a company which has already been incorporated by a company formation business: law stationers or firm of solicitors from whom it is then purchased by the promoters.

If this type of company is bought, the only part of the documentation which is likely to be entirely suitable to the trader's needs will be the objects clause of the memorandum, since stocks of companies carrying on most types of business are maintained. Companies will also be available with their object to 'carry on business as a general commercial company' (see **7.5.1.3**). However, while the objects clause will almost certainly be satisfactory, the name probably will not be and the articles may not be.

7.8.2.1 Company name

On incorporation, the shelf company will have been given a name which will have no connection with the company's owners or business. If the name of their company is

FORMATION OF A LIMITED COMPANY

unimportant to the promoters this will cause no problems; however, if they wish their company to trade under their own names or a chosen name, it will have to be changed (see 7.9).

7.8.2.2 Use of business name

An alternative is to use a business name for the purposes of trading, provided the promoters comply with the requirements of the Business Names Act 1985. This Act requires that where a company does not carry on its business under its corporate name:

(a) The corporate name must appear on all business letters, orders for goods or services to be supplied to the business, invoices and receipts issued in the course of the business as well as on written demands for payment of debts arising in the course of the business. In addition, an address in Great Britain at which service of any document relating to the business will be effective must be set out.

(b) In any premises where the business is carried on and to which the customers of the business or suppliers of any goods or services to the business have access, the company must display prominently a notice setting out this name and address.

The Act requires the company to supply this information in writing to anyone dealing in the course of business with the company who asks for it. Failure to comply with any of these requirements may lead to a fine.

7.8.2.3 Articles of association

As regards the articles, the shelf company will have been incorporated with either Table A alone or with standard amended articles. Great care must be taken to ensure that the articles are suitable. If they are not, they will have to be amended in accordance with s. 9 CA 1985, which requires the members to pass a special resolution approving the change (see **Chapter 26**). Having done so, a new print of all the articles will have to be delivered to the Registrar (together with a copy of the special resolution), which will take time and increase the expenses of formation.

7.8.2.4 Shelf company documentation

Representatives of the entity which formed the shelf company will have signed the memorandum and articles of association as subscribers, and been named in Form 10. This means that they become the first members, directors and secretary of the company, and their names should appear in the company's books as such. In order for ownership and control of the shelf company to be passed to the promoters, it is necessary that:

(a) the first members *transfer* their shares to the promoters;

(b) the first directors and secretary *resign* their positions; and

(c) new directors and a secretary (often the promoters) are appointed.

This entails, inter alia, the completion of stock transfer forms (see **11.2.3**) and company Form 288 (see **8.7.1.1** and **8.12**). Again, this will involve time and expense. Stamp duty is also payable, on the transfer of shares.

An alternative means by which ownership and control can be vested in the promoters is for a 'letter of renunciation' to be supplied with the shelf company. This letter contains a renunciation of rights as shareholders and company officers *by* the employees of the law stationers *in favour of* the promoters. This method should reduce the time and expense involved.

7.8.3 ADVANTAGES AND DISADVANTAGES

The greatest advantage of utilising a shelf company is generally considered to be speed. The promoters may obtain a company immediately, often for a comparatively low price. Against this must be set the disadvantage that the changes which may be necessary to make the company comply with the promoters' requirements can increase the cost (and time involved) considerably.

A tailor-made company will inevitably take longer to form (even using the expedited service — see **7.8.1**) due to the need to take instructions and complete documentation. The cost of the latter will almost certainly be greater than the initial cost of a shelf company. However, the promoters are ensured of obtaining a company which corresponds with their specific requirements.

There are no hard and fast rules as to when a tailor-made or shelf company should be used. The advantages and disadvantages above should be considered in conjunction with the circumstances of the particular case, including any time or budget limitations of the promoters.

7.9 Change of Name

7.9.1 PROCEDURE

Section 28 CA 1985 gives companies power to change their names by special resolution (which requires 75% of the votes cast in order to be passed — see **Chapter 12**). A copy of the special resolution must be sent to the Registrar, together with a fee of £10. (Note that Companies House offers a same-day change of name service on payment of a fee of £100.) Within 15 days of the change a printed copy of the memorandum with the name changed should be delivered to the Registrar. The change becomes effective when the Registrar issues a certificate of incorporation 'altered to meet the circumstances' (that is, showing the new name of the company) under s. 28(6). A *certificate of incorporation on change of name* is issued when the name is changed; however, the company remains the same legal person (its registered number remaining the same) so that its rights and obligations are not affected by the change (s. 28(7)). Once the name has been changed it must be used on the company's notepaper and other documents as required by ss. 348-349 CA 1985.

7.9.2 NOTIFICATION

The issue of a certificate of incorporation on change of name by the Registrar must be officially notified (that is, advertised by the Registrar in the *London Gazette*) under s. 711 CA 1985. The company is not entitled to rely on the change as against any person until it has been officially notified unless that person actually knew of the change, nor may it rely on the change for the first 15 days after official notification against a person who was unavoidably prevented from knowing about the change (s. 42 CA 1985). It is, therefore, in the company's interests to ensure that the change is officially notified.

7.9.3 CHOICE OF NAME

As on incorporation, a company has general freedom to choose whatever name it likes, but this is subject to the same restrictions which apply on incorporation and the powers of the Secretary of State to direct a change of name (detailed in **7.5.1.1**).

FORMATION OF A LIMITED COMPANY

7.10 Change of Objects

As we have already seen (7.5.1.3) most companies, especially those formed in recent decades, have objects clauses so widely drawn that the company can lawfully undertake almost any type of business without any danger of transactions being held to be ultra vires. However, it may occasionally be considered desirable for the company to widen its objects clause. There may also be occasions when a company wishes to alter its objects clause so that it is more obviously appropriate to present circumstances. For example, a company with a 'main object' giving it power to carry on business in manufacturing may now largely be in the wholesale business and may, therefore, wish to change its objects to reflect that fact.

Power to alter the objects clause is given by s. 4 CA 1985. A special resolution is required. A minority of shareholders may apply to court for an alteration to the objects to be cancelled under s. 5 CA 1985, within 21 days of the special resolution being passed. If no such application is made, the company is then required to deliver a printed copy of the amended memorandum to the Registrar of Companies within 15 days (s. 6 CA 1985).

7.11 Change of Accounting Reference Date

7.11.1 INTRODUCTION

A company's accounting reference period is the period for which a company must produce annual accounts, as required by the Companies Act 1985. The accounting reference period of a particular company is determined according to its accounting reference date ('ARD').

7.11.2 ACCOUNTING REFERENCE DATE OF A COMPANY

Unless a company has altered its ARD by giving notice in the prescribed form, its ARD is:

(a) if it was incorporated before 1 April 1990, 31 March; or

(b) if it was incorporated after 1 April 1990, the last day of the month in which the anniversary of its incorporation falls.

In case (b) therefore, a company incorporated on 14 July would have 31 July as its ARD.

7.11.3 ALTERING THE ACCOUNTING REFERENCE DATE

7.11.3.1 Reasons

A company may wish to alter its ARD for various reasons. Many companies wish to have their accounting period end at the end of the calendar or financial years. Others may be or become part of a group of companies where it makes administrative sense for each company in the group to have the same ARD and hence the same accounting period.

7.11.3.2 Method

A company may alter its ARD by giving notice to the Registrar of Companies using a form 225. The decision to alter a company's ARD will usually be taken by its board of directors.

EIGHT

DIRECTORS AND SECRETARY

This chapter covers the following topics:

8.1 Division of powers within a company
8.2 Appointment of directors
8.3 Retirement of directors
8.4 Removal of directors from office
8.5 Powers of directors
8.6 Directors' duties
8.7 Statutory provisions concerning directors
8.8 Managing directors
8.9 Alternate directors
8.10 Shadow directors
8.11 The directors and protection of outsiders
8.12 The company secretary.

8.1 Division of Powers Within a Company

The power to take decisions on behalf of a company is divided between the directors and members. There are a number of powers which are exercisable only by the members under various provisions of the Companies Act — for example, the power to change the name, objects, articles and nominal capital and various powers in relation to the issue of shares and meetings. The members' power to remove directors from office is considered in **8.4.2**. As far as the vast majority of powers are concerned, the company is free to choose its own procedures, which will be laid down in the articles. Usually these involve very wide powers being given to the directors.

8.2 Appointment of Directors

8.2.1 INTRODUCTION

The first directors of a company are the people who have agreed to take office by signing Form 10 (see **7.5.3**); they automatically become directors on the company's incorporation. From time to time it will be necessary to appoint further directors, either because one of the directors has ceased to hold office or because it is decided to increase the size of the board. Apart from a few statutory restrictions (dealt with below), the company is free to make whatever provision it wishes in its articles as to the appointment of directors. In particular, there is no general requirement that the directors should be shareholders, nor that they should be chosen by the

DIRECTORS AND SECRETARY

shareholders. The provisions of Table A will be considered first and then some other possibilities.

8.2.2 APPOINTMENT OF DIRECTORS UNDER TABLE A

Article 64 provides that the minimum number of directors is two and that there is no maximum number. However, the members can by ordinary resolution fix a different minimum number (including one) and/or fix a maximum number. The minimum and maximum can then be changed by further ordinary resolutions.

The main power to appoint directors is given to the members by art. 78. This provides for appointment by ordinary resolution (that is, by a simple majority at a meeting of the company or by unanimous written consent of the members).

Appointments to fill vacancies on the board and appointments of additional directors (up to the maximum, if any, fixed by the members) may be made by the board itself. A person co-opted in this way holds office until the following annual general meeting (art. 79).

8.2.3 OTHER MEANS OF APPOINTMENT

In most cases the provisions of Table A as to the appointment of directors will be entirely satisfactory. However, in some cases it may be considered appropriate to make permanent appointments to the board; this can be achieved by removing the retirement provisions discussed below. It is also possible for the articles to name the first directors and to make them permanent or life directors without affecting the method of appointment of other directors. However, such appointments are ineffective unless the directors are also named as the first directors in Form 10.

It should be noted that Table A does not require a director to be a shareholder. If the company wants to restrict membership of the board to shareholders, an article to that effect must be adopted on formation or by later amendment.

8.2.4 SERVICE CONTRACTS

It is common for managing directors (see **8.8** below) and other executive directors to enter into service contracts with a company on their appointment to the board. Notwithstanding that both events will usually occur within very close proximity to each other, it is important to understand the distinction between a person:

(a) being *appointed* to the *office* of director; and

(b) *entering* into a *service* contract.

On being appointed to the office of director, the director's conduct is defined primarily by the company's memorandum and articles, common law and legislation. He may receive a *fee* for holding office. On entering into a service contract to carry out an executive role, the director has various rights and obligations defined primarily by the terms of the contract as negotiated with the company. One of the main rights under the service contract will be that of receiving a *salary* in return for carrying out the defined obligations.

The distinction is of particular importance should a director be removed from office (see **8.4.1.3** below).

8.3 Retirement of Directors

8.3.1 RETIREMENT BY NOTICE

The most straightforward way in which a director may vacate office is to retire by giving notice to the company. Usually this takes the form of a letter to the board.

8.3.2 RETIREMENT BY ROTATION

If Table A or similar provisions apply, all the directors retire from office at the first annual general meeting and one third of them at each subsequent AGM (arts 73–74). The retiring directors are eligible for re-election and are automatically re-elected unless someone else is appointed, or the company resolves not to re-elect them, or to fill the vacancy (art. 75).

In the case of a private company, provisions for retirement by rotation are unnecessarily cumbersome and are often removed so that, once appointed, directors hold office permanently until death, voluntary retirement, disqualification or removal from office under s. 303 CA 1985 (see **8.4.1** below).

It should be noted that, under Table A, managing directors and directors holding any other executive office and are not subject to retirement by rotation (art. 84).

8.4 Removal of Directors from Office

8.4.1 REMOVAL OF DIRECTORS UNDER s. 303 CA 1985

8.4.1.1 Power to remove by ordinary resolution

Section 303 CA 1985 provides for removal of directors by ordinary resolution (i.e., by a majority vote of the shareholders in general meeting). The power given by the section overrides anything in the company's articles (even, for example, an article naming a life director) or in an agreement with the director. Section 303 provides the most effective means by which majority shareholders who object to the way in which their company is being run can keep control of the company. Where the directors themselves are the majority shareholders, as they very frequently will be in the case of a private company, the other (minority) shareholders have limited rights to object to the way the board is running the company (see below).

8.4.1.2 Procedure

No resolution purporting to remove a director from office is valid unless special notice has first been given to the company of an intention to remove a particular director. This usually emanates from the shareholder or shareholders who wish to remove the director. In effect this gives the company a minimum period of twenty-eight days 'grace' before any steps are taken by the shareholders in question to remove the director (s. 379(1)). On receipt of the notice, a company is obliged to send a copy to the director whose removal is proposed.

However, special notice is not sufficient to cause a meeting to be held at which the necessary resolution can be proposed or to have such a resolution included on the agenda of any forthcoming meeting (see *Pedley* v *Inland Waterways Association* [1977] 1 All ER 209). In most circumstances the shareholders concerned must either invoke their right under s. 368 CA 1985, or any special right they may have under the company's articles of association to cause the directors to call an EGM for the purpose of considering the director's removal.

DIRECTORS AND SECRETARY

8.4.1.3 Director's right to compensation and damages on removal

The shareholders have an absolute right to remove a director. However, this does not deprive the director of any rights to compensation or damages he may have (s. 303(5)). When considering these rights, it is important to maintain a distinction between the right to a payment for loss of office and the right to claim damages where there is a service contract between the director and the company.

Should the director be removed from office, then the only compensation for such loss of office he may receive is a payment approved by the company under s. 312 CA 1985. However, removal from office will almost certainly terminate any service contract as it will be impossible for the director to fulfil his obligations. Depending on the terms of the director's remuneration under the contract, damages could be extensive. It is therefore important for the shareholders to consider the financial cost of removing a director.

8.4.1.4 Special voting rights on resolution to remove director

The articles may validly give special voting rights to some of the shareholders either generally or in particular circumstances. In the case of *Bushell* v *Faith* [1970] AC 1099, the articles provided that 'in the event of a resolution being proposed at any general meeting of the company for the removal from office of any director, any shares held by that director shall on a poll in respect of such resolution carry the right to three votes per share . . .'. The director whose removal was proposed owned one third of the shares and so could not be removed. Nevertheless, the article was held to be valid, since all that s. 303 lays down is that an ordinary resolution may be used to remove a director and an ordinary resolution is one requiring a simple majority of votes. A clause of this type does not, therefore, prevent a resolution from being an ordinary resolution but effectively makes it impossible to remove the director without his consent.

The decision in *Bushell* v *Faith* has been criticised, but there are some circumstances where it may be appropriate to include in the articles a regulation which makes it impossible for the majority shareholders to get rid of a director who owns a minority of the shares. Such a regulation should be considered, for example, where a small number of people wish to run a company as a 'quasi-partnership' — that is, where they all intend to have a continuing right to take part in management. In other circumstances it may be appropriate to give the shareholders wider powers to remove directors than are given by s. 303 so that, for example, removal by ordinary resolution *without* special notice may be considered appropriate.

8.4.2 DISQUALIFICATION

8.4.2.1 Company Directors Disqualification Act 1986

Companies legislation contains a number of provisions under which directors are disqualified either automatically or by court order. The most important of these are contained in the Company Directors Disqualification Act (CDDA) 1986. This Act provides for disqualification from acting as a director, liquidator, receiver or manager of a company and from being concerned with the management of a company for up to 15 years (five years if the order is made by a magistrates' court). Disqualification can be imposed following:

(a) conviction for an indictable offence in connection with the management of a company;

(b) a finding that an offence involving fraud has been committed in the course of winding up a company;

(c) persistent default in filing returns with the Registrar (persistent default is conclusively presumed following three convictions for failure to file returns within five years); the maximum period of disqualification in this case is five years even if the penalty is imposed by a court other than a magistrates' court;

(d) a finding that a person is 'unfit' to be concerned in the management of a company. The order may only be made against a person who is or has been a director of a company which has become insolvent while or after he was a director. For these purposes a company is insolvent if it goes into insolvent liquidation, an administration order is made against it or an administrative receiver is appointed. Where an order is made on the ground of unfitness, the disqualification period must be for a minimum of two years and a maximum of 15.

The Insolvency Act 2000 has amended the CDDA 1986 such that directors may give an undertaking to the Secretary of State for Trade and Industry not to be involved in the management of a company for a specified period of time. This process of 'fast track' disqualification avoids the need for court proceedings and is intended to increase efficiency in dealing with errant directors.

8.4.2.2 Disqualification under the articles

The articles of a company may, of course, make provision for disqualification or automatic retirement in circumstances other than those specified in the Act. Table A art. 81 states that the office of director is to be vacated if a director:

(a) becomes bankrupt;

(b) is or may be suffering from mental disorder and is admitted to hospital under the Mental Health Act or a court order is made against him on matters concerning mental disorder;

(c) is absent from directors' meetings (without the board's permission) for at least six months and the directors resolve that the office be vacated.

Article 81 also provides for the resignation of directors by their giving written notice to the company. No particular period of notice is required. If the director has a service contract, as, for example, in the case of most full-time directors, there is an implied obligation to give reasonable notice but for the sake of certainty it is better to include a specific period in the contract.

Table A does not contain any express power for the directors to remove one of their kind. However, it is not uncommon for articles of association to reserve such a power either by a majority decision of the board or by a written request from all other directors. There is judicial authority for the fact that such a power is fiduciary and must be exercised in the best interests of the company (see *Samuel Tak Lee v Chou Wen Hsien* [1984] 1 WLR 1202).

8.5 Powers of Directors

8.5.1 DEFINING DIRECTORS' POWERS

The powers of the directors are laid down in the articles. Table A art. 70 gives the directors wide powers, including in particular power to manage the business of the company. Article 70 is in the following terms:

Subject to the provisions of the Act, the memorandum and the articles and to any directions given by special resolution the business of the company shall be managed by the directors who may exercise all the powers of the company. No alteration of the memorandum or

DIRECTORS AND SECRETARY

articles and no such direction shall invalidate any prior act of the directors which would have been valid if that alteration had not been made or that direction had not been given. The powers given by this regulation shall not be limited by any special power given to the directors by the articles and a meeting of directors at which a quorum is present may exercise all powers exercisable by the directors.

8.5.2 EXERCISE OF POWERS

It should be noted that under the general law and under art. 70, decisions of the directors must be taken either at a board meeting at which a quorum is present or by unanimous agreement. This is, however, subject to the directors' power to delegate (e.g., to a managing director, committee of directors or appointed agent — see **8.8** and **8.11**).

The powers of the directors must be exercised in accordance with the articles. Article 88, Table A allows the directors to decide how to regulate their own meetings and provides that any director may call a board meeting or require the company secretary to do so at any time. No particular period of notice is required, so that a meeting will be validly held if reasonable notice is given. Notice need not be given to a director or alternate director who is absent from the UK (arts 88 and 66).

8.5.2.1 Decisions at board meetings

Decisions at board meetings are taken by majority vote; if there is an equality of votes, art. 88 gives the chairman a casting vote. The chairman is chosen by the directors from among themselves (art. 91). The chairman's casting vote prevents deadlock (without it a resolution fails if there is an equality of votes), but it also means that the director who is the chairman has considerably more power than the others. In a company with only two directors he is, in effect, able to take decisions alone.

8.5.2.2 Prohibition on director voting on resolution in which he is interested

Article 94 prohibits a director from voting on any resolution concerning a matter in which he has an interest or duty which is material and conflicts or may conflict with the interests of the company. However, this prohibition does not apply to:

(a) a resolution concerning any guarantee, security or indemnity in respect of money lent to, or an obligation for the benefit of the company;

(b) an arrangement whereby the company gives a guarantee, security or indemnity to a third party in respect of an obligation of the company guaranteed or indemnified by the director;

(c) an interest arising from his buying any shares or other securities from the company; or

(d) a resolution relating to a retirement benefits scheme.

Article 94 can cause problems where a company has, for example, only two directors, one or both of whom are interested in specific resolutions. Prima facie, the relevant board meeting will be inquorate and the resolution will not be able to be passed validly. However, art. 96 allows a company to suspend or relax art. 94 by ordinary resolution. Alternatively, if it is thought that the problem will recur, art. 94 could be removed by special resolution.

8.5.2.3 Decision by way of written resolution

Article 93 allows the directors to pass valid resolutions without holding a board meeting provided *all* the directors entitled to receive notice of meetings (including alternate directors) sign a written resolution.

8.6 Directors' Duties

8.6.1 FIDUCIARY DUTIES

Directors do not hold the property of their company on trust since the company is a separate legal entity and therefore is able to own property directly. However, directors do owe fiduciary duties to their company, that is, they are in the same position in respect of their powers as trustees or agents with respect to the company. Because of their fiduciary duties directors must not make any secret profit out of their position and they must exercise the powers given to them bona fide for the benefit of the company.

The liability of directors for breach of duty is personal. However, the advice they receive may be relevant to whether they are in breach of duty. In *Norman v Theodore Goddard* [1992] BCC 14 it was held that a director was not liable for breach of fiduciary duty when he reasonably relied on advice given to him by a partner in a firm of solicitors.

8.6.1.1 Secret profit

Profit from position as director

The concept of secret profit is a rather intangible one; it does not, of course, prevent directors from receiving remuneration for their services. A profit is a secret profit if it comes to the director because of his position as a director:

In *Cook v Deeks* [1916] 1 AC 554, two directors of a company negotiated a construction contract with the Canadian Pacific Railroad on behalf of their company. At a late stage in the negotiations they decided to take the contract in their own names. The Privy Council held that they were accountable to their company for the profit; it was only through their position as directors of the company (which had previously contracted with the Canadian Pacific) that they were able to make the profit.

'Secret' means failure to obtain permission

Although the fiduciary duty is to hand over what are described as secret profits, it seems that secrecy in this context means failure to obtain permission rather than actual secrecy:

In *Regal (Hastings) Ltd* v *Gulliver* [1967] 2 AC 134 (note), the plaintiff company owned a cinema and wished to buy two others in the same town with a view to selling all three together. The company could not raise sufficient money to buy the other cinemas and so another company was set up partly owned by Regal (Hastings) Ltd and partly by some of the directors of Regal (Hastings) Ltd who had money of their own to invest. The new company then purchased the other two cinemas. The purchasers who wished to acquire all three cinemas then purchased all the shares in Regal (Hastings) Ltd and in the new company, thus acquiring control of the companies. The new board of directors then instituted proceedings on behalf of Regal (Hastings) Ltd against its former directors. It was held by the House of Lords that a secret profit had been made since the opportunity to invest in the new company only came to the defendants because they were directors of Regal (Hastings) Ltd. This profit was ordered to be paid to Regal (Hastings) Ltd even though that company had been unable to raise all the money needed for the purchase itself and even though, realistically, the consequences of the order was that the purchaser who had negotiated the purchase of the shares at a fair price got some of the purchase price repaid to their own company.

DIRECTORS AND SECRETARY

Secret profit to be paid to company

A secret profit must be paid over to the company even if the company itself could not have made the profit:

> In *Boston Deep Sea Fishing Co.* v *Ansell* (1888) 39 ChD 339, the defendant was a director of the plaintiff company and negotiated a contract on its behalf for the supply of ice to a fleet of fishing smacks owned by the company. The defendant was a shareholder in the ice-making company which had a policy of paying 'bonuses' to any of its shareholders who introduced work to it. The court held that the defendant was liable to the company for the bonuses even though the company itself could not have obtained them since it was not a shareholder in the ice-making company.

8.6.1.2 Exercise of powers bona fide in the interests of the company as a whole

The second requirement of directors' fiduciary duties is that the directors must exercise their powers bona fide in the interests of the company as a whole. This involves two separate restrictions on directors' powers:

(a) Directors must not exercise their powers other than for the purpose for which they were given; if they exercise their powers for some other reason, their decisions may be challenged.

> In *Hogg* v *Cramphorn Ltd* [1967] Ch 254, directors issued shares to trustees for the benefit of employees. The purpose of the directors in issuing the shares was found to be the prevention of a takeover of the company. It was held that the issue could be challenged (even though the directors believed it to be in the interests of the company as a whole), since the purpose of giving directors the power to issue shares is to enable them to raise capital.

(b) Directors must not exercise their powers for motives of personal gain (this often overlaps with the rule against directors making secret profits).

> In *Piercy* v *S. Mills & Co. Ltd* [1920] 1 Ch 77, shares were issued, at a time when capital was not needed, purely for the purpose of strengthening and maintaining the directors' control of the company. The issue was held to be invalid.

(Many of the cases on this type of breach of duty have been concerned with the issue of shares by directors, which power is now much restricted by legislation — see **Chapter 10**.)

8.6.1.3 Ratification of breach of fiduciary duty

A breach of fiduciary duty may be ratified by an ordinary resolution of the shareholders and the directors themselves (if shareholders) may vote in favour of the resolution. However, such ratification may be invalid where there has been a 'fraud on the minority' or where the directors are majority shareholders and use their voting power so as to prevent action being brought against them (see **9.6.2.1** and **9.6.2.2**). It is not easy to draw a distinction between cases where ratification is possible and those where it is not, but it seems that breach of fiduciary duty without personal gain to the directors is ratifiable, breach of fiduciary duty coupled with personal gain by the directors and actual loss to the company is not.

8.6.2 DUTIES OF CARE AND SKILL

Directors may be liable to their companies for their negligence as well as for breach of fiduciary duty. The courts are always reluctant to interfere with business decisions, however foolish they may seem with the benefit of hindsight. The duty of care and skill required from a director is, therefore, a low one. In particular, the test applied is a subjective one, that is, a director need not exhibit in the performance of his duties a greater degree of skill than may reasonably be expected from a person of his knowledge and experience. Directors may be liable for 'wrongful trading' if their company becomes insolvent: see **Chapter 24**.

8.6.3 STATUTORY DUTIES

8.6.3.1 Company records

The duty to make returns to the Registrar of Companies will normally be performed on behalf of a company by its secretary, but directors are in some circumstances also liable to a fine if returns are not made and persistent default can lead to disqualification. The directors are also under a duty to keep minutes of their own meetings and to deliver accounts.

8.6.3.2 Interests of employees

Section 309 CA 1985 provides that directors shall have regard to the interests of the company's employees in general as well as the interests of its members. However, this duty is only enforceable by the shareholders, not by the employees.

8.6.4 DIRECTORS' DUTIES TO THIRD PARTIES

A director does not generally owe any duty to a person dealing with his company. However, a director makes himself liable to such a person in a particular case if he claims an authority to bind his company which he does not have. The action resulting from such a liability is called an action for breach of warranty of authority (see **8.11**).

8.7 Statutory Provisions Concerning Directors

Because of the very high degree of control which directors are able to exercise over their companies a number of statutory provisions have been enacted for the protection of shareholders and the public generally.

8.7.1 DISCLOSURE OF INFORMATION

8.7.1.1 Register of directors

Section 288 CA 1985 requires every company to keep at its registered office a register of directors. In respect of each director (including any shadow director) the following information must be given:

(a) present Christian or other forename(s) and surname;

(b) any former names (there are limited exceptions, the most important being that married women need not state their maiden names or other names by which they were known before marriage);

(c) residential address;

(d) business occupation;

(e) other directorships held or which, during the last five years, have been held by the director other than directorships in dormant companies or in companies wholly owned by or wholly owning the company.

(It is also advisable to include dates of appointment and removal from office.)

DIRECTORS AND SECRETARY

The same information must also be sent to the Registrar of Companies. Form 10 is used for notification of particulars of the first directors and Form 288 must be sent to the Registrar within 14 days of any change in the particulars (whether because a director is appointed or ceases to hold office, or because of changes in the particulars of the continuing directors).

8.7.1.2 Register of directors' interests

A director is under an obligation to disclose to the company certain information about his interests in the company's shares and debentures (s. 324 CA 1985) and the company must keep a register of such interests. Any type of interest in shares or debentures must be reported, including, for example, outright ownership, options to purchase and charges — the register, therefore, includes information which cannot be obtained from the register of members which deals only with legal ownership. Notification and registration are also required of interests of the spouse and infant children (including step-children) of the director. This disclosure enables shareholders to see the level of control, direct and indirect, which directors have over a company through shareholdings.

8.7.1.3 Service contracts

Copies of directors' service contracts must be available for inspection by the members (s. 318 CA 1985). If a director does not have a written service contract then a written memorandum of his terms of service must be kept instead.

8.7.1.4 Publicity as to names of directors

Section 305 CA 1985 prevents a company from giving publicity to the names of directors in business letters unless the names (including forenames or initials) of *all* the directors are given.

8.7.1.5 Disclosure of interests in contracts

Section 317 CA 1985 requires a director who is directly or indirectly interested in a contract or proposed contract with his company to declare the nature of his interest at a board meeting. Notice must be given at the first meeting at which the contract is discussed or at the first meeting after the director becomes interested in the contract. Where the director is a member of another company or firm he may give general notice stating that he is interested in any contract with the company, and then he need not disclose his interest each time such a contract is discussed.

It should be noted that disclosure by a director under s. 317 does not affect the operation of art. 94 of Table A (see **8.5.2.2**).

8.7.2 RESTRICTIONS ON FREEDOM OF CONTRACT

8.7.2.1 Directors' service contracts

The terms of directors' service contracts will usually be determined by the board although members are entitled to information about the terms of such contracts and a director may not usually vote on his own service contract (Table A art. 94). Section 319 requires the approval of the members in general meeting of a term in a service contract of a director for a period exceeding five years under which he cannot be removed by notice. Approval is also required where an existing contract is extended if the aggregate term exceeds five years. Although only the service contracts of directors require approval of the members in this way, it is not possible to circumvent the section by providing for employment in a capacity other than as a director (for example, as a consultant) after the directorship ceases.

8.7.2.2 Property transactions

Section 320 CA 1985 requires the approval of the members in general meeting to be given to any arrangement whereby a director or a person connected with a director is to acquire from the company one or more non-cash assets of the 'requisite value' or whereby the company is to acquire such assets from such a person.

A non-cash asset is of the requisite value 'if at the time the arrangement in question is entered into its value is not less than £2,000 but, subject to that, exceeds £100,000 or 10% of the amount of the company's asset value'. The latter will normally be determined by reference to the company's most recent balance sheet.

The value to be attributed to the asset in question, raises two interesting issues. The first is that this value must be the market value of the asset, otherwise directors could manipulate the price paid to fall outside the ambit of the section. Secondly, should the market value be adjudged by reference to any special value which the asset may have to the relevant director? In *Micro Leisure Ltd* v *County Properties and Developments* [2000] TLR 12, this question was answered in the affirmative. Lord Hamilton put forward the example of a ransom strip which, when purchased by a director, would substantially increase the development potential of the director's existing land. It is submitted, however, that situations where the objective market value and the 'director-specific' value are different will be rare.

If a contract is made in contravention of the section it is voidable by the company unless:

(a) restitution is no longer possible;

(b) third party rights (acquired for value without notice) would be affected by avoidance; or

(c) the contract has been affirmed by the members in general meeting.

Furthermore, the directors who authorised the arrangement (not just the one who is a party to the contract) are liable to indemnify the company against any loss. The director or connected person who is a party to the contract is liable to account for any profit made, although a connected person is excused from liability if he did not know the circumstances. For the purposes of s. 320 a connected person includes (among others) a director's spouse, child or step-child.

The main purpose of s. 320 is to prevent directors from making substantial profits in transactions with their companies and so reinforces the rules of equity concerning secret profits. One fairly common type of contract which is subject to its provisions is a contract under which a director receives shares in return for assets: for example, if a director who owns business premises (of the requisite value) wishes to transfer them to the company in return for shares, the approval of the members in general meeting must first be obtained.

8.7.2.3 Loans to directors

The latest of the successively more stringent provisions preventing loans to directors are contained in ss. 330–347 CA 1985. A private company may not make a loan or loans of more than £5,000 in aggregate to a director of the company or a director of its holding company nor may it guarantee or provide security in connection with a loan made by any person to such a director. However, a loan of any amount may be made if its purpose is 'to provide a director with funds to meet expenditure incurred or to be incurred by him for the purposes of the company or for the purpose of enabling him properly to perform his duties' provided that the members in general meeting give approval in advance or the loan is repayable within six months of the next annual general meeting (s. 337).

DIRECTORS AND SECRETARY

8.8 Managing Directors

8.8.1 APPOINTMENT

It is very common for one of the directors of a company to be appointed managing director. The functions actually performed by the managing director vary from company to company, but in practice he will usually be either the most senior director in the company's hierarchy or second in command to the chairman. A managing director cannot be appointed unless the articles (or, rarely, the memorandum) so provide. Table A, art. 84 does so provide and art. 72 provides that: '[the directors] may ... delegate to any managing director ... such of their powers as they consider desirable to be exercised by him'.

8.8.2 POWERS

The board are also given the power to specify what his powers are to be and to impose conditions. The powers granted may even be to the exclusion of the powers of the board but can be revoked or altered at any time by the board.

8.8.3 SERVICE CONTRACT

The managing director will usually have a service contract. The terms of the contract will be negotiated by the managing director and the board; the members' approval will be required if he is given security of tenure for longer than five years and cannot be removed by notice (s. 319 CA 1985 — see **8.7.2.1**). The managing director is both a director and an employee of the company; like other employees he has certain statutory rights against the company if he is unfairly dismissed or made redundant. Since he automatically ceases to be managing director if he ceases to be a director, the members can remove him from both offices by passing an ordinary resolution (s. 303 CA 1985) but this may result in heavy damages being payable by the company for breach of the service contract (see **8.4.1.3** above).

8.9 Alternate Directors

Table A art. 65 gives a director power to appoint (subject to the approval of the board) an alternate director. Once appointed the alternate director has all the powers of the appointing director until he is removed by the appointing director or the appointing director ceases to be a director. However, the alternate director is not entitled to receive remuneration from the company for his services.

8.10 Shadow Directors

A 'shadow director' is defined by s. 741(2) CA 1985 as 'any person in accordance with whose directions or instructions the directors of a company are accustomed to act'. However, a person who gives advice in a professional capacity to the directors is not to be taken to be a shadow director. Similar provisions are contained in s. 251 of the Insolvency Act 1986.

Under a number of provisions of the Companies Act 1985, shadow directors are treated as directors of the company. For example:

(a) the statutory restrictions on the freedom of a company to contract with its directors (see **8.7.2**) apply equally to shadow directors of the company;

(b) shadow directors are required to disclose interests in contracts with the company to the board under s. 317 CA 1985 (see **8.7.1.5**) in the same way as directors;

(c) details of any service contract between a company and a shadow director should be open to inspection under s. 318 CA 1985 (see **8.7.1.3**); and

(d) details of any interests in shares of the company should be disclosed under s. 324 CA 1985; and

(e) the names of shadow directors should be included in the register of directors under s. 288 CA 1985.

In addition, and perhaps more significantly, shadow directors are deemed to be directors for the purpose of wrongful trading under s. 214 Insolvency Act 1986 (see **24.1**), by which they may become personally liable for the debts of an insolvent company. Under the Company Directors Disqualification Act 1986, shadow directors may also be disqualified from holding office or being concerned in the management of a company, as if they were directors.

8.11 The Directors and Protection of Outsiders

8.11.1 INTRODUCTION

A company is not a natural person and so can only exercise its powers through agents. Usually contracts will be made on behalf of the company either by the directors or by more junior officials acting on the directors' authority. If a contract is made in accordance with the articles of the company it will be binding on the company, so that the 'outsider' with whom the company is dealing can sue the company if it fails to perform the contract. Where, however, a contract is made by the wrong people (e.g., the directors exercise a power which is vested in the shareholders, or an employee acts without the authority of the directors), or in the wrong way (e.g., a meeting is held but it has not been properly convened), the whole transaction is, prima facie, void. Contracts and other transactions decided upon without proper authority (or without a proper exercise of authority) are described as 'irregular'.

In dealing with irregular contracts the law is faced with a dilemma. If the contract is declared irregular and void the outsider will not be able to enforce it against the company even though he may be unaware of the irregularity. On the other hand, if the company is held to be bound by irregular contracts the directors will, in effect, be able to ignore the requirements of the company's articles to the possible detriment of the shareholders. The law deals with this dilemma by providing that irregular contracts, though prima facie void, are binding on the company in certain circumstances only. These circumstances result partly from statute, partly from decisions of the court, and partly from the general law of agency. Amendments to the Companies Act 1985 have further extended the circumstances in which an irregular contract is valid.

8.11.2 STATUTORY PROTECTION

8.11.2.1 Section 35A CA 1985

The effect of s. 35A CA 1985 and related sections is that:

(a) where an unconnected third party

(b) acting in good faith

(c) enters into a contract with a company

(d) which contract has been decided on or authorised by the board of that company then, notwithstanding any restrictions on the board's powers under the company's constitution (and whether or not the third party is aware of any such restriction), the contract will be valid. However, the directors may be liable to the company for any loss caused. We shall now look at the relevant legislation in more detail.

Section 35A(1) provides:

> In favour of a person dealing with a company in good faith, the power of the board of directors to bind the company, or to authorise others to do so, shall be deemed free of any limitation under the company's constitution.

The reference to the company's constitution (for this purpose) includes a resolution of the company and agreements between the company and its members as well as the memorandum and articles.

It should be noted that a person dealing with the company is entitled to assume that the directors have unlimited power to bind it. A similar assumption may also be made where the directors have purported to authorise 'others' to do so.

Shareholder's power to seek injunction

If a shareholder believes that the directors are about to exceed their powers by entering into an irregular contract he can seek an injunction to restrain them. However, this right is lost once the company incurs any legal obligation to a third party (s. 35A(4)). If directors enter into an irregular contract they may be liable to the company for any loss (s. 35A(5)). (Section 35 gives them no protection personally.)

Requirements of good faith

The protection of s. 35A is given only to persons who act in good faith. However, good faith is presumed unless the contrary is proved (s. 35A(2)(c)) and knowledge that the directors are acting beyond their powers is not of itself sufficient proof of bad faith (s. 35A(2)(a)). Section 35B provides that a person dealing with a company is not under any obligation to enquire into the powers of its directors.

Transaction with connected party

Section 322A CA 1985 makes a limited exception to s. 35A. This applies where the board of a company exceed their powers in a transaction with a director or a person connected with a director. In such cases the transaction is voidable by the company. Whether or not it is avoided, the director or connected person and any director who authorised the transaction is liable to account to the company for any gain he makes and to indemnify the company against any loss. Where a transaction is irregular and is made between the company, a director and one or more third parties the court has a wide discretion which enables it to protect any innocent third party.

The company's right to avoid a contract under s. 322A is lost if restitution becomes impossible (i.e., if a third party who has acquired rights bona fide for value would be affected), if the transaction is ratified or if the company has been fully compensated by indemnity from the director.

8.11.2.2 Section 285 CA 1985

Section 285 provides that, 'the acts of a director or manager are valid notwithstanding any defect that may afterwards be discovered in his appointment or qualification'. This section protects the company, the outsider dealing with it, and the director, if there is some sort of procedural defect in the appointment (e.g., proper notice was not given of the meeting at which the appointment was made).

8.11.3 THE RULE IN *ROYAL BRITISH BANK* v *TURQUAND*

A number of common law decisions gave protection to outsiders where contracts were made without authority. In view of the enactment of ss. 35A and 35B the significance of these decisions is likely to be very slight in future.

These decisions held that a person dealing with a company was entitled to assume the correct procedures had been followed (*Royal British Bank* v *Turquand* (1856) E and B 327, 119 ER 886), that persons appearing to be directors had been properly appointed (*Mahony* v *East Holyford Mining Co.* (1875) LR 7 HL 869) and that a board meeting had been lawfully held (*Browne* v *La Trinidad* (1887) 37 ChD 1).

8.11.4 AGENCY

8.11.4.1 General position

A company can only act through agents; the authority of agents to act for a company depends on the general law of agency. The actions of an agent are binding on a principal if the agent has actual authority or authority arising from estoppel. The agent may also be personally liable to the third party (i.e., to the outsider) if the principal (i.e., the company) is not liable.

8.11.4.2 Actual authority

The scope of the actual authority of a company's agents depends upon the memorandum and articles of the company. The board of directors, acting collectively, usually has very wide powers to act on behalf of the company. The articles will usually permit delegation to committees of directors and to a managing director (or to a number of joint managing directors).

8.11.4.3 Agency by estoppel

A company may be bound by the acts of a person acting on its behalf when it is estopped from denying that person's authority. Agency by estoppel may result either from 'holding out' (that is, an actual representation that the agent has authority) or from a representation that the agent is a member of a particular class of agent which is recognised to have certain powers to bind its principals. The estoppel may prevent the company from denying that the alleged agent is its agent or that he has power to bind the company in a particular way.

'Holding out'

If a company is to be liable because an agent has been held out as having authority, the holding out must be done by the person or persons with actual authority to bind the company.

Usual or apparent authority

It is a well established rule of the law of agency that a principal is estopped from denying that an agent of certain recognised classes has the authority normally associated with that class (unless, of course, he tells the third party that there is a restriction on the power of the agent). In relation to companies, this rule has been applied to managing directors. If a company describes one of the directors as a managing director, it is estopped from denying that he is a managing director (even if he has not been appointed) and that he has the authority of a managing director (even if his appointment includes terms restricting his authority). This type of authority is sometimes called 'usual authority' or 'apparent authority'.

Directors other than managing directors do not generally have authority to act alone, so a company is not bound by the action of a single director who is not a managing director unless either he has actual authority or the board have held him out as having authority in the particular transaction.

A director may also have an authority because of some other office which he holds. For example in *First Energy (UK)* v *Hungarian International Bank*, *The Times*, 4 March 1993, a bank manager was held to have authority (by reason of his office) to make a statement as to a loan agreement which was binding on the bank. The bank manager in question was not a director but his authority would have been the same if he had been.

The company secretary has been held to have usual authority to bind the company to contracts concerning administration.

8.11.4.4 Liability of agent to third party

A person purporting to act as agent for a company will be personally liable to a third party for breach of warranty of authority if it turns out that he had no authority to bind the company.

8.11.4.5 Ratification

If a contract is made by an agent without authority so that the company is not bound by the contract, the company can ratify, and thus retrospectively validate, the contract. Ratification may be effected by the people with actual authority to bind the company (i.e., normally the board, but in some cases the members in general meeting). Ratification will usually be implied where the company has accepted performance of the contract.

8.12 The Company Secretary

Appointment

Section 283 CA 1985 requires every company to have a secretary. The secretary may also be a director but, to ensure there are always two officers of the company, a *sole* director cannot also be secretary. The first secretary of a newly formed company is the person named in Form 10; subsequently the secretary is appointed and removed by the board who also decide on the terms of appointment (Table A art. 99).

Responsibilities and powers

The secretary is responsible for keeping the various records of the company, such as minutes of board and general meetings and the various records which must be kept at the registered office. He is also an officer of the company and so is liable to a fine if the company is in breach of the provisions of the Companies Act which require information to be filed with the Registrar of Companies.

Many company secretaries are given powers far in excess of those contemplated by the Companies Act. Often the secretary is responsible for the administration of the company and performs the functions of an office manager as well as of a record-keeper. The courts have, therefore, recognised that an outsider is entitled to rely on a decision taken by the secretary which relates to administration even if it turns out that the decision was not authorised by the board (i.e., the secretary has usual authority to make such contracts). Thus in *Panorama*

(Developments) Guildford Ltd v *Fidelis Furnishing Fabrics Ltd* [1971] 2 QB 711, the Court of Appeal held that a company was bound to pay for the use of cars hired by the secretary purportedly on behalf of the company but in fact for his own use.

Register

Every company must keep a register of directors and secretaries and notify the Registrar of Companies within 14 days of any change (s. 288 CA 1985). In the case of a secretary the particulars to be given are the present and past names of the secretary (subject to the same exceptions as apply in the case of a director) and his usual residential address.

NINE

SHAREHOLDERS

This chapter covers the following topics:

9.1   Introduction
9.2   Registration of membership
9.3   Powers and duties of shareholders
9.4   Internal disputes — introduction
9.5   Section 14 Companies Act 1985
9.6   *Foss* v *Harbottle*
9.7   Actions by shareholders — procedure
9.8   Section 459 Companies Act 1985
9.9   Just and equitable winding up
9.10 Shareholders and profits
9.11 Procedure for declaring and paying a dividend
9.12 Restrictions on sources of dividends.

9.1 Introduction

This chapter will deal with the position of shareholders in relation to a company. We will look at the following issues:

(a) registration of membership;

(b) the powers of shareholders in relation to their company;

(c) the legal protection given to shareholders by the rules of equity and by the Companies Act;

(d) the payment of dividends to shareholders.

You will find references to shareholders throughout this Guide so that this chapter is intended to deal with their position in the company in general terms. Bear this in mind as you progress through your studies — it is always dangerous to pigeonhole things too much. You cannot understand the position of shareholders fully until you understand the position of directors (and vice versa).

9.1.1 THE RIGHT TO MEMBERSHIP

You already know (see **Chapters 6** and **7**) that all companies must have at least one 'member'. The vast majority of companies are incorporated with a 'share capital', that is with the right

SHAREHOLDERS

and expectation that one day they will issue shares to people who are in effect the owners of the company. Section 22(2) CA 1985 provides that: 'Every person who agrees to become a member of a company, and whose name is entered in its register of members, is a member of the company.' This means that membership begins when the member's name is entered in the register of members. The *right* to become a member may result from a contract between the company and the purchaser of new shares (this is called an allotment or issue of shares; see **Chapter 10**). The right may also arise because an existing shareholder transfers shares to someone else by sale or gift. It may also arise when a member dies or becomes bankrupt. At that time the shares are automatically transmitted to the personal representative or trustee in bankruptcy. From this we can see that it is the ownership of shares which makes someone a member of a company. Hence the terms 'member' and 'shareholder' mean almost the same thing.

When someone becomes a shareholder and is registered as a member he acquires some say in the way that the company is run.

9.1.2 PROTECTION OF SHAREHOLDERS

In most companies (including those which have Table A as their articles), it is the directors who actually run the company (see **Chapter 8**). As there may be a conflict between the interests of the directors and the shareholders the law steps in to provide a measure of protection to the shareholders. When giving advice on these matters it is vital to distinguish between shareholders in various categories. As we have already seen (see **8.3.2**) a shareholder with a majority of the votes has the power to remove the directors from office. When this power is available to a shareholder it is likely to be the most effective way in which he can control the company. Bear in mind also that with very many small companies the directors and shareholders are likely to be the same people so that they will have rights in both capacities. (These matters are dealt with more fully in **9.3** below.)

9.2 Registration of Membership

9.2.1 CONTENTS OF THE REGISTER

Every company must keep a register of its members and their shareholdings. The following information must be recorded (s. 352 CA 1985):

(a) the names and addresses of the members;

(b) the number of shares held and, where the company has more than one class of issued shares, the number of each class held by each member;

(c) the amount paid or agreed to be considered as paid on the shares of each member;

(d) the date at which each member was entered in the register;

(e) the date at which each member ceased to be a member;

(f) if the company has only one member, a statement to that effect and of the date when this occurred;

(g) if the company formerly had only one member a statement that the number has increased to two or more and the date when this occurred.

The register must normally be kept at the registered office of the company and if kept elsewhere the Registrar of Companies must be notified (s. 353 CA 1985). The register of members itself is not sent to the Registrar but the annual return made by the company after each AGM contains details of the membership. The register of members must be open to inspection (by members free of charge and by the public) during business hours for at least two hours during every business day.

No particular form of register is required (since 1967 it may be kept by a computer), but under s. 354 CA 1985 an index is required if the register is not kept in the form of an index and there are more than 50 members (this provision is of little relevance to private companies since very few of them have more than 50 members).

9.2.2 TRUSTS

Section 360 CA 1985 provides that 'no notice of any trust ... shall be entered on the register ...'. This means that the company must treat the *registered holder* of shares as beneficially entitled to those shares even if it knows that they are held on trust. The company must, therefore, pay dividends to the trustee and allow the trustee to exercise any voting powers attached to the shares.

Section 360 does not, of course, affect the position as between the registered owner and his beneficiary. The registered owner must, therefore, hand over to the beneficiary any dividend he receives and vote in accordance with the beneficiary's wishes.

9.2.3 RECTIFICATION OF THE REGISTER

Section 359 CA 1985 gives the court power to order rectification of the register of members if:

(a) the name of any person is, without sufficient cause, entered in or omitted from [the register]; ... or

(b) default is made or unnecessary delay takes place in entering on the register the fact of any person having ceased to be a member.

One of the circumstances in which rectification may be applied for is when the company *wrongly* refuses to register a transfer. However, a person to whom shares are transferred does not always have a right to be registered (see **Chapter 11**).

In addition to its powers under s. 359 the court may order rectification of the register in other circumstances where it is just and equitable.

9.3 Powers and Duties of Shareholders

9.3.1 SOURCES OF SHAREHOLDERS' POWERS

The powers of the shareholders are not easy to define succinctly. As we saw in **Chapter 8**, most of the decisions of a company are taken by the board of directors (unless the articles are very unusual), but certain powers are specifically given to the members by the Companies Act and these cannot be taken away by the memorandum or articles. In addition to these powers which are guaranteed by law, certain powers are also given to members by the articles. Thus, if Table A applies, the members have power to elect new directors and to declare dividends. It should be noted that the powers given to members are given collectively; therefore, a shareholder (or group of shareholders) who controls the majority of the votes at a company meeting is obviously in a far stronger position than a 'minority' shareholder.

9.3.2 POWERS OF CONTROL

In practical terms, a majority shareholder has extensive powers of control, exercisable ultimately by removing or threatening to remove the directors from office. A minority shareholder often has no real power (unless he is a director and/or can persuade the majority to agree with him), but his position is protected by a number of rights, mostly statutory, some of the most important of which are discussed later in this chapter.

The powers and rights given to members depend in many cases on the holding of a particular proportion of the company's shares (or votes). For example, a number of types of decision require a special resolution (75% majority) — a shareholder who controls 75% of the votes is, therefore, able to exercise powers which a shareholder with a simple majority could not exercise alone. Conversely, a shareholder with more than 25% of the votes can block a special resolution even though he may not have enough votes to be in control of the company (this is sometimes called negative control).

9.3.3 DUTIES OF SHAREHOLDERS

Just as the powers and rights of members largely depend on the proportion of votes that they control, so the duties of members differ depending on whether or not they are in control of the company. The basic rule is that members (whether or not in control) can exercise their right to vote as they wish, so that they can take account of their own interests to the exclusion of conflicting interest of other shareholders. However, this does not mean that shareholders are *entirely* free to vote as they please; thus certain breaches of duty by directors cannot be ratified by the members (see for example, *Cook* v *Deeks*, **8.5.1.1**) while other breaches can be ratified (*Regal (Hastings) Ltd* v *Gulliver*, **8.5.1.1**). In addition, shareholders may not commit a 'fraud on the minority', so that an alteration to the articles is invalid if it discriminates against some of the shareholders.

The powers of shareholders to control their companies are normally exercised by passing a resolution by the required majority at a meeting called by the appropriate notice at which a quorum is present. Alternatively, a written resolution may be used. Members who are absent do not count in the voting unless they have validly appointed a proxy to represent them. Company meetings and resolutions are dealt with in **Chapter 12**.

9.4 Internal Disputes — Introduction

The courts are very reluctant to get involved in disputes within a company. In particular they are not willing to do anything which might amount to interference with business decisions. Internal disputes must therefore usually be resolved under the terms of the company's articles. For example, if there are disputes about business policy the view of the majority of the board will prevail. In the case of an equal division on the board the dispute will be resolved by the chairman's casting vote if the articles so provide (as they usually will).

The power of the shareholders is rather limited. In this section we will look at four procedures which are, however, available to shareholders for their protection. The first of these (s. 14 CA 1985) provides any shareholder with a procedure for enforcing his personal rights in the company. The other three procedures are designed chiefly for the protection of minority shareholders when a dispute arises. In addition we dealt with removal of directors in **Chapter 8**. This gives a majority shareholder ultimate control of the company.

9.5 Section 14 Companies Act 1985

9.5.1 CONTRACT BETWEEN MEMBERS AND COMPANY

Section 14 states that:

> ... the memorandum and articles ... bind the company and its members to the same extent as if they respectively had been signed and sealed by each member, and contained

covenants on the part of each member to observe all the provisions of the memorandum and of the articles.

The effect of this important section is that the memorandum and articles form an agreement which contractually binds:

(a) a company to each of its members; and

(b) the members of the company to each other.

Thus, if specific provisions are not observed, an action may be taken to enforce the obligations imposed by the company's constitution. The extent to which obligations are enforceable is considered further below.

It should be noted that a company's articles are a contract complete in themselves. The court will not therefore imply any terms into the articles (*Bratton Seymour Service Co.* v *Oxborough* [1992] BCC 471).

9.5.2 MEMBERSHIP RIGHTS

An obligation imposed by the memorandum or articles on a member or on the company for the benefit of a member is only enforceable under s. 14 if it relates to membership rights. The most obvious examples of membership rights which have been enforced as a result of actions based on the section include:

(a) the right to a dividend once lawfully declared (*Wood* v *Odessa Waterworks Co.* (1889) 42 ChD 636);

(b) the right to share in surplus capital on a winding-up (*Griffith* v *Paget* (1877) 5 ChD 894); and

(c) the right to vote at meetings (*Pender* v *Lushington* (1877) 6 ChD 70).

The most obvious obligation of a member which may be enforced by s. 14 is the obligation to pay for shares issued by the company.

9.5.3 OTHER RIGHTS

Obligations imposed by the memorandum or articles which do not relate to membership rights are not enforceable under s. 14. A member may, therefore, be left without any remedy even though the company has failed to observe an article which would have benefited him. This is illustrated by the case of *Eley* v *Positive Government Security Life Assurance Co.* (1876) 1 ExD 88. When the company was formed a provision was included in the articles naming the plaintiff as solicitor of the company. He was never, in fact, appointed to the office but did become a member of the company. It was held that he could not sue the company (under the provisions of earlier legislation corresponding with s. 14) because the right to be appointed as solicitor was not a *membership right* of the plaintiff.

Just as a member cannot enforce rights against the company which do not relate to his rights as a member, neither can the company enforce obligations imposed by the articles other than in connection with membership. For example, in *Beattie* v *E. and F. Beattie Ltd* [1938] Ch 708, a dispute arose between a company and one of its directors concerning the latter's right to inspect documents. The company wished to refer the matter to arbitration in accordance with an article requiring arbitration of disputes with members, but was held not entitled to insist on arbitration since the dispute was between the company and the plaintiff in his capacity as *director* not in his capacity as shareholder.

9.5.4 IMPLIED CONTRACTS AND SHAREHOLDERS' AGREEMENTS

The terms laid down in the memorandum or articles may be impliedly incorporated into a contract made with the company. This is most likely to occur in relation to directors' service contracts. Thus, in *Read* v *Astoria Garage (Streatham) Ltd* [1952] Ch 637, a managing director whose service contract did not specify how long he was to remain in office was held to have an implied contract allowing for his dismissal in accordance with certain provisions in the articles.

If the members of a company wish to be able to enforce all the terms of the articles against the company and/or each other they are free to enter into a separate contract to that effect. Such a contract is generally referred to as a 'shareholders' agreement' (see **Chapter 28**).

9.6 *Foss* v *Harbottle*

9.6.1 MAJORITY RULE

A shareholder is not usually permitted to sue where a wrong is done to a company of which he is a member. This rule is known as the rule in *Foss* v *Harbottle* (1843) 2 Hare 461, and there are two justifications for it. Firstly, since a company is a separate legal person distinct from its members the company is the proper plaintiff in an action where a wrong has been done to the company. Secondly, the decision whether or not to sue can be taken either by the directors or by the members in general meeting, and the court is unwilling to interfere with this decision by imposing its own views on the company. At the same time, the courts have recognised that in some circumstances it is appropriate to allow a shareholder to sue on behalf of the company since otherwise justice cannot be done. There are, therefore, a number of exceptions to the rule in *Foss* v *Harbottle*, under which a shareholder can bring an action if the company will not.

These exceptional cases should be contrasted with cases where the personal rights of a shareholder are affected. In such cases, as we saw in the last paragraph, the shareholder need not rely upon an exception to *Foss* v *Harbottle* at all, but may sue because of the contractual rights which he has under s. 14. It is not always easy to decide which actions are permitted by the exceptions to *Foss* v *Harbottle* and which by s. 14. Minority shareholders are also given a number of statutory rights which may be directly enforced against the company (for example, to have the register to members rectified under s. 359 CA 1985). In addition, they have a statutory right to sue where they are 'unfairly prejudiced' by the way in which the company's affairs are being conducted (s. 459 CA 1985) (see **9.8** below).

9.6.2 EXCEPTIONS TO *FOSS* v *HARBOTTLE*

The following are the circumstances in which a member can sue to remedy a wrong done to the company.

9.6.2.1 Where the majority exercise their votes so as to 'defraud' the minority shareholders

'Fraud' in this context is quite a wide concept, covering forms of conduct which do not amount to the commission of a tort. Thus in *Clemens* v *Clemens Brothers Ltd* [1976] 2 All ER 268, a resolution was declared invalid, the effect of which was to increase the degree of control which the majority shareholder and her associates could exercise.

9.6.2.2 Where directors who are in control of a company have been guilty of a breach of fiduciary duty

This exception will often overlap with the first exception, since a breach of fiduciary duty will often involve a fraud on the minority. The reason for this exception is that if the directors control the company (through their shareholdings), they can use their voting power so as to prevent action being brought against themselves. Therefore, unless a minority shareholder can sue on behalf of the company, there is no real chance of a remedy for the breach of fiduciary duty. Where a breach of fiduciary duty can be ratified by the members in general meeting (see, for example, *Hogg* v *Cramphorn*), an action by a shareholder may be stayed pending the holding of a meeting, but the court will not permit ratification in every case (see, for example, *Cook* v *Deeks*).

Where the directors are not in control of a company, an action cannot be brought by a shareholder based on breach of fiduciary duty, since the company in general meeting is then in a position to decide to sue.

9.6.2.3 Where the company (usually as a result of a decision of the board) is proposing to act ultra vires or illegally

In such cases the action may result in an injunction against the directors or an order for compensation against the directors.

9.6.2.4 Where the company has purported to pass an ordinary resolution in circumstances where a special resolution or extraordinary resolution is required

Similarly, an action may be brought to restrain a threatened breach of the articles (which can only validly be altered by special resolution), although the exact scope of this exception is far from clear.

9.6.2.5 Where the company proposes to act on the authority of a resolution which is defective because inadequate notice was given

The notice may be inadequate either because the time between service and the holding of the meeting is too short or because the details given in the notice are insufficient to enable a member to decide whether to attend. For example, in *Baillie* v *Oriental Telephone Co. Ltd* [1915] 1 Ch 503, the notice referred to the fact that a resolution was to be proposed authorising certain payments of commission by a subsidiary company to the directors. It did not say that the payments effectively amounted to all the subsidiary's profits. This was held to be inadequate notice and, therefore, the resolution was set aside in an action brought by a shareholder.

9.7 Actions by Shareholders — Procedure

9.7.1 REPRESENTATIVE ACTION

When a member is able to bring an action under one of the exceptions to *Foss* v *Harbottle*, he is really doing so on behalf of the company. The plaintiff's interests are, therefore, the same as those of the other shareholders (other than any wrongdoers, usually the directors, who are defendants in the action). When a member sues to enforce the memorandum or articles under s. 14 he may be seeking a remedy for himself *or* for himself and a large number of other members whose rights have also been infringed. Order 15 r. 12(1) of the Rules of the Supreme Court (now contained in sch. 1 to the Civil Procedure Rules 1998) makes provision for a representative action where 'numerous persons have the same interest in any proceedings'. This type of action may be brought where the cause of action arises under one of the exceptions to *Foss* v *Harbottle* or under s. 14. The plaintiff shareholder then represents the interests of all the shareholders (except the wrongdoers) and the judgment is normally binding on, and enforceable by, them.

9.7.2 DERIVATIVE ACTION

If action is brought under one of the exceptions to *Foss* v *Harbottle*, the company will be made a nominal defendant. This type of action is sometimes described as a 'derivative action' because the right of the member to sue is not personal to him but derives from the right to sue which the company has failed to exercise. It should be noted that if this type of action is successful, the judgment will give a remedy to the company (which has been wronged) rather than to the plaintiff.

If action is brought under s. 14 it may or may not be representative but it will certainly not be 'derivative'. The right to sue is the plaintiff's own cause of action and in appropriate cases damages, specific performance or other directly beneficial orders will be made in his favour.

9.8 Section 459 Companies Act 1985

9.8.1 UNFAIR PREJUDICE

Section 459(1) provides that:

> A member of a company may apply to the court by petition for an order ... on the ground that the company's affairs are being or have been conducted in a manner which is unfairly prejudicial to the interests of some part of the members (including at least himself) or that any actual or proposed act or omission of the company (including an act or omission on its behalf) is or would be so prejudicial.

9.8.1.1 Grounds

A shareholder may petition under s. 459 if he can show that he has suffered unfair prejudice. The prejudice must have arisen from the way in which the affairs of the company were being conducted or from an actual or proposed act or omission by the company. The prejudice must have affected the interests of at least some of the members of the company. If these things can be shown then the court will have to consider what remedy would be appropriate.

9.8.1.2 Test for unfair prejudice

The test as to what amounts to unfair prejudice is objective. It is not, therefore, necessary for the petitioning shareholders to show that anyone acted in bad faith or with the intention of causing prejudice. In *Re R. A. Noble (Clothing) Ltd* [1983] BCLC 273 the judge suggested that the unfairness of the behaviour could be tested by the 'reasonable bystander test'; that is, prejudice will be regarded as unfair if a hypothetical reasonable bystander would believe it to be unfair.

9.8.1.3 Rights as shareholder must have been prejudiced

If the petitioner is to succeed he must show that his rights as a shareholder have been prejudiced. In *Re Postgate and Denby* [1987] BCLC 8 it was held that such rights include all rights given under the company's memorandum and articles, statutory rights and also rights arising out of agreements and understandings between members. The Law Commission recently reviewed shareholder remedies (Law Com No. 246). In this report a number of guiding principles were iterated, one of which was:

> A member is taken to have agreed to the terms of the memorandum and articles of association when he became a member, whether or not he appreciated what they meant at the time. The law should continue to treat him as so bound unless he shows that the parties have come to some other agreement or understanding which is not reflected in the articles

or memorandum. Failure to do so will create unacceptable commercial uncertainty. The corollary of this is that the best protection for a shareholder is appropriate protection in the articles themselves.

Thus, in *Re A Company (No. 004377 of 1986)* [1987] 1 WLR 102 the petition failed as the articles of the company laid down exactly what was to happen if the quasi-partnership ended for any reason. This included a right for a majority shareholder to buy the shares of the minority. The minority shareholder might indeed be prejudiced by such a provision but he could not claim that the prejudice was unfair as he had (by joining the company) agreed to this in advance.

Unfair prejudice is, however, a flexible concept, probably incapable of exhaustive definition. In *Re Elgindata* [1991] BCLC 959 it was held that in extreme cases mismanagement could be regarded as unfair prejudice.

However, it is submitted that it is difficult to prove one's claim under s. 459 for the simple reason that one is usually trying to establish on parol evidence and circumstances the terms upon which it was agreed that the company be run, as well as on the contents of the company's articles of association. Furthermore, one must normally prove an actual breach of such terms or show that they were being used in a way which offends against equitable considerations (see *O'Neill and another* v *Phillips and others* [1999] TLR 391).

9.8.2 POWERS OF COURT

9.8.2.1 Orders

If a petition under s. 459 is successful the court 'may make such order as it thinks fit for giving relief in respect of the matters complained of' (s. 461(1)). Subsection 461(2) lists particular types of order which may be made but is expressly stated to be without prejudice to the general power given by s. 461(1). The powers listed in s. 461(2) are to:

(a) regulate the conduct of the company's affairs in the future;

(b) require the company to refrain from doing or continuing an act complained of by the petitioner or to do an act which the petitioner has complained it has omitted to do;

(c) authorise civil proceedings to be brought in the name and on behalf of the company by such person or persons and on such terms as the court may direct;

(d) provide for the purchase of the shares of any members of the company by other members or by the company itself and, in the case of a purchase by the company itself, the reduction of the company's capital accordingly.

9.8.2.2 Power to authorise civil proceedings

The power to authorise civil proceedings subject to terms may prove particularly useful. A shareholder may be deterred from fighting a complicated action, based on an exception to *Foss* v *Harbottle*, by the prospect of heavy costs. It may, therefore, be attractive to petition under s. 459 in the hope of obtaining an order for the action to be pursued by the company. The court will ensure that such a petition can be dealt with (in suitable cases) without the substantive issue being tried in the s. 459 proceedings.

9.8.2.3 Purchase of petitioner's shares

In practice the most common remedy awarded to a successful petitioner is that his shares should be purchased by the wrongdoers who have caused the unfair prejudice. The question of valuation causes considerable problems in such cases. The courts have held that the shares

SHAREHOLDERS

should be valued as at whatever date is fair to the petitioner. This usually means that the shares are valued at the date when the prejudice to the petitioner began. If a different date is chosen the court will usually order that the valuer should value the shares as if the prejudice had not taken place.

9.8.2.4 Alteration of memorandum or articles

The order made by the court under s. 459 may require an alteration to the memorandum or articles. If this is done, an office copy of the court order must be delivered to the Registrar within (usually) 14 days.

9.9 Just and Equitable Winding Up

Companies may be wound up on a number of grounds. Winding up is the process by which a company's existence is brought to an end; it usually results from the insolvency of the company. However, one type of winding up is available as a remedy to shareholders of solvent companies — this is winding up under s. 122(1)(g) Insolvency Act 1986, which provides for winding up where 'the court is of the opinion that it is just and equitable that the company should be wound up'. Winding up is a rather drastic solution to problems arising within a company and is now much less important, due to the remedy for shareholders available for cases of unfair prejudice.

9.10 Shareholders and Profits

Basically there are four ways in which a company can deal with its profits:

(a) retain them in the business;

(b) use them to pay interest on debentures;

(c) pay directors' fees;

(d) pay them as dividends to the shareholders.

If profits are retained in the business the shareholders ought to benefit in the long run, since the capital value of the company (and thus of the shares in it) will increase. A payment of interest on debentures will often be a payment to an outsider, which reduces profits available to the shareholders. However, a long-term loan to a company is really a method of investing in the company without buying shares, and so the payment of interest on such a loan may properly be regarded as a payment to an investor in the business. Directors' fees are expenses of the business which an accountant would regard as reducing the profit available to shareholders, but in the case of most small, private companies the directors and shareholders are the same people; thus a payment of directors' fees is in a commercial sense equivalent to a payment of profit to the shareholders.

A company is not entirely free to choose between the four different uses of profits for the following reasons:

(a) it will often be contractually bound to make payments of interest and directors' fees;

(b) there are company law rules which prevent the company from paying dividends except to the extent of 'profits available for the purpose'. (The reason for this is that the original investment made in the company by shareholders may not be returned to them, except in limited circumstances, until the company is wound up.);

(c) it will often be commercially unwise for the company to pay out all its profits, since some will be required to provide for future contingencies or for the expansion of the business.

The tax consequences of each method of using profits will be considered and a comparison will be made between them in **Chapter 16**.

9.11 Declaration and Payment of Dividends

A dividend is a payment to the shareholders of the company which provides them with a return on their investment. It is not a payment of interest on the money invested, since the shareholder does not have an automatic right to the dividend — as we shall see, it becomes payable only if 'declared' by the company (or otherwise authorised under the articles) and only if the Companies Act permits payment in the circumstances.

9.11.1 PROCEDURE

9.11.1.1 Table A

The provisions of Table A in respect of dividend payments provide for the following procedure:

(a) After the accounts have been prepared the directors will consider what dividend, if any, ought to be declared, and will make a recommendation to the members in general meeting.

(b) A meeting of the company will be held at which the question of declaring a dividend will be considered. In practice, this will be done at the AGM, although Table A does not prevent consideration of dividends at an EGM. The members may reject the directors' recommendation or declare a dividend smaller than that recommended, but Table A art. 102 prevents them exceeding the amount recommended by the directors.

The reason why the members may not declare a dividend in excess of the directors' recommendation is that the directors are the managers of the company's business, and so are in a better position than the members to assess the economic ability of the company to pay dividends; it is therefore probably a sensible provision to include in the articles. If members with a majority of the votes object to the dividend policy of the directors they can exercise their right to remove the directors from office under s. 303 CA 1985.

(c) Once the dividend has been declared, the members will be paid the dividend by the company. The amount of dividend paid to each member depends on the nominal value of the shares held, no account being taken of any premium paid on the shares.

9.11.1.2 Interim dividends

During the course of an accounting period (i.e., a 12-month period in respect of which the company's accounts are prepared), the directors may decide to pay an interim dividend (art. 103). However, the directors may only pay an interim dividend if it appears to them to be 'justified by the profits of the company available for distribution'.

9.11.1.3 Other possible arrangements

The articles of the company may validly provide that directors are to declare dividends without holding a general meeting. It is also possible (although undesirable), for the articles to require payment of all the company's profits as dividends (subject to the legal restriction referred to below). If an elective resolution has dispensed with the need to hold an AGM, a

SHAREHOLDERS

dividend could also be declared by a written resolution if the company does not choose to hold an EGM.

9.11.2 CLASSES OF SHARE

If there are different classes of shares they may have different rights to dividends. Thus, if there are preference shares, the ordinary shareholders will usually not be entitled to any dividend until the preference shareholders have received their dividend (which will be expressed as a fixed amount per share or a fixed percentage).

For example, a company has 2,000 £1 shares of which 1,000 are ordinary shares and 1,000 are 10% preference shares; the company declares a dividend of £150. The preference shareholders are entitled to their 10% (i.e., £100) and the ordinary shareholders get the balance (i.e., £50 or 5p per share).

9.11.3 LEGAL ENTITLEMENT TO DIVIDEND

Once declared by the members in general meeting, a dividend is a debt due to the members from the company. The member is, therefore, entitled to sue the company if the dividend is not paid. An interim dividend is not, however, a debt due from the company, so that the members have no right to it until it is actually paid.

9.12 Restrictions on Sources of Dividends

9.12.1 THE BASIC RULE

So as to ensure that money invested by shareholders is not returned to them before the company is wound up, there have always been rules based on judicial decisions preventing the payment of dividends other than out of profits. The Companies Act 1985 now lays down clear rules as to what funds are available for the payment of dividends. These rules, which were first introduced in 1980, are designed to implement the European Communities' Second Directive on Company Law and differ somewhat from the rules previously established by the courts — the new rules are generally more restrictive.

Section 263(1) CA 1985 provides that: 'A company shall not make a distribution except out of profits available for the purpose.' The term 'distribution' is defined by s. 263(2) and includes all distributions of assets to members except:

(a) the issue of bonus shares;

(b) the redemption or purchase of its own shares by the company;

(c) reduction of capital (which requires the approval of the court; see **10.14.4**); or

(d) a distribution on winding-up.

Most dividends are paid in cash and are included in the definition of 'distributions', since cash is just as much an asset as other types of property.

9.12.2 'PROFITS AVAILABLE'

9.12.2.1 Definition

'Profits available for the purpose' of paying dividends are defined by s. 263(3) as 'accumulated, realised profits, so far as not previously utilised by distribution ... less ... accumulated, realised losses ...'. This means that each year it is necessary to calculate the company's trading profit and any capital profits that have been made on the disposal of fixed assets. These are the 'realised profits' from which must be deducted any realised losses, that is, any trading loss or loss made on the disposal of a fixed asset. However, a dividend is only payable if there are *accumulated* realised profits in excess of *accumulated* realised losses. This means that the balance of realised profits can be carried forward from year to year. It is not, therefore, necessary to make a profit every year in order to pay a dividend — all that is required is that there should be a balance of profits taking this year and previous years together.

For example:

	Realised Profit/(loss)	Dividend	Balance to carry forward
Year 1	4,000	1,000	3,000
Year 2	2,000	1,000	4,000
Year 3	(3,000)	1,000	nil

The dividend in year 3 is lawful because in year 1 the realised profits were £4,000 and the dividend only £1,000, so that £3,000 worth of profits could be carried forward. In year 2 the realised profits were £2,000 and the dividend £1,000, so that a further £1,000 could be carried forward. In year 3 there was a realised loss of £3,000 which had to be deducted from the accumulated profits of £4,000, thus leaving £1,000 for a dividend.

Just as realised profits not used to pay dividends may be carried forward to later years and used to pay dividends in those later years, so realised losses which are not balanced by realised profits accumulated from previous years must be carried forward to later years and set off against realised profits before a dividend can be paid. Thus (continuing the example above):

	Realised Profit/(loss)	Dividend	Balance to carry forward
Year 4	(2,000)	nil	(2,000)
Year 5	1,000	nil	(1,000)
Year 6	2,000	1,000	nil

In year 4 there was a loss, and since no accumulated profits were available from years 1–3, no dividend could be paid. In year 5 a profit of £1,000 was made but this could not be used to pay a dividend since the accumulated realised loss (£2,000 from year 4) was more than the realised profit. In year 6 the £1,000 dividend was the maximum which could be paid because £1,000 of the loss from year 4 had to be set off against the profit.

9.12.2.2 Calculation of profits and losses

Section 263 CA 1985 does not lay down particular rules as to how profits and losses are to be calculated; normal accountancy practice must be applied in deciding whether a profit or loss has been realised. However, a few situations are specifically dealt with:

(a) A profit which has been 'capitalised' (in this context a profit is capitalised only if it is used to pay up bonus shares or to replace capital repaid to members) cannot be treated as a realised profit.

(b) A loss which has been written off in a reduction of capital is not treated as a realised loss. This is because when the capital is reduced the shareholders' investment is wiped out, with the approval of the court, to the extent of the reduction and so does not have to be maintained.

SHAREHOLDERS

(c) If a 'provision' is made in the accounts of the company it must usually be treated as a realised loss (s. 275 CA 1985). A provision is an item shown in the accounts as an expense in respect of expected future expenses (e.g., it is usual practice to provide for depreciation of wasting assets — that is, to record the fact that they are declining in value). If the provision were not treated as a realised loss the company could write down the value of an asset in its accounts and then sell it for its written-down value thus (apparently) making neither a profit nor a loss, whereas in fact there was a substantial loss in value during the period of ownership of the asset.

9.12.2.3 Restriction on payment of dividends by a company's articles

The articles of a company may restrict the company's right to pay dividends further than is done by the Companies Act, for example, by preventing payment of a dividend out of a realised capital profit. Table A does not contain any such provisions. In most circumstances a company would be very unwise to distribute all the 'profits available' as defined by s. 263, since to do so would often create cash flow problems (a company always needs sufficient cash to buy stock, pay wages, etc.), and make expansion of the business more difficult.

9.12.2.4 Unrealised losses

It should be noted that, although realised losses must be made good out of realised profits before a dividend can be paid, there is no requirement that *unrealised* losses must be made good. For example, if a company owns land which it knows to be declining in value, it can still go on paying dividends out of realised profits, since the loss on the land is only realised when the land is sold. Similarly an unrealised profit cannot be used to pay a dividend. A company which is making small realised losses cannot, therefore, pay a dividend even if it knows its land is increasing in value by more than the losses.

9.12.3 THE 'RELEVANT ACCOUNTS'

9.12.3.1 'Properly drawn-up accounts'

Whether a company has got any profits available for distribution can only be judged by reference to properly drawn up accounts. Section 270 CA 1985 lays down rules as to which accounts are to be used at any particular time for deciding whether there are profits available. Usually the company must rely on the last set of accounts prepared in accordance with s. 226 CA 1985 (substituted by s. 4 CA 1989 — as we shall see in **Chapter 29**, these are the accounts which must be audited, laid before the members in general meeting and sent to the Companies Registry where they are available for public inspection).

9.12.3.2 Interim and initial accounts

If the company wants to pay a dividend which is not justified by its last accounts it can prepare 'interim' accounts specially for the purpose of showing that profits are available for distribution. This might be done, for example, if the company had made a loss and so could not pay a dividend but has now started to make profits again and does not want to wait until the next full set of accounts are produced. Similarly, if a company wishes to pay a dividend before it has prepared *any* accounts under s. 226 CA 1985 (i.e., broadly speaking, during its first year after incorporation) it can prepare 'initial' accounts to justify the dividend payment.

Interim and initial accounts must be prepared and audited in much the same way as the normal final accounts of the company. Because of the expense involved in preparing such accounts it will usually be better to wait until accounts are produced in the normal way before paying the dividend.

9.12.4 CONSEQUENCES OF UNLAWFUL DISTRIBUTIONS

Section 277 CA 1985 requires any member to repay a distribution which he 'knows or has reasonable grounds for believing' to be illegal. If a dividend is paid illegally the directors will normally be personally liable to the company, since they will have recommended and paid (or permitted payment of) the dividend in breach of their duty.

TEN

COMPANY FINANCE

This chapter covers the following topics:

10.1 Introduction
10.2 Issues of shares
10.3 Share capital
10.4 Financial assistance by company for purchase of shares
10.5 Classes of shares
10.6 The power to borrow
10.7 Secured loans
10.8 Registration of charges
10.9 Priority of charges
10.10 Remedies of debenture-holders
10.11 Receivers
10.12 Position of debenture-holders
10.13 Steps to be taken by a lender to a company
10.14 Alteration to the capital clause.

10.1 Introduction

Once a company is formed it will need to spend money to get its business going. It may need to buy stock, buy or rent premises, pay wages, advertise and pay the general expenses involved in running a business. The money that the company needs to start its business is often called capital. Technically, however, 'capital' is the liability of the company to the people who have provided it with money on a long-term basis.

A company can raise money either in the form of an investment by shareholders or in the form of loans. Once the business is established profits may be retained in the business thus producing a third source of finance.

This chapter will look at how companies raise money through share allotments and borrowing. It is important to note that an important source of information as to how a company is capitalised is the balance sheet, which will provide both details of debt and share funding. It is, therefore, recommended that **29.7**, which provides an introduction to the balance sheet, is read in conjunction with this chapter.

10.2 Issue of Shares

10.2.1 LEGAL NATURE OF SHARES

A share in a company is a chose in action. Its value to the shareholder depends on the particular contractual rights which he obtains from owning the share. These contractual rights are obtained when the shares are issued to him by the company if he is the original owner, or when they are transferred or transmitted to him. This section is concerned with the issue of shares by a company; transfer and transmission are dealt with in **Chapter 11**.

10.2.2 RIGHTS ATTACHING TO SHARES

The rights attached to shares vary from company to company and a company may issue different classes of shares with different rights attached to them. It is, therefore, difficult to generalise about the exact nature of a share but the following general points may be of assistance:

(a) Nearly all shares give the shareholder a *right to a dividend* (i.e., a share in profits), but a dividend is only payable if the company has made profits and it is decided to declare a dividend (see **Chapter 9**).

(b) Most, but not all, shares give the shareholder a *right to vote* at general meetings of the company.

(c) If the company is wound up the shareholder will have a *right to repayment* of his investment (in the comparatively unlikely event that the company is then solvent) and in most cases a *right to participate* in any undistributed profit.

(d) The Stock Transfer Act 1982 lays down a procedure for the transfer of shares but does not guarantee the shareholder a *right to transfer*.

(e) Shareholders are given certain *rights as a matter of law* by the Companies Act. Many of these rights are, however, only given to shareholders who have a right to vote at company meetings (e.g., the rights to remove directors and to appoint and remove auditors referred to in **Chapter 8**).

In the case of a private company the voting rights will often be as important as the financial rights. This is especially so in the case of a shareholding which gives voting control, since it effectively carries with it the right to control many major decisions of the company.

10.2.3 THE VALUE OF SHARES

The capital value of shares clearly depends to some extent on the rights attached to them but it also depends on other factors — particularly the profitability of the company and its asset worth.

All shares must have a 'nominal value' (also called 'par value') which is set out in the capital clause of the memorandum. This figure says little about the true value of the shares since, as we shall see shortly, shares can be issued for more (but not less) than nominal value and, once issued, their true value will fluctuate either upwards or downwards as the company is more or less successful.

10.2.4 PROCEDURE FOR THE ISSUE OF SHARES

When new shares are created by a company they are said to be 'issued' or 'allotted' by the company to the people who have contracted to buy them. The articles of the company may give the directors the power to issue shares. Any power granted to the directors to issue shares is subject to the following restrictions:

(a) *Company must have sufficient nominal capital to allow issue*

Shares may only be issued to the extent of the nominal capital of the company. If the articles give power to do so, the nominal capital may be increased under s. 121 CA 1985, but this requires the approval of the members by ordinary resolution in general meeting (see **10.14**).

(b) *Directors must be authorised to issue shares*

The powers of the directors to issue shares is restricted by s. 80 CA 1985. This requires the directors to be authorised to issue shares either by the company in general meeting or by the articles. The authorisation may be given either for a particular exercise of the directors' power or generally, and may be unconditional or subject to conditions. Whether the authorisation is given by ordinary resolution of the members in general meeting or by the articles, it must state the maximum amount of shares which the directors may issue and the date when the authority will expire. The authority cannot be given for more than five years from formation of the company or the passing of the resolution (as the case may be) and can be revoked or varied by the company in general meeting at any time. Once given, the authority can be extended by up to five years by the further resolution of the company. (Following the enactment of the Companies Act 1989, in the case of private companies, it is possible to dispense with this five-year limitation if the authority is given by an elective resolution in accordance with the provisions of s. 80A CA 1985.)

Resolutions under s. 80 may be passed as ordinary resolutions (so that a simple majority is sufficient), even though they alter the articles. The resolution must, however, be registered with the Registrar of Companies as if it were a special resolution.

If the directors issue shares without authority they commit an offence and presumably would be liable to the company for breach of duty but the issue of shares remains valid (s. 80(10)). At first sight this section gives very considerable protection to the shareholders but in most private companies the directors and majority shareholders are the same people, so that all that will be required is an extra procedural step (the calling of a meeting of the company) at some time within five years before the issue. The section is, therefore, of most importance to the comparatively few private companies where the directors are not the controlling shareholders, and to public companies.

(c) *Consideration must be given to rights of pre-emption*

Under s. 89 CA 1985 if it is proposed to issue shares to any person, they must first be offered to the existing shareholders, in proportion to their existing holdings, on terms at least as favourable as those proposed for the issue to that person. The members must be given 21 days to make up their minds. This right of pre-emption does not apply if the shares are to be issued for a non-cash consideration and can, in the case of a private company, be varied or removed by contrary provision in the articles (s. 91 CA 1985). A special resolution can be passed by a private *or* public company, without altering the articles, to allow the directors to issue shares on a particular occasion as if s. 89 did not apply (s. 95 CA 1985).

Section 89 gives shareholders a useful degree of protection in cases where the effect of issuing shares would be to water down their control of the company. A higher degree of protection will be given if the articles provide for pre-emption rights on *any* issue of shares, so that the company will not be able to offer shares for a non-cash consideration unless the members are willing to give up their rights. It should be noted that s. 89 is only concerned with the *issue* of shares. It is fairly common for *articles* to provide for pre-emption rights where an existing shareholder wants to *transfer* his shares (see **Chapter 11**).

(d) *Directors must observe fiduciary duties*

The directors may not issue shares in breach of their fiduciary duty, so that the approval of the members is required if the motive behind the issue is anything other than the raising of further investment in the company.

(e) *Any restrictions in the articles must be observed*

The articles themselves may impose restrictions. For example, the power may extend only to issuing ordinary shares, the sanction of the members in general meeting being required for the issue of shares with special rights.

10.2.5 PAYMENT FOR SHARES

10.2.5.1 Consideration

A contract for the issue of shares may provide for payment in cash or for some other consideration. If the agreement is for the payment of cash the full amount may be payable immediately or part of it may be left outstanding until the company makes a 'call' for the unpaid amount or the company goes into liquidation. Payment in full on issue of the shares is now usually required, so that partly paid shares are rather uncommon.

Companies may not issue shares at a discount. This is prohibited by s. 100 CA 1985.

10.2.5.2 Premium

Shares are quite commonly issued at a premium, that is, for more than their nominal value. The premium is treated as 'capital' of the company (for the consequences of this, see **10.3.2**).

10.2.6 'RETURN AS TO ALLOTMENTS'

Section 88 CA 1985 requires a return of allotment to be made to the Registrar of Companies within one month of the issue of shares on Form 88(2). The form requires details as to the number and nominal amount of the shares, the names, addresses and descriptions of the shareholders, and the amount paid up on each share including any premium. Where there is a non-cash consideration, a written contract for the sale of the shares must also be sent to the Registrar or, if the contract was oral, particulars of the contract should be set out on Form 88(3) and also returned to the Registrar.

10.2.7 ISSUE OF SHARES TO THE PUBLIC

Section 81 CA 1985 makes it an offence for a private company to offer shares (or debentures) to the public or to issue them with a view to an offer for sale to the public.

10.3 Share Capital

10.3.1 MAINTENANCE OF CAPITAL

Once shares have been issued they are said to form part of the 'capital' of the company.

'Share capital' is really a liability of a company to its shareholders, since the company will one day be liable to repay the shareholders' investment (usually, in fact, only when the company is wound up). For the protection of people dealing with the company, share capital has to be 'maintained' by the company. This does not mean that the money invested has to be deposited or set aside as a fund to guarantee the company's creditors. The money is available to be used by the company as 'working' capital, to pay for the expenses of its business. What maintaining capital means is that it must not, normally, be returned to the members in any way while the company is a going concern.

Two major consequences of this rule are:

(a) That dividends may only be paid out of profits (see **9.12**).

(b) That capital invested cannot be returned to the members except:

(i) with the approval of the court (s. 135 CA 1985 deals with the cases where capital can be returned or the liability to members cancelled with the approval of the court); or

(ii) where the company redeems or purchases its own shares (see below and **Chapter 11**).

10.3.2 SHARE PREMIUM ACCOUNT

As has already been explained, it is common for shares to be issued for more than their nominal value. The excess is not strictly speaking share capital but is required by s. 130 CA 1985 to be credited to a 'share premium account' (i.e., an account showing the company to be liable to the members for the amount of the premium). The share premium account has to be maintained in the same way as share capital; thus assets representing it cannot be returned to members.

10.3.3 COMPANY AS MEMBER OF ITSELF AND PURCHASE OF OWN SHARES

10.3.3.1 The company as its own shareholder

A company may not be registered as its own shareholder. However, shares can be transferred to a trustee or nominee for the company.

10.3.3.2 Original prohibition on buy-back of shares

The traditional position was that it was illegal for a company to buy its own shares (*Trevor v Whitworth* (1887) 12 App Cas 409). This is because use of its money by a company to purchase its own shares is in effect a return to the shareholder of his investment and so is a reduction of capital.

10.3.3.3 Redeemable shares

Section 159 CA 1985 gives companies (if authorised by their articles) power to issue redeemable shares, that is shares which can be bought back by the company at the option of the company or the shareholder. Table A art. 3 gives the company power to issue redeemable shares.

10.3.3.4 Buy-back of shares

It was thought to be desirable for companies, particularly small family companies, to have the power to purchase their own shares as this would provide an additional market for the shares. Section 162 CA 1985, therefore, gives companies power to purchase their own shares if authorised to do so by their articles (Table A art. 35 gives such authorisation). Examples of cases where the power is useful include buying out dissident shareholders and the provision of funds to the estate of a deceased shareholder to assist in the payment of inheritance tax.

COMPANY FINANCE

The contract for purchase must be approved by special resolution before the company enters into it. The members whose shares are to be purchased must not use the votes given to them by the shares which are to be purchased on that resolution. The resolution will be invalid unless a copy of the contract (or a memorandum of its terms) is made available for inspection by the members at the company's registered office for a period of at least 15 days ending with the date of the meeting and also at the meeting itself. Once the shares have been purchased by the company they are treated as cancelled.

Within 28 days after the shares have been purchased a return must be made to the Registrar of Companies stating the number and nominal value of the shares purchased and the date of purchase (Form 169).

10.3.3.5 Financing buy-back or redemption

When shares are redeemed or purchased by the company the money used to pay for them must generally come out of profits or the proceeds of a fresh issue of shares. Where the shares are purchased or redeemed with assets representing profits the legislation requires the capital of the company to be maintained. Thus, s. 170 CA 1985 requires the company to open a 'capital redemption reserve' equal to the reduction in the share capital. This reserve is treated in the same way as share capital or the share premium account, that is, it is shown in the balance sheet as a liability due to shareholders which has to be maintained until the company goes into liquidation.

Example

BALANCE SHEET OF JCT LIMITED

FIXED ASSETS		
Premises		200,000
Fixtures		20,000
		220,000
CURRENT ASSETS		
Stock	30,000	
Debtors	40,000	
Cash	70,000	
	140,000	
CURRENT LIABILITIES		
Creditors	40,000	
		100,000
		320,000
CAPITAL		
Share capital		250,000
Share premium		10,000
Profit & loss		60,000
		320,000

COMPANY FINANCE

JCT buys back 10,000 ordinary shares of £1 each at a price of £20,000. The purchase is made wholly out of profits. The amendments to the balance sheet are:

(a) Reduce cash by £20,000.
(b) Reduce share capital by £10,000 (i.e., the nominal value of the shares).
(c) Reduce profit & loss by £20,000 (to reflect the use of profits to buy back the shares).
(d) Create capital redemption reserve of £10,000 (equivalent to the reduction in capital, as per s. 170 CA 1985).

BALANCE SHEET OF JCT LIMITED FOLLOWING BUY-BACK

FIXED ASSETS
Premises		200,000
Fixtures		20,000
		220,000

CURRENT ASSETS
Stock	30,000	
Debtors	40,000	
Cash	50,000	
	120,000	

CURRENT LIABILITIES
Creditors	40,000	
		80,000
		300,000

CAPITAL
Share capital	240,000	
Share premium	10,000	
Capital redemption reserve	10,000	
Profit & loss	40,000	
	300,000	

In the case of a *private* company, payment out of assets representing capital is permitted. The use of assets representing capital to redeem or purchase its own shares means that a private company can reduce its capital without seeking the sanction of the court. In order to protect the interests of members and creditors the following detailed procedural requirements must be satisfied:

(a) The articles must contain an express power to use capital assets for this purpose (the general power to purchase its own shares is not sufficient) Article 35 of Table A does contain such a power.

(b) The directors must certify that the company will remain solvent and will, in their view, be able to carry on business as a going concern for at least a year. The directors' certificate must be supported by an auditors' report in which the auditors certify that they are not aware of anything which would indicate that the directors' view of the situation is unreasonable.

(c) Not later than one week after the date of the certificate a general meeting of the company must be held at which a special resolution approving the payment is passed. The members whose shares are to be purchased may not use the votes on those shares on this resolution.

(d) The payment for the shares must be made by the company not less than five nor more than seven weeks after the date on which the resolution is passed. This period is laid down so that members or creditors who object to the purchase have time to challenge the purchase in court.

In addition, where a payment is made out of capital, the company's accounts must reflect this. Under s. 171(4) CA 1985, where the permissible capital payment (as defined by s. 171(3)) is less than the nominal value of the shares redeemed, the amount of the difference must be transferred to a capital redemption reserve. Where the permissible capital payment is greater than the nominal value of the shares redeemed, the situation is different. The company may then reduce the amount of any capital redemption reserve, share premium account, fully paid share capital or unrealised profits of the company standing in any reserve by a sum not exceeding the amount by which the permissible capital payment exceeds the nominal amount of the shares (s. 171(5) CA 1985). There are also accounting requirements where a company uses the proceeds of a fresh issue of shares to buy back shares.

Example

BALANCE SHEET OF BHW LIMITED

FIXED ASSETS
Premises   100,000
Fixtures   20,000
                                                      ———————
                                                      120,000

CURRENT ASSETS
Stock   30,000
Debtors   40,000
Cash   70,000
                               ———————
                               140,000

CURRENT LIABILITIES
Creditors   40,000
                               ———————
                                                      100,000
                                                      ———————
                                                      220,000
                                                      ———————

CAPITAL
Share capital   150,000
Share premium   50,000
Profit & loss   20,000
                                                      ———————
                                                      220,000
                                                      ———————

COMPANY FINANCE

BHW buys back 20,000 ordinary shares of £1 each at a price of £30,000. The purchase is made from a combination of available profits (£20,000) and a permissible capital payment of £10,000. The amendments to the balance sheet are:

(a) Reduce cash by £30,000.
(b) Reduce share capital by £20,000 (i.e., the nominal value of the shares).
(c) Reduce profit & loss by £20,000 (to reflect the use of profits to buy back the shares).
(d) Create capital redemption reserve of £10,000 (equivalent to the amount by which the permissible capital payment is less than the nominal value of shares redeemed, as per s. 171(4) CA 1985).

BALANCE SHEET OF BHW LIMITED FOLLOWING BUY-BACK
(Permissible capital payment is less than nominal value of shares redeemed)

FIXED ASSETS
Premises   100,000
Fixtures   20,000

                                                                 120,000

CURRENT ASSETS
Stock   30,000
Debtors   40,000
Cash   40,000

                                         110,000

CURRENT LIABILITIES
Creditors   40,000

                                                                  70,000

                                                                 190,000

CAPITAL
Share capital   130,000
Share premium   50,000
Capital redemption reserve   10,000
Profit & loss   =======
                                                                 190,000

If BHW had bought the 20,000 ordinary shares of £1 each at a price of £50,000, then the accounting treatment would be different. In this case, the purchase was made from a combination of available profits (£20,000) and a permissible capital payment of £30,000. The amendments to the balance sheet are:

(a) Reduce cash by £50,000.
(b) Reduce share capital by £20,000 (i.e., the nominal value of the shares).
(c) Reduce profit & loss by £20,000 (to reflect the use of profits to buy back the shares).
(d) Reduce share premium account by £10,000 (equivalent to the amount by which the permissible capital payment exceeds the nominal value of shares redeemed, as per s. 171(5) CA 1985).

COMPANY FINANCE

BALANCE SHEET OF BHW LIMITED FOLLOWING BUY-BACK
(Permissible capital payment exceeds the nominal value of shares redeemed)

FIXED ASSETS
Premises   100,000
Fixtures   20,000
                                                      ───────
                                                      120,000

CURRENT ASSETS
Stock   30,000
Debtors   40,000
Cash   20,000
                               ──────
                               90,000

CURRENT LIABILITIES
Creditors   40,000
                               ──────
                                                       50,000
                                                      ───────
                                                      170,000
                                                      ───────

CAPITAL
Share capital   130,000
Share premium   40,000
Profit & loss
                                                      ═══════
                                                      170,000
                                                      ───────

10.4 Financial Assistance by Company for Purchase of Shares

Section 151 CA 1985 makes it illegal for a company to give financial assistance directly or indirectly to assist someone to purchase shares in the company (or its holding company) but there are important exceptions to this rule which will be considered in **Chapter 11**.

10.5 Classes of Shares

In most companies, all the shares issued have the same rights attached to them. It is possible, however, for a company to issue shares with different rights. The shares are then said to belong to different classes. For example, a company may issue preference shares, that is, shares which have a better right to receive a dividend than ordinary shares. It is also possible to give some shareholders a greater measure of control over the affairs of the company either by creating voting and non-voting shares or by providing that all shares are to carry a right to vote but that some will have more votes than others.

The rights attaching to a specific class of shares will usually be set out in the company's articles (although they can be contained in the memorandum). Where it is proposed to effect a variation of class rights, it is necessary first to obtain the approval of a three-quarters majority of the holders of the relevant class of shares (s. 125 CA 1985).

10.6 The Power to Borrow

10.6.1 EXPRESS AND IMPLIED POWER

A trading company has an implied power to borrow for the purpose of its trade. This is because the trade will be authorised by its objects and the borrowing will be reasonably incidental to the power to carry on the trade.

A company with power to borrow also has an implied power to give security for the loan. It is preferable to include express powers if a full objects clause is adopted rather than to rely on implied ones. In practice, banks (and other professional lenders) would probably continue to check the company's express powers despite the abolition of the consequences of the ultra vires rule referred to in **10.6.2**.

10.6.2 ULTRA VIRES BORROWING

A lender to a company was formerly well advised to check the company's memorandum so as to ensure that the loan was within the powers of the company. However, s. 35 CA 1985 removes the need to do so by providing that 'the validity of an act done by a company shall not be called into question on the ground of lack of capacity by reason of anything in the company's memorandum'.

10.6.3 EXERCISE OF BORROWING POWERS

The power to borrow must be exercised in accordance with the company's articles of association. If the company has adopted Table A the directors will have power to borrow at least where the loan is to be used for the purposes of the business (art. 70).

The Table A in force *before 1 July 1985* limited the powers of the directors to borrow on behalf of the company. Many companies formed before that date will therefore only be able to borrow substantial sums following approval of the loan by the members in general meeting. In the case of newly formed companies, restrictions on the power of the directors to borrow can be imposed by the adoption of a special article to that effect.

10.7 Secured Loans

10.7.1 TYPES OF SECURITY

A prudent lender will usually require security for a loan made to a company. Any assets of the company may be charged by way of security. Usually security will be in the form of a mortgage, a fixed charge, a floating charge or all three. Therefore, a key issue for any lender taking security is that the company in question actually owns the assets which will be charged. Also a lender will want to know if there are other charges already attaching to such assets. Such investigations are commonly referred to as 'due diligence' and one of the key responsibilities of a lawyer acting for a lender will be to carry out due diligence on the client's behalf. (See further at **10.13** for some of the usual investigations made.)

In addition to charges over the assets of the company a lender may frequently require personal guarantees from the directors. Where a personal guarantee is given by a director who is also a shareholder, the benefit of limited liability is effectively lost to the extent of the guarantee.

When companies borrow money, they will more often than not enter into a 'debenture' with the lender. (For a discussion of the contents of this document see **Chapter 27**.) Unfortunately, the term 'debenture' covers a variety of loan instruments and has no one specific usage. In its simplest form it means a document issued by a company acknowledging debt of that company. This will clearly cover unsecured loan agreements. However, in commercial circles the term very often implies that the debt is backed up by some form of security. (In fact, such documentation may be called a 'mortgage debenture'.)

To complicate matters further, companies may issue 'loan stock' or 'debenture stock' which consists of transferable *securities* in a company, carrying with them a contractual right to interest and repayment of the sum paid for them. These can also be classed as debentures (s. 744 CA 1985). Therefore, care should always be exercised in both the use and interpretation of the term and the actual documentation in question should be inspected to establish the nature of a company's indebtedness.

Finally it is equally important to distinguish between the terms 'security' and 'securities'. The former is a generic term for charges over property; the latter covers all forms of transferable instruments in a company, most commonly shares and loan stock.

10.7.2 MORTGAGES AND FIXED CHARGES

A lender may take security in the form of a mortgage or a fixed charge. The essential difference between the two is that a mortgage requires the formal transfer of title in the asset to the mortgagee, subject to an automatic right for title to be transferred back to the mortgagor once the debt is repaid — the so-called 'equity of redemption'. There are no such formalities required to create a fixed charge, merely an intention by the parties that the asset in question can be appropriated by the chargeholder and sold by it. However, in most security documentation, it will be clear from the wording that a fixed charge is intended. Both types of security must attach to specific, identifiable assets or assets which can be ascertained and defined.

In the case of a mortgage, the mortgagee actually owns title to the asset and can, thus, sell it without reference to the mortgagor, provided that the mortgagor is in default under the loan. In the case of a fixed charge, title remains with the chargor, but the chargor is not entitled to sell the asset without the consent of the chargeholder.

It is important to note that mortgages specifically of freehold and leasehold land are somewhat different and are governed, inter alia, by Part III of the Law of Property Act 1925. In particular, the creation of a mortgage over land is not possible by the transfer of the legal estate (s. 85 LPA 1925). Instead it must be created by way of a charge by deed expressed to be by way of legal mortgage.

Mortgages can either be equitable or legal. Legal mortgages require specific formaities to be fulfilled, in particular the transfer of title in the property according to the law. An equitable mortgage is created where there is evidence of a desire to create a mortgage without fulfilling all such formalities.

> **Example 1** Gibson borrows money from Fender. By way of security for the debt, Gibson transfers some shares in Washburn Limited to Fender. Fender is entered on the register of members of Washburn Limited. Thus Fender has a legal mortgage over the shares.
>
> **Example 2** Instead of Gibson transferring shares to Fender, he deposits with Fender his share certificate and an executed, undated stock transfer form in Fender's favour, on the understanding that Fender shall be entitled to present the form and the certificate to Washburn Limited, should Gibson default on repaying the loan. As such, Fender has an equitable mortgage over the shares.

An equitable mortgage is weaker than a legal one, in that a bona fide purchaser for value without notice of the equitable mortgage takes the property free from it. However, there are in place specific registration requirements which make it more difficult for such a purchaser to claim ignorance of such a fact, particularly in relation to registered and unregistered land. Also, the circumstances of the equitable mortgage may mean that the owner cannot sell the property in any event, as in the above example, where the shareholder would be unable to sell the shares without possession of the share certificate.

Fixed charges are essentialy creatures of equity. Confusingly, they may sometimes be referred to as equitable mortgages. In fact, commentators and judges often use the terminology loosely. Rather than worry about specific labels, the main distinction mentioned above should be borne in mind, that is, a mortgage either grants or purports to grant a proprietary interest in property, whereas a charge grants a right over property which can be exercised in certain situations.

An important distinction, however, is that between fixed and floating charges, which are discussed next.

10.7.3 FLOATING CHARGES

A floating charge is an equitable charge over assets of a particular description owned by the company from time to time. A floating charge can be given over assets which are repeatedly dealt with by the company. Perhaps stock-in-trade is the clearest example. A company cannot give a fixed charge over its stock since to do so would prevent it from selling that stock without first obtaining the consent of the mortgagee. This would obviously hinder the ability of the company to carry on its business. However, if it gives a floating charge over the stock, the charge will 'float' over whatever stock the company owns from time to time — it can therefore sell the stock free from the charge and buy new stock to which the charge will automatically attach.

The nature of a floating charge was defined by Romer LJ in *Re Yorkshire Woolcombers' Association Ltd* [1903] 2 Ch 284, in the following way:

> ... if a charge has the three characteristics I am about to mention it is a floating charge.
>
> (a) if it is a charge on a class of assets of a company present and future;
>
> (b) if that class is one which, in the ordinary course of business of the company, would be changing from time to time; and
>
> (c) if you find that by the charge it is contemplated that, until some future step is taken by or on behalf of those interested in the charge, the company may carry on its business in the ordinary way as far as concerns the particular class of asset I am dealing with.

At first sight a floating charge would seem to give no security at all to the lender since the company can continue to deal with the assets which are charged. However, a floating charge 'fixes' on the charged assets owned by the company at the time when the charge 'crystallises'. A floating charge crystallises when:

(a) The winding-up of the company commences (in the case of a winding-up by the court this is usually when the winding-up petition is presented (s. 129(2) Insolvency Act 1986); in the case of voluntary winding-up it is when the winding-up resolution is passed (s. 86 Insolvency Act 1986)).

(b) A receiver is appointed by the court.

(c) A receiver is appointed by the lender under a power given by the debenture.

(d) Any other event occurs which the debenture specifies will cause crystallisation.

COMPANY FINANCE

It should be noted that companies are the only type of business association which can create a floating charge.

10.7.4 ADVANTAGES AND DISADVANTAGES OF FLOATING CHARGES

As far as the borrowing company is concerned a floating charge has one great advantage over a fixed charge; that is, until crystallisation, it can deal freely with the charged assets without the permission of the lender.

From the lender's point of view a floating charge suffers from a number of disadvantages when compared with a fixed charge. In particular:

(a) Its value as a security is uncertain until crystallisation.

(b) It is postponed to execution and distress for rent completed before crystallisation.

(c) It is postponed to preferred creditors on a liquidation of the borrowing company.

(d) It is postponed to later fixed charges in certain cases (see **10.9.1**).

(e) It may be invalid as a security if the company goes into liquidation within a year (see **Chapter 24**).

10.8 Registration of Charges

10.8.1 SECTION 395 CA 1985

10.8.1.1 Requirement to register charges

Section 395 requires registration with the Registrar of Companies of most types of charge and mortgage created by a company. Registration is required of all floating charges and charges over the company's land, goodwill, book debts and many other types of property. A complete list would be beyond the scope of this Guide. Certain types of charge are not covered by s. 395, so that a charge over shares in another company owned by the borrowing company is not registrable, nor is an unpaid vendor's lien nor any other charge arising by operation of law. For the purposes of this section (**10.8**), the term 'charge' is used to include mortgages and fixed and floating charges, unless specific reference is made.

10.8.1.2 Method of registration

Registration must be made by delivering to the Registrar the instrument creating the charge (which is returned after registration), the particulars of the charge (on Form M395) and a fee of £10 within 21 days. This means within 21 days of the execution of the instrument creating the charge (which may be longer than 21 days after the indebtedness secured by the charge is incurred by the company). The duty to register is imposed on the company (s. 399 CA 1985) and if it fails to register in time it, and every officer of the company in default, is liable to a fine. However, any person interested in the charge may register it (as we shall see below, it is very much in the interests of the lender to make sure that the charge is registered). A charge is not registered in time if Form M395 is submitted for registration within 21 days but incorrectly completed (R v *Registrar of Companies, ex parte Esal (Commodities) Ltd* [1985] 2 All ER 79).

10.8.1.3 Register of charges at Companies House

The Registrar keeps a register of the charges created by each company (s. 401 CA 1985) from which the following information can be discovered:

(a) the date of creation of the charge;

(b) the amount secured by the charge;

(c) short particulars of the property charged;

(d) the persons entitled to the charge.

This register is open to public inspection along with the other information on the company's file at Companies House on payment of the Registrar's fee (currently £1).

10.8.1.4 Certificate of registration

Once he has registered the charge the Registrar gives a certificate of registration which is conclusive evidence that the requirements of the Act as to registration have been complied with. Registration gives constructive notice of the charge to anyone dealing with the company and since the Registrar's certificate is conclusive evidence of *proper* registration, a later chargee cannot complain that the registered particulars are inaccurate. (For example, in *National Provincial and Union Bank of England* v *Charnley* [1924] 1 KB 431, the registered particulars understated the amount of the loan and yet a later creditor was held to have constructive notice of the proper registration and therefore could not object to full payment of the earlier charge in priority to his charge.) Although the registered particulars will seldom be inaccurate (since the Registrar checks them against the charge before issuing his certificate), a prudent lender should check the instruments creating any prior charges so as to be certain of the amount secured and the extent of the property given as security (this can be done by searching at the company's own registered office; see **10.8.4**).

10.8.1.5 Extension of time limit for registration

If the charge is not registered within 21 days the court may extend the time limit provided that it is satisfied that the failure to register was:

> '... accidental, or due to inadvertence or to some other sufficient cause, or is not of a nature to prejudice the position of creditors or shareholders of the company, or that on other grounds it is just and equitable to grant relief ...'.

The court may impose terms and will, in practice, always impose a condition that the registration is not to prejudice rights acquired by other persons before registration finally takes place.

10.8.2 EFFECT OF NON-REGISTRATION

Section 395(1) provides that the security given by a registrable charge shall be '... void against the liquidator and any creditor of the company'. The importance of this provision is that if the company goes into liquidation before the loan has been repaid the unregistered chargee loses his security. This is so even if a later secured creditor had actual notice of the charge when he took his security (*Re Monolithic Building Co.* [1915] 1 Ch 643). It should be noted that non-registration makes the security void against the liquidator or creditor but not against the company. The lender is, therefore, entitled to enforce his security against the company up to the time when winding-up commences (but not after that time since the security is then void against the liquidator).

Furthermore, s. 395(1) is stated to be '... without prejudice to any contract or obligation for repayment of the money secured ... and when a charge becomes void under this section, the money secured by it immediately becomes payable'. The chargee can, therefore, demand payment immediately if the charge is not registered even if the instrument creating the charge provided for repayment at a later date.

The practical problem is that, although the secured debt is not extinguished by non-registration of the charge, the chargee will only rank as an ordinary creditor in a liquidation of the company. This means that the chargee will have to wait until those with valid, registered fixed and floating charges (and preferential creditors) have been paid out of the company's assets. The chargee ranks with all the other ordinary creditors and, if there are insufficient assets to pay all the ordinary creditors, may only receive a fraction (or none) of the money due to it (see **23.8** for a more detailed discussion of the order of entitlement to assets on a liquidation).

Section 400 CA 1985 requires a company which acquires property subject to a charge to register particulars within 21 days of acquiring the property. Failure to register in this case renders the company and any officer in default liable to a fine but does not render the security void.

10.8.3 COMPANIES ACT 1989

The Companies Act 1989 provided for the introduction of a new system of registration. At the time of writing this system has not been introduced. It is believed that the Department of Trade are having second thoughts following the opposition of lending institutions to the proposed system.

10.8.4 COMPANY'S REGISTER OF CHARGES (ss. 406–408 CA 1985)

Section 407 CA 1985 requires the company to keep a register of all the charges affecting its property at its registered office. The register must contain a description of the charged property, the amount of the charge and the name of the chargee. Failure to comply with the requirement may result in a fine but does not make the security of the charge invalid.

Section 408 CA 1985 requires the company to make the register of charges available to public inspection (fee 5p but no charge to members and creditors). Section 406 also requires the company to keep *copies* of all charges registered under s. 395 at its registered office where they are open to inspection by members and creditors. A person lending money to the company should check these copies carefully so that he can see what, if any, charges the company has created over the property which is to be charged to him.

The Companies Act does not require a company to keep a register of debenture-holders. Some public companies do keep such a register in respect of loan stock (i.e., long-term loans freely transferable from holder to holder), so that they have a record of the person currently entitled to the interest. A private company, which cannot issue debentures to the public, will not need such a register.

10.8.5 OTHER TYPES OF REGISTRATION: CHARGES OVER LAND

In addition to registration under the Companies Act, mortgages of, and charges on, land by a company may have to be registered at HM Land Registry or at the Land Charges Department (depending on whether the land is registered or unregistered respectively).

10.9 Priority of Charges

10.9.1 FIXED CHARGES

A company which creates a floating charge retains the right to deal with its assets. As we have already seen, this means that the value of the security may be reduced by the sale of the assets over which the charge floats. Furthermore, the company is free to deal with the assets by charging them. A floating charge, even though properly registered, is, therefore, normally postponed to a later fixed legal charge. This is because 'where the equities are equal the law prevails'. If the later fixed charge is equitable rather than legal the position is more complicated but the fixed charge will usually prevail since the fixed chargee will normally have a stronger claim to the security than the floating chargee.

The reason for the priority of later fixed charges is that, under the floating charge, the company is left free to deal with its property as it wishes. The floating charge will usually only have priority over later fixed charges if:

(a) the instrument creating the charge prohibits the creation of later fixed charges ranking in priority to or *pari passu* (i.e., equal) with the floating charge; *and*

(b) the later fixed chargee has *notice of this prohibition* at the time when he takes his charge.

10.9.2 FLOATING CHARGES

As between several floating charges, the *first in time* will have priority provided that it is properly registered. However, a later floating charge over some particular type of asset will probably take priority over an earlier floating charge over the whole of a company's property (*English and Scottish Mercantile Investment Co.* v *Brunton* [1892] 2 QB 700).

10.9.3 AVOIDANCE OF CHARGES

In certain circumstances charges may be avoided, other than for non-registration, if made within a short period before the commencement of insolvency proceedings. This topic is dealt with in **Chapter 24**.

10.10 Remedies of Debenture-holders

10.10.1 EXPRESS AND IMPLIED POWERS

If the company fails to pay interest or principal money (i.e., the debt itself) the debenture-holder may sue as a creditor or petition for winding-up. In addition, the debenture may contain an express power of sale and a power to appoint a receiver (see below). The debenture will state the circumstances in which these powers are to arise. It may, for example, give such powers to the lender when his interest is in arrears for a specified period, when the company breaks any term of the debenture, when any other creditor of the company appoints a receiver and when the company suffers execution by a judgment creditor.

Section 101 of the Law of Property Act 1925 gives the lender implied power to sell and to appoint a receiver if the debenture is made under seal and interest is two months in arrears or principal money has not been paid three months after it becomes due. In drafting a debenture, express powers should be given since they can be made wider than the implied powers; if the debenture is not under seal, express powers are essential.

10.10.2 APPLICATION TO THE COURT

In the absence of express powers an application may be made to the court for sale or appointment of a receiver or manager if:

(a) liquidation of the company has commenced; or

(b) the company is in arrears with payment of principal or interest; or

(c) the lender's security is in jeopardy.

If the court orders sale the chargee will be paid principal money and interest and any balance will be paid to the company. The assets will be treated as disposed of by the company so that a chargeable gain or allowable loss may result — thus affecting the company's corporation tax position (see **Chapter 15**).

10.11 Receivers

A receiver is appointed to realise the security of a debenture-holder. His position is, therefore, different from that of a liquidator, whose function is to wind up the company entirely. Once the receiver has paid the debenture-holder he will return any surplus to the company, which may then continue to trade. In fact, very often the appointment of a receiver by a debenture-holder will lead to the liquidation of the company, for example, because, after his appointment, the receiver finds that he can only obtain payment by winding up the company or because other creditors petition for winding-up.

For the effect of an appointment of an administrative receiver see **Chapter 23**.

10.12 Position of Debenture-holders

Many debentures are short-term loans to a company (typically by a bank) on which interest will be paid by the company at a fixed or variable rate in accordance with the loan agreement. The lender who takes such a debenture will consider the interest part of his general profits rather than as a source of investment income — he may take an interest in the running of the business as a financial adviser but will not consider that he is an investor in the business.

Some types of debenture are issued to people who have lent money to the company on a long-term basis and who may, therefore, be regarded as investors in the business. The nature of their investment is quite different from the investment made by shareholders. As we shall see in **Chapter 16**, the tax treatment of debenture interest is usually different from the treatment of dividends paid to shareholders. There are a number of other important differences between the two types of investment, which may be summarised as follows:

(a) Debenture-holders are not members and so do not have the right usually given to the members of voting at meetings.

(b) Debenture interest is payable out of capital if the company fails to make profits, so that a debenture is a safer investment (although if the company makes large profits the debenture-holders will not usually benefit).

(c) Debenture-holders are creditors on a winding-up and will usually have a charge over some or all of the company's assets, whereas shareholders are repaid their investment only if the company is solvent.

(d) Debenture-holders, unlike shareholders, may be repaid while the company is a going concern (usually at a fixed date or at the option of the company). Shareholders may only be repaid where capital is reduced or where the company redeems or purchases its own shares.

10.13 Steps to be Taken by a Lender to a Company

A person who wishes to lend money to a company should take the following steps either personally or through his advisers. Some of them are dictated by common sense, others by legal requirements:

(a) Investigate the financial standing and management of the company.

(b) Search at the Companies' Registry to see the company's last few sets of accounts and of what charge particulars have been registered.

(c) Search at the company's registered office — inspect copies of charges and obtain evidence of discharge of any registered charges.

(d) Search at the Land Registry or Land Charges Department (as appropriate) if a charge is to be taken over land.

(e) If there are any floating charges, make sure that they have not crystallised (until regulations requiring registration of crystallisation are made there is no machinery for ensuring this, but the directors of the company should be asked to certify that no events leading to crystallisation have occurred and, if possible, confirmation should be obtained from the chargees).

(f) Include in the debenture power to appoint a receiver and a power of sale. If the charge is a floating charge, provide for its crystallisation.

(g) Ensure that the charge is registered within 21 days.

10.14 Alteration to the Capital Clause

10.14.1 THE CAPITAL CLAUSE

As stated earlier, the capital clause merely states the company's authorised capital and how it is divided into shares of particular nominal value. In **10.2** we saw how shares are issued. The capital clause may be altered in a number of ways, the most important of which is by increasing the authorised capital. It should be noted that an issue of shares even long after incorporation does not always require an alteration to the capital clause. For example, the capital clause may say: 'The share capital of the company is £5,000 divided into 5,000 shares of £1 each.' Shortly after incorporation 1,000 of these shares may have been issued but this still leaves 4,000 unissued shares, so that an increase of capital will only be required if it is decided to issue more than 4,000 shares. If a further issue of shares is being considered, it is necessary to find out what the authorised capital is (by looking at the capital clause) and how much of it has been issued (by looking at the last annual return and any allotments since then).

10.14.2 THE POWER TO ALTER CAPITAL

10.14.2.1 Increase

Section 121 CA 1985 gives a limited company power to alter its capital in a number of ways provided that the articles authorise the alteration. The most important alteration permitted by s. 121 is the power for a company to 'increase its share capital by new shares of such amount as it thinks expedient'. If Table A applies, then the authorisation for an increase is given by art. 32, which says: 'The company may by ordinary resolution increase its share capital by new shares of such amount as the resolution prescribes'. Section 121(4) requires that the decision to alter capital must be taken by the company in general meeting.

10.14.2.2 Other alterations

Most alterations of capital under s. 121 will be increases of nominal capital but it is also possible under that section to *consolidate* or *subdivide* shares. Shares are consolidated if shares of a smaller amount are consolidated into a smaller number of shares of a larger amount (e.g.,

COMPANY FINANCE

1,000 £1 shares become 100 £10 shares); subdivision is the opposite (1,000 £1 shares become 10,000 10p shares). If Table A applies the company has power to consolidate or subdivide under art. 32. However, since the change is really only a nominal one, there will seldom be any advantage in making it unless the value of each share is either extremely large or extremely small, in which case subdivision or consolidation may be of some cosmetic value.

10.14.3 STEPS TO BE TAKEN ON INCREASE OF CAPITAL

The directors will normally propose the increase and so will summon a general meeting to consider an increase. The ordinary resolution will then be considered at the meeting. In the extremely unlikely event that the articles do not give the company power to increase capital, the articles will have to be changed first. In *MacConnell* v *E. Prill and Co. Ltd* [1916] 2 Ch 57, it was held that the same special resolution could be used both to alter the articles and to exercise the power to increase capital.

After the meeting, if the alteration has been approved by the members, s. 123 CA 1985 requires that notice must be given to the Registrar of the increase, together (on Form G123) with a copy of the resolution and (within 15 days of the change) a printed copy of the amended memorandum. (This is one of the comparatively few circumstances in which an ordinary resolution requires registration.) Following the increase of capital steps will, of course, usually be taken to issue further shares (usually an increase will only be considered when such an issue is intended).

10.14.4 REDUCTION OF CAPITAL

Under ss. 135–141 CA 1985, companies may reduce their share capital. The reasons for wanting to do this vary and are often quite technical. For example, public companies are only permitted to pay dividends if their net assets exceed their share capital (s. 264 CA 1985). If this is not the case, one solution is to reduce the share capital. (For public companies listed on the Stock Exchange a failure to pay out a dividend can be prejudicial to the share price of the company.)

It is beyond the scope of this book to deal with this issue in any detail. However, in order to have a basic understanding the following important issues should be borne in mind:

(a) the shareholders must approve the reduction by special resolution;

(b) the reduction must be sanctioned by the court;

(c) in a number of circumstances, creditors have a right to object to the reduction;

(d) should the reduction affect separate classes of shareholders differently, there may be a class rights issue under s. 125 CA 1985.

ELEVEN

DISPOSAL OF SHARES

This chapter covers the following topics:

11.1 Introduction
11.2 Transfer of shares
11.3 Transmission by operation of law
11.4 Buy-back and redemption by a company
11.5 Financial assistance.

11.1 Introduction

In this chapter we shall consider the various ways in which a shareholder in a company may dispose of his interest in the company either during his lifetime or on death.

On disposal of shares tax will often become payable, although there are a number of reliefs available; this topic is dealt with in **Chapter 14**.

A disposal of shares by a substantial shareholder will alter the control of the company and possibly affect the rights of the remaining shareholders. The interests of the incoming shareholder and the remaining shareholders have to be balanced against each other. Arrangements for achieving a balance between those interests have to be anticipated and made in advance (usually by drafting suitable articles when the company is formed). It is, therefore, essential that potential problems should be foreseen and suitable arrangements made for the particular circumstances of each company.

We shall also consider financial involvement by a company in buying back its own shares or providing financial assistance for the purchase of its own shares or those of a holding company.

11.2 Transfer of Shares

11.2.1 INTRODUCTION

A transfer of shares may be made by means of a sale or a gift *inter vivos*. The death or bankruptcy of a shareholder gives rise to an automatic transmission of shares (which will be followed by a transfer) and the special rules for transmission are dealt with later in the chapter.

DISPOSAL OF SHARES

11.2.2 CONTRACT FOR SALE

A shareholder who wishes to sell his shares may make a contract in any form that he wishes. The contract for sale is sufficient to give the purchaser an equitable interest in the shares. As between vendor and purchaser, the vendor will be liable to account to the purchaser for any dividends received and to vote as directed by the purchaser. However, *membership of the company* does not begin until the purchaser is registered as a member in the register of members which the company is required to keep. An entry cannot be made in the register of members until the company has received an 'instrument of transfer': this will take the form of a stock transfer form.

11.2.3 PROCEDURE FOR TRANSFER

Section 1 of the Stock Transfer Act 1963 provides that a transfer of fully paid shares may be made on a stock transfer form signed by the transferor and specifying:

(a) particulars of the consideration;

(b) description of the number or amount of the shares;

(c) particulars of the person by whom the transfer is made; and

(d) the full name and address of the transferee.

Once the sale of the shares has been agreed the vendor should execute a stock transfer form and send it together with the share certificate to the purchaser, who pays the stamp duty (see **11.2.4** below). The purchaser then applies to the company for registration by sending the stamped transfer and share certificate to the company. The transfer must be registered within two months of the application unless the directors have power to refuse registration, and the company must send the purchaser a share certificate within the same period (s. 185 CA 1985). The procedure explained above applies on a gift of shares as well as on a sale (save that no stamp duty is payable).

(It should be noted that shares of publicly quoted companies may be transferred electronically under the CREST system, which came into operation in July 1996. A detailed description of this system is beyond the scope of this text.)

11.2.4 STAMP DUTY ON TRANSFER OF SHARES

Stamp duty on a transfer of shares is charged at a rate of 0.5% of the consideration payable with the resulting figure being rounded up to the nearest £5. There is a minimum stamp duty payment of £5. The purchaser of the shares pays the relevant amount of duty.

Examples

Consideration payable	Stamp duty charged
£1	£5
£70	£5
£830	£5
£1,620	£10
£45,763	£230

DISPOSAL OF SHARES

Certain transfers of shares are exempt from stamp duty. One of the most common types is a gift of shares, i.e., a transfer for no consideration in money or money's worth. Certain other types of transfer are not exempt from stamp duty but are not liable to the duty described above. These transfers are subject to a fixed duty of £5. The various types of transfer which are exempt or subject to a fixed duty are described on the reverse of the standard stock transfer form. In order to claim exemption or a fixed duty, it is necessary to complete a form of certificate which is set out on the reverse of the form.

11.2.5 RESTRICTIONS ON RIGHT TO TRANSFER

Unless the articles provide to the contrary, every shareholder has a *right* to transfer his shares (which in effect means that the transferee has a right to be registered). However, the articles of the company can impose a restriction on the right to transfer shares. In the case of private companies a restriction is extremely common. A restriction is often thought to be desirable since it enables the company (usually through the directors) to refuse to allow unsuitable outsiders to join the company. Article 24 of Table A provides as follows:

> The directors may refuse to register the transfer of a share which is not fully paid to a person of whom they do not approve and they may refuse to register the transfer of a share on which the company has a lien. They may also refuse to register a transfer unless:
>
> (a) it is lodged at the registered office or at such other place as the directors may appoint and is accompanied by the certificate for the shares to which it relates and such other evidence as the directors may reasonably require to show the right of the transferor to make the transfer;
>
> (b) it is in respect of only one class of shares; and
>
> (c) it is in favour of not more than four transferees.

Thus, the directors can refuse to register a transfer of shares in the following circumstances:

(a) where the transfer is of partly paid shares;

(b) where the transfer is of fully paid shares over which the company has a lien (where Table A applies unamended, there is only a lien for calls on partly paid shares); or

(c) where the transfer is of fully paid shares (whether or not the company has a lien) and the requirements set out in (a), (b) and (c) of art. 24 are not complied with.

The person responsible for drafting the articles of a company should consult his clients to see what restrictions, if any, they require.

Where there are restrictions on the right to transfer shares, the company must decide within two months of application for registration, whether or not to permit the transfer. If within that time the company has not given notice of refusal of registration to the transferee, the company and its officers who are in default are liable to a fine (s. 183(5) and (6) CA 1985) and the transferee becomes *entitled* to be registered.

It is not possible to consider all the possible types of restriction on the right to register but some of the more common restrictions will now be considered.

11.2.5.1 'The directors may, in their absolute discretion and without assigning any reason therefor, decline to register any transfer of any share, whether or not it is a fully paid share'

At one time a company could not be a private company unless there was a restriction, in its articles, on the right to transfer shares. (This requirement was removed by CA 1980, now

DISPOSAL OF SHARES

consolidated in CA 1985.) The inclusion of this particular restriction in Table A before the enactment of the Companies Act 1980 means that it is very common. As with most restrictions on transfer it is the directors who have power to refuse registration. The power is a negative one, that is, the directors have power to *refuse* registration — their positive approval is not required. This may seem an unimportant distinction but it means that a resolution of the directors is required to refuse registration, and since a resolution requires a majority in favour, an equality of votes will not be sufficient (unless, of course, the chairman has a casting vote and is against registration). This should be borne in mind in the case of 'two-man' companies, since either director will be able to ensure a transfer of his own shares merely by voting *against* the resolution to refuse registration. The directors' power to refuse registration must be exercised in good faith but it is very difficult to prove bad faith. The directors do not need to give reasons for refusal even if the article does not specifically excuse them from doing so.

It should be noted that this restriction is a restriction on the right to *transfer* shares, it is not a restriction on the right to *sell* them. If shares are sold but the purchaser is not registered, the vendor will hold the shares on trust for the purchaser. The purchaser will not be able to sue the vendor for damages (or his money back) unless the vendor guaranteed that registration would take place.

11.2.5.2 'The directors may decline to register a transfer of any share in favour of a person of whom they disapprove or of a share over which the company has a lien'

This restriction gives the directors two grounds for refusing registration. If required to do so, the directors must say on which ground they rely but need not give reasons justifying their decision. However, if they specified refusal on the grounds of a lien and there was no lien over the shares, the transferee would be able to insist on registration. If, however, the directors specified disapproval of the transferee the latter would find it impossible in most cases to establish that they did not disapprove of him. If the directors choose to give reasons justifying their decision the court will enquire into them to see if they are cogent reasons for refusal.

11.2.5.3 'The directors may decline to register a transfer of any share except a transfer to [a member of the company or to a member of the family of the transferor]'

This type of restriction may be appropriate to restrict a shareholder in his right to bring in outsiders against the wishes of other members of the company; it leaves him free to transfer to insiders (i.e., the existing members of the company) or his own family. The words in square brackets could be adapted to include various other groups of permitted transferees, e.g., named persons or employees of the company. The term 'family' must, of course, be defined by the articles.

11.2.6 PRE-EMPTION RIGHTS

The object of restrictions on the right to transfer shares is to keep a private company private. However, the restrictions referred to above are not entirely sufficient for that purpose since they are merely restrictions on *transfer* and do not prevent sale or gift of the equitable title to the shares. If it is decided that the company should be kept completely private, the articles should include pre-emption rights. The usual provision is that a member who wishes to transfer shares must first offer them to the existing members of the company. In drafting an article providing for pre-emption rights the following points should be considered:

(a) Should the transferring member be free to transfer to *any* existing member of the company or should he be obliged to offer his shares to *all* the existing members in proportion to their present holdings?

(b) Should the transferring member be obliged to transfer part of his holding to the existing members if they do not wish to take all the shares which he proposes to transfer?

(c) Should any exceptions be made to the pre-emption rights? For example, the articles may provide that the pre-emption rights do not apply on a transfer to a member's family as defined by the article.

(d) How is the price payable to be fixed? It is quite common for the price to be fixed by agreement or by the auditors if no price can be agreed between vendor and purchaser.

(e) How long are the other members to be given to make up their minds? A period should be specified for the avoidance of doubt.

(f) How is the transferring member to give notice of his intention to sell? It is quite common for the article to require notice to be given to the company. The secretary will then inform the other members of the offer.

A pre-emption right is a right given to the other members of the company. It is also possible for the articles to provide that a member who wishes to transfer shares shall have a right to *require* the other members to buy his shares.

11.3 Transmission by Operation of Law

When a member of a company dies, his shares vest automatically in his personal representative, who is entitled to any dividend paid by the company but may not vote at general meetings. The personal representative does not, however, automatically become a member of the company since membership begins only with an entry in the register of members. A personal representative will have to prove his title to the shares, by production of the grant of representation. Having done so, he has two courses of action open to him:

(a) The personal representative can apply, by means of a letter of request, for registration by the company as a member (the entry in the register of members will not refer to his representative capacity). The articles of the company will usually contain a provision (such as Table A art. 30) permitting the personal representative to be registered as a member. If he is registered as a member, a subsequent transfer to a beneficiary will require a stock transfer form to be completed.

(b) Alternatively, if the personal representative wishes to sell the shares so as to raise cash for the purposes of the deceased's estate or when he wishes to vest the shares in the deceased's beneficiary, he can do so without himself being registered, by means of a stock transfer form.

A restriction on the right to transfer shares does not apply to a transmission on death unless the articles specifically so provide.

11.4 Buy-back and Redemption by a Company

As we have already seen (**10.3.3.4**), a company can issue redeemable shares or buy its own shares in certain circumstances. If the company buys its own shares it must normally do so out of profits, although purchase out of capital is permitted provided: a special resolution is passed; the directors can certify that the company will be solvent after the purchase and will be able to continue in business for a year; and the creditors or dissenting members do not successfully apply to the court for cancellation of the resolution.

OF SHARES

Financial Assistance

INTRODUCTION

Section 151(1) CA 1985 states that it is prima facie unlawful for a company to give financial assistance to any person for the purchase of its shares or those of any parent company. In addition, s. 151(2) makes it prima facie unlawful for a company to give financial assistance for the purpose of reducing or discharging any liability incurred by a person in buying such shares. Both subsections apply to indirect and direct financial assistance and it may be unlawful whether it was given before, at the same time as, or following, the time of acquisition.

Section 152 provides a definition of financial assistance and some examples are given below:

(a) A Limited provides a loan to one of its directors to allow him to buy shares in that company.

(b) B Limited gives a guarantee to a bank in respect of the obligations of C, who has borrowed money from the bank in order to buy shares in D Limited, the parent company of B Limited.

(c) E Limited is acquiring F Limited from G Limited. To finance the purchase, E Limited is borrowing money from a bank. As security for the loan, the bank requires security over all the assets of both E and F Limited. F Limited is therefore giving financial assistance by way of security (s. 152(1)(a)(ii)) for the purchase of its shares by E Limited.

It should be noted that the financial assistance provisions in the Companies Act apply in relation to a purchase of either issued or unissued shares.

One of the main purposes behind the general prohibition on financial assistance created by s. 151 is the maintenance of share capital. However, there may be circumstances where companies may wish to provide financial assistance. There are two exceptions to the general prohibition and these are discussed below.

11.5.2 GENERAL EXCEPTION FOR ALL COMPANIES

Section 153(1) contains the first exception to the prohibitions referred to above. It applies to all companies, public and private, and says that a company is not prohibited from giving assistance 'for the purpose of an acquisition of shares in it . . .' if:

(a) the company's principal purpose in giving the assistance is not to give it for the purpose of any such acquisition, or the giving of the assistance for that purpose is but an incidental part of some larger purpose of the company; and

(b) the assistance is given in good faith in the interests of the company.

Demonstrating that the provision of financial assistance falls within this exception may involve difficult questions of proof and it is very rare to seek to rely on these grounds.

11.5.3 SPECIFIC EXCEPTION FOR PRIVATE COMPANIES

Section 155 CA 1985 contains the second exception to the prohibitions and gives *private companies* wide powers to give financial assistance for the purchase of their own shares (or for the reduction or discharge of liabilities incurred on purchase). The main requirement of the section is that the assistance must not reduce the net assets of the company or, if it does reduce them, must be provided out of profits available for dividend (s. 155(2)). Financial assistance by way of a loan would not normally reduce net assets since the reduction in assets (cash) caused by the lending would be balanced by the debt owed to the company by the borrower. Financial assistance by way of gift would, of course, reduce net assets.

Before financial assistance can be given under s. 155, the general requirements are that:

(a) a special resolution must be passed approving the assistance (unless the company is a wholly-owned subsidiary) (s. 155(4)); and

(b) the directors must make a statutory declaration setting out the nature of the assistance and stating the directors' opinion that the company is solvent and will remain so for at least 12 months. The directors' opinion must be confirmed by the auditors in a report annexed to the statutory declaration.

Where the financial assistance is made by a company in connection with an acquisition of shares in its holding company, then the directors of the holding company and any intermediate companies are also required to make a statutory declaration in the terms described above (s. 155(6)). The shareholders of the holding company (and any intermediate company which is not a wholly-owned subsidiary) are required to pass a special resolution approving the giving of the financial assistance (s. 155(5)).

Under s. 157 CA 1985 the special resolution must be passed within a week of the statutory declaration and 10% of the shareholders may apply to the court for cancellation of the resolution within 28 days.

The company must send copies of the special resolution, statutory declaration and auditors' report to the Registrar of Companies.

The financial assistance approved by the special resolution must not be given until four weeks after the resolution (or until the court approves it if an application for cancellation is made), and must not be given more than eight weeks after the directors make the statutory declaration. However, the four week 'waiting period' does not apply if the resolution approving the provision of financial assistance was passed unanimously; in such a case the financial assistance can be given immediately.

TWELVE

COMPANY MEETINGS AND RESOLUTIONS

This chapter covers the following topics:

12.1 Types of general meeting
12.2 Resolutions
12.3 Calling a general meeting
12.4 Notice of meetings
12.5 Proceedings at meetings
12.6 Dispensing with meetings — written resolution procedure
12.7 Minutes and returns.

In this chapter we shall look at meetings of shareholders and the resolutions which are passed at such meetings. In **Chapter 9** we saw that there are certain powers which can only be exercised within a company by the shareholders. In this chapter we are concerned with how those powers are exercised. The rules about these matters are sometimes quite technical but their importance cannot be overestimated. Unless correct procedures are followed the rights of shareholders may often be lost. A solicitor advising a company or shareholder may often be called upon to see that the correct procedures are adopted.

We are not concerned in this chapter with directors' meetings (which were dealt with in **Chapter 8**), we are only concerned with meetings of shareholders. Shareholders' meetings are also called 'company meetings' or 'general meetings'.

12.1 Types of General Meeting

The meetings of a private company are of two types: annual general meetings and extraordinary general meetings. The meetings are called 'general' meetings to distinguish them from board meetings (that is, meetings of the directors).

12.1.1 ANNUAL GENERAL MEETINGS

An annual general meeting (AGM) must normally be held once in every calendar year and must be within 15 months of the last AGM. However, a company need not hold an AGM during the (calendar) year of incorporation or during the next calendar year provided the first AGM is held within 18 months of incorporation.

Private companies are able to dispense with the need to hold an annual general meeting. In order to do so they must first pass an elective resolution (see **12.2**).

COMPANY MEETINGS AND RESOLUTIONS

12.1.2 EXTRAORDINARY GENERAL MEETINGS

Any meeting which is not an AGM is an extraordinary general meeting (EGM). An EGM is held as and when necessary. The procedure for calling such a meeting will be considered shortly, but first it is necessary to consider the types of resolution needed to transact business at general meetings.

12.2 Resolutions

A company in general meeting can only transact business by passing the appropriate type of resolution. There are four types of resolution: ordinary, extraordinary, special and elective.

12.2.1 ORDINARY RESOLUTIONS

An ordinary resolution is one which requires a simple majority of votes in favour if it is to be passed (a simple majority means more votes in favour than against — an equality of votes is not sufficient). Where there is an equality an ordinary resolution may, however, be passed on the chairman's casting vote if the articles so provide. Table A art. 50 gives the chairman a casting vote. In the case of a small company the decision as to whether to allow an article giving a casting vote may be crucial. The presence of a casting vote resolves the problem of deadlock but may in some cases be considered to give the chairman too much power. An ordinary resolution is sufficent to transact any business at a general meeting save in those cases where the Companies Acts require special, extraordinary or elective resolutions or where the articles require special or extraordinary resolutions.

12.2.2 SPECIAL AND EXTRAORDINARY RESOLUTIONS

A special resolution and an extraordinary resolution both require a three-quarters majority — that is, at least three votes must be cast in favour of the resolution for every one cast against it. The difference between these forms of resolution is that an extraordinary resolution (like an ordinary resolution) requires the same length of notice as the meeting at which it is to be considered (14 days at an EGM, 21 at an AGM), whereas a special resolution requires 21 days' notice even if it is to be considered at an EGM.

12.2.2.1 When a special resolution is required

The Companies Act lays down many circumstances in which a special resolution is required. Among the most important from the point of view of the shareholder are resolutions to alter the articles or objects, and resolutions to exclude pre-emption rights on the issue of shares. Any generalisation as to when a special resolution is required is perhaps a dangerous simplification, but if there is a factor common to all the circumstances it is probably that they are all circumstances where minority shareholders need protection. It is a common mistake to suppose that all alterations to the memorandum require a special resolution. This is not so since, for example, capital can be increased by ordinary resolution if the articles so provide (s. 121 CA 1985).

A special resolution may be required by the articles of the company in any other circumstances where the Act does not require some other kind of resolution. However, it is very uncommon for the articles to require a special resolution where the Act does not do so. If the company wishes to give the minority shareholders the greater protection of a three-quarters majority, the articles will usually provide for an extraordinary resolution.

12.2.2.2 When an extraordinary resolution is required

An extraordinary resolution is provided for by the Companies Act in a small number of circumstances where it is considered that minority shareholders require protection but the matter is urgent. The most important of these circumstances is where a resolution is passed to commence a voluntary winding-up because of the company's liabilities (s. 84(1)(c) Insolvency Act 1986). As with a special resolution, the articles can require an extraordinary resolution in any circumstances where the Act does not require some other sort of resolution.

12.2.3 ELECTIVE RESOLUTIONS

Section 379A CA 1985 (interpolated by CA 1989) allows a private company to simplify its own internal management by passing elective resolutions. An elective resolution depends on the unanimous approval of all the shareholders or their proxies (unanimous agreement by all who attend and vote is not sufficient) and 21 days' notice is required. Such resolutions may:

(a) authorise the directors to allot shares for an indefinite period (see **Chapter 10**);

(b) dispense with the need to hold a shareholders meeting for the consideration of accounts;

(c) dispense with the holding of an AGM (see **12.1**);

(d) permit the holding of a meeting with short notice with the approval of 90% of the members (see **12.4**); and

(e) dispense with the need to make annual appointment of auditors.

Once passed, an elective resolution may be revoked by an ordinary resolution.

12.3 Calling a General Meeting

As we saw in **Chapter 8**, directors' meetings can be called quite informally at the request of any one of the directors. The position in relation to general meetings is much more complicated. As with so many aspects of company law, the rules are partly statutory and partly depend on the provisions of the company's own articles. Most of the statutory rules are designed to protect the shareholders whose voting rights would be worthless if they were not backed up by rights to call meetings. The provisions of Table A will be considered first and then the statutory rules.

12.3.1 TABLE A

Table A art. 37 gives the directors power to decide when to call the AGM and to call an EGM at any time. *The vast majority of EGMs will be called in this way.* Article 37 also provides that if there are not sufficient directors present in the UK to constitute a quorum at a board meeting, a single director or any member may convene a meeting.

12.3.2 STATUTORY RULES

12.3.2.1 Shareholders' right to requisition meeting

Section 368 allows shareholders who are registered as owners of 'not less than one tenth of such of the paid-up capital of the company as ... carries the right of voting at general meetings' to requisition a meeting. The requisition must be in writing and signed and must be deposited at the registered office. It is then up to the directors of the company to take steps to convene an EGM. Should they fail to do this (that is, give shareholders notice) within 21 days of the date of the deposit of the requisition, then the requisitionists may themselves convene a meeting at the company's expense. The requisitionists may also do this should the directors convene an EGM for a date more than 28 days after the date of the notice sent by

COMPANY MEETINGS AND RESOLUTIONS

the directors to the shareholders. Where the requisitionists convene the EGM as a result of either of the above, it must be held within three months of the date of the deposit of the requisition.

Section 368 does not say that the requisitionists have a right to specify what resolutions are to be discussed at the meeting but s. 368(3) clearly implies that they have such a right. In most private companies it should be rare for s. 368 to be used, since the director will usually call meetings when required.

12.3.2.2 Power to call meeting under section 370 CA 1985

Section 370 provides a separate power for 'two or more members holding not less than one tenth of the issued share capital' to call a meeting. In the majority of circumstances this adds little to s. 368, but it should be noted that under s. 370 the shares need not represent one tenth of the *paid-up* capital but only of the *issued* capital, nor need the shares carry the right to vote. Section 370 has one substantial advantage over s. 368 — that is, the members can themselves call the meeting (although they must, of course, give proper notice), so that there will be less delay before the meeting is held than in the case of s. 368. However, unlike s. 368, s. 370 only has effect 'in so far as the articles of the company do not make other provision in that behalf': that is, it can be excluded or varied by the articles.

12.3.2.3 Court power to order meeting

Section 371 gives the court power to order meetings 'if for any reason it is impracticable to call a meeting of a company in any manner in which meetings of that company may be called'.

12.3.2.4 Default in holding AGM

Section 367 CA 1985 provides that if default is made in holding an annual general meeting when required, the Department of Trade can call a meeting on the application of any member and can order that one person shall constitute a quorum at the meeting.

12.4 Notice of Meetings

12.4.1 SERVICE OF NOTICE

Business at a meeting cannot be properly transacted or relied upon unless proper notice has been given of the meeting. Section 370(2) provides that 'notice of the meeting of a company shall be served on every member of it in the manner in which notices are required to be served by Table A (as for the time being, in force)'. The articles in Table A dealing with notices are numbers 38–39 and 111–116.

Article 38 requires notice of general meetings (of both types) to be given to all the members, persons entitled to a share in consequence of the death or bankruptcy of a member, the directors and auditors. Article 112 relieves the company from the duty to give notice to members who have no registered address in the UK, and art. 116 provides that notice need only be given to personal representatives and trustees in bankruptcy if they have supplied the company with an address to which notices are to be sent; if they have not done so, service on the dead or bankrupt member is deemed effective if sent to his registered address as if the death or bankruptcy had not occurred.

Article 112 provides for personal service or service by post. Where service is by post, it is presumed to have been served 48 hours after posting (art. 115).

Article 39 provides that accidental omission to give notice to someone entitled to it, does not invalidate the meeting. Accidental omission would include clerical errors but not a failure to give notice resulting from a failure to apply the articles properly (*Young* v *Ladies Imperial Club Ltd* [1920] 2 KB 523).

12.4.2 LENGTH OF NOTICE

12.4.2.1 Full notice procedures

The length of notice required depends on the nature of the meeting and the resolutions to be proposed at it. For an AGM, 21 days' notice is required. For an EGM, 14 days' notice is required, *unless there is proposed*:

(a) a special resolution;

(b) an elective resolution; or

(c) where Table A applies, a resolution appointing a director;

in which case 21 days' notice is required.

Table A, art. 38 provides that notice periods are to be 14 and 21 'clear days', that is, *exclusive* of the date of service and the date of the meeting. This is illustrated in the example which follows:

The directors wish to hold an EGM at which a special resolution is to be proposed. They post the notices on 1 March. The date of deemed service is 3 March (48 hours after posting — art. 122). The 21 clear day period is 4–24 March inclusive. The earliest the meeting can be held is therefore the next day, 25 March.

12.4.2.2 Short notice procedure

Section 369(3) and art. 38 provide that shorter notice than that normally required may validly be given if:

(a) in the case of an AGM all the members entitled to attend and vote at the meeting agree to short notice; and

(b) in the case of an EGM a majority in number of members owning 95% of the voting shares and entitled to attend and vote at the meeting agree to short notice.

It should be noted that, in the case of an EGM, a lesser percentage (to a minimum of 90%) may be substituted by elective resolution.

For many private companies (especially family companies or companies where the members are all directors) this allows a meeting to be held at very short notice; however, it is not a practical alternative to the giving of proper notice for companies with large numbers of members.

12.4.3 CONTENTS OF NOTICE

The notice of a meeting must state the date, time, and place of meeting. It must also describe the business which is to be transacted sufficiently for members to be able to decide whether they wish to attend. It is a question of judgment in each case how much detail of the business needs to be stated, so that decided cases do not give much guidance to those drawing up the notice. However, it is clear that any personal interest of directors in the business of the meeting must be disclosed. In drawing up a notice it is better to err on the side of inclusion rather than exclusion.

COMPANY MEETINGS AND RESOLUTIONS

If a special, elective or extraordinary resolution or a resolution which requires special notice (for example, a resolution to remove a director under s. 303 CA 1985) is to be proposed, it must be set out verbatim in the notice. Section 372 CA 1985 requires that the notice should tell the members that each of them is entitled to send a proxy (who need not be a member) to attend and vote on his behalf.

12.5 Proceedings at Meetings

12.5.1 QUORUM

A meeting cannot consider business unless a quorum is present at the time when the meeting proceeds to business. Unless the articles otherwise provide or the company has only one member, two members personally present are the quorum (s. 370(4)).

12.5.2 AGENDA

Discussion of resolutions is limited by requirements as to the notice of meetings, that is, sufficient notice and description of the business should be given to enable members to decide whether to attend. Amendments may be moved but only within the scope of the notice; therefore, no amendment of substance is permitted to a special, elective or extraordinary resolution and amendments to ordinary resolutions are limited. Proxies as well as members may speak at a meeting of a private company.

12.5.3 VOTING

12.5.3.1 Show of hands

A vote on a resolution will normally be decided on a show of hands unless a poll is demanded (art. 46). On such a vote each member personally present has one vote (regardless of the number of shares owned), and a proxy cannot vote unless the articles provide to the contrary (Table A does not give a proxy a right to vote on a show of hands).

12.5.3.2 Poll

Section 373 gives a right to demand a poll to:

(a) any five voting members; or any member or members with 10% of the voting rights; or any member or members with 10% of the paid-up capital with a right to vote.

(b) Table A art. 46 extends this by allowing any two members (instead of five) or the chairman to call for a poll. Proxies have the same right to call for a poll as the member or members they represent. When a poll is called, the votes are counted according to the voting rights of the members rather than according to the number of members. If necessary the meeting can be adjourned while the votes are counted but this is unlikely in the case of a private company.

12.6 Written Resolution

12.6.1 PROCEDURE

A private company may pass resolutions in writing under s. 381A CA 1985, without a meeting or any previous notice being given. This is achieved by *all* the members of the company entitled to vote approving the resolution by signing a copy of it. The date of the resolution is determined by the time at which the last member signs.

The company may pass any type of resolution — ordinary, extraordinary, special or elective — using this procedure, save for two exceptions. These are the removal of a director under s. 303 CA 1985 or removal of an auditor under s. 391 CA 1985.

12.6.2 DOCUMENTATION

Commonly the board will arrange for the resolution to be distributed to members. There is no need for all signatures to be on a single document, provided that each is on a document which accurately sets out the terms of the resolution.

There are a number of resolutions the procedure for which is amended when using the written resolution procedure. These are:

- s. 95 — disapplication of pre-emption rights
- s. 155 — financial assistance for the purchase of shares
- ss. 164, 165 and 167 — authority for purchase of own shares
- s. 173 — approval for payment out of capital
- s. 319 — approval of director's service contract
- s. 337 — funding director's expenditure

The detail of the amended procedure is set out in sch. 15A CA 1985. The basic requirement in each case is the supply or disclosure of specific information to members at or before the time at which the resolution is supplied.

12.6.3 NOTIFICATION OF AUDITORS

Section 381C CA 1985 requires a copy of a proposed written resolution (or details of its terms) to be sent to the company's auditors at or before the time the resolution is sent to the members for signature. Failure to do so does not invalidate the resolution but a director or secretary who fails to comply with the requirement may be liable to a fine.

12.6.4 RECORDING

A written resolution must be entered into a company's minutes book in the same way as minutes of a general meeting.

12.6.5 PROVISIONS IN ARTICLES

The written resolution procedure under s. 381 CA 1985 does not affect any provision in a private company's articles which allows it to pass resolutions using a written procedure.

12.7 Minutes and Returns

Minutes must be kept of all decisions taken at general meetings and must be available for inspection by the members at the registered office. Copies of certain resolutions must be sent to the Registrar of Companies within 15 days of being passed (s. 380 CA 1985). Included in this requirement are all special, elective and extraordinary resolutions, together with ordinary resolutions under ss. 80 and 121.

TAXATION

THIRTEEN

THE TAXATION OF THE INCOME PROFITS AND LOSSES OF SOLE TRADERS AND PARTNERSHIPS

This chapter covers the following topics:

13.1 Introduction
13.2 Income profits
13.3 The basis of assessment for income tax
13.4 Losses under the income tax system
13.5 Income tax liability of partnerships.

13.1 Introduction

In this chapter we will look at the way the income profits and losses of sole traders and partnerships are determined and assessed. We will first look at the general rules as they apply to any unincorporated business and then look at the specific rules relevant to partnerships.

13.2 Income Profits

13.2.1 THE TAX SCHEDULES

Businesses pay income tax on income. For a receipt to be income it must usually be recurrent or capable of recurrence (but 'one-off' receipts can be income in some circumstances), and must be included in the definition of income under one of the five schedules of the Income and Corporation Taxes Act 1988 (commonly called 'the Taxes Act'). It is beyond the scope of this book to deal with the various definitions of income in the schedules but the following table will give an idea of what is covered:

Schedule A	Rents
Schedule C	Government securities
Schedule D Case I	Profits of a trade
Schedule D Case II	Profits of a profession or vocation
Schedule D Case III	'Pure income' (interest, annuities and annual payments)

TAXATION OF INCOME PROFITS AND LOSSES OF SOLE TRADERS AND PARTNERSHIPS

Schedule D Cases IV & V	Income from foreign securities or possessions
Schedule D Case VI	Miscellaneous income (casual profits and certain items specifically allocated to this case)
Schedule E	Income from offices, employments or pensions
Schedule F	Dividends

Each schedule lays down rules for the deductibility of expenses in calculating income and for the allocation of receipts to a particular year of assessment (each year of assessment starts on 6 April and ends on the following 5 April and is commonly called a tax year).

For businesses Schedule D Case I (trade) or II (profession or vocation) is usually the most important case. The rules for these two cases are almost identical, and are in many respects quite different from the other cases of Schedule D and from the other schedules. To determine the amount of profits it is necessary to calculate the amount of income generated from trading activities and deduct from that the amount of deductible expenditure.

Once the income has been calculated the taxpayer is liable to income tax on the whole amount less certain payments known as charges on income and certain sums known as personal reliefs. Charges on income are defined by s. 8(8) Taxes Management Act 1970 as 'amounts which fall to be deducted in computing total income'. This somewhat unhelpful definition is not explained further. Charges on income include annuities and other annual payments and certain interest payments. A personal relief is a sum deducted in computing the taxable part of income, the amount of which depends on the taxpayer's circumstances. The tax is progressive, that is, the rate increases as income increases.

13.2.2 DEFINITION OF INCOME

Income must be distinguished from capital receipts. In most cases there is no problem in deciding which an item is. Thus profits received from the sale of stock-in-trade are income: profits made from the sale of fixed assets are capital. For example, if the business is a grocer's shop, the food which is sold is stock but the shop itself, its shelves and counters are fixed assets. The evidence of accountants as to general accountancy practice is valuable but not conclusive in deciding whether an item is income or capital.

Almost all businesses produce final accounts on an annual basis. These show the amount of profit made according to normal accountancy practice and how it is allocated to the proprietor(s). These accounts are not, however, necessarily suitable for tax purposes, as often there are special tax rules which define what is taxable as income and what is deductible as an expense.

13.2.3 DEDUCTIBLE EXPENDITURE

Deductible expenditure is not fully defined in the Taxes Act. Expenditure is deductible if it is of an income rather than a capital nature. This distinction is similar to the distinction between income and capital receipts, so that, again, evidence of accountancy practice is valuable. Section 74 ICTA 1988 prevents the deduction of expenses in a number of circumstances.

The first paragraph of s. 74 provides that, 'in computing the amount of the profits or gains to be charged under Case I or II of Schedule D, no sum shall be deducted in respect of any disbursements or expenses, not being money *wholly and exclusively* laid out or expended for the purposes of the trade, profession or vocation'. Expenditure, if it is to be deducted, must, therefore, be 'wholly' incurred for the purposes of the trade, so that if a sum of money represents partly a business expense but is excessively large so that it also partly represents a gift it is not deductible. Expenditure must also be 'exclusively' incurred for the purposes of the trade, so that if money is spent and the motive is partly connected with the trade and partly not so connected (e.g., there is an element of personal enjoyment), then the payment is not deductible.

TAXATION OF INCOME PROFITS AND LOSSES OF SOLE TRADERS AND PARTNERSHIPS

Certain types of expenditure are not deductible because of the provisions of paras. (b)–(q) of s. 74. Many of these paragraphs refer to types of expenditure which would be non-deductible anyway because they are not revenue expenditure or not wholly and exclusively incurred for the purposes of the trade. The section, among other things, prohibits the deduction of provisions for bad debts (but not of actual bad debts); and most business entertainment expenses are non-deductible under the provisions of s. 577 ICTA 1988.

13.2.4 ACCOUNTING BASES

When calculating profit, it is important for any business to apply a consistent method to determine whether receipts and expenses relate to one accounting period or to a later period. If it fails to do so its accounts are useless to the business for the purposes of comparison; what is more, the business could manipulate its receipts and expenses so as to avoid tax.

For tax purposes accounts have to be agreed with the Inland Revenue and must be prepared on one of three bases: the earnings, the cash, or the bills delivered bases.

(a) *The earnings basis*

Accounts are prepared on the basis of income earned (even if not received) and expenses incurred (even if not paid) during the relevant accounting period.

The value of stock unsold at the end of an accounting period and/or the value of work-in-hand at the end of the accounting period must be included when calculating profit (see **13.2.5** below).

(b) *The cash basis*

Accounts are prepared on the basis of sums actually received and paid. No account is taken of amounts owed or owing or of the value of unsold stock or work-in-hand. This basis may give a misleading picture of the true profit where credit is given and/or received.

(c) *The bills delivered basis*

Accounts are prepared on the basis of bills delivered to customers and received from suppliers irrespective of whether the bills have been paid. No account is taken of amounts owed or owing but not billed or of the value of unsold stock and work-in-hand. The fact that work-in-hand need not be valued makes this basis particularly popular with professional partnerships.

Most trading partnerships are assessed on the earnings basis. The Revenue is normally reluctant to allow the cash basis except in special cases.

13.2.5 THE NEED TO VALUE STOCK AND WORK-IN-HAND

As explained above, when a business is taxed on the earnings basis, it is necessary to value stock and work-in-hand at the end of an accounting period, otherwise the accounts are misleading. If a trading business which makes a profit by buying and selling goods or other property simply compared its receipts and expenses, the accounts would give no real idea of the amount of profit. For example, £1,000 worth of goods are bought during a particular period and half of them are sold for £1,200 — clearly the profit is more than £200 since half the goods remain. Ignoring other expenses (wages, rates, electricity bills, etc.) the profit could be said to be £700 since goods purchased for £500 have been sold for £1,200.

Clearly it would be impractical to record the sale price of each item and deduct from it the original purchase price. To calculate a trading profit, stock must be valued at the end of the period. If the closing stock figure (i.e., the value at the end of the year) is deducted from the total of the opening stock figure and the amount spent on stock during the year (which accountants call 'purchases') the cost of goods sold has been calculated. This figure can then be deducted from the receipts from the sale of stock (called 'sales') to calculate the gross profit.

Example

	£	£
Sales		50,000
Opening stock	10,000	
Add: Purchases	35,000	
	45,000	
Less: Closing stock	(12,000)	
		33,000
Gross profit		17,000

Other deductible expenses such as wages are then deducted from the gross profit to arrive at the net profit which enters into the tax calculation.

Clearly the amount of profit depends on the value placed on stock — the lower the closing stock figure the smaller is the profit (and, therefore, the tax on it). Stock is valued according to normal accountancy principles, which allow each item of stock to be valued at the lower of cost or market value. Thus where stock has risen in value an upward valuation is not required, but where it has fallen in value immediate relief is given by the revaluation. Once a closing stock figure has been arrived at for a period it becomes the opening stock figure for the next period.

A business which supplies services will not have trading stock left at the end of an accounting period. It will, however, have work-in-hand at that date (that is, work commenced but not yet billed). The same principles are applied as with trading stock. Thus, where the earnings basis applies, the work-in-hand at the end of the year will increase profits, whereas work-in-hand at the start of the year will reduce them.

13.3 The Basis of Assessment for Income Tax

Almost all traders find that a suitable accounting period is twelve months. The period chosen need not correspond with the year of assessment (tax year which runs from 6 April to the following 5 April). A trader pays tax on the income of the year of assessment according to the rates fixed for that year by the annual Finance Act (taking into account his tax-free personal reliefs for the year). Because the accounting period and year of assessment do not usually correspond, rules are needed for allocating the profits of accounting periods to years of assessment. This system is known as the current year basis.

Before this system is looked at in detail, it should be noted that the whole system of collection of income tax was altered by the introduction of self-assessment from the tax year 1996/97. As with the previous system, tax returns are sent out in the usual way. However, rather than

TAXATION OF INCOME PROFITS AND LOSSES OF SOLE TRADERS AND PARTNERSHIPS

simply providing the Revenue with the relevant details of income and expenditure etc. taxpayers are now obliged to calculate the actual amount of their taxble income. They may also, if they wish, calculate the actual tax due thereon as well although this may still be left to the Revenue.

It is assumed that the reader will have access to details of the general mechanics of the income tax calculation from other materials. Therefore, no details will be given here. However, as confirmation of the rates of income tax for the tax year 2001/2002:

Starting — 10% (£0–£1,880 of taxable income)
Basic – 22% (£1,881–£29,400 of taxable income)
Higher – 40% (amount in excess of £29,400 of taxable income)

Put simply, taxable income is the amount of income received by a tax payer in a tax year after all relevant deductions, most notably the personal allowance. For the tax year 2001–2002 this stands at £4,535. (There are a number of other reliefs, but these are beyond the scope of this book.)

13.3.1 CURRENT YEAR BASIS

13.3.1.1 Current year basis

The effect of the system is that the Revenue can assess profits for an accounting year ending in a tax year as the income of that year. For example, if an unincorporated business makes its accounts up to 30 April each year, the profits made in the business for the year ended 30 April 1997 would have been the profits on which the sole proprietor or partners (as the case may be) were assessed in the tax year 1997/98.

The dates for payment of tax under the system are 31 January in the year of assessment, 31 July following the year of assessment and 31 January following the year of assessment. The first two instalments will be estimated (in effect payments on account based on the previous year's tax liability) and the third will deal with any balance due, either because of over or under-estimation of tax, once full details of actual profits have been received by the Inland Revenue.

> **Example** Jones & Co. (a partnership) makes up its accounts to 30 September each year. The tax liability of the partners for the tax year 1998/99 would have been based on profits to the year-end 30 September 1998. Tax is payable on 31 January 1999 and 31 July 1999 (estimated according to previous year's profits) and any adjustment will be due on 31 January 2000 once actual profits are known.

13.3.2 OPENING AND CLOSING YEAR RULES

13.3.2.1 Introduction

The general rule expressed above regarding assessment is modified when a business has just begun trading or has ceased to trade. These rules are known as the opening and the closing year rules. They will be looked at in turn.

13.3.2.2 Opening year rules

The opening years rules under the new regime apply to the first two tax years of the unincorporated business's 'life'. They are as follows:

TAXATION OF INCOME PROFITS AND LOSSES OF SOLE TRADERS AND PARTNERSHIPS

Year of commencement	Profits from date of commencement to following 5 April
Second year	Profits of first 12 months of trade or the current year basis when an accounting period of at least 12 months ends in the tax year
Third and subsequent years	Current year basis

> **Example** X commences business as an electrician on 1 June 1998, taking 30 September as the accounting year end. The business has, therefore, started in the tax year 1998–99 and this will constitute the first year of assessment. Consequently, the relevant periods for assessment will be:
>
> First Year (98–99) — Profit from 1 June 1998 to 5 April 1999
> Second Year (99–00) — Current year basis, i.e., profits from 1 October 1998 to 30 September 1999
> Third Year (00–01) — Current year basis
>
> Instead, if X had chosen an accounting year end of 30 April, the relevant profit for the second year would be the first 12 months of trading, i.e., 1 June 1998 to 31 May 1999. This is because the accounting date which falls within the second year of assessment (30 April 1999) would be less than 12 months from the commencement of the business.

It will be noted from the above example that, unless an accounting period corresponds exactly with the tax year, some profits will be assessed twice in the first and second years of assessment. Overlap relief will operate in such circumstances (see s. 63A ICTA 1988).

13.3.2.3 Closing year rules

When a business ceases there will be a notional accounting period which runs from the day after the end of the last accounting period to be taxed up to the date of cessation. For example:

> A business is ended on 31 December 1999 (i.e., in the tax year 1999/00). Accounts for the business are made up to 30 April.
>
> The relevant accounting periods for the tax years in question are as follows:
>
> 1997/98   1 May 1996–30 April 1997
> 1998/99   1 May 1997–30 April 1998
> 1999/00   1 May 1998–31 December 1999.

13.4 Losses Under the Income Tax System

If a trader makes a trading loss (i.e., deductible expenses exceed income profits) during an accounting period, the relevant assessment to tax on that sum will amount to a 'nil' liability. In addition, tax relief will be available in respect of the loss in the following ways.

13.4.1 SET-OFF AGAINST SAME YEAR INCOME

Under s. 380(1)(a) ICTA 1988 the amount of the loss may, if the taxpayer so elects, be deducted from any other income of the taxpayer taxable in the year of assessment during which the loss is made. Where, as is usual, the loss-making period is partly in one tax year and partly in another the Revenue will, in practice, allow the whole of the loss to be set off against the income of the tax year during which that period ends.

TAXATION OF INCOME PROFITS AND LOSSES OF SOLE TRADERS AND PARTNERSHIPS

If a loss is not fully relieved under s. 380(1)(a) either because the other income of the year of the loss was insufficient or because the taxpayer did not elect to take the relief, a similar election may be made in respect of the immediately preceding tax year, provided that the trade is still being carried on by the taxpayer on a commercial basis (s. 380(1)(b)).

It should be noted that under both subsections the loss may be set off against *any* of the taxpayer's income from whatever source. A claim under s. 380 must be made in writing within 12 months of 31 January immediately following the year of assessment in which the loss arose.

Special rules apply to prevent relief under s. 380 being given where the trade is not being carried on with a view to profit.

Trading losses can, in limited circumstances, be set against the taxpayer's capital gains in the tax year when the loss arises and in one following tax year under s. 72 Finance Act 1991. The relief under s. 72 only applies to such losses as have not been used up following a claim under s. 380.

13.4.2 SET-OFF AGAINST FUTURE INCOME

Under s. 385 ICTA 1988 a loss may be set against income from the same trade (but not from any other source) in future years (without time limit) to the extent that it has not been completely relieved under s. 380, either because no relief was claimed or because the income was insufficient. Relief is given by means of a deduction from the income of the next tax year in which there are profits and then the year after that and so on until the loss is completely relieved.

The following example should make the operation of ss. 380 and 385 clear. The profits and loss of a trade made during accounting periods ending on 31 December each year are as follows:

1996	£ 5,000	profit
1997	£20,000	loss
1998	£ 6,000	profit
1999	£ 7,000	profit

In addition to his trade, the taxpayer has a part-time employment producing an income of £2,000 per annum throughout the period. If claims for relief under ss. 380 and 385 are made the income tax position is as follows:

	1996/97	1997/98	1998/99	2000/01
DI income	5,000	nil	6,000	7,000
Schedule E income	2,000	2,000	2,000	2,000
	7,000	2,000	8,000	9,000
Loss relief	7,000*	2,000**	6,000***	5,000***
Final income	nil	nil	2,000	4,000

*s. 381(1)(b)   **s. 380(1)(a)   ***s. 385

Note:

(a) The loss occurred in the tax year 1997/98 which means that it can be set-off against other profits being taxed in that year, or against the previous year's profits. As there is still some unrelieved loss once this has been done, the balance can be carried forward.

TAXATION OF INCOME PROFITS AND LOSSES OF SOLE TRADERS AND PARTNERSHIPS

(b) On these figures full relief is not given until 2000/01 even though the loss was made in 1996.

(c) It would probably be better not to claim relief for 1997/98 since the income for that year would have been covered by personal reliefs which are tax-free anyway. The loss relief is, therefore, wasted.

(d) The deduction in 1998/99 is only £6,000 because in that year no relief is given against income from other sources. After the deduction of £5,000 in 2000/01 full relief has been given for the loss.

13.4.3 CARRY BACK OF TERMINAL LOSSES

Under ss. 388 and 389 ICTA 1988 a loss made during the last year of a trade may be deducted from income from the same trade in the three years of assessment before the discontinuance (relief under s. 380 will be available for the year of discontinuance), taking later years before earlier years. It should be noted that the relief only applies where the loss is made in the last year of a trade. If a business makes losses for a number of years before discontinuance there will be no loss relief unless the trader has other sources of income — s. 385 cannot help since there will be no future profits, nor can ss. 388 and 389, since the loss can only be carried back three years and those years will have had nil assessments because of the earlier losses.

13.4.4 LOSSES IN EARLY YEARS OF TRADE

Under s. 381 ICTA 1988 losses made during the first four years of a trade may be set off against income of the three tax years before the loss, taking earlier years before later years. The loss can be deducted from all the income of those years from whatever source and the rules of s. 380 dealing with the order in which relief is given where there is more than one source of income apply to s. 381. The principal effect of s. 381 is to allow a sole trader who starts a trade to set the loss off against income received before the business started.

13.4.5 GENERAL CONSIDERATIONS

As would be expected, all the sections giving relief prevent double relief being claimed in respect of the same sum (for example, if relief is claimed under s. 381 only the unrelieved balance, if any, may be carried forward under s. 385). In many cases relief is given by setting a loss off against income which has already been taxed; where this happens the relief is given by means of repayment of tax.

It should be noted that loss relief is not intended as a subsidy for unsuccessful business; there is no guarantee that just because a loss is made relief will one day be given. Where relief is given the saving is, of course, the amount of the tax on the amount of the relief, so that for the basic rate taxpayer a loss of £100 saves £22 in tax.

13.5 Income Tax Liability of Partnerships

13.5.1 GENERAL

A partnership is not a separate legal person. It is a group of individuals each of whom is taxed on his own share of the partnership profits or losses in the light of his own personal reliefs, charges on income and other sources of income. For the purposes of *assessment* and *collection* of tax each partner is treated as a notional sole trader.

The income on which the partnership is assessed to tax in a particular tax year is calculated according to the current year basis, as is the case for all unincorporated businesses.

TAXATION OF INCOME PROFITS AND LOSSES OF SOLE TRADERS AND PARTNERSHIPS

A trading partnership will be charged to tax under Schedule D Case I. It is normally assessed on the earnings basis. A professional partnership will be charged to tax under Schedule D Case II. It is also assessed on the earnings basis initially, although the Inland Revenue will normally agree to the bills delivered basis in the fourth and subsequent accounting periods, provided an undertaking to bill promptly is given (for a fuller discussion of the three bases see **13.2.4** above).

13.5.2 PROFIT SHARE OR BUSINESS EXPENSE?

The taxable profit is calculated by applying normal income tax principles to ascertain taxable receipts and deductible expenses. However, in the case of a partnership, it is necessary to examine any payment made by the business to a partner to determine whether it is a deductible expense or merely an allocation of the taxable profit amongst the partners. A payment which falls into the latter category cannot reduce the taxable profit of the partnership.

The following items merit special attention:

(a) *Salary*

The tax treatment of a 'salary' payable to a 'partner' depends on whether the Revenue regard the recipient as a true partner sharing in the profits in a particular, agreed way (the decision to allocate profits in this way is normally taken to ensure that one partner is entitled to an agreed portion of profit in priority to the other partners) or whether the recipient is merely an employee in receipt of a salary who is described as a 'partner'. In making their decision, the Revenue will consider all the facts and the terms of the partnership agreement entered into by the parties. The terms of the agreement are not conclusive (*Stekel* v *Ellice* [1973] 1 WLR 191). Where salary is treated as an allocation of profit, it is not deductible from the firm's taxable profits. Where it is a true salary, it is deductible and will be assessed under Schedule E with tax deducted at source under the PAYE procedure.

(b) *Interest*

'Interest' payable to a partner will not be a deductible expense if it is payable on a partner's contribution of capital to the firm. Such a payment is regarded as part of the agreed method of allocating profits. However, if a partner makes a loan to the partnership, interest payable on the loan will normally be a deductible expense.

(c) *Rent*

Where a partnership pays rent to a partner for the use of assets owned by the partner the amount of the rent will be a deductible expense (unless it is excessive).

13.5.3 MECHANICS OF ASSESSMENT — CURRENT YEAR BASIS

Partners are assessed to tax on an individual basis rather than being jointly liable as with all other partnership liabilities (see **3.2**). As a result, each partner is required to include his share of partnership profits in his own tax return and is liable for the tax on his profit share but not that of any other partner. However, the partnership is required to submit a set of accounts and a tax return in respect of total partnership profits. Once these are agreed with the Inland Revenue, the final profit figure will be apportioned amongst the partners according to the profit-sharing ratio in force during the accounting period in question. The deadline of submission of a return will depend on whether or not the partership wishes to have the Inland Revenue calculate the tax liabilities or whether it wishes itself to do so under the system of self-assessment. If it chooses the former option, the deadline is 30 September following the year of assessment. If it chooses the latter, the deadline is 31 January following the year of assessment.

TAXATION OF INCOME PROFITS AND LOSSES OF SOLE TRADERS AND PARTNERSHIPS

The rules applicable if a partner dies or retires or joins the firm are considered in **Chapter 18**.

Prior to the 1996/97 tax year, the liability of partners to taxation was different in that the Revenue calculated an aggregate partnership tax liability for which all partners were jointly liable. This had three consequences: if there was a dispute between the Inland Revenue and a partner about that partner's tax liability in respect of partnership profits, this would delay the finalisation of the partnership tax bill; it was important that the partners made provision to deal with the satisfaction of such liability out of partnership funds; there was substantial risk of exposure for partners, if another failed to meet his or her liability. Now that partners are, in effect, individual profit centres for tax, these consequences have disappeared.

13.5.4 LOSSES OF A PARTNERSHIP

When a partnership makes a loss, each partner can choose what type of relief to claim in respect of his share of the loss. For example, some of the partners may prefer to claim relief under s. 380 ICTA 1988 immediately; others may prefer to wait and claim relief under s. 385 ICTA 1988.

13.5.5 NATIONAL INSURANCE

Partners, being self-employed, are liable to make national insurance contributions at a rate lower than the rate applicable to employees (but the benefits are correspondingly lower), and they are entitled to deduct one half of their contributions when calculating their income tax liability.

FOURTEEN

CAPITAL GAINS TAX AND INHERITANCE TAX ON BUSINESS ASSETS

This chapter covers the following topics:

14.1 Introduction
14.2 Capital gains tax
14.3 Partnerships
14.4 Shareholdings
14.5 Business assets owned by investor
14.6 Inheritance tax
14.7 The purchase by a company of its own shares.

14.1 Introduction

One of the principal motivations for people going into business, is to earn a living from the income they derive from the enterprise. For many people an equally important motivation is to create a capital asset which they can either sell or give away (whether during their lifetime or on death). The tax charges which can arise if any of these events occur will, therefore, be of importance to most business people and in this chapter we will examine the capital gains tax and inheritance tax charges which can arise.

14.2 Capital Gains Tax

14.2.1 GENERAL

Capital gains tax is payable, under the provisions contained in the Taxation of Chargeable Gains Act 1992 (TCGA 1992), when a taxable person makes a disposal of chargeable assets giving rise to a chargeable gain unless an exemption or relief applies. Capital gains tax is charged by reference to gains made during a tax year (as with income tax).

14.2.2 THE CHARGED TAX

A taxable person for CGT purposes is anyone who is resident or ordinarily resident in the UK (including the personal representatives of a deceased person). For the charge to tax to arise, the taxable person must make a 'disposal', a term which is not exhaustively defined in the Act but which covers a sale, gift or part disposal. The definition of 'assets' for capital gains tax purposes is contained in s. 21(1) TCGA 1992 which widely defines it as including 'all forms

CAPITAL GAINS TAX AND INHERITANCE TAX ON BUSINESS ASSETS

of property ...'. Only *chargeable* assets can give rise to a liability to the tax but virtually all 'assets' are chargeable assets subject to a few exceptions (such as motor cars and sterling).

14.2.3 CALCULATING THE CAPITAL GAIN

For the tax to become payable, the disposal of chargeable assets has to give rise to a gain, which will occur if the 'consideration for disposal' exceeds the 'allowable expenditure' permitted by the Act. The 'consideration for disposal' equals the sale price of the asset unless there is a gift or a gift element in which case the market value of the asset is substituted. 'Allowable expenditure' consists of:

(a) the initial expenditure (that is, the original purchase price or market value if the asset was acquired by way of gift) plus incidental costs incurred in acquiring the asset;

(b) subsequent expenditure (such as money spent on enhancing the value of the asset); and

(c) incidental costs of disposal.

14.2.4 PART DISPOSALS

Special rules apply in relation to the allowable deductions if there was a partial disposal of the asset. The effect of these rules is to permit the taxpayer to deduct only a proportion of the 'allowable expenditure'. This proportion is equal to the proportion which the part of the asset disposed of bears to the whole asset. For example, if the total 'allowable expenditure' in respect of a piece of land owned by a sole trader are £100,000 and he sells one half of the land for £75,000, he is only allowed to deduct one half of the total 'allowable expenditure' (namely, £50,000) when calculating his liability to capital gains tax on the subsequent partial disposal.

14.2.5 INDEXATION ALLOWANCE

14.2.5.1 Basic rationale and calculation

When capital gains tax was originally introduced, no allowance was given for inflation. The result was that, in times of raging inflation, taxpayers had to pay tax on 'gains' arising as a result of inflation, rather than as a result of a real increase in the asset's value. This unfairness was addressed by the introduction of an 'indexation allowance' which permits taxpayers to remove inflationary gains from the charge to tax. The allowance is calculated by multiplying the initial and subsequent allowable expenditure by a decimal fraction produced by the following formula:

$$\frac{RD - RI}{RI}$$

where RD is the retail prices index for the month of disposal and RI is the retail prices index for the month in which the expenditure was incurred. The resulting figure can then be deducted from the consideration for the disposal, together with any allowable expenditure, to reduce further the actual gain subject to tax. As will be seen below, inflation before March 1982 is not taken into account.

14.2.5.2 Availability of indexation allowance for individual taxpayers

For assets acquired on or after 1 April 1998, no indexation allowance is allowable in computing the chargeable gains on the disposal of such assets. For gains realised on or after 6 April 1998, indexation allowance is given for periods of ownership up to April 1998 but not thereafter. (This is because indexation has been replaced by a tapering relief on chargeable gains. This relief is explained in detail in **14.2.7** below.)

CAPITAL GAINS TAX AND INHERITANCE TAX ON BUSINESS ASSETS

For all disposals no capital gains tax is levied on gains arising in respect of periods of ownership prior to 31 March 1982. Effectively, taxpayers are treated as having disposed of assets on 31 March 1982 and then immediately reacquired them at their market value at that date.

The general effect of the above rules is demonstrated in the examples below.

> **Examples**
>
> *Asset bought in July 1976 and sold in September 1998*
> The taxpayer is treated as having disposed of the asset on 31 March 1982 and then immediately reacquired it at its market value at that date. Indexation allowance is then calculated on that value from that date (plus any subsequent expenditure) until 31 March 1998. No indexation allowance is allowed from April 1998 to the date of sale.
>
> *Asset bought in June 1993 and sold in September 1998*
> Indexation allowance is calculated on the initial June 1993 expenditure (plus any subsequent expenditure) until 31 March 1998. No indexation allowance is allowed from April 1998 to the date of sale.
>
> *Asset bought in May 1998 and sold in September 1998*
> No indexation allowance is allowed since the asset was acquired after 1 April 1998.

14.2.5.3 Availability of indexation allowance for companies

Companies pay corporation tax on capital gains they may make. Capital gains are calculated in the same way as for individual taxpayers, with the one major exception that companies do not receive the benefit of the new tapering relief. Instead, companies continue to receive indexation allowance without the cut-off date of 1 April 1998 applying.

14.2.6 CREATION OF LOSSES BY ALLOWABLE EXPENDITURE AND INDEXATION ALLOWANCE

It may be that the 'allowable expenditure' in respect of a particular asset exceeds the sale price or market value. In those circumstances, the loss arising can be set off against other gains made during the current tax year. The gains in the current year must be reduced to nil. Only the balance of the loss once all other gains have been completely wiped out can be carried forward. Such losses can be carried forward indefinitely until gains arise in future years (although a carried forward loss must be set off against future gains as they arise). In contrast to the position for the year in which the loss initially arises, carried forward losses need only be set against the gains of future years to the extent necessary to bring that year's gains down to the amount of the then current annual exemption.

It may be that the indexation allowance alone will create a loss or will increase one already created by allowable expenditure. For gains made after 30 November 1993 this is now no longer possible and the indexation allowance can only be used to extinguish any gain.

> **Example** If A disposes of an asset for £60,000 and the base cost for that asset is £45,000, A is left with a gain of £15,000. If the base cost also attracted indexation allowance of £20,000, this could be used to wipe out the gain, but could not create a loss of £5,000.

CAPITAL GAINS TAX AND INHERITANCE TAX ON BUSINESS ASSETS

14.2.7 TAPERING RELIEF ON CHARGEABLE GAINS

14.2.7.1 Introduction

Indexation allowance (see **14.2.5**) has been replaced by a tapering relief on chargeable gains. The taper operates by reducing the amount of chargeable gain according to how long an asset has been held for periods after 5 April 1998. The longer an asset is held before disposal, the lower the chargeable gain will be. The rationale for this relief is to encourage longer-term investment and entrepreneurship. The taper operates on a more generous basis for business assets than non-business assets.

14.2.7.2 'Business assets'

For the purpose of the relief, business assets are broadly defined as:

(a) an asset used for the purposes of a trade carried on by the individual (either alone or in partnership) or by a qualifying company of that individual;

(b) an asset held for the purposes of a qualifying office or employment to which that individual was required to devote substantially the whole of his time; or

(c) the following categories of shareholdings:

  (i) all shares in unquoted trading companies;

  (ii) all shares held by employees in their employer trading companies;

  (iii) shares in quoted trading companies where the holder can exercise at least 5% of the voting rights.

  (iv) shares held by employees in their employer non-trading companies, if the employee does not have a material interest in the employer company or in a company that controls that company. A material interest is classed as:

  — more than 10% of any class of share in the company; or

  — more than 10% of the voting rights in the company; or

  — a right to more than 10% of the distributable profits of the company; or

  — an entitlement to more than 10% of the assets of the company on winding up or in other circumstances.

  The rights of connected persons (such as a spouse and certain relatives) are to be included in calculating the employee's interest.

  (Unquoted companies are those whose shares are not listed on a recognised exchange. This includes companies whose shares are traded on the AIM.)

CAPITAL GAINS TAX AND INHERITANCE TAX ON BUSINESS ASSETS

14.2.7.3 Operation of taper

The taper will operate to reduce chargeable gains in the manner set out below.

Business assets		**Non-business assets**	
Number of complete years after 5 April 1998 for which asset held	*Percentage of gain chargeable*	*Number of complete years after 5 April 1998 for which asset held*	*Percentage of gain chargeable*
0	100	0	100
1	87.5	1	100
2	75	2	100
3	50	3	95
4	25	4	90
		5	85
		6	80
		7	75
		8	70
		9	65
		10 or more	60

> **Example** A taxpayer sells a business asset for £300,000 in February 2003. The asset was bought in July 1998 for £250,000. The asset has been held for four complete years after 5 April 1998. The chargeable gain will, therefore, be £12,500 (25% of £50,000).

14.2.7.4 Special situations

(a) *Transfer of asset between spouses*

Where there has been a transfer of an asset between spouses, the relief is based on the *combined* period of holding by both spouses.

(b) *Assets used partly as business assets*

Where an asset has been used partly as a business asset and partly as a non-business asset during its period of ownership or the last 10 years of ownership, whichever is shorter, the taper on the chargeable gain will be apportioned pro rata. Part of the gain will qualify for the business asset taper and the other part for the non-business asset taper, in each case over the whole period of ownership.

14.2.8 RELIEFS AND EXEMPTIONS IN GENERAL

Assuming that a gain has arisen after both indexation allowance and taper relief have been taken into account, whether a *chargeable* gain will arise will depend on the availability of the exemptions and reliefs. The TCGA 1992 contains a variety of exemptions, the details of most of which are beyond the scope of this book. They include:

(a) exemption for the taxpayer's only or main residence (s. 222 TCGA 1992);

(b) items of tangible movable property having a predictable useful life not exceeding 50 years (s. 45 TCGA 1992); and

(c) chattels where the consideration for disposal does not exceed £6,000 (s. 262 TCGA 1992).

CAPITAL GAINS TAX AND INHERITANCE TAX ON BUSINESS ASSETS

If an exemption is not available in respect of a particular disposal, the following reliefs from tax may help reduce (or extinguish) the liability to tax:

(a) the first £7,500 of gains arising on disposals in the current tax year (the 'annual exemption') (s. 3 TCGA 1992); and

(b) gains on disposal of business assets by a taxpayer aged 50 (or older), or a taxpayer who as retired on ill health grounds below that age ('retirement relief') (ss. 163-164, Sch. 6 TCGA 1992). In outline, this relief means that gains up to a specified amount are either 100% or 50% exempt. However, the maximum relief is available only if the taxpayer has owned the business assets for 10 years or more and no relief is available for business assets owned for less than one year. Note that this relief is being phased out — see **14.2.9** below.

In addition to the exemptions and reliefs outlined above it is possible, in certain circumstances, to postpone or defer the payment of tax, as follows:

(a) If the disposal is by way of a gift, or there is a sale at an undervalue, the donor and donee can elect to 'hold over' any gain arising. This will result in the donee being treated as acquiring the asset at the donor's acquisition value (see **14.2.10**).

(b) In certain circumstances, where the owner of certain types of assets sells them (even at full value), he can elect to 'roll over' the gain arising into replacement assets. The effect will be to reduce the acquisition cost of the new assets by the amount of the 'rolled over' gain (see **14.2.11**).

(c) Gains realised on the disposal of any asset may be deferred into an investment in shares in a private limited company (see **14.4.2**).

14.2.9 RETIREMENT RELIEF

As a result of the introduction of taper relief, retirement relief is being phased out from 6 April 1999 by a gradual reduction of the relief thresholds. The way in which the relief thresholds are being reduced is set out below.

Year	100% relief on gains up to:	50% relief on gains up to:
1998–1999	250,000	250,001–1,000,000
1999–2000	200,000	200,001–800,000
2000–2001	150,000	150,001–600,000
2001–2002	100,000	100,001–400,000
2002–2003	50,000	50,001–200,000
2003–2004	relief withdrawn	relief withdrawn

As such, when the full relief was available, a gain, for example, of £500,000 would have been exempt from tax as to £375,000 of its value. In the current tax year, such a gain would be exempt as to £250,000 of its value.

The figures given in the table are maxima. It is possible to qualify for the relief but not to its full extent. This is discussed at **14.2.8** and **14.4**.

The balance of any gain after the application of the relief will attract taper relief in the usual way.

Retirement relief is available on gifts as well as sales. In these circumstances, to the extent that the chargeable gain exceeds the amount of retirement relief available, the unrelieved gain can be held-over under s. 165 TCGA 1992.

CAPITAL GAINS TAX AND INHERITANCE TAX ON BUSINESS ASSETS

> **Example** In the tax year 2001/2002, T realised a chargeable gain of £600,000 which attracts full retirement relief. Applying the table above:
>
> £0–£100,000 of the gain is 100% exempt   =   £100,000 gain tax exempt
> £100,000–£400,000 of the gain is 50% exempt   =   £150,000 gain tax exempt
> £400,000 upwards attracts no exemption   =   £Nil gain tax exempt
>
> As such, T will pay tax on £350,000 worth of the total gain.

14.2.10 HOLD-OVER RELIEF

Hold-over relief is available in circumstances including:

(a) transfers between spouses (s. 58 TCGA 1992);

(b) gifts or sales at undervalue of business assets (s. 165 TCGA 1992), in which case a joint election can be made by the transferor and transferee and any gain arising will be held-over (for these purposes, business assets are those used for the purposes of a trade, profession or vocation carried on by the transferor or his personal company and also include shares in an unquoted company or in the transferor's personal company; 'personal company' means that the donor holds at least 5% of the voting rights).

It should be noted that a claim for hold-over relief will mean that the whole gain in question must be held-over and cannot be reduced by the donor's annual exemption.

> **Example** A gifts an asset to C when the asset is worth £20,000. A's base cost for the asset is £10,000. Ignoring any other allowable expenditure and any indexation allowance, the gain on the disposal is £10,000. If A and C elect to hold-over the gain, C takes over the asset with a base cost of £10,000.

A sale at an undervalue produces different results in that the whole of the actual chargeable gain cannot be held over and is, instead, reduced by the amount actually received by the seller in excess of the base cost of the asset sold, ignoring any indexation allowance.

> **Example** S bought an asset for £10,000. S sells this asset to T for £20,000 when it is worth £30,000. The indexed rise on the asset at that date is £5,000. S is deemed to receive £30,000, and so, the actual gain is £15,000.
>
> If S and T elect to hold over the gain, the amount of the gain which can be held over is £5,000. The amount received by S in excess of the base cost is £10,000, which, when deducted from the gain, leaves £5,000.
>
> Accordingly, S will be taxed on £10,000 worth of the gain and T will take the asset with a base cost of £25,000.

Note that where there has been a transfer between spouses or hold-over relief claimed on a gift, taper relief on a subsequent sale of an asset will operate in the first case with reference to the combined holding period and in the second case with reference only to the holding period of the new holder of the asset.

CAPITAL GAINS TAX AND INHERITANCE TAX ON BUSINESS ASSETS

14.2.11 ROLL-OVER RELIEF

There are two main types of roll-over relief:

(a) roll-over on the replacement of certain business assets, pursuant to s. 152 TCGA 1992; and

(b) roll-over of any gain from the disposal of any asset into a qualifying investment in shares.

Details of (b) are given at **14.2.12**. Point (a) is explained below. The conditions which must be fulfilled to benefit from replacement asset roll-over relief are:

(a) The original and the replacement asset must both fall within limited categories. The most common are land, buildings and plant and machinery. Both the original and the replacement asset must be used as business assets throughout their periods of ownership.

(b) The purchase of the replacement asset must take place within the twelve month period before, or the three year period after, the disposal of the original asset.

(c) To roll-over the whole gain realised on the original asset, the full proceeds of sale must be used to purchase the replacement asset. If a lesser sum is used, an amount equivalent to that by which the proceeds of sale of the original asset exceed the cost of the replacement asset will become chargeable to tax immediately. This may reault in the whole gain becoming chargeable, even though the relief is theoretically available.

It is important to note that this relief is available both to individuals and companies disposing of business assets.

> **Example** Ovid Limited is considering selling its trading premises and buying new ones. The proceeds from the sale are likely to be £155,000. It is considering three potential sites; one at £175,000 (Premises A); one at £145,000 (Premises B) and one at £130,000 (Premises C).
>
> Assuming the gain on any sale of the original premises would be £20,000, the following would result:
>
> **Premises A** — Total gain rolled over, as whole of proceeds of sale used; base cost of new premises for future CGT calculations = £155,000 (£175,000 − £20,000).
>
> **Premises B** — Percentage of gain rolled over (£10,000); base cost of new premises for future CGT calculations = £135,000 (£145,000 − £10,000). Tax payable on £10,000 of gain.
>
> **Premises C** — No amount of gain rolled over — difference in value between original and replacement asset is greater than amount of gain; base cost of new premises for future CGT calculations = £130,000.

The interaction between this relief and taper relief must be considered. On the sale of any replacement asset, the relevant taper relief will be calculated by reference to the ownership period of the replacement asset only. Therefore, if the original asset has been owned for a considerable time after 5 April 1998, resulting in a large amount of taper relief having been accrued, it may be more sensible to take this immediate benefit rather than postpone a gain.

CAPITAL GAINS TAX AND INHERITANCE TAX ON BUSINESS ASSETS

14.2.12   EIS DEFERRAL OF CHARGEABLE GAINS

As well as being a method of filling the public coffers, the taxation system can also be used to 'engineer' certain types of behaviour. Over the last few years, efforts have been made to encourage high net worth individuals to invest in growing private companies, by affording such investment preferable tax treatment. Up until the March 1998 Budget, there existed two schemes: the Enterprise Investment Scheme and Reinvestment Relief. Very simply, the former resulted in income tax relief for investors on the amount invested and also capital gains tax relief for any gains realised on their investment after five years of ownership of the same. The latter was another system of capital gains deferral, with the gain from any disposal being deferred into an investment of appropriate shares, such gain only being realised on a subsequent disposal of those shares.

The Finance Act 1998 resulted in a merger of these systems. However, it should be noted that the overall effect was left very much the same, merely the detail altered. It is beyond the scope of this chapter to examine the intricacies of the scheme as it applies to income tax, so discussion will be limited to its impact as a capital gains tax deferral mechanism.

Any gain realised upon the disposal of any asset by an individual can benefit from the relief. However, to qualify the investment can only take a specified form, that is it must be:

(a) an allotment of fully-paid ordinary shares, with no rights of redemption or preference in whatever form for five years;

(b) in a company whose shares are unquoted;

(c) which only carries on regular trading activities, e.g., is not an investment, property development, farming or forestry company or the like, mainly in the UK;

(d) which does not have a gross assets value of more than £15m before nor £16m after the investment (such value to include the value of assets owned by subsidiaries);

(e) and which is not controlled by another company and which does not have any subsidiaries other then ones which fulfil the requirements in (b) to (d) also.

In addition, the investment must take place at least twelve months before or three years after the original disposal.

Because this is a scheme to encourage start-up/development capital for companies, any attempt to use the system solely to achieve a tax benefit or failure to use the funds realised in the trading activities of the company will result in the relief being withdrawn, resulting in an immediate liability to tax on the gain deferred. Also, for the same reason, it is not possible to sell shares in a company and then re-invest in that same company.

The investor will not be liable for tax on the original disposal until such time as the shares are sold. However, should the investor cease to be UK resident before the period of five years has elapsed from the date of investment, the relief will be withdrawn.

It is not necessary to invest all of the proceeds of the original disposal to claim the deferral, an investment of an amount equivalent to the gain will be sufficient to defer the full value of it. Once the shares are sold any increase in their actual value will be subject to capital gains tax. (Although note the commentary after the following example.) Taper relief will have to be applied in the usual way.

CAPITAL GAINS TAX AND INHERITANCE TAX ON BUSINESS ASSETS

> **Example** Sumiya disposes of an asset in January 2001 and realises a gain ('the original gain') of £40,000. She bought the asset in September 1996. In June 2002 she invests in EIS-qualifying shares worth £85,000. These shares are sold in May 2006 realising a gain of £35,000. Issues to note are:
>
> (a) The deferral takes place within three years of the original gain, so is within the time limits.
>
> (b) The amount of the EIS investment exceeds the original gain, so the full amount of this gain is deferred.
>
> (c) The sale in 2006 results in the original gain being taxed. The gain will be reduced by taper relief because the asset was owned for two complete years after 5 April 1998. Therefore, 75% of the gain will be taxed.
>
> (d) The sale in 2006 also results in the gain of £35,000 being taxed. This will attract three years taper relief. (In fact, if the disposal had occurred a month after, four years relief would have been available. Therefore, the timing of a sale can be very important.)

It is important to note a qualification to the above. As was stated at the outset, the other facet of the EIS system results in income tax relief and a capital gains-free investment. There is no reason why any investment under the deferral arrangements may not also result in these benefits for the taxpayer. Note, however, that such benefits are limited to the first £150,000 of shares acquired and that the conditions which must be fulfilled to achieve these benefits are quite strict, most notably that the shares must be owned for at least three years from subscription and that for a period of two years before subscription and five after the investor must not have been connected with the company in question. Therefore, in the above example, the taxpayer would qualify for capital gains exemption on the sale of the shares because she owned them for just under four years.

Finally, it is possible to make an EIS investment and on the realisation of this make a further EIS investment and defer the gain. In this case, on a disposal of the second investment, taper relief can be claimed for the cumulative period of ownership of EIS shares.

It is possible to combine the deferred relief with retirement relief pursuant to s. 164BA TCGA 1992. In effect, the amount of retirement relief available in respect of a chargeable gain must be calculated to establish how much of the gain is unrelieved by retirement relief. If the taxpayer re-invests the unrelieved amount, this will result in no tax being paid at the time of the disposal.

14.2.13 RATE OF TAX

If after taking into account all available exemptions, reliefs and deferments, a chargeable gain still remains, capital gains tax is payable calculated as if the gain was the top slice of the taxpayer's taxable income. Any gain which falls within the starting rate band will be taxed at 10%, any gain falling within the basic rate band will be taxed at 20% and any gain falling above the basic rate band will be taxed at 40%.

14.2.14 DEATH OF TAXPAYER

No capital gains tax is payable when a person dies. The beneficiaries of the estate under the will or intestacy are deemed to acquire the asset at market value at the time of death.

CAPITAL GAINS TAX AND INHERITANCE TAX ON BUSINESS ASSETS

14.3 Partnerships

14.3.1 GENERAL

When a firm disposes of one of its assets, normal CGT principles apply in determining what gain, if any, the firm has made. There are difficulties involved in applying the normal CGT principles to a partnership context. The premise on which the Revenue operates is that each partner is to be treated as owning a fractional share of each of the chargeable assets of the partnership (including goodwill) and not, for this purpose, as owning an interest in the business as a whole. When the firm disposes of an asset to an outsider, each partner is treated as making a disposal of his fractional share in the asset.

What follows is concerned with the disposal by a firm of its assets. CGT issues can also arise when partners leave and join partnerships. These are discussed in **Chapter 18**.

14.3.2 ASSESSMENT

The assessment and collection of CGT is treated differently from the assessment and collection of income tax. The precedent partner delivers a return to the Inland Revenue giving full details of disposals. The assessment is made on the individual partners. Each partner's share in the gain is calculated in accordance with his share in the asset disposed of.

In order to calculate the CGT liability of the individual partners in relation to the disposal of assets it is, therefore, necessary to know the proportions in which assets are owned. This is often referred to as the partners' 'assets surplus ratio'.

14.3.3 ASSET SURPLUS RATIO

The partnership deed may specify the proportions in which asset surpluses are to be shared. If it does, it is conclusive. If there is no express provision in the partnership deed the asset surplus sharing ratio is deemed to be the ratio in which profits are shared. It is common for a partnership deed to provide an asset surplus sharing ratio which is different from the profit sharing ratio. For example, the agreement may provide for an individual partner's right to share in an asset surplus to be greater than his right to share in income profits, to reflect the fact that he has made a substantial capital contribution to the firm while contributing comparatively little to earning income profits.

When an asset is acquired by a partnership, each partner's share in the acquisition value is determined by his share in the asset surplus *at that time*. Similarly, in a disposal, each partner's share in the proceeds of disposal is determined by his share in the asset surpluses *at that time*.

Example A and B are in partnership. They share profits equally and have made no special agreement as to sharing asset surpluses. They acquire an asset for £20,000. The acquisition value for each partner is:

A	½	£10,000
B	½	£10,000

They sell the assets for £36,000. The share in the proceeds of the disposal of each partner is:

A	½	£18,000
B	½	£18,000

The chargeable gain of each partner is (ignoring indexation):

A	£18,000 − £10,000 = £8,000
B	£18,000 − £10,000 = £8,000

Each partner is personally liable for his own chargeable gain and will be assessed for tax at the rates appropriate to his level of income.

CAPITAL GAINS TAX AND INHERITANCE TAX ON BUSINESS ASSETS

14.3.4 RELIEFS

If there is a gain realised on the disposal, the exemptions and reliefs referred to in **14.2** may be available. To the extent that there is a gift element in a disposal, hold over relief is available to postpone the payment of tax. This relief can be claimed not only in respect of partnership assets but also in respect of assets owned by an individual partner which are used by the firm. (However, in this case, there may be a potential inheritance tax liability to take into account as well.)

A disposal of partnership property in circumstances where the partners intend to reinvest the sale proceeds can attract roll-over relief (under ss. 152–160 TCGA 1992). This option to postpone payment of tax is also available to a partner who owns an asset which is used by the partnership (irrespective of the terms on which the asset is used by the firm). (See **14.2.11**.)

Very simply, retirement relief is unavailable to individual partners when the firm disposes of an individual asset. This is because the relief is only available to partners when they make a disposal of their share in the partnership, rather than when the partnership is selling an asset. Therefore, the most likely situation in which a partner may be looking for retirement relief is when that partner retires from the business and sells his stake in it to the remaining partners (subject to all other conditions being satisfied).

However, it is possible that the disposal of an asset actually owned by a partner, but used by the firm, may attract retirement relief. Further details are given at **14.5.2**.

14.4 Shareholdings

A capital profit on the sale of shares will in most cases attract a liability to capital gains tax and the general principles and reliefs set out in **14.2** will apply. However, there is a notable exception to this rule when the purchaser of the shares is the company in which the shares were issued. This is dealt with at **14.7**.

It is not our intention to repeat those general principles but there are certain points in relation to the availability of retirement relief on the disposal of shares in a company which merit particular attention.

In addition to the general conditions set out at **14.2.8** and **14.2.9**, the conditions to be satisfied on the disposal of shares are that they are shares in a personal trading company or a personal holding company and the individual must be a full-time working officer or employee of the personal trading or personal holding companies or of another company in the group. (We explained in **14.2.10** that a personal company is one in which the transferor owns 5% of the voting rights.)

To be entitled to relief at all, the individual must be able to show that these conditions have been satisfied throughout a period of at least one year prior to the disposal. Normally, this period of one year must end with the date of disposal. However, in certain cases, the relief is still available provided the conditions are satisfied by reference to a period ending on an earlier date. Thus, for example, a full-time officer or employee who decides to devote less of his time to the company can still claim the relief on a subsequent disposal of his shares if all the conditions were satisfied at the time he ceased to work full-time. However, having gone part-time, he can only preserve his rights to relief if he remains a director of the company and devotes at least 10 hours per week to the service of the company in a technical or managerial capacity throughout the period, starting with the date he ceases to work full-time and ending with the date of the disposal. There is no limit on the length of time the officer or employee can work part-time.

CAPITAL GAINS TAX AND INHERITANCE TAX ON BUSINESS ASSETS

If the conditions for relief are fulfilled, a disposal of shares will attract the relief. There is no actual requirement that the shareholder must retire.

To be entitled to the full relief, the taxpayer must have fulfilled all the relevant conditions for the ten-year period prior to the disposal. Any period less than this will result in a reduction of 10% of the relief for each year below the ten-year period.

> **Example** In the tax year 1998–99, A realised a chargeable gain of £400,000 on the disposal of shares in P Ltd. A had been a shareholder of P Ltd for 8 years and a full-time director for six years. As such, A was entitled to 60% of the maximum relief as follows:
>
> Relief available = £0–250,000 × 60% = £150,000 tax-free gain
> = £250,000–1,000,000 × 60% = Up to £450,000 50% tax-free
> Impact of relief = £0–150,000 tax free
> = £150,001–400,000 50% tax-free
> Chargeable Gain = £125,000
>
> Contrast this with the situation where all the requirements were fulfilled for 10 years, in which case the relief available to A would have been:
>
> £0–250,000 = Tax-free sum
> £250,001–400,000 = 50% Tax-free sum
> Chargeable gain = £75,000

The relief is only given in relation to 'chargeable business assets', that is, assets which if sold themselves would attract a capital gains tax liability. In the case of a disposal of shares it is, therefore, necessary to calculate how much of the gain reflects chargeable business assets of the company (or of the whole trading group where shares in a holding company are being disposed of) and how much reflects other assets (such as stock in trade, which is not chargeable at all, and investments, which are not business assets). The relief is then restricted to the part of the gain resulting from chargeable business assets.

> **Example** A company is valued at £1,000,000. However, this value is made up of £750,000 worth of chargeable business assets and £250,000 non-chargeable business assets. A 50% shareholding in this company will, therefore, very simply have a value of £500,000. However, for retirement relief purposes this shareholding represents 50% of £750,000 worth of assets. As such, on a disposal of the whole shareholding at its current market value only £375,000 worth of the consideration will attract retirement relief.

14.5 Business Assets Owned by an Investor

14.5.1 GENERAL

It is not uncommon for shareholder/directors or partners to own assets which are used by their respective companies or partnerships. The disposal of such assets may result in a CGT liability for the person concerned.

Many of the reliefs mentioned above will be available. This section will briefly set out such availability. However, because of the complexities of this area, reference should always be made to the statute for full details.

CAPITAL GAINS TAX AND INHERITANCE TAX ON BUSINESS ASSETS

14.5.2 RETIREMENT RELIEF

When a partner or shareholder is withdrawing from a business and retirement relief is available on the partnership share or shareholding in question, a related disposal of an asset by the individual but used by the business may also attract relief. Such disposals are known as 'associated disposals', due to the fact that they accompany the disposal of a qualifying share in a business or shareholding. It is important to note that the taxpayer must be withdrawing from the business at the time the disposals take place. This does not necessarily mean retiring completely, but a negligible reduction in responsibilities probably would not be enough. Failure to prove this issue will not affect the relief available for the main disposal, but will remove it completely for the associated one.

Two other hurdles to attracting the relief are:

(a) if the partner or shareholder charged a commercial rent to the partnership or company for the use of the asset; and

(b) if the asset was not used for the purposes of either the partnership or the company throughout.

In both instances the amount of relief available can be curtailed to the extent that the Inland Revenue thinks is just and reasonable, which in many cases will be the absolute denial of the relief.

14.5.3 ROLL-OVER (REPLACEMENT ASSET) RELIEF

Subject to the main conditions of the relief being fulfilled, assets owned by a partner or shareholder but used by their partnership or personal company respectively will attract the relief. (See **14.2.11**.)

14.5.4 HOLD-OVER RELIEF

To reiterate what has already been mentioned in **14.2.10**, any business asset owned by a partner or a shareholder, where the company in question is that shareholder's personal company, is eligible for this relief.

14.6 Inheritance Tax

14.6.1 GENERAL

Inheritance tax is payable under the provisions of the Inheritance Tax Act 1984 (IHTA 1984) where there is a *chargeable transfer*. The chargeable transfer is defined as 'any *transfer of value* which is made to an individual but is not ... an exempt transfer'. A transfer of value is defined as 'a *disposition* made by a person ... as a result of which the value of his estate immediately after the transfer is less than it would be but for the disposition ...'. Inheritance tax is payable on the *value transferred* which is the amount by which the value of the transferor's estate is reduced as a result of the disposition.

Transfers of value can be made either *inter vivos* as a result of gifts or sales with a gift element or on death. In this section, we only give an outline of the principal aspect of the tax. The reader is referred to one of the standard tax text books for full details of all of the aspects of the tax.

CAPITAL GAINS TAX AND INHERITANCE TAX ON BUSINESS ASSETS

14.6.2 TYPES OF TRANSFER

There are three types of transfer which can give rise to inheritance tax (subject to the availability of any exemptions or reliefs). These are:

(a) a transfer on death which will attract tax at the full rate of 40%;

(b) a potentially exempt transfer which is an *inter vivos* transfer of value made by an individual as a result of which property becomes part of the estate of another individual or is transferred to certain types of trust. (As such, transfers to companies do not qualify as potentially exempt.) A potentially exempt transfer will become fully exempt if the transferor lives for seven years after the transfer. Death within those seven years will result in the transfer becoming chargeable at the rates of tax in force at the date of death; and

(c) a chargeable transfer made before death which is immediately taxable but at only half the rates which apply on death, that is, 20%. The death of the transferor within seven years will lead to the transferee becoming liable to tax at the full rates in force at the date of death.

14.6.3 CUMULATION

There are only the above two rates of inheritance tax. There is a nil rate band of £242,000 and any excess is taxed at the rate of 40% (subject to the points made above). Whether or not the nil rate band has been used up in relation to a particular chargeable transfer will depend on the total value of all previous chargeable transfers which the transferor has made within the immediately preceding seven years. This process of cumulation will mean that the tax on the present transfer will be calculated as if it were the top slice of a single transfer equal in value to all of the transfers (including the one with which we are concerned) made during the last seven years.

The full rate of 40% only applies where the transfer is made on death or within three years of death. Subject to that, if the chargeable transfer is made before death, inheritance tax is charged at the time of the transfer at half the full rate (currently 20%), assuming the nil rate band has been exhausted. If the transfer is a potentially exempt transfer or a chargeable transfer and the transferor dies within seven years, but not less than three years of the transfer, a sliding scale applies to determine the value of the transfer which will be subject to tax at the full rates in force at the time of death. Here as a gift is made *inter vivos*, the transferor and the transferee can agree which of them will pay the inheritance tax. If the tax is paid by the donor, the loss to the donor will be the value of the gift plus any inheritance tax on it. This will mean that the inheritance tax calculation will be based on the gross loss to the donor. In those circumstances, it will be necessary to 'gross-up' the net gift before the calculation of the tax can be made.

It is not our intention to cover in this book any of the other detailed rules on the calculation of tax, such as the rules relating to gifts with a reservation or changes in values of gifts within seven years of death.

14.6.4 VALUE TRANSFERRED

Clearly, the value of the property transferred plays an important part in the calculation of the liability to inheritance tax. For the purposes of inheritance tax, the value of particular items which have been given away will be the price which the property might reasonably be expected to fetch if it was to be sold in the open market at the time of the gift. However, there is no presumption that the value of the property will be reduced because it was all placed on the market at the same time. The latter reference will be of particular relevance when valuing a large holding of shares in a private company. In addition, there are certain special valuation rules which apply to shares. Quoted stocks and shares are usually valued by taking the lower of the two prices quoted in the Stock Exchange Daily Official List for the relevant day and adding to it one quarter of the difference between the lower and the higher quoted prices or, if it produces a lower figure, by taking a figure half way between the lowest and highest prices at which bargains were struck on the relevant day. The value of unquoted shares will be determined by the normal market value rule but it is sometimes extremely difficult to value such shares accurately. The facts that have to be taken into account include the company's profitability, its dividend record, the level of retained earnings and the value of the assets which the company owns. Should the shares be sold subject to pre-emption rights, the market value will be determined on the assumption that the pre-emption rights did not apply to the hypothetical sale. However, those rights will be assumed to apply to the hypothetical purchaser (which will mean that the value so determined would be the one which a purchaser was likely to pay in the full knowledge that the pre-emption rights will apply to their shares in the future).

Although not exclusively applicable to shares, a further rule which is of particular relevance when valuing shareholdings is the rule relating to 'related property'. This rule recognises the fact that some assets can be more valuable when combined with other assets of the same type than when they are owned individually. Shares which form part of a majority holding in a company will, for example, be more valuable than shares which form part of a minority shareholding. The IHTA 1984 defines a variety of items of property as being related property. This can include any item of property owned by the transferor's spouse at the time of the transfer. If the transfer is made of related property, the property actually transferred and the property to which it is related are valued as a single asset and tax is then calculated on the proportion of the total value which is transferred.

Finally, when valuing any property, transferred liabilities are taken into account to the extent that they were incurred for consideration in money or money's worth or imposed by law and provided there is no right to reimbursement.

14.6.5 EXEMPTIONS

At the start of this section, we stated that a chargeable transfer was any transfer of value which is not an *exempt* transfer. An exempt transfer will not attract tax and it will not be included in the transferor's cumulative total. The exemptions which can be claimed include the spouse exemption which is available both *inter vivos* and on death (and means that all gifts, irrespective of the value, between spouses are exempt from inheritance tax provided the recipient spouse is domiciled in the UK). An annual exemption of £3,000 per year is available on transfers made before death. If the annual redemption for any year is not used either wholly or partially, the unused part can be carried over for one year but no longer. Furthermore, outright *inter vivos* gifts worth up to about £250 per transferee are exempt.

14.6.6 BUSINESS PROPERTY RELIEF

14.6.6.1 General

In addition to the exemptions, the IHTA 1984 also makes various reliefs available which include quick succession relief, agricultural property relief and business property relief. The effect of a relief being available is to reduce the value of the relevant property with a resultant reduction in the amount of inheritance tax payable.

In this section we will look only at business property relief which is available provided the property was 'relevant business property'. This term is defined as:

(a) property consisting of a business or an interest in a business (and so it includes the interest of a sole proprietor or a partner in a business);

(b) shareholdings in unquoted companies or companies quoted on the Alternative Investment Market;

(c) shareholdings in quoted companies which alone or with other shares owned by the transferor or with related property gave the transferor control immediately before the transfer (control means being able to exercise more than 50% of the votes in general meeting — temporary control will suffice);

(d) land or buildings, or machinery or plant used immediately before the transfer wholly or mainly for the purposes of a company controlled by the transferor or of a partnership of which he was a member.

(e) land or buildings, machinery or plant used immediately before the transfer for the purposes of a business carried on by the transferor and which was settled property in which the transferor had an interest in possession.

The relief on such a property is a reduction in the value transferred of 100% (in the case of property falling within (a)–(b) above) or 50% (in the case of property within (c)–(e) above).

14.6.6.2 'Business'

For the purposes of this relief, 'business' includes a profession or a vocation but does not include a business carried on otherwise than for gain. Agriculture is a type of business and so business property relief may be available to the extent that agricultural relief is not. If the business consists of dealing in securities, stocks, shares, land or buildings or of holding investments, the relief is not available. However, business property relief will be available where the business is the active management of land.

The reduction in value is given on the net value of the business property (that is to say, after the liabilities have been deducted).

Even if the property falls within the categories set out above, relief will not be available unless the transferor has owned the property throughout the two years before the transfer. If property replaces other relevant business property (other than in the case of minority shareholdings), relief is available provided the aggregate period of the ownership of the original and replacement property exceeds two years in the five years before the time of transfer. If the transferee of relevant business property himself makes a transfer of the same property before he has owned the property for two years, this will not prevent the relief being claimed provided the relief was available on the original transfer and one of the transfers was a transfer on death. If property is received on the death of a spouse, the surviving spouse can aggregate the deceased spouse's period of ownership with his own in order to satisfy the two year period of ownership requirement.

14.6.6.3 Period of ownership

If a business (or other relevant business property) has been owned for two years (or more), business property relief at the appropriate percentage is available on the full value at the time of transfer. There is no obligation to show that particular assets of business have been owned for two years. Having said that, the value of an asset will be excluded from relief if it has not been used wholly or mainly for the purpose of the business throughout the two years preceding the transfer or throughout the period since it was acquired, if later.

CAPITAL GAINS TAX AND INHERITANCE TAX ON BUSINESS ASSETS

14.6.6.4 Anti-avoidance

As a way of preventing taxpayers placing private assets in a business and then trying to obtain business property relief on them, s. 112 IHTA 1984 provides that relief is not available on 'excepted assets'. These are assets which are neither:

(a) used wholly or mainly for the purposes of the business concerned throughout the whole of the previous two years; nor

(b) required at the time of the transfer for future use.

These are alternative requirements. An asset which fulfils either one of the requirements will not be an excepted assets. However, (b) is not available where relief is claimed on an asset used by a company controlled by the transferor or by a partnership of which he is a member.

14.6.6.5 Potentially exempt transfers

Where a transfer is made before death (whether it is chargeable or potentially exempt) and the transferor dies within seven years, the relief is available only if the property originally given or qualifying property representing it has remained as relevant business property in the ownership of the transferee from the date of the transfer to the date of the death of the transferor. If the transferee dies before the transferor within the seven year period, relief is only available on the death of the transferee if the same condition is satisfied. The property must remain relevant business property in the hands of the transferee. If only a proportion of the property originally given or qualifying property representing it remains in the ownership of the transferee at the date of death, relief is available on the proportion of the property owned at that date. It is sufficient if 'property representing' the original property is in the hands of the donee at the relevant date. It should, however, be noted that:

(a) the whole of the consideration must have been applied on acquiring the replacement property;

(b) replacement property must be acquired within three years after the disposal of the original property; and

(c) the provision applies only to the first replacement and not to subsequent ones.

It is not our intention to deal with the complex rules for determining who is liable to account for inheritance tax to the Inland Revenue on death, nor to consider the rules on the burden or incidence of inheritance tax.

18.6.7 PAYMENT OF IHT

Tax on a chargeable transfer made before death must be paid six months after the end of the month in which the transfer is made or, if the transfer is made after 5 April and before 1 October, at the end of April in the next year. Tax in relation to a death is payable six months after the end of the month in which the death occurred. If tax is paid late, interest will be charged.

Inheritance tax on certain types of property can be paid by ten annual instalments. The instalment option is available in respect of:

(a) land of any description;

(b) shares or securities in a company giving the transferor control of the company immediately before death;

CAPITAL GAINS TAX AND INHERITANCE TAX ON BUSINESS ASSETS

(c) unquoted shares or securities which do not give the transferor control (provided paying the tax in one lump sum will not cause any hardship);

(d) unquoted shares or securities not giving the transferor control in the company, provided at least 20% of the tax paid by the person paying the tax on the shares is either tax on those shares or on those shares and other instalment options;

(e) unquoted shares which did not give the transferor control and the value of which exceeds £20,000, provided they are at least 10% of all the shares of the company or are ordinary shares and at least 10% of the ordinary shares in the company; and

(f) business or interest in a business including a profession or vocation.

Shares quoted on the Alternative Investment Market are still 'unquoted' for these purposes. Control means voting control on all questions affecting the company. The relief is available whether the transfer is on death or *inter vivos* but, in the latter case, the relief is only available if the *transferee* pays the inheritance tax. The instalment option must be claimed by a written notice to the Revenue and the outstanding instalments must be paid off if the assets are sold within the ten year period.

If the instalment option is available, the first instalment is generally due six months after the end of the month in which the gift has been made. No interest is charged on the tax provided the instalments are paid on time. Although the instalment option does not reduce the amount of tax, the relief is nonetheless beneficial.

14.6.8 PARTNERSHIPS

The IHT legislation contains few provisions dealing specifically with partnerships. According to the general principle of IHT, any transfer of a partnership asset, or of an interest in a partnership, will be a transfer of value by the individual partners if the transfer is by way of gift or there is an element of gift in the disposition.

The transfer will be exempt if it is made between spouses. It will also be exempt if it was not intended to, and was not made in a transaction intended to, confer any gratuitous benefit and either it was an arm's length transaction between unconnected persons or was such as might be expected to be made between unconnected persons.

As a result of this provision, many *inter vivos* transfers which might appear to be transfers of value will escape inheritance tax. For example, when a new partner is admitted and is given a share in the assets without making a payment, there would be a transfer value were it not for this provision. This is considered in **Chapter 18**.

On death, a deceased partner's interest in the partnership will be part of his estate. The position is considered more fully in **Chapter 18** but business property relief (see **14.6.6**) will normally be available.

14.6.9 SHAREHOLDINGS

The gift of shares may give rise to inheritance tax (and capital gains tax) since inheritance tax is chargeable on the 'loss to the donor's estate'. This normally means the market value of the asset given away, but in some cases the loss is considerably more than market value. For example, if a controlling shareholder gives away enough shares to lose control of the company, the loss to his estate will be very much more than the value of the shares given away.

The most important (but not only) 'reliefs' which will be relevant when shares in a company are given away are 'business property relief' and the instalment option (considered in **14.6.7**).

These reliefs exist because the Government recognises that too high a tax burden on the disposal of shares in a company could lead to the break-up of a company as being the only way of raising funds to pay the tax. It should not be forgotten that the general exemptions (such as the spouse exemption and the annual exemption) will be available in respect of business property as well as the business property relief.

Anybody in business, should consider the possible impact of tax on his family from a relatively young age. It should be clear from the rules described in this chapter that there is a very considerable fiscal advantage in disposing of assets *inter vivos* so as to take account of the fact that the IHT lifetime rates are lower than the death rates, and tax can be avoided altogether if the donor survives seven years after a potentially exempt transfer has been made. Since transfers of value are only cumulated for seven years after they are made (i.e., transfers made more than seven years ago are ignored in calculating the amount of tax), there is an advantage to be gained from making gifts of shares over a considerable period of time rather than all at once. The burden of IHT can also be reduced in the long run by making use of the spouse exemption to ensure that both husband and wife leave enough to take maximum advantage of the nil rate band that they each have.

14.7 The Purchase by a Company of its Own Shares

14.7.1 THE INCOME TAX TREATMENT

Where a company redeems, repays or buys its own shares under the provisions of ss. 159–181 Companies Act 1985 (see **Chapter 10**), tax will usually become payable. The amount received from the company is in most cases treated as a dividend (and so is subject to income tax in the hands of the recipient) to the extent that it exceeds the original investment in the company (see **16.3**). The return of the original cost of the shares is a capital sum.

> **Example** Purchase Ltd buys back shares from A for £9,000. A originally subscribed for his shares at a nominal value of £1,000. Purchase Ltd is treated as making a dividend of £8,000. A receives the return of his investment of £1,000 at the same price as he paid for it, so there are no capital gains tax consequences (ignoring any items of actual allowable expenditure etc.). A also receives a dividend of £8,000 which has borne basic rate income tax at source. The consequences of this are as follows:
>
> (a) if the dividend falls to be taxed entirely at basic rate income tax, A need pay no further tax;
>
> (b) if some or all of the dividend falls to be taxed at higher rate income tax, A must account for the balance of the tax due;
>
> (c) if some of the dividend is exempted from tax by falling within A's personal allowance, A will be unable to claim back any of the tax already deducted;
>
> (d) if A has tax-exempt status, for example, as a charity or pension fund, again, as in (c), A will be unable to claim back any tax.

Payments to buy back members' shares are not deductible in calculating the company's profits for corporation tax purposes.

14.7.2 THE CAPITAL GAINS TAX TREATMENT

Section 219 ICTA 1988 contains provisions excluding such a payment from the definition of a distribution in certain circumstances. Where the payment is so excluded, capital gains tax will be payable on any increase in the value of the shares during the period of ownership (the redemption or repayment is treated as a disposal for CGT purposes as if it were a sale).

A redemption, repayment or purchase by the company is excluded from the definition of a distribution if the company is a trading company and the transaction is made 'wholly or mainly for the purposes of benefiting a trade carried on by the company'. Presumably, the transaction will be made for such a purpose if the object of it was to enable a shareholder of the company who disagreed with the policy of the directors to retire from the business if the company had more capital than it required. A transaction designed to enable the proprietors to take an income tax-free profit would not be covered, and this is reinforced by the further requirement that the main purpose or one of the main purposes of the scheme must not be 'to enable the owner of the shares to participate in the profits of the company without receiving a dividend or the avoidance of tax'. A redemption, repayment or purchase is also excluded from the definition of a distribution if the proceeds are intended to be used (and are used within two years) for the payment of IHT. The IHT must have arisen on a death and the shareholder must show that undue hardship would have arisen if the shares had not been purchased by the company.

In addition to the basic requirements of s. 219, income tax is only avoided if the following conditions are satisfied:

(a) that the owner of the shares is resident and ordinarily resident in the UK at the time of the purchase;

(b) that he has owned the shares for five years;

(c) that the sale is of a substantial part of his shareholding taking into account any holding of his associates (which terms includes close relatives, partners and trustees of certain settlements); and

(d) certain special conditions apply only in the case of groups of companies.

The object of these rules is to ensure that tax avoidance or tax advantages cannot be obtained by a purchase of its own shares by a company, but that 'genuine' transactions should give rise to CGT liability only. It is possible to apply for advance clearance when a scheme to buy back shares is proposed which, if granted, will ensure that putting the proposal into effect will not give rise to an income tax charge.

> **Example** Suppose in the above example the receipt by A fell within s. 219. A would receive a capital sum of £9,000, from which the base cost of his shares could be deducted (ignoring any indexation allowance) resulting in a capital gain of £8,000.

Historically, a taxpayer would normally wish the buy-back to fall within s. 219 because the rate of CGT was lower than that for income tax. This difference has been eradicated, so ensuring that the transaction is treated as capital is no longer so crucial. However, it may be that the taxpayer has reasons for wanting a charge to capital gains tax, for example, if there are capital losses which could be set-off against the gain; or if a capital gain would be a lesser amount than an income gain; or if the shareholder could claim a valuable relief, such as retirement relief or taper relief.

FIFTEEN

THE CORPORATION TAX SYSTEM

This chapter covers the following topics:

15.1 Introduction
15.2 Calculation of profits — corporation tax
15.3 Assessment — corporation tax
15.4 Loss relief under the corporation tax system
15.5 Close companies.

15.1 Introduction

In this chapter, we will look at how the corporation tax system works and the chapter will concentrate on the tax liability of companies. The tax liabilities of the recipients of income from companies (whether the income be in the form of dividends, debenture interest or directors' fees) will be considered in **Chapter 16**. The inheritance tax and capital gains tax liabilities of shareholders in respect of shares were considered in **Chapter 14**.

15.2 Calculation of Profits — Corporation Tax

15.2.1 PROFITS IN GENERAL

15.2.2 INCOME

Companies pay corporation tax on their profits. For the purposes of the tax, unincorporated associations (such as members' clubs), other than partnerships, local authorities and local authority associations, are taxed as companies (s. 832(1) ICTA 1988). 'Profits' means income profits and capital gains (s. 6(4)(a) ICTA 1988). It is this aggregate profit figure which is assessed to corporation tax.

Income profits are calculated according to income tax principles (see **13.2**), so that the various schedules of income are as relevant for corporation tax as for income tax. Similarly, the rules for deduction of expenses which apply for income tax purposes also apply to corporation tax (s. 9 ICTA 1988). There are some exceptions to these rules, particularly in relation to dividends, losses and charges on income. Companies, unlike individuals, have no right to claim any personal allowances.

THE CORPORATION TAX SYSTEM

15.2.3 CHARGES ON INCOME

A charge on income is defined for corporation tax purposes as an annuity or other annual payment. It used to be that interest on borrowings could constitute a change in income but since the Finance Act 1996, all interest is treated as a trading expense and no longer as a charge on income. Sums which are deductible as business expenses are not within the definition. A charge on income payable out of profits may be deducted from profits liable to corporation tax. Deduction is not, however, permitted unless the charge was incurred for valuable and sufficient consideration. Individuals may also deduct certain items as charges on income in computing tax liability (see **13.2**), but the definition of charges on income is in some respects wider (for example, mortgage interest relief is available) and in others narrower (some covenanted payments are not deductible) than for corporation tax purposes. Charges should be distinguished from business expenses (which are deductible from receipts in calculating income profits rather than from overall taxable profits once calculated). A charge on income is deducted when paid, whereas a business expense is deducted when it accrues due.

15.2.4 CAPITAL ALLOWANCES

Companies are entitled to claim the allowances at the same rates as individuals (see **Chapter 17**). Capital allowances of companies are treated as trading expenses of the accounting period in respect of which they are claimed, and balancing charges are treated as trading receipts of that period.

15.2.5 CAPITAL GAINS

Capital gains realised by companies are calculated according to general capital gains tax principles (see **Chapter 14**). However, there are certain key points to note:

- Companies are not entitled to the annual exemption.

- Companies do not receive the benefit of taper relief.

- Companies do, however, receive full indexation allowance.

- Most reliefs available to individuals, for example retirement relief, are not available to companies, with the exception that companies can claim roll-over relief on the replacement of business assets.

Retaining appreciating assets in a company can lead to an element of double taxation since, on realisation of the asset, the company pays tax (subject to the relief for replacement assets). The company's gain after tax may be reflected in an increase in the value of the company's assets. This will cause the value of the shares in the company to increase which will result in a greater gain being realised (subject to exemptions and reliefs) on a subsequent disposal of shares by the shareholder.

15.3 Assessment — Corporation Tax

15.3.1 BASIS OF ASSESSMENT

Although income tax and capital gains tax rules are used to calculate the amount of profit, the basis of assessment for corporation tax is quite different from either of those taxes. For corporation tax purposes, tax is calculated by reference to profits (that is, the aggregate income and capital profits) made in each accounting period of the company (s. 12 ICTA 1988). An accounting period is normally 12 months ending with the company's accounting date, that is, the date to which its accounts are made up. If the accounts are made up for a period of less than 12 months, then the accounting period is also less than 12 months; if for a longer period, special rules apply and the profits are divided on a time basis between two or more accounting periods, none of which may be longer than 12 months.

Corporation tax is currently payable nine months after the end of the accounting period so that the date chosen does not affect the length of time between the end of the period and the date of payment. However, large companies are obliged to account for corporation tax on an instalment basis. (A large company is treated as one which has annual profits of not less than £1.5 million.) Such instalments are payable on the seventh and tenth months of the accounting period being assessed and on the thirteenth and sixteenth months thereafter.

> **Example** Wolfe Industrials plc has an accounting reference date of 31 December. In relation to its accounting year ending on 31 December 2001 its corporation tax payments will be payable in July and October 2001 and January and April 2002.

The onus is on the companies concerned to estimate their profits for the purpose of making tax payments. Where under- or over-payments of tax are made, interest (at rates set by statutory instrument) will be payable.

Since 30 September 1993, companies have been required to make their own assessments of their liability to corporation tax. This pay and file system requires companies to determine their own tax liabilities and to submit a return together with accounts to substantiate this. Companies have up to 12 months from the end of each of their accounting periods to submit this return but must always satisfy their tax liabilities within the times mentioned above.

15.3.2 RATES OF TAX

15.3.2.1 Main rate

The rates of corporation tax for the year 2001/2002 are set out in the table below.

Rate	Company profits (£)
Starting rate: 10%	0–10,000
Marginal relief	10,001–50,000
Small companies rate: 20%	50,001–300,000
Marginal relief	300,001–1,500,000
Main rate	1,500,001 or more

The following paragraphs detail the way in which these rates operate.

Although companies pay tax on the profits of their own accounting periods, the rate of tax is fixed for financial years, that is, periods starting on 1 April and ending on the following 31 March. For the financial year 2001 (i.e., the period 1 April 2001 to 31 March 2002) the main rate is 30%.

THE CORPORATION TAX SYSTEM

Unless the company happens to make up its accounts to 31 March the profits will have to be apportioned (on a time basis) between two financial years if the rate changes.

> **Example** A company makes up its accounts to 31 December. Its profits for the accounting period ending on 31 December 1999 were £1,600,000 — the rate of corporation tax for the financial year 1998 (1 April 1998–31 March 1999) was 31% and for the financial year 1999 (1 April 1999–31 March 2000) the rate was 30%. Corporation tax for the accounting period would be:
>
> £
>
> $\frac{90}{365} \times 1{,}600{,}000 \times 31\% = 122{,}301.34$
>
> $\frac{275}{365} \times 1{,}600{,}000 \times 30\% = 361{,}643.79$
>
> 483,945.13

15.3.2.2 Small companies' rate

Although the main rate of corporation tax for the financial year 2001 is 30%, s. 13 ICTA 1988 makes provision for a reduced small companies' rate. The rate for the financial year 2001 is 20% and applies where the profits are greater than £50,000 (see **15.3.2.3** below) but do not exceed £300,000 (the 'lower relevant maximum amount'). Where profits exceed the 'higher relevant maximum amount' (£1,500,000 for the financial year 2001) all profits, not just the excess over that figure, are taxed at the main rate of 30%. Where the amount of the profits falls between the two maximum amounts the effective rate of tax is between the small companies' and main rates of tax. In such a case the rate can be calculated for 2000 by treating the first £300,000 as taxable at 20% and the balance up to £1,500,000 as taxable at an effective rate of 32.5%. This rate is known as the marginal rate.

> **Example**
> Clarke Knitwear Limited has total taxable profits of £600,000 for the accounting year being assessed as follows:
>
> £0–300,000   × 20%   = £60,000
> £300,000–600,000   × 32.5%   = £97,500
> Total tax   = £157,500
>
> It should be noted that the marginal rate of 32.5% is not an actual rate of corporation tax but is the by-product of what is known as marginal relief, an explanation of which is given in **15.3.2.4** below. The marginal relief formula applied to the above profits results in exactly the same liablity to corporation tax:
>
> £600,000   × 30%   = £180,000
> Marginal relief   = (£1,500,000 − £600,000) × (600,000/600,000) × 1/40
>   = £22,500
>
> Deducting the marginal relief from tax liability at the full rate gives a figure of £157,500.
>
> It is obviously much easier in these circumstances to apply the marginal rate. However, it is not always possible to do so, as explained in **15.3.2.4** below.

THE CORPORATION TAX SYSTEM

15.3.2.3 Starting rate of corporation tax

For the financial year beginning on 1 April 2001, there is a starting rate of corporation tax of 10% on taxable profits of up to £10,000. For those companies with taxable profits from £10,001 to £50,000, there will be marginal relief available. The fraction for calculating this relief will be one-fortieth, giving an effective marginal rate of 22.5%. Companies with profits between £50,000 and £300,000 will continue to pay corporation tax at the small companies' rate of 20%.

> **Example**
> Metro Kitchens Limited has total taxable profits of £30,000 for the accounting year being assessed as follows:
>
> | | | |
> |---|---|---|
> | £0–10,000 | × 10% | = £1,000 |
> | £10,000–30,000 | × 22.5% | = £4,500 |
> | Total tax | | = £5,500 |
>
> Again, the application of the marginal rate produces the same result as the application of the formula for marginal relief:
>
> | | | |
> |---|---|---|
> | £30,000 | × 20% | = £6,000 |
> | Marginal relief | | = (£50,000 − £30,000) × (30,000/30,000) × 1/40 |
> | | | = £500 |
>
> Deducting the marginal relief from tax liability at the small companies' rate of 20% gives a figure of £5,500.

15.3.2.4 Profits in the form of dividends

Where a company's profits include dividends from another company the situation is more complex. The first matter to note is that these dividends are not actually taxable in the hands of the recipient company. However, they do impact on those profits which are taxable because they must be included in the company's profits total to determine whether or not that company benefits from the small companies' rate.

The law provides that if taxable profits *including dividends* fall within the bands in which marginal relief applies (£10,001–£50,000 — see table in **15.3.2.1** above), they should be taxed at small companies' rate of 20% or main rate of 30% respectively. The resulting liability will then be reduced by marginal relief in the manner set out below. Should profits including dividends be £10,000 or less, between £50,000 and £300,001, or more than £1,500,000 then marginal relief is irrelevant and the normal rates apply. This is summarised in the table below.

Profits *including dividends* (£)	Rate of tax
0–10,000	Starting rate: 10%
10,001–50,000	Small companies' rate: 20% *then* reduced by marginal relief
50,001–300,000	Small companies' rate: 20%
300,001–1,500,000	Main rate: 30% *then* reduced by marginal relief
More than 1,500,000	Main rate: 30%

THE CORPORATION TAX SYSTEM

For the purposes of this rule, dividends do not include dividends paid from another company in the same group as the recipient. It is beyond the scope of the book to examine what constitutes a 'group', suffice it to say that a common example of a payment within a group would be from a wholly-owned subsidiary to its parent.

To establish the amount of marginal relief, the following statutory formula must be applied:

$(M - P) \times (I/P) \times$ Statutory Fraction

Where:
M = Higher relevant maximum amount
P = Total profits including non-group dividends
I = Profits excluding non-group dividends
Statutory Fraction = 1/40 (set each year by the Finance Act)

The basic result of this formula is that the higher the proportion of total profits which is made up of dividends, the less marginal relief available for the actual profits taxed.

Example In the financial year 2001, Fallon Limited has trading profits of £300,000 and gross dividend receipts (non-group) of £200,000. Although such dividends will not be taxed in the hands of Fallon Limited, it is not possible simply to tax the first £300,000 at 20% and ignore the balance.

Applying the statutory formula, the corporation tax liability will be £78,000. This is because tax at 30% on the trading profits of £300,000 is £90,000 and marginal relief reduces this by £15,000 to £75,000. The amount of marginal relief is calculated as follows:

£
(1,500,000 − 500,000) × 300,000/500,000 = 600,000
600,000 × 1/40   = 15,000

It will be noted that 20% of £300,000 is £60,000, so dividends, although not actually taxable, have a considerable impact on the company's tax liability.

15.4 Loss Relief under the Corporation Tax System

15.4.1 INTRODUCTION

Trading losses of companies are relieved in a number of ways; the scheme of the legislation is very similar to the one which applies for income tax (see **Chapter 13**).

15.4.2 CARRY FORWARD

Under s. 393 ICTA 1988, a company can carry forward a trading loss and use it to reduce profits derived from the same trade in future accounting periods. The claim for relief under this section must be made within six years of the end of the accounting period in which the loss was made. This relief is similar to s. 385 for sole traders or partners.

THE CORPORATION TAX SYSTEM

> To illustrate the application of s. 393, the company has an accounting period corresponding with calendar years and its profits and losses are as follows:
>
> | | Trade I
£ | Trade II
£ | Capital Gains
£ |
> |---|---|---|---|
> | 1996 | 75,000 | 25,000 | Nil |
> | 1997 | 100,000 | 50,000 | Nil |
> | 1998 | 100,000 | 50,000 | 20,000 |
> | 1999 | (300,000) loss | 50,000 | 30,000 |
> | 2000 | 100,000 | 50,000 | Nil |
> | 2001 | 200,000 | 50,000 | Nil |
>
> Under s. 393 the £300,000 loss incurred in Trade I in 1999 can only be carried forward against future profits of that same trade. Therefore, the profits made by Trade I in 2000 and 2001 will be wiped out but the profits from Trade II and the capital gains realised in the years 1999, 2000 and 2001 will all remain taxable.

15.4.3 USE WITHIN SAME ACCOUNTING PERIOD

In addition to or instead of the relief given by s. 393, a company may set off a loss made during an accounting period against any profits of the same accounting period if a claim for relief is made within two years of the end of the accounting period in which the loss was made. 'Profits' for corporation tax include both income and capital gains so that the company may set an income loss (from a trade) against a chargeable capital gain. If the loss is not entirely relieved by setting it off against profits of the same accounting period in which the loss was made, the company may also make a claim requiring the unrelieved part of the loss to be set against profits (including capital gains) for the immediately previous accounting period (s. 393A ICTA 1988). A loss cannot be carried back under this provision to a period when the company was not carrying on the business and there are no corporation tax provisions corresponding with s. 381 ICTA 1988 (income tax loss relief for the early years of a new trade). Where relief is being claimed in respect of a loss which has been carried back under this provision, the carried back loss will be taken into account before charges on income incurred in the earlier accounting period are deducted but any loss made in the earlier year is taken before the carried back loss.

To illustrate the application of ss. 393 and 393A and using the figures set out in **15.4.2**, the £300,000 loss made in Trade I in 1999 can be used to wipe out the Trade II profits and capital gains for that year, resulting in a loss to be carried back of £220,000. Total profits for 1998 amount to £170,000, resulting in £50,000 of the loss being unrelieved. This may then be carried forward against the profits for Trade I in 2000.

15.4.4 TACTICAL CONSIDERATIONS

In deciding which method of relief to use, the company will wish to ensure, so far as possible, that the maximum tax saving is achieved (by setting the loss against those profits which are subject to tax at 30% rather than any lower rate). However, the cashflow problem of having to meet a tax bill at a time when the cash reserves may be low often means that it is preferable not to carry forward the relief but to claim the relief as soon as possible.

The possibility of carrying forward losses is lost in certain cases where there are substantial changes in both the ownership of the company and in the nature of its trade. This is an anti-avoidance provision designed to prevent the purchase of a company simply to take advantage of its tax losses.

THE CORPORATION TAX SYSTEM

15.4.5 CAPITAL LOSSES

If a company makes a capital loss (calculated in the same way as a capital gain), it may be set off against capital gains of the same accounting period and, if unrelieved, may be carried forward and set off against capital gains of later accounting periods. Although trading losses may be set off against capital gains there are no provisions allowing capital losses to be set off against income profits.

15.4.6 GROUP RELIEF

Section 402 ICTA 1988 makes provision for group relief. In outline, where a company is a member of a group it may surrender its loss to another company in the same group. The latter then deducts the loss from its profits as if it were its own loss. Companies are in the same group, broadly speaking, if one is the 75% subsidiary of the other or both are 75% subsidiaries of a third company.

15.5 Close Companies

15.5.1 DEFINITION

A close company is a company controlled by five or fewer participators or any number of participators who are also directors (s. 414 ICTA 1988). 'Participators' are shareholders, loan creditors and certain others entitled to participate in the distributed income of the company. 'Control' includes, inter alia, ownership of a majority of the share capital or a majority of the votes or a right to a majority of the dividends. In assessing control, the rights of 'associates' must be added to the rights of a participator — associates include, among others, the participator's spouse, parents, remoter forebears, children, remoter issue, brothers and sisters. The above definition is only a very brief summary but it is sufficient to show that nearly all private companies are close companies (for example, if a company has nine or fewer shareholders, it must be under the control of some five of them even if none of them is related to each other — it will therefore be a close company unless it falls into one of the small number of cases excluded from the definition).

15.5.2 TAXATION CONSIDERATIONS

Close companies are subject to certain special tax rules. These are designed to prevent the use of the company as a vehicle for tax avoidance.

If a loan is made to a participator or his associate, then under s. 419 ICTA 1988 the company must pay a levy equal to 25% of the loan within nine months of the end of the accounting period in which the loan was made. This currently means that for every £4 lent an additional £1 must be paid to the Revenue. The levy will be repaid to the company whenever the loan is repaid, waived or written off.

If the borrower pays back the debt in full, no taxation issues arise for the borrower. (Except, perhaps, for the fact that any interest which has been foregone or which has been paid at less than the official rate, may result in an income tax liability for the debtor based on that sum.) However, if the loan is written-off or waived by the company, the borrower benefits from a 'windfall'. As such, income tax will be payable. If the borrower is a basic rate taxpayer, no extra tax will be payable. However, if the borrower is a higher rate taxpayer, the amount written-off will be grossed up at the 10% rate of income tax and the resulting sum taxed at 32.5%.

One very important exception is that the above rules do not apply if the amount of the loan does not exceed £15,000 and the borrower owns less than a 5% shareholding in the company.

THE CORPORATION TAX SYSTEM

Remember that loans to directors are generally prohibited by s. 330 CA 1985 (see **8.7.2.3**).

If close companies provide living accommodation or other 'benefits in kind' for a participator or his associates the company will be treated as making distribution. This charge will *not* apply if the recipient of the benefit is subject to the normal benefit in kind rules under Schedule E. It is, therefore, designed to ensure that the provision of such benefits to shareholders who are neither directors nor higher paid employees of the company is assessed to tax. If a charge is applicable, the cost of providing these benefits is treated like any other 'distribution' (see **Chapter 16**).

If the close company is a 'close investment holding company', the small companies rate of corporation tax will not be available. The company will instead pay corporation tax on its profits, whatever the amount, at the full rate. To fall within this category of close companies, the company must not be a trading company nor a member of a trading group. Companies which deal in land, shares or securities and companies carrying on property investment on a commercial basis are all treated as trading companies and so outside the scope of this anti-avoidance provision.

Companies are not normally liable to inheritance tax if they make gifts. However, if a close company makes a gift (or other transfer of value) this is deemed to be a gift made by all the shareholders in the company (except those with very small interests) in proportion to their shareholdings. If the shareholders fail to pay inheritance tax on this deemed gift, the company becomes liable (ss. 94–102 and 202 IHTA 1984).

SIXTEEN

TAXATION OF RETAINED PROFITS, DIVIDENDS, DIRECTORS' FEES AND DEBENTURE INTEREST

This chapter covers the following topics:

16.1 Introduction
16.2 Retained profits
16.3 Taxation of distributions
16.4 Directors' fees
16.5 Interest on debentures
16.6 Conclusion.

16.1 Introduction

In **Chapter 15** we looked at the corporation tax system for charging companies tax on their profits (or allowing them relief on their losses). Assuming that the company makes profits, the company has three main ways of dealing with those profits:

(a) retaining them in the business;

(b) paying them as dividends to the shareholders; or

(c) paying directors' fees.

If profits are retained in the business, the proprietors ought to benefit in the long run as the capital value of the company (and thus the value of the shares in it) will increase. The payment of a dividend can be looked at as a 'reward' to the shareholders for their investment in the company. Indeed, as regards companies whose shares are traded on the Stock Exchange, the regularity and size of a dividend may influence potential investors to choose that company. With regard to smaller, private companies, dividends are one method of extracting profits, as the shareholders will normally only be involved because of the opportunity to enjoy the rewards of profitability.

A company is not entirely free to choose between the different uses of profits. Firstly, it may be contractually bound to make payments of interest and directors' fees. Secondly, there are company rules which prevent the company from paying dividends except to the extent of profits available for the purpose. (The reason for this is that the original investment made in

TAXATION OF RETAINED PROFITS

the company by shareholders may not be returned to them, except in limited circumstances, until the company is wound up.) Thirdly, it will often be commercially unwise for a company to pay out all of its profits since some will be required to provide for future contingencies or for the expansion of the business.

In this chapter, we will consider the tax consequences of each method of using profits. The company rules dealing with the distribution of profits are set out at **9.11** and **9.12** and those relating to the company's power to borrow are set out at **10.6**. We will not repeat those rules in this chapter.

16.2 Retained Profits

16.2.1 CORPORATION TAX

Profits retained by the company are liable to corporation tax at the rates explained in **Chapter 15**. It does not generally matter why the profits are retained, although sums used for certain types of capital expenditure are eligible for relief under the capital allowance system (see **Chapter 17**).

16.2.2 FUTURE TAXATION OF RETAINED PROFITS

The only tax liability on retained profits *at the time they are made* is corporation tax. However, such profits will usually be subject to tax at some time in the future. Thus, if those profits are distributed in a later year Schedule F tax will be payable by the recipient shareholders. If the profits are retained for many years they will be reflected in the value of the shares in the company so that CGT and IHT liability on disposal of the shares will be increased (capital tax liability on disposal of shares is considered in **Chapter 14**).

16.3 Taxation of Distributions

16.3.1 DEFINITION OF DISTRIBUTION

A shareholder is liable to income tax under Schedule F on any 'distribution' which he receives in respect of shares. The definition of distribution for this purpose is extremely complicated but the following types of receipt are the most important of those included in the definition:

(a) any dividend paid by the company including a capital dividend (s. 209(2)(a) ICTA 1988);

(b) any other distribution out of assets of the company ... in respect of shares ... (s. 209(2)(b));

(c) any interest on securities (e.g., debentures) where the interest varies with the profits of the company (s. 209(d)(iii));

(d) in some circumstances, the issue of bonus shares following a reduction of share capital or the repayment of share capital after a bonus issue.

It should be noted that an issue of bonus shares (that is, shares treated as paid up out of the profits of the company) is not a distribution for tax purposes unless share capital has previously been reduced. However, if the shareholders are given a *choice* between receiving a cash dividend (which is, of course, a distribution) or bonus shares, those who choose to take the bonus shares are taxed on the amount of cash dividend forgone in almost the same way as if it were a distribution (s. 249 ICTA 1988).

When a company redeems or purchases its own shares there is usually a tax liability on the members (this topic is dealt with in **Chapter 14**).

16.3.2 TAX CONSEQUENCES OF THE PAYMENT OF A DIVIDEND

The payment of a dividend or other distribution is neither an expense of a company's business nor a charge on its income. The amount of any dividend paid does not, therefore, reduce a company's liability to corporation tax.

16.3.2.1 Advance corporation tax

Until 5 April 1999, companies were required to pay advance corporation tax ('ACT') on qualifying distributions at a rate which for 1998/99 was equivalent to ¼ of the distribution. The requirement to pay ACT was abolished from 6 April 1999. However, there are tax consequences which, for some companies, may continue to flow from this requirement.

When a company was required to pay ACT, this had to be done within, at the most, three months of the payment of a distribution and within 14 days of assessment. This meant that payments of ACT could be made during the course of an accounting period. The company could later set off any ACT paid against its overall corporation tax bill for that accounting period. This was, however, limited to a maximum of '... the amount of advance corporation tax ... in respect of a distribution ... of an amount which, together with the advance corporation tax so payable in respect of it, is equal to the company's profits charged to corporation tax for that period'. (On 1998/99 tax rates, this was equivalent to 20% of the company's profits for the accounting year in question.) It was therefore possible for a company to be unable to set off all its ACT.

> **Example** A company had income profits of £2.2 million in the accounting period ending 31 March 1998 and paid a dividend of £2 million. ACT was £500,000. To establish whether or not all of this ACT could be set-off against the year-end MCT bill, the above-mentioned rule was applied to find the amount of theoretical dividend, which, when aggregated with ACT thereon, equalled profits of £2.2 million. This sum is £1,760,000, which, when added together with ACT thereon of £440,000, gives £2.2 million. This calculation established the maximum amount of ACT set-off. The result here is that the company had an ACT liablity during the year of £500,000 and a corporation tax liability of £682,000 (£2.2 million × 31%) against which only £440,000 of ACT could be set-off.

In the above example, the company 'overpaid' corporation tax to the extent of £60,000. Any such amount was known as surplus advance corporation tax ('SACT'). SACT could be carried back to the company's six previous accounting periods (taking latest periods first) and reclaimed to the extent that *gross* distributions in those years were less than income profits. If the SACT could not be reclaimed, it could be carried forward without time limit and used to pay ACT in future accounting periods (subject to the same maximum limit as to the amount which could be set off). The overall effect of these rules was that a company which paid gross distributions in excess of its income profits would suffer a cash flow disadvantage. However, the ability to use SACT would ensure that the overall amount of corporation tax would not be increased in the long run.

The long term effect of these rules is that, notwithstanding the abolition of ACT, there remain a number of companies with SACT. To ensure that these companies are not disadvantaged, a system is in place to allow them to use their SACT. It works as follows:

TAXATION OF RETAINED PROFITS

(a) The existing maximum set-off limits for ACT remain.

(b) A deemed amount of ACT (known as shadow ACT) is calculated on dividends paid after 6 April 1999. This amount is not actually paid but is deducted from the maximum set-off limit to determine the amount of SACT which can be set off against corporation tax.

> **Example** Coverdale Electronics Limited pays a dividend of £20,000 during its accounting period 1 January 2000–31 December 2000. Its taxable profits in that same period are £160,000 and it has SACT of £30,000. Under the new system:
>
> (a) Maximum SACT set-off during this year will be £32,000 (20% × £160,000).
> (b) There will be shadow ACT of £5,000 (1/4 × £20,000);
> (c) The amount of SACT which can be set-off against MCT for the accounting period will be £27,000 (£32,000 – £5,000).
> (d) The unrelieved balance of SACT will be carried forward to the next accounting period.

16.3.3 TAXATION OF A RECIPIENT OF A DIVIDEND

16.3.3.1 Corporate recipient

Where a UK company receives a dividend or other distribution from another, the general rule is that these sums are not subject to corporation tax in the hands of the recipient.

16.3.3.2 Individual recipient

An individual shareholder who receives a dividend from a company is treated, for tax purposes as receiving a sum equivalent to the actual dividend *plus* a tax credit. The latter is equivalent to 10% of the dividend as grossed up by a tax credit fraction. The current fraction is 10/90.

> **Example**
>
> Shareholder receives a dividend of £500. For tax purposes, he is treated as receiving:
>
> | | |
> |---|---:|
> | The actual dividend | £500 |
> | *plus* | |
> | 10% of £500 grossed up (i.e., £500 plus (10/90 × £500)) | £55.56 |
> | Total | £555.56 |

The shareholder is liable to pay tax on this amount under Schedule F. From 6 April 1999, the lower and basic tax for individuals on dividends is 10%, with the higher rate at 32.5%.

Dividend income is treated as the top slice of the shareholder's income. Where dividend income falls entirely within the lower or basic rate bands of taxable income, the tax credit will satisfy their liability to tax. If dividend income falls entirely within the higher rate band of income, an additional amount of 32.5% of the grossed-up dividend will be due from the shareholder. Where the income cuts across the basic and higher rate bands, the dividend must be apportioned between them and the tax credit deducted from the resulting sum. The balance will be the amount of tax outstanding. Should a shareholder not be liable to tax, there is no ability to claim a repayment of the tax credit.

> **Examples**
>
> *Example 1*
>
> A has taxable income of £15,000 and receives a gross dividend of £555.56 (i.e., £500 cash plus tax credit of £55.56). The total dividend falls within the basic rate income tax band. Tax is therefore:
>
> £555.56 × 10% = £55.56
>
> The tax liability is fully satisfied by the tax credit.
>
> *Example 2*
>
> B has taxable income of £32,000 and receives a gross dividend of £1,666.67 (i.e., £1,500 cash plus tax credit of £166.67). The total dividend falls within the higher rate income tax band. Tax is therefore:
>
> £1,666.67 × 32.5% = £541.67
>
> The tax liability is satisfied to the extent of the tax credit, i.e., £166.67. The shareholder is required to pay the remaining tax due of £375. (N.B., £375 is equivalent to 22.5% of £1,666.67.)
>
> *Example 3*
>
> C has taxable income of £27,000 and receives a gross dividend of £3,333.34 (i.e., £3,000 cash plus tax credit of £333.34). The dividend falls within both the basic and higher rate income tax bands. Tax is payable as follows:
>
> £2,400 × £10% = £240
> £933.34 × 32.5% = £303.34
> Total tax payable = £543.34
>
> The tax liability is satisfied as to the extent of the tax credit, i.e., £333.34. The shareholder is required to pay the remaining tax due of £210.

16.4 Directors' Fees

16.4.1 THE EMPLOYING COMPANY'S PERSPECTIVE

16.4.1.1 General

If a trade or profession is carried on through the medium of a company, the company will want to ensure that any payment of salary, pension or compensation for loss of office or any provision of a benefit in kind entitles it to claim a pre-tax deduction so as to reduce its profits taxable under Schedule D Cases I or II. It will be remembered from **Chapter 13** that to be deductible, any expense must satisfy two conditions, namely that the payments must be:

(a) of an income nature as opposed to a capital outlay; and

(b) incurred wholly and exclusively for the purpose of the trade or profession and must not fall within any of the disallowed deductions listed in the ICTA 1988.

TAXATION OF RETAINED PROFITS

In this section of the chapter, we will look at the tax rules as they apply to the payments to directors of companies but the rules can apply to other employees (including employees of sole proprietors or partnerships).

16.4.1.2 Limitation on deductibility

The payments that *are* deductible include the payment of salaries, wages, pensions and even lump sum payments in compensation for loss of the employee's office. However, this is subject to certain qualifications.

(a) *'Wholly'*

In respect of all such payments, the word 'wholly' in s. 74 relates to quantum, so that excessive payments cannot be deducted. In *Copeman* v *William J. Flood and Sons Ltd* [1941] 1 KB 202, it was decided that where such a payment is held to be excessive, such proportion of the payment as is reasonable in the light of the employee's work can be deducted.

With regard to pensions, the pension paid to an ex-employee is deductible even if it is paid voluntarily by the employer. In practice most employers who provide pensions do so by setting up a fund managed by an insurance company. Contributions paid into the fund by the employer are deductible as business expenses provided that the scheme is a retirement benefit scheme as defined by s. 590 ICTA 1988.

(b) *Compensation for loss of office*

Lump sum payments for loss of office are deductible provided they satisfy the conditions set out above, even though they may be one-off payments. Thus, in *Mitchell* v *B. W. Noble Ltd* [1927] KB 719, compensation payments made to directors who were liable to dismissal because of their misconduct but who resigned to avoid bad publicity, were held to be deductible on the basis that the retirement was in the interests of the business. Conversely, payments made to former employees to persuade them to enter into restrictive covenants have been held not to be deductible, since the payments were intended to buy off potential competitors and so amounted to a capital payment (*Associated Portland Cement* v *Kerr* (1945) 27 TC 108 (CA)). This position has now been changed statutorily, such that the payment will be both taxable as income in the hands of the recipient and an income deductible expense for the company (see **16.4.2.5** below). If the employee is redundant and receives a redundancy payment, s. 579 ICTA 1988 provides that such payments are deductible under Schedule D Cases I and II and are treated as having been paid on the last day on which the business was carried on if made after the discontinuance of the trade, profession or vocation.

(c) *The provision of benefits*

Many employers provide their employees with benefits over and above their salary, such as company cars, free meals and so on. The cost of providing such benefits will be deductible if the payments are made wholly and exclusively for the purposes of the trade. Thus if cars are provided for salesmen, the outlay will be deductible, but if they are for private use they will only be deductible if they can be regarded as reasonable remuneration.

16.4.1.3 Social security contributions

Although it is beyond the scope of this book to consider the social security legislation in detail, it should be noted that the employer is obliged to make national insurance contributions in respect of each employee (as well as deducting the contributions of the employee before

TAXATION OF RETAINED PROFITS

paying over the net wages). The employer's contributions are deductible in computing the tax liability of the employer.

16.4.2 THE EMPLOYEE'S PERSPECTIVE

16.4.2.1 The Schedule E charge

Under s. 19 ICTA 1988, as amended, tax under Schedule E is charged in respect of *emoluments* from an *office* or *employment* as well as pensions and income (such as compensation payments) specifically charged to tax under the schedule. Tax is collected on a receipts year basis. That is to say, the employee pays tax on the emoluments received during the tax year whether or not they are earned in that year or in some other year. The tax is usually collected by deduction at source under the PAYE scheme.

(a) *Office*

The word 'office' is not defined in the statutes but Rowlatt J in *Great Western Railway Co.* v *Bater* [1920] 3 KB 266, said it meant 'a subsisting, permanent, substantive position which had an existence independent of the person who filled it, which went on and was filled in succession by successive holders', although Lord Wilberforce and Lord Lowry, in *Edwards* v *Clinch* [1981] 3 All ER 543, felt the definition should be refined. Lord Wilberforce accepted 'that a rigid requirement of permanence is no longer appropriate ... and continuity need not be regarded as an absolute qualification. But still, if any meaning is to be given to 'office' in this legislation ... the word must involve a degree of continuance (not necessarily continuity) and of independent existence: it must connote a post to which a person can be appointed, which he can vacate and to which a successor can be appointed'. Over the years office holders have been held to include directors of UK companies, NHS consultants, bishops, judges and personal representatives.

(b) *Employment*

'Employment' is equally difficult to define, but Pennycuick V-C said in *Fall* v *Hitchen* [1973] 1 All ER 368, that, 'unless some special limitation is to be put upon the word 'employment' in any given context, the expression 'contract of service' appears to be coterminous with the expression 'employment''. The case involved a ballet dancer who entered into a contract having the attributes of a contract of service, in that he was paid weekly regardless of whether a performance was given or a rehearsal attended, the 'employer' paid national insurance contributions on the dancer's behalf as if he were an employee and the dancer worked only for the employer. This contract was therefore assessable under Schedule E, even though it had been entered into in the normal course of carrying on his profession of dancer. Conversely, if it can be shown that the taxpayer's method of earning a livelihood does not consist of obtaining a post and remaining in it (as was the case in *Fall* v *Hitchen*), but consists of engagements and moving from one engagement to another, he is assessed under Schedule D and not Schedule E, provided the engagements are entered into as part of his profession (*Davies* v *Braithwaite* [1931] 2 KB 628).

(c) *Emolument*

Section 131 of ICTA 1988 defines emoluments as including 'all salaries, fees, wages, perquisites and profits whatsoever'. To be assessable the emoluments must arise out of the office or employment and be in money or convertible into money (although there are special statutory rules dealing with benefits in kind which are dealt with below).

TAXATION OF RETAINED PROFITS

16.4.2.2 Taxable receipts by employees

(a) *What is taxable?*

A director or other employee who receives salary or wages from his employer is obviously assessable under Schedule E. Gifts, bonuses or tips, will be taxable if the taxpayer holds an office or employment and the receipt derives from the employment even if paid by third parties. A pension paid to a former director or employee (or his dependants) is taxable under Schedule E even if it is voluntary or can be discontinued.

(b) *Payments made on employee's behalf*

Such payments will be assessable if the employer discharges a debt owed by the director or employee (*Nicholl* v *Austin* (1935) 19 TC 531).

16.4.2.3 Benefits in kind

(a) *The general rule*

The emoluments on which an employee is assessed to tax may include 'perquisites' as well as salary or wages. (The term 'perquisites' in this context includes assets or benefits provided by the employer.) For such receipts to be assessable emoluments, according to normal tax principles, they must be in the form of money or convertible into money (although it is not necessary that the asset or non-cash benefit *is* actually converted into money). Thus, free meals in a staff canteen fail this convertibility test (and so are tax-free) since the employee cannot sell the meal; the mere fact that it saves the employee money is not enough. However, a cash allowance in lieu of such a benefit attracts a tax charge (*Sanderson* v *Durbridge* (1955) 36 TC 239).

(b) *The amount taxed*

If the benefit is convertible into money, the employee is taxed on the monetary value of the benefit to him at the time it was received. This was held, in *Wilkins* v *Rogerson* [1961] Ch 7 (where suits were provided for employees) to mean that the employee should be assessed on the second-hand value of the benefit. If the emolument is a benefit in the form of money (such as a cash allowance), the cash value of the benefit will be the taxable emolument.

(c) *Replacement by statute*

These rules make the provision of benefits in kind very attractive since the employees who receive them will either not be taxed at all on them (because their nature is such that they cannot be converted into cash) or be taxed on the second-hand value of the asset (which in the case of clothes, cars and similar items will be considerably less than the 'new value' of the asset). Therefore, to prevent abuse, various statutory provisions have been introduced (these are considered below). While, strictly speaking, the convertibility test applies to all employees, effectively the test is superseded when the special rules apply (see paragraphs (d) and (e) immediately below).

(d) *Statutory rules applicable to all employees*

(i) *Living accommodation*

Under s. 145 ICTA 1988, an employee who occupies premises by reason of his employment is taxed on the greater of the rent paid by his employer or the 'annual value' of the accommodation less the rent actually paid by the employee. 'Annual value' means the market rent that could be obtained for the premises on the assumption that the landlord will bear the costs of repair and insurance (s. 837 ICTA 1988).

Under s. 146 ICTA 1988, employees who receive the benefit of taxable living accommodation which costs more than £75,000 to provide will be treated as receiving an emolument equal to the official rate of interest (which will be kept in line with typical mortgage rates) on the excess over the £75,000 limit (less any rent paid in excess of the annual value of the accommodation calculated as above).

(ii) *Vouchers*

Where vouchers, stamps or similar documents are provided, which can be converted into money or goods, the employee is taxed on the cost of providing the voucher, etc., incurred by the employer (s. 141 ICTA 1988).

(e) *The statutory rules applicable to directors and higher-paid employees*

(i) *The persons subject to the rules*

Where the recipient of a benefit is a 'director or higher-paid employee', certain provisions of ICTA 1988 as amended by FA 1989 apply. Under s. 167 the special rules apply if the taxpayer receiving the benefit is an employee earning £8,500 per annum or more or a director.

For the purpose of deciding whether an employee is earning over £8,500, it is assumed that the special rules apply, (i.e., that the cost of providing the benefit incurred by the employer is added to the employee's salary). Thus if an employee earning £8,400 is given a suit that cost the employer £250 to buy, the cost to the employer is added to his salary to make his emoluments £8,650 and therefore sufficient to make him a 'higher-paid employee' for all purposes. This will be the case even if the second-hand value of the suit was only £50. Furthermore, although the special rules only apply to benefits provided for the director or employee by reason of his employment, s. 168 ICTA 1988 prevents the tax charge being avoided by giving the benefit to the director's or employee's family.

(ii) *The special rules*

—Expense accounts. Under s. 153 ICTA 1988 if an expense account is provided, the director or employee is taxed on its full amount less any expenses incurred wholly, exclusively and necessarily in the course of his employment. Thus, if, for example, the employee has an expense allowance of £1,000 and he uses only £750 'wholly, exclusively and necessarily in the course of his employment' and the rest for his personal benefit, he adds £250 to his taxable emoluments. (See **16.4.2.6**.)

—Benefits given to employees and directors. In the case of other benefits in kind which are given outright to the employee, he is treated as receiving emoluments equal to the 'cash equivalent' of the asset, which means the cost to the employer of providing them less any sums paid by the employee.

—Company cars. The 'cash equivalent' is added to the employee's emoluments where a car is made available for use by the director or higher paid employee or their families is based on 35% of the list price of the car. (The market value of the car is the basis of the charge if the car is 15 years or more old and worth £15,000 or more.) The 'cash equivalent' is reduced to 25% if the employee does at least

TAXATION OF RETAINED PROFITS

2,500 business miles per year and to 15% where the business mileage exceeds 18,000. The resulting 'cash equivalent' is further reduced by one-quarter if the car is four years or more old at the end of the relevant tax year. Cars taken from a pool do not attract the tax charge. The provision of car fuel attracts a charge to tax subject to certain limitations.

At the time of writing, the Government has announced its intention to alter this system radically from 6 April 2002. The main change will be that the taxable amount will be based on a percentage of the car's value, the percentage being determined by the car's carbon dioxide emissions. The percentage limits will be a minimum of 15% and a maximum of 35%. The discounts for extra mileage and for the age of the car will be abolished.

—Beneficial loan arrangements. Generally, beneficial loans would not be benefits in kind, since they are not convertible into money. However, s. 160 ICTA 1988 provides that if an employer makes an interest-free or cheap loan, the recipient director or employee is taxed on its cash equivalent unless this does not exceed £300 or the loan would qualify for interest relief. The 'cash equivalent' is the difference between the official rate of interest fixed by statutory instrument and the rate paid by the employee (for example, for the tax year 2000/2001 the rate was 6.25%). The tax charge also arises if the loan is made to the director's or employee's relatives unless he personally derives no benefit from the loan.

If any loan is written off in whole or in part, the amount released is treated as a taxable emolument. Where the release is made on the termination of the employment, there is a tax charge unless the release is caused by the director's or employee's death.

16.4.2.4 Terminal payments

(a) *General principles*

The mere fact that the payment is made on the termination of the contract (or the alteration of its terms) does not preclude its taxation under the rules of Schedule E, if it is 'something in the nature of a reward for services, past, present or future' (per Upjohn J in *Hochstrasser* v *Mayes* [1959] Ch 22). As a result of this, sums paid in accordance with the terms of the employment contract will be taxable since they will represent deferred or advance remuneration (*Dale* v *De Soissons* [1950] 2 All ER 460). Thus, if an employee is to be paid £10,000 a year for 10 years but under the contract is to receive a lump sum of £50,000 on either the commencement or termination of the term, the sum is fully taxable under Schedule E (see *Williams* v *Simmonds* [1981] STC 715). However, it is more common for an employee's contract to be terminated and for the employee to be allowed to work out his notice or to be denied this right and paid a lump sum to reflect the money that he would have earned had he been allowed to do so, i.e., a payment in lieu of notice. It is at this point that some important distinctions must be made.

If an employee is allowed to work his notice period or is kept on for the period of his notice, but not allowed to work (so-called 'gardening leave'), the payments made to the employee will be taxable in the usual way. This should be contrasted with the situation where the employee is dismissed without notice and is paid in lieu of notice. Such a payment constitutes damages for breach of contract by the employer, and as such, will not be treated as taxable as an emolument. Instead it will be taxable under s. 148 ICTA 1988 (see (b) below).

Some employment contracts specifically provide the option for an employer to make a payment in lieu rather than give notice. This is in an attempt to avoid the deeming of a breach of contract, thus preserving many of the terms of the contract, specifically any restrictive covenants. Any payment made under such a provision is taxable as an emolument, as it arises from the operation of the contract.

As such, the exact nature of any lump sum termination payment made to an employee needs careful consideration to determine its status for tax purposes.

(b) *Payments under s. 148 ICTA 1988*

A lump sum payment made to an employee on early termination of the contract by the employer which is not assessable under the general principles may be taxable under s. 148 ICTA 1988. This taxes a payment on retirement or removal from office or employment that is not otherwise chargeable to tax (under the general principles), 'which is made, whether in pursuance of any legal obligation or not, either directly or indirectly in consideration or in consequence of, or otherwise in connection with, the termination of the holding of the office or employment or any change in its functions or emoluments, ...'.

Section 148 does not apply if:

(i) the terminal payment is paid on the death, injury or disability of the holder of the office or employment (s. 188(1)(a));

(ii) the sum falls to be taxed under s. 313 (see **16.4.2.5**) (s. 188(1)(b));

(iii) the payment does not exceed £30,000 (s. 188(4)). However, any excess over this figure is taxable and the subsection prevents the tax charge being avoided by paying the terminal payments in instalments.

If a terminal payment exceeds the £30,000 limit, the excess is taxable in the year of receipt as earned income.

A common example of a s. 148 payment is a payment in lieu of notice which amounts to damages for breach of contract (see (a) above). This can lead to the unusual situation that an employee who is paid £25,000 in lieu of notice pursuant to a contractual provision will pay tax on this amount, whereas an employee who is paid the same sum, but which amounts to damages for breach, will pay none.

Another example of payments falling within the ambit of s. 148 are ex gratia payments or 'golden handshakes'.

A terminal payment paid to a director near retirement age needs careful consideration, as such a payment may instead be treated by the Revenue as a payment out of an unapproved pension scheme, in which case it will not attract the £30,000 exemption and will be taxed in full under s. 596A ICTA 1988.

Statutory redundancy payments and, since *Mairs v Haughey* [1993] 3 All ER 801, non-statutory redundancy payments are only taxable under s. 148. However, only genuine redundancy payments are caught. So an attempt to class a payment of less than £30,000 to a director as a redundancy payment to take advantage of s. 188 will be closely scrutinised by the Inland Revenue.

TAXATION OF RETAINED PROFITS

16.4.2.5 Restrictive covenant payments

If an employee receives a payment in consideration of entering into a restrictive covenant, this is regarded as being a capital outlay by the employer. As such, it should be a capital receipt in the hands of the employee and so not taxable as part of the employee's income. However, s. 313 ICTA 1988 levies income tax on such payments. They are fully taxed in the recipient's hands and the paying employer can deduct them when calculating income profits.

16.4.2.6 Expenses

If an employee incurs expenses, they will only be deductible by that employee if they are incurred wholly, exclusively and necessarily in the actual performance of his duties. This is narrower than the expenses rule for Schedule D Case I or II taxpayers. Two separate requirements can be extracted. These rules are of limited practical importance since an employee is usually indemnified by his employer for any such expenses which he incurs.

16.4.2.7 Social security contributions

The contributions deducted by the employer from the employee's salary (see **16.4.1.3**) are not deductible when calculating the employee's tax liability. Employees' contributions are greater than those levied on the self-employed but, in compensation, the benefits available to employees are greater than those available to the self-employed. (The details of the benefits are beyond the scope of this book.)

16.5 Interest on Debentures

16.5.1 INTRODUCTION

Although not mentioned specifically at the start of this chapter, the tax treatment of interest on debentures will be looked at for two reasons:

(a) It should be contrasted with the tax treatment of dividends.

(b) It may influence whether or not an investment is made into the company by way of equity or loan funding.

16.5.2 TAX CONSEQUENCES FOR THE PAYING COMPANY

Interest is a 'payment by time for the use of money' (per Rowlatt J in *Bennett* v *Ogston* (1930) 15 TC 374). A payment of interest by a company will usually result in a tax saving to the company because the interest will be a business expense deductible in computing trading profits.

16.5.2.1 Loan relationships

Since the Finance Act 1996 ('FA'), the taxation treatment of a company's borrowing falls to be dealt with under the provisions relating to 'loan relationships'. For the purpose of s. 81, FA 96, a company has a loan relationship where (inter alia) a 'company stands ... in the position of a ... debtor as respects any money debt' and the debt 'is one arising from a transaction for the lending of money'. As such, borrowing in the form of debentures comes within the definition. (Loan relationships also encompass situations where a company is a creditor but that is not relevant for discussion here.)

16.5.2.2 Interest on borrowing for the purposes of trade

Section 82 of FA 96 sets out the method by which expenditure resulting from a loan relationship is brought into account: any 'debits', of which the main type is interest, can be treated as income expenses which can be deducted from income profits. Also, charges and expenses incurred in setting up the loan relationship (in this instance, legal or administrative) are treated as debits.

16.5.2.3 Non-trading borrowing

If a company raises money by borrowing but this does not support the trade carried on by the company, interest thereon is treated as a 'non-trading debit'. Such a sum must first be deducted from any 'non-trading credits' (i.e., profits which a company has made from lending money where this is not the trade of the company). If such credits exceed debits, the resulting sum is charged to tax under Schedule D, Case III. However, where the situation is in reverse, the company may, very simply, use that deficit and set it off against any profits of the same accounting period or carry it back against any profits of earlier accounting periods (in addition to any deductible sums in **16.5.2.2**).

16.5.2.4 Timing of deductibility

Prior to the FA 96, the law contained numerous technical distinctions between the treatment of profits and expenses incurred on lending and borrowing. To simplify the situation and to reflect the accounting reality, the treatment of payments arising out of loan relationships is now determined by their accounting treatment. Consequently, most interest payments payable by a company will be deductible on an accruals basis, that is, when they accrue due to be paid, rather than when they are actually paid.

16.5.3 DEDUCTION OF TAX

The company must deduct basic rate income tax from interest which it pays (s. 349(2) ICTA 1988). The current rate applicable on all savings and distribution income (other than from dividends) is 20%. (Deduction is not, however, made where interest is short interest or where it is yearly interest paid to a bank in the UK.) When the company deducts tax it must account to the Revenue for the tax deducted. For example, a company borrows £1,000 at 10% interest from an individual. Each year (assuming tax rates remain the same) it will pay £80 to the lender and £20 to the Revenue.

16.5.4 TAXATION OF THE RECIPIENT

The gross amount of interest received by a debenture-holder is taxed under Schedule D Case III. As we have just seen, the company usually deducts the 20% tax from the payment so that the amount received is a net amount. To calculate the amount of tax payable it is, therefore, first necessary to calculate the gross amount of interest. This is done by multiplying the net amount actually received by 100/80 (e.g., £80 × 100/80 = £100). If the tax rate changes so will the fraction — the '80' represents 100 minus the rate of tax. Of course, if no deduction of tax has been made at source, this calculation is unnecessary.

The gross amount of interest is investment income in the hands of the recipient and is liable to higher rate tax if the recipient's income is large enough. If the recipient has unused personal reliefs the 20% tax can be reclaimed to the extent that the reliefs are not set against other income.

TAXATION OF RETAINED PROFITS

> **Example** P has taxable income of £21,900. He, therefore, has £6,500 of the basic rate band still unused. He received £10,000 interest on a loan to the company.
>
> (a) Net receipt of £8,000 plus credit for £2,000 deducted.
> (b) Tax to pay (on gross sum):
>
> £0 – 6,500 × 20%   = £1,300
> £6,501 – 10,000 × 40% = £1,400
>   = £2,700
>
> (c) Tax deducted satisfies £2,000 of the above liability – balance to pay of £700.
> (d) Net cash receipt = £7,300

16.6 Conclusion

It is impossible to come to any general conclusion as to which type of extraction of profits is most beneficial because the circumstances of each case can be different. Only a specific examination of the business in question will provide the most suitable method, taking into account considerations beyond pure taxation ones, such as cashflow issues and pension provision. This chapter will conclude with an examination of some of the major factors which will determine the choice made.

16.6.1 DIRECTORS' FEES OR INTEREST

Whether profit is distributed to the proprietor by way of directors' fees or interest, the tax effect is the same for the company. Both payments are deductible.

So far as the proprietor is concerned, the only tax distinction between fees and interest is that one is earned income and the other is investment income. This distinction is normally of no significance. (Investment income, unlike earned income, can never be taken into account when assessing pensionable income.)

The deductible nature of both these payments can, quite often, produce a taxation advantage for the company which will result in their being a favoured method of extracting profits, especially if this can be used to reduce a company's taxable profits below the small companies threshold.

Caution is, however, required. Any attempt to charge an excessive amount of interest or to link the amount of interest to profits may result in s. 209(2), ICTA 1988 applying; the effect being that the element of interest which is excessive will not be deductible and will be treated as a distribution in the hands of the recipient.

16.6.2 DIVIDENDS

Distributing profit by way of dividend is less tax-effective for the company than either of the other two methods. Dividends are not deductible expenses nor are they charges on income. So far as the proprietor is concerned, distributions by way of dividend may also be less tax-effective than the two previous methods. Where profit is distributed by way of dividend by a company which pays tax at a rate of 30%, the company can only pass on to the shareholder a 10% tax credit (see **16.3.3** above). In such a case the full benefit of the profit distributed by way of dividend is not received by the shareholder.

In effect, there is an element of double taxation of the sum in question. As a result, if the shareholder is a higher rate taxpayer, the effective rate of tax which the distributed profit has borne is 47.25%. This disadvantage is reduced where a company is only paying the small companies rate of corporation tax.

16.6.3 RETAINED PROFITS

Because of the tax-deductible nature of salaries and debenture interest in the hands of a company, the proprietors of a company can structure such payments in the most tax-efficient manner. They may wish to pay out all a company's earnings in such form during an accounting year, thus reducing the amount of profits taxable in its hands to nil. Alternatively, they may wish only to pay out a proportion of such earnings, resulting in a tax liability being split between the company and the recipient.

Very often, such decisions will be driven by practical or commercial reasons; the company needs funds to expand or a director would like a higher salary. However, the proportions in which earnings are paid out or retained can have a crucial effect for tax purposes.

16.6.4 OTHER CONSIDERATIONS

Tax considerations alone cannot decide the matter. Other relevant factors to be considered are:

(a) There may be shareholders who are not directors and who, therefore, cannot receive directors' fees. This is particularly relevant where the company is listed on the Stock Exchange and the majority of its investors will be institutions. In part, such shareholders will be expecting dividend payments to justify their investments.

(b) A company may *have* to borrow money for commercial reasons. Thereafter, it will be obliged to pay interest.

(c) Payment of any form of salary to a director will attract a national insurance liability which is met by both the director and the company. It may be that the director's contributions are already at their maximum level, so any increase in salary will not result in further contributions for the director. However, the company's contributions are subject to no such limit. Liability to national insurance can erode to a great extent the apparent advantage which payment of a salary has over that of a dividend. (Attempts have been made by many employers to pay their employees in various ways other than by cash payments, such as gold bullion. Successive legislation has attempted to counter these methods, such that very careful planning is required to provide a 'reward' which is not subject to national insurance.)

SEVENTEEN

CAPITAL ALLOWANCES

This chapter covers the following topics:

17.1 Introduction
17.2 Plant and machinery
17.3 Industrial buildings
17.4 Other expenditure which attracts capital allowances.

17.1 Introduction

17.1.1 GENERAL

Most businesses will need to acquire fixed assets for use in the business. The depreciation in the value of those assets due to wear and tear arising from their use in the business is not an allowable deduction from the business's profits for income tax purposes, even though their acquisition is essential to the future profitability of the business. However, certain limited types of fixed assets do attract relief in the form of capital allowances which can be deducted when calculating taxable profits. In effect, the allowance is an amount which represents deprivation in the asset in question, calculated according to a fixed formula.

Relief is only available if the capital expenditure has been incurred in respect of the items of expenditure prescribed by the governing statute, the Capital Allowances Act 1990. Under this Act, the principal allowances relate to expenditure incurred on 'plant and machinery' and 'industrial buildings' (although expenditure on other items is deductible under the terms of the Act). The Act has been superseded by the Capital Allowances Act 2001. The latter will only make minor amendments to the existing regime, its principal purpose being a simplification of the existing legislation.

The allowances can be claimed by companies, partnerships or individuals.

Capital allowances are treated as trading expenses incurred in the accounting period in which they are claimed. They are, therefore, deductible from income receipts from the same period.

17.2 Plant and Machinery

17.2.1 DEFINITION

The Capital Allowances Act 1990 does not define either 'plant' or 'machinery' and therefore whether the expenditure will attract the allowances will depend on the facts in each case. In *Yarmouth* v *France* (1887) 19 QBD 647, Lindley LJ said that the term 'plant':

CAPITAL ALLOWANCES

> ... includes whatever apparatus is used by a businessman for carrying on his business, not his stock-in-trade which he buys or makes for sale; but all goods and chattels, fixed or movable, live or dead, which he keeps for permanent employment in his business.

On the basis of this guidance (which has been followed in subsequent cases), the term 'plant' will not apply to (and so allowances will not be available in respect of) an item which is not used for carrying on the business, the stock in trade of the business or the premises or place in which the business is carried on. However, the Finance Act 1994 has introduced a new sch. AA1 into the 1990 Act providing that land, buildings and structures cannot be plant.

A fuller description of the definition of the term is beyond the scope of this book. The reader is referred to one of the standard tax textbooks for further detail.

17.2.2 THE WRITING DOWN ALLOWANCES

17.2.2.1 Qualifying expenditure

If the expenditure is incurred on an item of 'plant or machinery', it will qualify for a 'writing down allowance' of up to 25% of the 'qualifying expenditure' in the first and subsequent years. The term 'qualifying expenditure' means the original cost of the asset less any allowances already given. The allowance may be claimed in whole or in part by sole traders or partners.

Example Machinery is purchased for £50,000 on 1 January 2000 and the full writing down allowance of 25% is claimed. This would mean that an allowance of £12,500 will be available in the first year of ownership. If the owner of the machinery decides to claim the full 25% allowance in the three subsequent years, the allowance available will be as follows:

	Written down value		Allowance for the year
Second year	£50,000 − £12,500 (1st Year WDA)	= £37,500	£9,375
Third year	£50,000 − £21,875 (£12,500 + £9,375)	= £28,125	£7,031
Fourth year	£50,000 − £28,906 (£12,500 + £9,375 + £7,031)	= £21,094	£5,273

17.2.2.2 Balancing charge allowance

When the asset is sold there is a balancing charge on the difference between the sale price and the written down value. In the above example, the written down value after the fourth year was £15,821 (£21,094 − £5,273), so if the machinery was sold for £17,821 there would be a charge to tax (under Schedule D Case VI) of £2,000. This charge is known as the 'balancing charge'. This means that, taking all the years together, the amount on which relief is finally given is equal to the amount of the actual depreciation. (Should the item be sold for *less* than the current written down value, a 'balancing allowance' will be available as a way of granting relief.) The balancing charge can never be on more than the amount of allowance given — any actual profit made on the sale of the assets being liable to capital gains tax, if taxable at all.

The illustration set out above shows that the allowances are of up to 25% of the *unrelieved expenditure* (that is to say, the purchase price less the allowances already taken). Thus, the annual allowance is a percentage of an ever-reducing balance so that it can take many years for the entire expenditure to be set against profits, subject to a balancing charge becoming payable.

17.2.3 'POOLING'

17.2.3.1 General

So far, we have looked at the rules as they apply to the acquisition and subsequent disposal of a single item of plant or machinery. If several items of plant and machinery are owned by the business (as is more likely to be the case) the allowances are given by reference to a 'pool' of expenditure. This will mean that all of the assets in the pool are treated as if they were one asset. The amount of the writing down allowance on the 'pool' of expenditure will be up to 25% of the total of expenditure on machinery and plant less all allowances so far claimed. Where one item included in the pool is disposed of, the sale price of that item is deducted from the written down value of the pool (this deduction being known as a 'balancing adjustment'), so that smaller allowances will be available in later years. A 'balancing charge' will only apply where pooled items are sold for more than the written down value of the whole pool.

17.2.4 USING THE ALLOWANCES

Writing down allowances are available both in the accounting period in which the asset was purchased and in all subsequent accounting periods during which the asset is owned.

While the system does not lend itself to simplification (especially from the corporation tax perspective), the basic use of a writing down allowance for either a company or a partnership or a sole trader is that of a deductible trading expense. If such allowances exceed income receipts, the loss incurred attracts loss relief in the usual way.

17.2.5 SPECIAL RULES ON PLANT AND MACHINERY

17.2.5.1 Enhanced first year allowances for small and medium-sized companies

Small and medium-sized companies (which account for around 99% of companies in the United Kingdom) are entitled to claim capital allowances of 40% in the first year of ownership of plant and machinery. This is designed to encourage investment.

17.2.5.2 Long-life assets

Any plant and machinery acquired after 26 November 1996 which falls under this category attracts a writing down allowance of 6%. Long-life assets are those with a useful economic life of more than 25 years.

This legislation, introduced by the Finance Act 1997, is intended to affect only large concerns. As such, any business which spends less than £100,000 a year on long-life assets is excluded and will still be able to claim the full 25% allowance. Certain cagetories of assets are also excluded, the most relevant for the purposes of this chapter being motor cars.

Because these rules result in allowances being claimed at a slower rate than normal, businesses could be tempted to sell off assets prematurely at less than their written down value so as to bring an immediate balancing allowance into effect. The legislation contains provisions to defeat such activity by deeming the sale to have been at the relevant written down value.

17.2.5.3 Leased assets

The Capital Allowances Act 1990 contains special rules on the availability of capital allowances to the lessor when plant and machinery is bought in order to be leased (see Part II, Chapter V, Capital Allowances Act 1990). There are also special rules for the lessees of equipment. It is important to distinguish between arrangements which are 'pure' leasing contracts, where

CAPITAL ALLOWANCES

the title in the assets leased always remains with the lessor, and those which constitute lease-purchase (and hire-purchase) arrangements where the lessee (or hirer) becomes the ultimate owner of the assets, normally upon payment of a final capital sum. In the former case, the lessor will be able to claim writing down allowances; in the latter it will be the lessee. Because of the amount of assets either leased or subject to lease-purchase in the UK, these rules should not be overlooked. The detail of these rules is beyond the scope of this manual and the reader is referred to one of the standard tax textbooks.

17.2.6 MOTOR CARS

Cars which are used only for business purposes qualify for full writing down allowances. However, cars which are used for private as well as business purposes qualify for a 25% writing down allowance.

17.3 Industrial Buildings

17.3.1 DEFINITION

The Capital Allowances Act 1990 allows for allowances to be claimed in respect of the construction and purchase of industrial buildings and structures (such as factories, but not offices) for manufacturing (but not distributive) trades. The Act defines the term 'industrial building' at some length and it can include a mill, a factory and a warehouse. The allowances are not available in respect of the expenditure laid out to acquire the land. Expenditure incurred subsequently when the industrial building is improved can attract the allowances. If part of a building which satisfies the definition of an 'industrial building' is used for non-industrial purposes, the allowance can still be claimed provided expenditure on the non-industrial purpose does not exceed 25% of the expenditure incurred in respect of the whole building.

17.3.2 THE ALLOWANCE

A writing down allowance of 4% of the original cost of construction (or purchase) of an industrial building can be claimed for every year when the building is in use. Since the writing down allowance is a percentage of the *original* cost price, full relief for the expenditure will have been obtained once 25 years have elapsed. If an industrial building has declined in value and is sold, a balancing charge will be levied if the decline in the building's value is less than the allowances which have been given to date. A balancing allowance will be available if the decline is greater than the allowances given to date. These adjustments will not, however, be made once the 4% annual writing down allowance has been claimed for 25 years. This is because the value of the building will be regarded as having been written down to nil by then.

17.3.3 SALE OF A BUILDING

Where the vendor who has been claiming this allowance sells the building, the purchaser can claim a writing down allowance. In this case, the allowance is calculated by spreading the 'residue of expenditure' over the balance of the period of 25 years commencing when the building was originally built or purchased by the first claimant of the allowances. The 'residue of expenditure' is the written down value of the building at the date of the sale plus any balancing charge or less any balancing allowance. For example, a taxpayer buys a factory for £200,000 and claims the 4% writing down allowance for each of the first five years of his ownership (giving a total of allowances claimed of £40,000). After five years, the original owner sells the building for £175,000, which represents £15,000 above the written down value of the building of £160,000 for the purposes of the allowance. The vendor will suffer a balancing charge on the sum of £15,000. The purchaser will be able to claim the writing down allowance in respect of the sum of £175,000. The purchaser will be able to spread the 'residue of expenditure' of £175,000 over the balance of the original period of 25 years, that is to say, over the next 20 years. It should be noted that the writing down allowance which the purchaser in these circumstances can claim is not limited to the 4% figure.

17.4 Other Expenditure which Attracts Capital Allowances

The Capital Allowances Act 1990 provides that capital allowances may be available in respect of:

(a) agricultural forestry buildings;

(b) scientific research;

(c) patents and 'know-how';

(d) mines, oil wells, mineral rights, cemeteries, crematoria and dredging; and

(e) hotels.

EIGHTEEN

THE TAX CONSEQUENCES OF LEAVING AND JOINING A PARTNERSHIP

This chapter covers the following topics:

18.1   Introduction
18.2   The tax consequences of the dissolution of a partnership
18.3   The tax consequences of the retirement of a partner
18.4   The tax consequences of death
18.5   The tax consequences of expulsion from a partnership
18.6   The tax consequences of admission of a new partner.

18.1   Introduction

In **Chapter 5** we saw that it was possible for an individual to cease to be a partner on the happening of one of the following events:

(a)   the dissolution of the partnership;

(b)   his retirement or death; or

(c)   expulsion from the partnership.

Having considered the legal consequences of the occurrence of these events in **Chapter 5**, we will concentrate in this chapter on the tax consequences (particularly the circumstances in which tax charges can arise). We will only consider the tax exemptions and reliefs where they are of special relevance.

We will also consider the position of a new partner joining the firm, whether or not as a replacement for a deceased, retired or expelled partner.

In this chapter we will not repeat the legal consequences so the reader is recommended to review **Chapter 5** for this information.

Reference is made throughout this chapter to both capital gains tax and inheritance tax. It is recommended, therefore, that **Chapter 14** has been read beforehand.

THE TAX CONSEQUENCES OF LEAVING AND JOINING A PARTNERSHIP

18.2 The Tax Consequences of the Dissolution of a Partnership

18.2.1 INTRODUCTION

If a partnership is dissolved by one of the methods explained in **Chapter 5**, the partnership relationship ceases and the assets of the business may be realised. From this will flow various tax consequences.

18.2.2 INCOME TAX

If there is a permanent cessation (on a closure of the business) the relevant closing year rules will be applied (see **13.3.2.3**).

If the partnership has been claiming capital allowances on, for example, the plant and machinery used in the business, balancing charges may be levied if the assets are disposed of for more than their written-down value on cessation. Balancing allowances may be claimed if the market value of the assets is less than their written-down value.

Finally, if the partnership has made losses, loss relief under ss. 380 and 382 ICTA 1988 in respect of the final tax year of the trade may be claimed. Terminal loss relief under ss. 388 and 389 ICTA 1988 will permit the partners to carry back losses made in the final 12 months of the trade against the profits of the same trade during the immediately preceding three tax years or set them off against other income in the year of cessation (see **13.4**).

18.2.3 CAPITAL GAINS TAX

If the partnership property is sold to outsiders following dissolution any gains realised by each partner on the disposal of his fractional share of the assets will be taxable in accordance with general principles. The general principles will also apply when a partner disposes of assets he owns personally but which have been used by the partnership.

18.2.4 INHERITANCE TAX

If the assets of the partnership are disposed of at full market value on dissolution, there will be no reduction in the value of the transferor's estate and, therefore, no transfer of value. If there is no transfer of value there cannot be any IHT liability.

18.3 The Tax Consequences of the Retirement of a Partner

18.3.1 INTRODUCTION

As we explained in **Chapter 5**, while 'retirement' implies a person retiring from full-time work having reached normal retirement age, in the partnership context 'retirement' simply means leaving the partnership voluntarily so that the age of the 'retiring' partner is irrelevant. In this section we have examined the tax charges which can arise when there is such a change in the partnership.

18.3.2 INCOME TAX

18.3.2.1 Deemed cessation under s. 113 ICTA 1988

Until 6 April 1997 whenever there was a change in the persons engaged in carrying on any trade, profession or vocation under Case I or Case II of Schedule D, this resulted in a deemed discontinuance of the partnership under s. 113(1) ICTA 1988. One such instance is the retirement of a partner.

A deemed discontinuance would result in the closing years rules applying to the partnership as originally constituted and the opening years rules applying to the changed partnership.

It was possible to displace the statutory presumption by making an election under s. 113(2) to treat the business as continuing.

Because of the need for all the partners, both old and new, to concur in the s. 113(2) election, a partnership agreement normally provided that new partners must agree to the election before joining the firm and that retiring partners (and the personal representatives of a deceased partner, if appropriate) be required to concur with the election if the continuing partners so requested.

18.3.2.2 No deemed cessation under current year basis

From 6 April 1997 the effect of s. 113 is different in that only a complete change of partnership personnel will result in a deemed discontinuance. As such, if one of the original partners is still involved with the business after the change in the partnership, no discontinuance will occur. Consequently, the s. 113 election will cease to be of any relevance. It may be, of course, the case that many partnership agreements drafted to take the old regime into account will still contain a provision for it.

However, despite the fact that there is no deemed discontinuance of the partnership business as a whole, when a partner retires, the closing year rules will apply in order to calculate that partner's final partnership tax liability (see **13.3.3.3**).

18.3.3 CAPITAL GAINS TAX

18.3.3.1 Disposals amongst partners

Where one partner retires from the business he will normally relinquish his interest in the partnership assets in consideration of a capital sum and/or the provision of an income. The retiring partner's present interest in the business is shown on his capital account. He will be treated as making a disposal of that interest to the continuing partners (and to any new partners who are being admitted on his retirement). The continuing (and new) partners will acquire his interest and will thereafter have a greater interest in the business.

Disposals by a firm are subject to the normal CGT principles in determining whether a gain has arisen. However, the lack of a comprehensive body of legislation dealing with the taxation of capital gains realised by partners led to difficulties. The Revenue's Statements of Practice D/12, SP 1/79 and SP 1/89 set out the Revenue's view of the way in which general capital gains tax principles apply in a partnership context. The underlying principle on which the Statement of Practice D/12 is based is that each partner is to be treated as owning a fractional share of each of the chargeable assets of the partnership (including goodwill). This concept forms the basis of the rules which follow.

In this section we will consider the capital gains tax consequences which arise, according to the Statements of Practice, when there is a change in the personnel of the partnership (principally on the retirement of a partner or when a new partner is admitted).

THE TAX CONSEQUENCES OF LEAVING AND JOINING A PARTNERSHIP

> **Example** A, B, C and D share profits (and asset surplus) equally. The assets of the firm were acquired for £60,000. A is retiring and once he has retired, all the profits will be divided equally between B, C and D. The asset-sharing ratio will change as follows:
>
> | | Before
£ | After
£ |
> |---|---|---|
> | A | 15,000(¼) | (—) |
> | B | 15,000(¼) | 20,000(⅓) |
> | C | 15,000(¼) | 20,000(⅓) |
> | D | 15,000(¼) | 20,000(⅓) |
>
> A has disposed of his ¼ interest to the continuing partners and is left with nothing. Each of the continuing partners receives ⅓ of A's ¼ share (i.e., $^1/_{12}$th share in the partnership property). They will, naturally, each pay A for such share.

It can be clearly seen from the above example that the retiring partner has made a disposal to the continuing partners. The question then arises of whether or not the disposal has realised a gain (or a loss). Where the assets have not been revalued in the accounts and the retiring partner receives an amount equivalent to the balance on his capital account, he is simply receiving the return of his original capital contribution. There will be no gain and no loss (D/12 para. 4). For example, in the above illustration, if A was paid £15,000 he would realise neither a gain nor a loss.

However, there will be a gain on disposal where assets have been revalued in the accounts (D/12 para. 5). Where assets have increased in value since the date of acquisition the partners may wish to record this increase in the accounts; the process is referred to as a 'revaluation'. The values of the various assets are increased in the accounts and the balances on the partners' capital accounts are increased by a corresponding amount in order to reflect the increase in the worth of the business. A revaluation of itself gives rise to no charge to CGT since there has been no disposal. However, if after a revaluation there is a change in the asset surplus sharing ratio, for example on retirement, the disponer partner will receive more than his original capital contribution and (subject to reliefs) there will be a charge to capital gains tax.

> **Example** The facts are as in the previous example but the partnership decides that prior to A's retirement the assets should be revalued from £60,000 to £90,000. A's £ share will be worth £22,500. Therefore A will be treated as disposing of assets for £22,500 which were acquired for £15,000, and will have a capital gain of £7,500.
>
> | | Before
£ | On revaluation
£ | After
£ |
> |---|---|---|---|
> | A | 15,000(¼) | 22,500(¼) | — |
> | B | 15,000(¼) | 22,500(¼) | 30,000(⅓) |
> | C | 15,000(¼) | 22,500(¼) | 30,000(⅓) |
> | D | 15,000(¼) | 22,500(¼) | 30,000(⅓) |
> | | 60,000 | 90,000 | 90,000 |
>
> B, C and D will each be treated as acquiring £7,500 worth of A's share in the assets and therefore their respective base costs will increase from £22,500 to £30,000. They are, therefore, holding assets which have increased in value to them from £15,000 to £30,000. When they realise the assets, there will be a CGT liability.

The members of the partnership, in order to minimise the burden of finding large capital sums, may agree not to revalue assets as and when partners retire. It could be argued that this is a gift by each retiring partner of his share in the increased value of the asset. In the case of a gift (or sale at an under-value), the Revenue can treat the disposal as made for market value unless it was a bargain made at arm's length. In the case of connected persons, transfers are always treated as otherwise than by way of bargains made at arm's length. Partners are normally connected but will not be when transferring property to each other provided the disposal *was pursuant to a bona fide commercial arrangement*. Thus, provided there is some bona fide commercial reason for not revaluing, the Revenue will not seek to substitute market value.

Even where the partners are connected other than by partnership (for example, father and son) the Revenue have stated that they will only seek to substitute market value where the transaction would not have been entered into by persons who were not at arm's length.

18.3.3.2 Entitlement to reliefs

If a charge to tax arises on the disposal by a partner of his interest in partnership property, the disponer will be entitled to claim the benefit of the CGT exemptions and reliefs in the normal way.

Details of the relevant reliefs are given in **Chapter 14**. The three most likely reliefs will be retirement relief, EIS deferral of chargeable gains and taper relief. Each will be looked at briefly in turn.

(a) Retirement relief will only apply until the end of the tax year 2002/2003. Despite its gradual erosion until that time, it is still a valuable relief and every effort should be made to try to benefit from it. A key decision, therefore, for partners considering retirement within the next few years will be whether to time their retirement to take advantage of the last year of retirement relief.

(b) EIS deferral. If the partner can find an appropriate company to invest in, this relief can be used to defer the payment of CGT. The partner need only be a shareholder in such a company and need take no part in management.

(c) Taper relief. Maximum relief is available for assets owned for at least four complete years after 5 April 1998. Therefore, it is quite likely that many disposals which occur after 5 April 2002 will attract the full relief. In addition, long-standing partners may also have acquired rights to indexation allowance on ownership of their partnership share until 6 April 1998. It may be, therefore, that the actual gain subject to taxation is quite small.

18.3.3.3 Goodwill

Goodwill presents particular problems. In recent years partners (particularly in professional firms) who paid for a share in the goodwill of the firm when they were admitted to partnership have agreed not to charge incoming partners for a share (the burden of finding a large capital sum being regarded as too great). The effect of this is that the old partners write off goodwill. It is clear that when an old partner retires and receives no payment for the goodwill he makes a loss on that asset. Many partnerships have argued that the old partners are entitled to make a claim for CGT loss relief when the value of goodwill is written off. (Section 24(2) Taxation of Chargeable Gains Act 1992 provides that where an inspector is satisfied that the value of an asset has become negligible he may allow an immediate loss.) The Revenue resist such claims, taking the view that the goodwill still has a value and does not become negligible simply because the partners choose not to charge for it. However, claims for immediate loss relief have been successful in front of the General and the Special Commissioners. The position is unsettled and the practice varies between inspectors, some being prepared to allow such claims and some not.

THE TAX CONSEQUENCES OF LEAVING AND JOINING A PARTNERSHIP

18.3.3.4 Payment of annuities

A partnership may agree to pay a retiring partner an annuity. The annuity will be subject to income tax in the hands of the recipient partner. If it is more than can be regarded as reasonable recognition of the past contribution of work and effort by the partner to the partnership, the Revenue will treat the capitalised value of the annuity as consideration for the disposal of the retiring partner's share in the assets. An annuity will be regarded as reasonable for this purpose if:

(a) the former partner had been in the partnership for at least 10 years;

(b) the annuity is no more than of his average share of profits in the best three of the last seven years in which he was required to devote substantially the whole of his time to acting as a partner.

18.3.3.5 Disposal of assets owned by partners personally

Where a partner disposes of an asset which he owns personally but which is used by the partnership, the Statements of Practice are not relevant. On such disposals the normal CGT principles are applied to ascertain whether a gain or loss has arisen. Similarly, the disposing partner will be able to claim any relevant exemptions or reliefs, save that retirement relief will only be available to relieve the gain realised on the disposal of such an asset if the disposal is associated with the partner's disposal of his share in the partnership on reaching 50 or on retirement under that age on ill-health grounds.

18.3.4 INHERITANCE TAX

18.3.4.1 Gratuitous benefit

Normal principles of IHT apply in the partnership context. Thus, where a partner sells an interest in the partnership for full consideration there is no transfer of value and therefore no charge to IHT arises. If a partner sells an interest for less than full consideration or transfers it for no consideration at all, prima facie a charge to IHT will arise. However, s. 10 IHTA 1984 provides that a disposition is *not* a transfer of value if it was not intended to confer gratuitous benefit and was either made at arm's length between unconnected persons or, if between connected persons, was such as might be expected to be made between unconnected persons. Partners are not connected persons in respect of transfers between partners of partnership assets pursuant to bona fide commercial arrangements. Thus many transfers which might appear to be chargeable may escape IHT on the ground that there was no intention to confer a gratuitous benefit.

18.3.4.2 Goodwill

It is common for partners to agree that on their retirement (or death) their share of goodwill is to accrue automatically to the other partners without payment. This has the benefit of relieving the partnership of the need to pay for portions of goodwill as and when partners retire. Section 163(1) of IHTA 1984 provides that where a person enters into a contract which excludes or restricts the right to dispose of any property the exclusion or restriction will be ignored in valuing the asset when it is next transferred except to the extent that consideration for the exclusion or restriction was given. The effect of s. 163 is that, unless consideration is given for the accruer clause, the clause will be ignored when the goodwill is valued on the transfer to the other partners and the full value of the retiring (or deceased) partner's share in the goodwill will be charged to tax.

18.3.4.3 Business property relief and other reliefs

In the event that an inter vivos transaction is regarded as a transfer of value it will be potentially exempt. If the transferor dies within seven years the transfer will be treated as if it had always been chargeable. An interest in the partnership is relevant business property qualifying for business property relief at 100% provided:

(a) the transferor had owned the property for at least two years up to the time of the transfer;

(b) the transferee still owns the property (or replacement property) and it still qualifies as relevant business property.

Where there is a gift of land, buildings, plant or machinery owned by a partner personally but used wholly or mainly for the purpose of the partnership of which he is a member, a reduction of only 50% is available.

The transferor's annual exemption may be available from the tax year of transfer and the preceding tax year, in which case it will reduce the value transferred.

Should a PET become chargeable tapering relief will be available if the transferor survives three years from the date of the transfer. The burden of the inheritance tax will fall on the transferee (unless the transferor provides otherwise in his will). In cases where the potential liability is large the transferee may wish to consider insuring the transferor's life. The option to pay inheritance tax by instalments will be available. The first will be due six months after the end of the month of the transferor's death. Interest will not be payable unless an instalment is late.

18.4 The Tax Consequences of Death

18.4.1 INTRODUCTION

As we saw in **Chapter 5**, under the Partnership Act death causes the automatic dissolution of a partnership, although it is common to provide in partnership agreements that this will not happen. In this section, we look at the tax consequences of the death of a partner.

18.4.2 INCOME TAX

Whether the death is treated in the same manner as a retirement (because of the provisions of the partnership agreement) or as causing a dissolution of the partnership (because the partnership agreement is silent on the point), the death will result in a change in the persons engaged in carrying on the partnership's trade, profession or vocation. However, from 6 April 1997 this has no longer resulted in a deemed discontinuance for taxation purposes if the remaining partner(s) continue to trade after the event (see **18.3.2.2**). The deceased partner, however, will be subject to the closing year rules.

18.4.3 CAPITAL GAINS TAX

The deceased partner's interest in the partnership assets is *acquired* by his personal representatives at market value on the date of death. Since a disposal is a prerequisite for liability to CGT, this means that no CGT is payable on death and that unrealised gains arising during the deceased's lifetime escape the charge to tax.

18.4.4 INHERITANCE TAX

18.4.4.1 General

The estate of a deceased partner will include his interest in the partnership assets. Under s. 4(1) IHTA 1984, the partner is deemed to make a transfer of value on his death and the value transferred is the value of the assets in his estate immediately before his death. Accordingly, subject to exemptions, reliefs and the deceased partner's cumulative total at the date of death, IHT will be payable in respect of the market value of his share in the partnership.

Changes in the value of assets resulting from death are taken into account for IHT purposes. If all or part of the value of the goodwill of the business was personal to the deceased partner the value of the goodwill, and therefore of the business, will fall as a result of the death. The reduced value of the deceased partner's share in the business will then be included in his estate for IHT purposes.

18.4.4.2 Business property relief

Where an IHT liability does arise on death it may be reduced by virtue of the relief for business property given by ss. 103–114 IHTA 1984 (and considered in **18.3.4.3**).

However, there is no entitlement to claim the relief if the assets are the subject of a binding contract for sale at the time of death. A clause in the partnership agreement to the effect that the surviving partners are *obliged* to buy and the personal representatives of the deceased partner are *obliged* to sell the deceased partner's share may have been included in the agreement for sound commercial reasons but it will result in the loss of business property relief. This is because the Revenue regard such clauses as amounting to binding contracts (see Statement of Practice 12/80 dated 13 October 1980). If there is no *obligation* to buy and sell, the relief is available and so this difficulty can be avoided by the use of an option arrangement or an automatic accruer clause.

18.4.4.3 Instalment option

IHT attributable to an interest in partnership property can be paid in 10 yearly instalments under ss. 227 and 228 IHTA 1984. The first instalment is due six months after the end of the month of death and no interest is due unless an instalment is late. If the interest in partnership property is sold all outstanding IHT must be paid off. Where the continuing partners purchase the interest of a deceased partner the instalment option will not thereafter be available to the deceased partner's estate.

18.5 The Tax Consequences of Expulsion from a Partnership

In **Chapter 5** we saw that s. 25 of the Partnership Act 1890 provides that the majority of the partners can expel any partner unless a power to do so has been conferred by express agreement between the partners. If the partnership agreement does contain such a power and it is exercised, the tax consequences of expulsion are the same as for retirement.

18.6 The Tax Consequences of Admission of a New Partner

18.6.1 INTRODUCTION

Although this chapter is primarily concerned with leaving a partnership, the admission of new partners is a topic so closely connected that it seems appropriate to deal with it here.

THE TAX CONSEQUENCES OF LEAVING AND JOINING A PARTNERSHIP

18.6.2 INCOME TAX

Because partners are treated as notional sole traders for tax purposes, when a partnership starts up, all partners will be equally subject to the opening year rules (see **13.3.2.2**). Accordingly, when a new partner is admitted to an existing partnership, that partner will be treated as if starting up a trade and will initially be subject to the opening year rules, while the original partners will continue to be taxed on the normal current year basis.

> **Example** Y and T are in partnership sharing profits equally. The accounting year end for the business is 30 June. On 1 January 1998, W is admitted to the partnership and will share profits equally with Y and T. W joins, therefore, in the tax year 1997–98.
>
> The tax liability of Y and T for the tax year 1997–98 will be based on profits to the year end 30 June 1997.
>
> W's tax liability for his year of joining will, according to the opening year rules, be based upon his profit entitlement from 1 January 1998 to 5 April 1998.
>
> The tax liability of Y and T for the 1998–99 tax year will be based on the share of profits earned during the accounting year ending on 30 June 1998; one half of profits each up to the date of W's joining and one third each thereafter.
>
> The tax liability of W for the 1998–99 tax year will be based on W's share of profits for his first 12 months of notional trading, i.e., from 1 January 1998 to 31 December 1998. (This is because the relevant year end in this tax year is not more than 12 months from the date of W's joining.)
>
> For the tax year 1999–00 all three partners will be assessed on a current year basis on profits up to the year end 30 June 1999.
>
> It will be noted that W's tax liability is based upon a certain amount of double taxation; the profits from 1 January 1998 to 5 April 1998 are taxed twice along with profits from 1 July 1998 to 31 December 1998. C may be able to claim overlap relief in respect of this.

If the new partner has to borrow money to raise the funds to buy into the partnership, the borrower will be able to deduct the interest as a charge on his income. The same relief is available if the borrower uses the funds to contribute additional capital to the partnership or to make a loan to the partnership, if it is used exclusively for the partnership's business purposes.

18.6.3 CAPITAL GAINS TAX

A newly admitted partner will acquire an interest in the partnership assets either by purchase or by gift. Thus, for example, if the old partners give the incoming partner a one-third share in profits and asset surpluses, he will acquire one third of the value of the partnership assets at that date. That value will be his acquisition value.

THE TAX CONSEQUENCES OF LEAVING AND JOINING A PARTNERSHIP

Example A and B, who share profits and assets equally, decide to admit C and to share profits and assets equally thereafter. The partnership assets are shown in the accounts as worth £120,000 at the date of C's admission.

	Before £	After £
A	60,000 (½)	40,000 (⅓)
B	60,000 (½)	40,000 (⅓)
C	—	40,000 (⅓)

C's acquisition value is, therefore, £40,000. A and B have disposed of a part of their share in the assets surplus. As discussed above there will be no charge to CGT on such a disposal provided there has been no upward revaluation of the assets in the accounts and provided no payment is made. The old partners are treated as making a disposal for a consideration equal to their capital gains tax cost so that there will be neither a chargeable gain nor an allowable loss at that point. They will carry forward a smaller proportion of cost to set against a subsequent disposal of their assets. The Inland Revenue will not seek to substitute market value in such a case since the transaction is likely to be a bona fide commercial transaction where the continuing partners dispose of a share in the asset surpluses but in consideration of the incoming partner covenanting to devote himself to the partnership.

If there has been an upward revaluation in the accounts there will be a potential charge to CGT.

Example Taking the same facts as those for the previous example, suppose that the assets are revalued at £180,000 a month prior to C's joining. The accounts would differ as follows:

	Before £	After £
A	90,000	60,000
B	90,000	60,000
C	—	60,000

Both A and B have disposed of one third each of their entitlement to the assets, such share originally being worth £20,000 (⅓ × £60,000) but which after revaluation stands at £30,000. Each has, therefore, realised a gain (ignoring indexation, etc.) of £10,000. C takes the share of the assets with a base cost of £60,000.

18.6.4 INHERITANCE TAX

Inheritance tax is unlikely to be an immediate problem for a newly admitted partner. However, he might be the recipient of a potentially exempt transfer of value. If so, it is possible that the transfer will become chargeable if one or more of the transferor partners dies within seven years. The donee of an inter vivos transfer of partnership property may exercise the right to pay by way of 10 equal yearly instalments, the first due six months after the end of the month of transfer. Interest is not charged unless an instalment is late.

NINETEEN

VALUE ADDED TAX

This chapter covers the following topics:

19.1 Introduction
19.2 Registration
19.3 Taxable supplies and the charge to VAT
19.4 Accounting for VAT.

19.1 Introduction

Value Added Tax ('VAT') is charged on supplies of goods and services made in the United Kingdom. Where a person makes taxable supplies in excess of a set limit in any one year period, he must register with Customs and Excise. He is then liable to account to Customs and Excise for VAT on all taxable supplies which he makes. The total amount payable may be reduced by the amount of VAT which he has paid on certain taxable supplies made *to him*.

The liability to pay VAT to Customs and Excise rests on suppliers of goods and services. However, the cost of the tax is actually borne by suppliers' customers (unless they can recover VAT) who are charged VAT on the goods and services provided to them by the suppliers.

VAT is charged in the UK under the provisions of the Value Added Tax Act 1994 ('VATA 1994'). The obligation to charge the tax arose from the United Kingdom becoming a member of the European Economic Community in 1973. VAT is the common tax on business turnover within the European Union and is intended to be applicable in the same manner in each member state.

19.2 Registration

19.2.1 TURNOVER LIMITS FOR REGISTRATION

Under sch. 1 VATA 1994, a person becomes liable to register for VAT with Customs and Excise if:

(a) at the end of any month, the value of taxable supplies made during the past year exceeds £54,000; or

(b) at any time, a person has reasonable grounds to believe that the value of taxable supplies which will be made in the coming 30 days will exceed £54,000.

VALUE ADDED TAX

Where a person makes taxable supplies which do not exceed the relevant turnover limits, he may apply to be registered for VAT on a voluntary basis. It should be noted that the relevant turnover limits for registration are those in force from 1 April 2001 and may be altered in the future.

19.2.2 'PERSON' FOR VAT PURPOSES

VATA 1994 requires registration by a 'person'. The latter includes an individual, a body corporate or a partnership (notwithstanding that the latter has no separate legal personality). A person is only entitled to one VAT registration (irrespective of the number of businesses run) and is therefore liable for VAT on taxable supplies made by *all* of their businesses. There are exceptions to this rule, one being that a company which is organised into several divisions may seek registration for each division.

19.2.3 REGISTRATION DOCUMENTATION

A person applying for VAT registration must complete an application form VAT 1. A partnership must also submit details of all the partners on a form VAT 2.

19.2.4 EFFECT OF REGISTRATION

Once registered, a person is liable to account for VAT to Customs and Excise on all taxable supplies of goods and services made in the United Kingdom.

19.2.5 DE-REGISTRATION

A person may apply to be de-registered for VAT if he ceases to make taxable supplies or if he can satisfy Customs and Excise that taxable supplies for the next 12 months will not exceed £52,000. It should be noted that the relevant turnover limit for de-registration is that in force from 1 April 2001 and may be altered in the future.

19.3 Taxable Supplies and the Charge to VAT

19.3.1 TAXABLE SUPPLIES

VAT is charged on taxable supplies of goods and services made in the UK. A taxable supply is one which is made in the course of furtherance of business and is not classified as exempt from VAT under sch. 9 VATA 1994. (Examples of exempt supplies include most sales of land and buildings, insurance, doctors' services and certain types of education services.)

19.3.2 RATES OF VAT ON TAXABLE SUPPLIES

A taxable supply will be charged at one of two rates: standard or zero. Since April 1991, the standard rate of VAT has been 17.5%. Zero-rated supplies do not actually give rise to a VAT charge; however, they may allow a person to recover input tax paid on supplies *received by the supplier* (see **19.4.4**).

Zero-rated supplies are set out in sch. 8 VATA 1994 and include:

Food (except restaurant and hot take-away)
Children's clothing and shoes
Books and newspapers
Sales of new houses.

19.4 Accounting for VAT

19.4.1 CHARGING VAT TO CUSTOMERS

A person should start charging VAT to his customers and keep relevant records as soon as he realises that he is liable to register for VAT with Customs and Excise.

19.4.2 INVOICE TO CUSTOMERS

Once registered, a person will be given a VAT registration number. This must be included on tax invoices sent to customers for supplies of goods or services. The tax invoice should also include the date of supply, type of supply, total amount payable and the amount of VAT chargeable at the relevant rate. This VAT, charged to customers, will meet the liability to Customs and Excise.

19.4.3 VAT RETURN

A registered person is required to make a VAT return on form VAT 100 every three months (although monthly or annual returns may be agreed with Customs and Excise). It is on the basis of this return that a person makes VAT payments to Customs and Excise: thus a system of *self-assessment* operates. The form must be completed and returned, together with the tax payable, within a month of the end of the three month period to which it relates.

19.4.4 AMOUNT OF VAT PAYABLE

The amount of VAT payable by a taxable person will effectively be the standard rate of 17.5% as charged on all supplies of goods and services made in the relevant three month period. This is often referred to as *output tax*, i.e., the amount of VAT charged to customers on supplies *made* by a taxable person.

Output tax may be reduced by *input* tax. The latter is VAT which the taxable person has paid on supplies *made to* him. However the amount of input tax which a taxable person may set off against output tax is limited to such input tax as is attributable to taxable supplies made by that person. Put another way, a taxable person can only set off input tax which relates to supplies which are then used in some way in his making taxable supplies to others.

If a person makes zero-rated supplies, there is no output tax charge levied. In terms of the effect on a customer, it is as if it is an exempt supply. However, from the point of view of the taxable person, he is entitled to recover any input tax attributable to zero-rated supplies made by him. This is the benefit derived from zero-rated supplies, compared with exempt supplies.

It should be noted that it is possible, particularly where a person makes predominantly zero-rated supplies, for recoverable input tax to be in excess of output tax. In such cases, Customs and Excise will repay any excess.

The ability to recover input tax and the effect of zero-rated supplies is illustrated in the following examples. The following should be noted:

(a) each example relates to a single three month VAT period;

(b) the input tax has been assumed to be wholly attributable to the taxable supplies made; and

(c) the supplies received and made figures are shown *exclusive* of any VAT, the latter being shown in a separate column.

VALUE ADDED TAX

> **Example 1**
>
> | Cost of supplies received | VAT on supplies received (input) | Standard rate supplies made | VAT on supplies (output) | Net VAT payable |
> |---|---|---|---|---|
> | 1,000 | 175 | 1,600 | 280 | 105 |
>
> **Example 2**
>
> | Cost of supplies received | VAT on supplies received (input) | Zero-rate supplies made | VAT on supplies (output) | Net VAT recovered |
> |---|---|---|---|---|
> | 1,000 | 175 | 1,600 | 0 | 175 |

19.4.5 CALCULATION OF TAX ON VAT INCLUSIVE FIGURE: THE VAT FRACTION

As a final point, calculation of standard rate VAT or payable on *VAT exclusive* figures (as used in the above examples) is comparatively easy. It merely requires calculation of 17.5% of the VAT exclusive figure.

A figure which represents both the price of the supply *and* the VAT payable on the supply is said to be *VAT inclusive*. To calculate the element of a VAT inclusive figure which represents the tax payable, you need to multiply the figure by a fraction which will give you the equivalent of 17.5% on the VAT exclusive price. That fraction is $7/47$ and is known as the *VAT fraction*. It will obviously change with the standard rate of VAT.

> VAT inclusive price of goods supplied is £2,800.
>
> $7/47$ of £2,800 = £417.02. This latter figure is the amount of VAT payable.
>
> Therefore, the VAT exclusive price of the goods is £2,800 − £417.02 = £2,382.98.
>
> (N.B. 17.5% of £2,382.98 = £417.02.)

THE EUROPEAN COMMUNITY

TWENTY

THE RIGHT OF ESTABLISHMENT, THE RIGHT TO PROVIDE SERVICES AND THE FREE MOVEMENT OF GOODS

This chapter covers the following topics:

20.1 Introduction
20.2 Establishment and services
20.3 Limitations on the rights of establishment and provision of services
20.4 The free movement of goods.

20.1 Introduction

In this chapter we will examine two closely related rights established by European Community law. These are the 'right of establishment' and the right to provide services. The right of establishment is the right of a national of one member State to set up business in another member State. The right to provide services is a right to do business in another member State in ways which fall short of setting up a business. Under Articles 48 and 55 the right of establishment and the right to provide services are extended to 'companies or firms formed in accordance with the law of a member State and having their registered office, administrative centre or principal place of business within the Community'.

We will also examine the related issue of the free movement of goods within the European Community as enshrined in Articles 28 and 30 of the Treaty of Rome.

20.2 Establishment and Services

Article 43 provides (in part):

> ... restrictions on the freedom of establishment of nationals of a member State in the territory of another member State shall be abolished ... such ... abolition shall also apply to the setting up of agencies, branches or subsidiaries by nationals of any member State established in the territory of any member State.

> Freedom of establishment shall include the right to take up and ... manage undertakings in particular companies or firms ... under the conditions laid down for its own nationals by the law of the country where such establishment is effected ...

Article 49 provides (in part):

> ... restrictions on freedom to provide services within the Community shall be ... abolished ... in respect of nationals of member States who are established in a State of the Community other than that of the person for whom the services are intended.

Services are defined as services 'normally provided for remuneration'.

These provisions effectively mean that nationals of all member States are to be treated as being on the same footing as far as doing business in any member State is concerned. A French national is, for example, free to set up business in the UK either on his own account, in partnership or through the medium of a company. Furthermore it would be illegal in terms of Community law for UK law to discriminate against him in respect of such a business.

However, companies formed in a member State are effectively excluded from this right unless their business is established in one of the member States. The reason for this is that such a company is not really an economic entity within the Community.

20.3 Limitations on the Rights of Establishment and Provision of Services

The basic principle of the provisions we have just examined is that nationals of any member State should be treated the same as nationals of the member State where they have set up their establishment where they are providing services. For example a Greek national who is undertaking a business in Germany should be treated in the same way, under German law, as a German conducting the same business.

At first sight this would seem to give complete protection to the Greek national. However, the Community has decided that further protection is needed in some cases. This is because national law might lay down requirements for its own nationals which they could easily achieve but which nationals of other states could not easily achieve. Any restriction must be objectively justified on the grounds of 'the general good or to ensure the protection of the [person for whom the services are provided]' (*Ministère Publique* v *Willy van Waesemael* [1979] ECR 35). In this case a restriction in Belgian law on the right of establishment of employment agencies was held to conflict with EC law.

Similar restrictions apply where, for example, a language requirement is imposed simply for the purpose of giving a preference to nationals of the member State concerned. The Community is therefore progressively abolishing such restrictions. However, it is recognised that such restrictions are reasonable in certain cases where the restriction relates to the education and training requirement of particular types of work or where it relates to rules of professional conduct in any member State.

The Community is, therefore, undertaking a process whereby Directives will be made under which professional and other qualifications will be recognised throughout the Community subject to safeguards in respect of reasonable requirements of the host State. To implement this process the basic requirement is that all States should recognise qualifications acquired in all other States. There are limited exceptions to this in the form of satisfying the host State's requirements in term of length of training. In certain cases an adaptation period may also be required during which the national of a member State may not practise on his own account in the host State. The period of additional training and the adaptation period together cannot exceed four years. The applicant to the profession (who is qualified in another member State) may take an aptitude test instead of undergoing the adaptation period.

A special exception is made for the legal profession and other professions which require knowledge of the law of the host State. In these cases the proper authority in the host State may require all applicants to take an aptitude test rather than undergoing a period of adaptation (they may not, however, require both). Such aptitude tests have been instituted in a number of member States. In England and Wales the test requires the applicant who is qualified in another EC jurisdiction to demonstrate his or her ability in English and to take a number of tests to demonstrate his or her aptitude to be a lawyer in this jurisdiction.

20.4 The Free Movement of Goods

20.4.1 INTRODUCTION

In order to open up markets within the European Community and to allow traders the opportunity to market their goods 'on a level playing field', there was included in the Treaty of Rome Article 28, the effect of which is to remove barriers to the sale of goods across and within all member States.

These Articles cover all measures taken by member States, including not just those emanating directly from government but also from institutions or bodies which have governmental or legislational approval or backing (R v *Royal Pharmaceutical Society of Greater Britain* [1989] 2 All ER 758).

20.4.2 ARTICLE 28 — RESTRICTIONS ON IMPORTS

Article 28 states that 'quantitative restrictions on imports and all measures having equivalent effect shall ... be prohibited between member States.'

It will be noted that the wording covers both measures which are prohibitions or restrictions of themselves (quantitative restrictions) and measures which amount to or have as their effect a prohibitive or restrictive effect on imports (measures for equivalent effect). For example, the Article will equally defeat an import ban on matches as it will a provision requiring that all imported matches be sold in metal, fire-proof containers. (Although it could be argued that the latter measure is for the protection of the consumer — see **20.4.5**.)

20.4.3 THE 'DASSONVILLE' FORMULA

The case of *Procurer du Roi* v *Dassonville* [1974] ECR 837 established the following definition of measures of equivalent effect:

> All trading rules enacted by member States which are capable of hindering directly or indirectly, actually or potentially, intra-community trade ...

20.4.4 THE CASSIS PRINCIPLE — TREATMENT OF MEASURES OF EQUIVALENT EFFECT

Measures of equivalent effect need not necessarily be aimed specifically at imported goods. For example, a law of a member State requiring all alcoholic drinks to be sold only in half litre bottles, irrespective of where they are produced, could hinder trade in drinks because drinks companies wanting to import into that country would have to have specific bottling facilities to comply with such legislation. Although not necessarily so in this example, legislation of this kind may be based on sound, objectively justifiable reasoning, such as the protection of public health or the consumer.

As such, the ECJ has acknowledged the fact that certain laws should be upheld even if they appear contrary to Article 28. What the court devised has become known as the 'Cassis principle', which draws a distinction between legislation which is applicable to all goods wherever their origin ('indistinctly applicable') and that which applies only to imported goods ('distinctly applicable') (see *Rewe-Zentral AG v Bundesmonopolverwaltung für Branntwein* [1979] 3 CMLR 494). Any restriction which is *indistinctly* applicable will only offend against Article 28 to the extent that the restriction it seeks to impose is out of proportion to the ends it is trying to achieve. In other words, if these ends can be achieved by lesser methods which have a reduced impact on inter-State trade, the relevant legislation will be caught by Article 28. (The treatment of distinctly applicable restrictions is covered by Article 30 — see **20.4.5**.) However, this so-called 'rule of reason' is only applicable where the legislation under scrutiny is concerned with:

(a) fiscal supervision;

(b) protection of public health;

(c) fairness of commercial transactions;

(d) defence of the consumer.

Perhaps a surprising (but inevitable) effect of this rule has been its use as a proposed defence in certain prosecutions involving the regulation of trading in member states, those involving Sunday trading laws in the UK being a good example (see *B&Q Ltd v Shrewsbury & Atcham Borough Council* [1990] 3 CMLR 535). This has led to the European Court in the case of *Keck and Mithuard* [1993] ECR I-6097 attempting to redefine the impact of *Dassonville* to allow greater freedom for member states to regulate trade on a national level without concern for Article 28. The decision distinguishes between 'requirements to be met' by goods, such as those relating to size, designation, labelling and packaging, and those rules which govern 'selling arrangements'. When considering a 'requirements to be met' issue, one must still consider *Dassonville* and, if caught, must then consider the impact of the 'Cassis Principle'. However, 'selling arrangements' will prima facie not come within the ambit of *Dassonville*, provided that those arrangements apply to all affected traders equally and they do not involve discriminatory treatment between domestic and imported products. As such, it is less likely that traders will be able to rely upon Article 28 to challenge or avoid prosecution under national regulations. (In the *Keck and Mithuard* case itself, the parties had been prosecuted under a French law which governed predatory pricing and were claiming invalidity of such law. Ironically, their case was not based upon Article 28 but the European Court focused on Article 28, no doubt, it is submitted, in an attempt to seize the opportunity to provide some clarification on the article.)

20.4.5 ARTICLE 30 — DEROGATION FROM ARTICLE 28

In addition to the 'rule of reason', Article 30 allows member States to derogate from Article 28 on the following grounds:

(a) public morality;

(b) public policy;

(c) public security;

(d) protection of health;

(e) protection of national treasures;

(f) protection of intellectual property rights.

Such grounds are narrowly construed and any member State must be able to justify objectively any ban or restriction it is imposing.

By far the most relevant of the above to businesses is that relating to intellectual property. Whilst it is beyond the scope of this book to look at such a topic in any detail, brief explanation should be given.

By way of example, suppose that a company in one member State manufactures compact discs. It owns copyright in those recordings. It arranges to have those discs sold in another member State by a different company but this company decides to re-import the discs back into their country of origin where they are not available. Such an action would constitute breach of copyright and could, therefore, be prevented by the manufacturer. However, such action is contrary to Article 28, and so must fall within the ambit of Article 30 to be justified. In such a case, the ECJ decided that derogation from Article 28 only extends to protection of the actual intellectual property itself and action beyond this will not be permitted (see *Deutsche Grammophon GmbH* v *Metro-SB-Grossmärkte GmbH* [1971] CMLR 631).

This is a complex and sophisticated area of law and the reader is first recommended to become familiar with the basic concepts of intellectual property and then to consult the relevant texts for a full explanation. However, a rule of thumb with regard to this area is that:

(a) Once the intellectual property owner has permitted its goods which are the subject of the intellectual property rights onto the market in any member State, its rights are said to be 'exhausted' and any attempt to use such rights to prevent importation of those goods into another member State will contravene Article 28.

(b) There is nothing, however, to prevent an owner of intellectual property exercising its rights to prevent blatant infringement by counterfeiters etc.

TWENTY ONE

TREATY OF ROME ARTICLES 81 AND 82

This chapter covers the following topics:

21.1 Introduction
21.2 Article 81
21.3 Article 82
21.4 Enforcement of competition policy
21.5 The Competition Act 1998.

21.1 Introduction

Articles 81 and 82 relate to the competition policy of the European Community. They are among the most important provisions of the Treaty. The object of the Treaty is to ensure that there is a free market which enables goods to move freely between the member States. Article 81 furthers this objective by outlawing certain agreements which prevent, restrict or distort competition within the Community. Article 82 prohibits abuse of a dominant position in the common market or a significant part of it in so far as it may affect trade between member States.

In addition to the provisions of the Treaty itself regulations have been made by the Council of Ministers and by the Commission which supplement the provisions of the Treaty. The Court of Justice of the European Community and the Court of First Instance have also been called upon to develop a considerable body of case law relating to the competition policy of the Community.

The Council of Ministers has granted wide powers to the Commission in relation to competition law. In particular the Commission both makes policy decisions and enforces them (as to enforcement, see below). Parties aggrieved by a decision of the Commission are entitled to appeal, on points of law, to the Court of First Instance, and ultimately from there to the Court of Justice of the European Community itself.

21.2 Article 81

Article 81(1) prohibits 'all agreements between undertakings, decisions by associations of undertakings and concerted practices which may affect trade between member States and which have as their object or effect the prevention, restriction or distortion of competition within the common market'.

Agreements are defined as including informal agreements which may fall short of being contracts. The concept of a 'concerted practice' is even wider. This has been held to include any case where 'practical co-operation' between undertakings (i.e., businesses) have been set up in opposition to the concept of competition. An example of a concerted practice is where different undertakings keep their prices in line with each other. The fact that prices have risen at the same time is not, however, sufficient to prove a concerted practice. There must be evidence that the activities of the undertakings involved are such as to distort the market.

Decisions by associations of undertakings include such things as price fixing by trade associations. Decisions which have the effect of fixing prices are subject to Article 81 even if they are not binding on the members of the association, provided they are likely to be complied with at least to the extent that the free market will be affected.

The object of this provision is to ensure free movement of goods within the Community. However, it should be noted that what is prohibited is any agreement which may *affect trade between member States*. This does not, however, mean that an agreement which is made between undertakings in only one member State is automatically valid. An agreement between undertakings which only relates to activities within one country may indirectly prevent other companies from entering that market from a different member State.

21.2.1 VERTICAL AGREEMENTS

A vertical agreement is one between undertakings at different levels within the market. For example a manufacturer's agreement with a wholesaler or a wholesaler's agreement with a shop are vertical agreements. Examples of vertical agreements include agency agreements and supply agreements. Such agreements may fall foul of Article 81.

21.2.2 HORIZONTAL AGREEMENTS

Horizontal agreements are made between undertakings which are at the same level of the economic chain. For example, an agreement between two manufacturers is a horizontal agreement. These agreements are unlikely to be valid in view of the provisions of Article 81.

For example in *Heintz van Landewyck Sàrl v Commission* [1981] 3 CMLR 134 an instruction from a trade association representing tobacco manufacturers in Belgium and Luxembourg was held invalid. This was on the basis that the trade association was able to give directions which were binding on its members. This case also decided that Article 81 can apply to non-profit organisations (such as the trade association) if they are carrying on economic activities.

21.2.3 ARTICLE 81(3)

Article 81(3) provides an exemption from the basic rule contained in Article 81(1) where the operation of the rule would be inconsistent with the more general principles of competition law. Article 81(3) allows the Commission to consider agreements notified to it. The Commission can then issue a Decision to the parties which may exempt them from Article 81(1). The Commission will grant exemption to an agreement or decision of an association if it:

> contributes to the improvement of the production or distribution of goods or to promoting technical or economic progress, while allowing consumers a fair share of the resulting benefits, and ... only imposes restrictions on the parties which are indispensable to the attainment of these objectives and does not allow the parties concerned the possibility of eliminating competition within the relevant product market.

21.2.4 IS IT POSSIBLE TO AVOID FALLING FOUL OF ARTICLE 81?

Article 81 is widely drawn so it is not possible to contract out of it. However, there are a number of effective exemptions.

21.2.4.1 Agreements of Minor Importance

The Commission has itself issued a notice on Agreements of Minor Importance which lays down guidelines allowing small scale agreements in circumstances where a similar agreement on a larger scale would be void. Put very simply, where the parties to a horizontal agreement own no more than 5% of the market share for the product in question and 10% of the market in relation to a vertical agreement, the agreement falls outside the ambit of Article 81. (Full details of this are given in 33.3.2.3.)

21.2.4.2 Article 81(3)

We have already seen that Article 81(3) itself provides for exemption where the agreement is beneficial. An undertaking which believes that its agreement should be exempt under that provision can apply for an individual exemption which confirms the exempt status of this agreement.

21.2.4.3 Block exemptions

A system of block exemptions has been devised by the Commission. This provides that certain types of agreement are not to be regarded as infringing Article 81. In relation to each type of agreement the Commission will usually produce lists of contract terms which will be regarded as acceptable in such agreements ('the white list') and terms which will exclude the agreements from the block exemption ('the black list').

There are currently a number of block exemptions in existence, each one targeting particular arrangements. From 1 June 2000, those which apply to exclusive distributorship agreements, exclusive purchasing agreements and franchise agreements will be supplanted by Regulation (EC) 2790/1999, which will operate to provide exemption from the effect of Article 81(1) to various types of vertical agreements.

Vertical agreements are those which are entered into between businesses at different levels in the production and distribution chain and which govern the circumstances under which those businesses buy and sell goods and/or services.

However, the exemption will only apply when the market share of the supplier or the buyer (where the agreement has exclusive supply obligations) does not exceed 30%. Market share of the supplier is calculated on the basis of the market sales value of the goods or services in question sold by the supplier, which are regarded as interchangeable or substitutable by the buyer, by reason of the price of the goods or services, intended use and characteristics. Market share of the buyer is based upon the market purchase value of the relevant market.

The Regulation anticipates that such market share may fluctuate and provides that:

(a) if market share increases beyond 30% up to 35%, the exemption will continue to apply for a period of two calendar years after the year in which the first increase over 30% occurred;

(b) if market share increases beyond 35% the exemption will continue to apply for a period of one calendar year after the year in which the first increase over 35% occurred.

Not all vertical agreements which satisfy the above criteria will be exempt. Exceptions are:

(a) agreements which have as their object, inter alia, the restriction of the price at which the buyer may sell on or the restriction of the territories into which the buyer may sell. A notable exception to the latter is the restriction of active sales into an exclusive territory reserved for the supplier or allocated by the supplier to another buyer;

(b) agreements which contain certain non-competition clauses which are operative for a period of more than five years;

(c) agreements which restrict the buyer from manufacturing, purchasing or selling goods or services after termination of the agreement.

The main concern for lawyers and their clients will be how to draft an agreement to benefit from the Regulation. As with so many things, the devil will be in the detail and there are a number of areas of the Regulation which require further clarification. Until this is provided, lawyers will have the difficult task of making value judgments about the suitability of contracts and the market shares of their clients.

Any agreements in force on 31 May 2000 which satisfy the conditions of any of the block exemptions mentioned above will continue to be exempt from Article 81(1) until 31 December 2001. Thereafter, if they do not fall within the Regulation, they will cease to be exempt, so another issue will be how far parties will want to review and revise their agreements if they are advised that they will fail to satisfy the Regulation.

21.3 Article 82

Article 82 provides:

> Any abuse by one or more undertakings of a dominant position within the common market or in a substantial part of it shall be prohibited as incompatible with the common market in so far as it may affect trade between member states.

Notice that Article 82 (unlike Article 81) may be infringed by one undertaking acting alone. The key requirements here are that there must be a dominant position in the market and that that position must have been abused. The European Court of Justice has decided that a dominant position is one which 'enables the undertaking [or undertakings] to prevent effective competition ... by giving it the power to behave to an appreciable extent independently of its competitors, customers and ultimately of its consumers' (*United Brands Co. v Commission* (Case 27/76) [1978] 1 CMLR 429). To be actionable the dominance must exist in a particular market. This is sometimes defined as the relevant product market which means the market for the goods in question together with any other goods which are effective substitutes for the goods in question.

Article 82 itself provides a list of activities which may be regarded as an abuse. This list is not intended to be exhaustive:

(a) imposition of unfair prices or trading conditions;

(b) limiting production markets or technical development to the prejudice of consumers;

(c) discriminating between different trading parties;

(d) by including terms in contracts which are collateral to the subject of the contract.

The abuse which is prohibited by Article 82 might also constitute a breach of Article 81. The two Articles are not designed to be mutually exclusive.

21.4 Enforcement of Competition Policy

21.4.1 DIRECT EFFECT

The provisions of Articles 81 and 82 have 'direct effect' in each of the States of the EC. This means that they are part of the law of each of the member States (in the UK as a result of the European Communities Act 1972). If there is any conflict between the provisions of EC law and the pre-existing UK law the EC law is to prevail. This means that UK courts must recognise and give effect to the competition law of the Community.

Agreements made in the UK which according to the principles of contract law may be valid, may be rendered void as a result of the competition law of the Community. In some cases, however, it may be possible for an English court to apply the principle of severance; that is, the court may be able to declare the clause in the agreement which offends competition law to be void, but uphold the rest of the contract. Whether the court can do this depends on the principles of English law. The traditional approach is that the court will not order severance if to do so would effectively require a re-writing of the agreement, either because the offending part cannot be separated within the agreement or because it is so fundamental to the agreement that to sever it would amount to imposing a new contract on the parties.

In addition to the possibility of action by another party to the contract it is also possible for third parties to sue under either Article if they have suffered loss. The position in English law is not entirely clear, but it would seem that the court can impose an injunction or award damages for breach of 'statutory' duty.

21.4.2 ENFORCEMENT BY THE COMMISSION

Many of the Commission's powers to investigate possible breach of Articles 81 and 82 are contained in Regulation 17/62. This enables the Commission to obtain information by (for example) inspecting premises, books and other records. The Commission has powers to impose fines of up to 1,000,000 Euros (formerly ECUs), or 10 per cent of the undertaking's turnover in the last accounting period, whichever is higher. Perhaps the most famous instance of this is where the Commission levied a fine of 75 million Euros (formerly ECUs) on Tetra-Pak for breaches of Article 82.

21.5 The Competition Act 1998

Since the introduction of the above, the relevance of EC competition law has become more acute. See **33.5** for further discussion.

INSOLVENCY

TWENTY TWO

BANKRUPTCY

This chapter covers the following topics:

22.1 Introduction
22.2 The bankruptcy procedure
22.3 The trustee in bankruptcy
22.4 Effect of the bankruptcy order on the bankrupt personally
22.5 Assets in the bankrupt's estate
22.6 Distribution of the bankrupt's assets
22.7 Duration of the bankruptcy and discharge of the bankrupt
22.8 Voluntary arrangements.

22.1 Introduction

The risk of personal bankruptcy is a spectre which haunts many partners and sole traders. If a partner or sole trader finds that he is unable to pay his debts as they fall due, he may be made personally bankrupt. Thus, the partner or sole trader may be made bankrupt if his liabilities exceed his assets; he faces the same risk if he has insufficient liquid assets to pay his current liabilities even if the value of his total assets exceeds the value of his total liabilities.

It is to avoid this risk that many entrepreneurs choose to trade through a limited company. However, it should not be forgotten that the directors and members of a company may face personal bankruptcy where, for example, a director or shareholder has personally guaranteed a loan to the company or where a director is liable for 'wrongful' trading.

The members or partners may, of course, also find themselves facing bankruptcy as a result of a financial collapse entirely unconnected with the business of their own company or partnership.

The law of bankruptcy is now mostly contained in the Insolvency Act 1986 together with delegated legislation made under its provisions.

In this chapter we will summarise the law under the following headings:

(a) The procedure for making a person bankrupt.

(b) The appointment, function and removal of the trustee in bankruptcy.

BANKRUPTCY

(c) The effect of the bankruptcy order on the bankrupt personally.

(d) The provisions relating to the assets in the bankrupt's estate.

(e) The distribution of the bankrupt's assets.

(f) The duration of the bankruptcy and the discharge of the bankrupt.

(g) The rules governing voluntary arrangements contained in the Insolvency Act 1986.

A debtor who finds himself unable to meet all his debts in full may:

(a) be adjudicated bankrupt; or

(b) have his estate administered by a qualified insolvency practitioner under a voluntary arrangement (see **22.6** below).

22.2 The Bankruptcy Procedure

22.2.1 INTRODUCTION

Bankruptcy proceedings are commenced by the presentation of a petition for a bankruptcy order. The petitioners (who, broadly speaking, simply have to prove that the debtor is unable to pay his debts) are:

(a) a creditor (or creditors jointly) whether secured or unsecured; or

(b) the debtor personally; or

(c) a supervisor of, or a person bound by, a voluntary scheme; or

(d) the Director of Public Prosecutions.

22.2.2 PROCEDURE ON A CREDITOR'S PETITION

22.2.2.1 Prerequisites for presentation of a creditor's petition

The court will only entertain a petition presented by a creditor or creditors if certain conditions are satisfied:

(a) The debtor must normally be domiciled or personally present in England and Wales when the petition is presented.

(b) The debt (or debts) which are the basis of the petition must be for a liquidated sum.

(c) The debt (or debts) must amount to at least £750. (This sum can be changed from time to time by statutory instrument.)

(d) The debt must be unsecured. A secured creditor can present a petition but only if he relinquishes his security or petitions only for the unsecured part of the debt.

22.2.2.2 Grounds for presenting a creditor's petition

The petitioning creditor must allege that the debtor appears either:

BANKRUPTCY

(a) to be unable to pay, or

(b) to have no reasonable prospect of paying

the debt or debts specified in the petition and that there are no outstanding applications to have a 'statutory demand' set aside. (A 'statutory demand' is a demand in a form which complies with the Insolvency Rules 1986, r. 6.1.) The functions of the demand are described below.

22.2.2.3 Proving inability to pay debt

Before the court will make the order, the debtor's inability to pay his debt or debts may be proved in one of two ways:

(a) By showing that a 'statutory demand' served on the debtor requiring him to pay, secure or compound for the debt to the satisfaction of the petitioning creditor has not been complied with within three weeks.

(b) By showing that execution or other process issued in respect of the debt as a judgment or order of any court has been returned unsatisfied in whole or in part.

22.2.2.4 Grounds on which court may dismiss petition

Once a petition has been presented by a creditor the court may dismiss the petition if it is shown that the debtor can pay all his debts, including contingent and prospective debts; if the creditor has unreasonably refused any offer made by the debtor in response to a 'statutory demand'; or if it is appropriate to dismiss the petition for any reason, including a breach of the rules.

The court *must* dismiss a petition if a 'statutory demand' has been complied with.

22.2.3 PROCEDURE ON A DEBTOR'S OWN PETITION

The debtor himself may present a petition provided he has a connection with England and Wales. Accordingly the debtor must be able to show that he satisfies the requirements set out in **22.2.2.1 (a)** above.

The only ground on which the petition can be based is that the debtor is unable to pay his debts. When presenting the petition, the debtor must lodge a 'statement of affairs' giving full details of his assets, liabilities and creditors. Once presented, the petition can only be withdrawn with leave of the court.

In most cases the court will order an insolvency practitioner to inquire into the debtor's affairs and report on whether the debtor is willing to make a proposal for a composition with his creditors and/or whether the creditors should be summoned to a meeting at which they will consider such a proposal. Having considered the report of the insolvency practitioner the court can, if it considers it appropriate, make a bankruptcy order. Otherwise the voluntary composition will be pursued or the court can issue a certificate of summary administration.

22.2.4 PRESENTATION OF A PETITION BY A SUPERVISOR OF, OR A PERSON BOUND BY, A VOLUNTARY SCHEME

The supervisor of, or a person bound by, a voluntary scheme (the details of which are considered below in **22.8**) may base a petition on the following grounds:

BANKRUPTCY

(a) that the debtor has failed to comply with his obligations under the scheme (or failure to comply with the supervisor's reasonable requests in connection with the scheme);

(b) that the debtor has provided false or misleading information in connection with entry into the scheme.

22.2.5 PRESENTATION OF A PETITION BY THE DIRECTOR OF PUBLIC PROSECUTIONS

The DPP has power (under the Powers of Criminal Courts Act 1973) to apply to have a person made criminally bankrupt if the person has been convicted of an offence where loss in excess of a specified value has occurred.

22.2.6 CONSEQUENCES OF PRESENTING A PETITION

22.2.6.1 Restrictions on dispositions

A debtor who is the subject of a bankruptcy petition may be tempted to dispose of property before he is adjudicated bankrupt. The Insolvency Act 1986 makes void any disposition of property or payment of money made after the presentation of a petition if the debtor is subsequently adjudicated bankrupt unless the court approves the transaction either before or after it takes place.

22.2.6.2 Restrictions on proceedings

The court has power to stay any action, execution or legal process against the debtor or his assets while bankruptcy proceedings are pending.

22.2.7 MAKING THE BANKRUPTCY ORDER

Once the petition has been presented, the court may exercise its discretion to make a bankruptcy order (or, in the case of a petition presented by the debtor personally, to make an interim order so that a voluntary composition with the creditors can be arranged).

22.2.8 PROCEDURE FOLLOWING THE MAKING OF THE BANKRUPTCY ORDER

22.2.8.1 The official receiver becomes receiver and manager of the estate

Unless a trustee in bankruptcy is appointed at the time the bankruptcy order is made, the official receiver (who is an official of the court) will become the receiver and manager of the bankrupt's estate on the making of the order, pending the appointment of a trustee in bankruptcy.

22.2.8.2 Statement of affairs by the bankrupt

The bankrupt must, unless the official receiver dispenses with the requirement, prepare a statement of his affairs within 21 days (although this time-limit may be extended by the official receiver). Failure to do so is contempt of court.

When the debtor presents his own petition he must prepare a statement of affairs which is lodged with the petition.

22.2.8.3 Public examination of the bankrupt

At any time after the order is made and before the bankrupt is discharged, the official receiver can apply for an order that the bankrupt be required to attend a public examination of his affairs.

22.2.8.4 Appointment of a committee of creditors

Following the making of the bankruptcy order, a committee of creditors can be appointed by the creditors (unless the official receiver has been appointed as trustee in bankruptcy in which case the Secretary of State performs the function of the committee).

22.3 The Trustee in Bankruptcy

22.3.1 INTRODUCTION

The Insolvency Act 1986 provides that the administration of a bankrupt estate should be carried out by a trustee in bankruptcy.

22.3.2 APPOINTMENT

The procedure for appointing a trustee in bankruptcy and the date on which his appointment takes effect differ depending on who makes the appointment.

22.3.2.1 Appointment by creditors

If the official receiver is acting as receiver and manager of the bankrupt's estate, he has 12 weeks from the making of the order to decide whether to call a meeting of the creditors for the purpose of appointing a trustee. If he decides to call such a meeting he must notify the creditors within the 12-week period. He *must* call such a meeting if one-quarter (by value) of the creditors demand it and if he decides not to call a meeting, one-quarter (by value) of the creditors can override his decision. Provided the creditors do not object to no meeting being called, on notifying the court that no meeting will be held, the official receiver automatically becomes the trustee.

22.3.2.2 Appointment by the court

If the order is based on the debtor's own petition, the insolvency practitioner who is appointed to report on the debtor's affairs can be appointed as the trustee.

22.3.2.3 Appointment by the Secretary of State

The Secretary of State has power to appoint the trustee if the creditors fail to make an appointment at their meeting.

22.3.3 FUNCTIONS OF THE TRUSTEE

The function of the trustee is to get in, realise and distribute the bankrupt's estate in accordance with the provisions of the Act.

22.3.4 POWERS OF THE TRUSTEE

The Act gives the trustee wide powers which he may exercise in the course of administering the bankrupt's affairs. He may:

(a) Sell any part of the property for the time being comprised in the bankrupt's estate, including the goodwill and book debts of any business.

(b) Give receipts for any money received by him.

(c) Prove, rank, claim and draw a dividend in respect of such debts *due* to the bankrupt as are comprised in the bankrupt's estate.

(d) Exercise in relation to any property comprised in the bankrupt's estate any powers which the Act vests in him as trustee.

(e) Exercise all the powers of a receiver appointed by the High Court to enable him to collect or retain the bankrupt's estate.

(f) Exercise all the powers the bankrupt could exercise to transfer shares, stock or other property.

(g) Exercise extensive powers to require delivery, production or inspection of books, documents and records.

(h) Apply to the court for orders directing the bankrupt to do any act in connection with the administration of the estate.

(i) Hold property, make contracts, sue and be sued, employ agents, execute documents and do any act which may be necessary or expedient for the exercise of his powers.

(j) Disclaim onerous property (e.g., unprofitable contracts).

There are certain further powers which are only exercisable with the consent of the committee of creditors (if there is one) or of the court. These include:

(a) Power to carry on the bankrupt's business with a view to a beneficial winding up.

(b) Power to mortgage or pledge assets with a view to raising money for the estate.

(c) Power to make any compromise or arrangement as may be expedient with the creditors of the estate.

(d) Power to require the bankrupt to do any acts in the management or carrying on of the bankrupt's business.

22.3.5 RETIREMENT, REMOVAL AND RELEASE

22.3.5.1 Resignation

A trustee in bankruptcy may resign only if the resignation is accepted either by a creditors' meeting or by the court. Resignation must arise out of ill-health, retirement from practice, conflict of interest or other sufficient causes.

22.3.5.2 Removal

The appointees of creditors can be removed either by the court or by the creditors themselves at a general meeting summoned specially for the purpose.

22.4 Effect of the Bankruptcy Order on the Bankrupt Personally

If the court exercises its discretion to make a bankruptcy order against the debtor, he will become an undischarged bankrupt and will be deprived of the ownership of his property.

An undischarged bankrupt suffers certain disabilities, for example he cannot practise as a solicitor or barrister nor act as a director, nor be involved in the management, of a company. Furthermore, an undischarged bankrupt faces criminal liability if he commits one of the offences specified in the 1986 Act. These include making gifts of property, concealing property, and obtaining credit without disclosing the bankruptcy.

22.5 Assets in the Bankrupt's Estate

22.5.1 INTRODUCTION

The trustee in bankruptcy is under an obligation to collect the bankrupt's assets and distribute them among the bankrupt's creditors. In this section, we consider which assets can be claimed by the trustee towards payment of the bankrupt's debts.

22.5.2 AVOIDANCE OF DISPOSITIONS MADE AFTER THE PRESENTATION OF THE PETITION

Any disposition made by the bankrupt in the period between presentation of the petition and the date the estate of the bankrupt vests in the trustee in bankruptcy is void, unless the court gave prior consent (or subsequently ratifies) the disposition.

22.5.3 VESTING THE ASSETS IN THE TRUSTEE

Once the bankruptcy order is made, the undischarged bankrupt is deprived of the ownership of his property.

22.5.4 PROPERTY NOT AVAILABLE TO THE TRUSTEE

If the bankrupt enjoyed a purely personal right, such as the benefit of the Rent Act statutory tenancy, this is not available to the trustee. The following items are also not available for distribution:

(a) Property held by the bankrupt in trust for any other person.

(b) The tools of his trade, as well as such wearing apparel and bedding as is necessary to satisfy the basic needs of the bankrupt and his family.

(c) The personal earnings of the bankrupt to the extent that those earnings are not in excess of what is required to satisfy the reasonable domestic needs of the bankrupt and his family.

22.5.5 EXTENSION OF TRUSTEE'S TITLE TO BANKRUPT'S PROPERTY

The Act gives the trustee power to claim assets which are no longer in the possession or ownership of the bankrupt in the circumstances set out below.

22.5.5.1 Transactions defrauding creditors (sections 423 to 425)

Grounds

Section 423 of the Insolvency Act 1986 can be used to give relief in respect of transactions defrauding creditors. To be within the scope of s. 423 a transaction must be:

(a) a transaction at an undervalue entered into between one person and another; and

(b) be accompanied by the requisite intent, namely that it is done for the purpose of putting assets beyond the reach of a person who is making, or may at some time make, a claim against the relevant person, or of otherwise prejudicing the interests of such a person in relation to the claim which he is making or may make.

Time limit

The transaction which is the subject of an action under s. 423 can have taken place at any time; there is no time-limit.

22.5.5.2 Undervalue transactions

If a person who is subsequently made bankrupt has transferred property to, for example, a member of his family or to trustees to hold for the benefit of his family with a view to putting assets beyond the reach of his creditors the transaction may be voidable under s. 339 of the Insolvency Act 1986.

Grounds on which transaction voidable

If the transaction is at an undervalue and is with a person who is not an associate of the transferor, it is voidable at the instance of the trustee in bankruptcy (or administrator where a voluntary arrangement has been made) if the transaction took place within the five years ending with the day on which the bankruptcy petition which ultimately led to the individual being adjudged bankrupt was presented (unless the debtor was solvent at the time of, and despite entering into, the transaction). However, if the individual entered into the transaction at an undervalue within two years of the presentation of the relevant bankruptcy petition, the transaction is voidable irrespective of whether the debtor was insolvent at the time of, or as a result of, the transaction.

Transfer to associate

In circumstances where the transferee is an 'associate' of the transferor, transactions entered into during the period of five years preceding the presentation of the petition are presumed, unless it can be *proved* to the contrary, to have taken place at a time when the transferor was insolvent. 'Associate' is defined as the bankrupt's spouse or former or reputed spouse, and, in relation to any of them or the bankrupt, a brother, sister, uncle, aunt, nephew, niece, lineal ancestor or lineal descendant (including relatives of the half-blood, stepchildren, adopted and illegitimate children. A company controlled by the bankrupt or any associate(s), as defined, is an associate.

22.5.5.3 Voidable preferences

A debtor who is in financial difficulties may not only make an undervalue transaction (as described in **22.5.5.2** above) but he may also be tempted to give a 'voidable preference' (Insolvency Act 1986, s.340).

Grounds

A 'voidable preference' consists of the debtor doing or suffering anything to be done at a time when he is insolvent which 'has the effect of putting [the person who benefits from the preference] into a position which, in the event of the [debtor's] bankruptcy, will be better than the position he would have been in if that thing had not been done'. Thus, a debtor discharging one of his unsecured, ordinary creditor's debts in full at a time when his assets are insufficient to discharge *all* his debts in full may have given a voidable preference.

If the trustee in bankruptcy considers that a voidable preference has been made, he may apply to the court to remedy the preference. However, an order can only be made where it can be proved that the debtor was 'influenced in deciding to give it by a desire' to improve the position of the creditor. Under these provisions the intention to prefer the particular creditor need not be the *dominant* intention.

Preference given to 'associate'

In cases where the preference is given by an individual to his 'associate' (see **22.5.5.2** above), there is a *presumption* that the debtor was influenced by the desire which would make the preference voidable, unless the contrary is proved.

Time limits

A preference is voidable if it takes place within the two years ending with the presentation of the bankruptcy petition, if the person preferred is an associate, but in other cases the preference is only actionable if it took place in the six months preceding the presentation of the petition.

22.5.5.4 Family homes

The Insolvency Act contains provisions designed to protect the family home of the bankrupt for the benefit of his family.

If the family home is owned in the sole name of the bankrupt the 1986 Act charges the right of occupation of the spouse of the bankrupt on the interest of the trustee in bankruptcy in the matrimonial home. If an application is made to realise the bankrupt's interest in the house the court will consider certain factors when deciding whether to grant an application for sale of the house. These factors include the creditors' interests, the needs and resources of the spouse, the needs of the children, whether the spouse's conduct contributed to the bankruptcy and all other relevant circumstances. (If the matrimonial home is owned in joint names by the bankrupt and his spouse, the discretionary factors listed above will be taken into account when the trustee applies under s.30 of the Law of Property Act 1925 to realise the bankrupt's interest.) If the application is made after one year has elapsed since the bankrupt's property vested in the trustee in bankruptcy, the interests of the creditors will be paramount.

If the bankrupt's minor children lived in the home at the time of presenting the petition and when the bankruptcy order was made, the bankrupt cannot be evicted without a court order. The court will consider the creditors' interests, the bankrupt's financial resources, the needs of the children and all the circumstances when deciding whether to make the eviction order. If the application is made after one year has elapsed since the bankrupt's estate vested in his trustee the interests of the creditors will outweigh all other considerations, unless the circumstances are exceptional.

22.6 Distribution of the Bankrupt's Assets

22.6.1 DISTRIBUTION PROCEDURE

Having realised as much of the bankrupt's assets as possible without needlessly protracting the administration of the estate, the trustee must notify the creditors that he intends to declare a final dividend (or that no dividend will be declared). The notice must also state a final date for the proving of claims (although the court has power, on application by any person, to postpone this date). Subject to any postponement, any creditor who fails to prove by the final date may be ignored in the final dividend.

BANKRUPTCY

22.6.2 ORDER OF PRIORITY FOR PAYMENT OF DEBTS

The distribution of the bankrupt's assets must be made strictly in accordance with the statutory order for payment of debts which is as follows:

(a) Secured creditors, who take the mortgaged or charged property in priority to all other claims. However, if the security is insufficient to meet the debt, as far as the excess is concerned, the secured creditor claims as an ordinary creditor.

(b) The administration costs of the bankruptcy paid to the official receiver, the trustee in bankruptcy and others, including professional advisers who have given assistance.

(c) Certain sums paid to masters by their apprentices.

(d) The preferential debts which are the same as those relevant on a company liquidation. These debts are calculated by reference to the 'relevant date', which, generally, is the date the bankruptcy order is made (unless an interim receiver is appointed following the presentation of the petition in which case the date is that on which the receiver is first appointed), and include:

  (i) Sums due from the debtor in respect of deductions of PAYE from his employees' wages in the 12 months prior to the relevant date.

  (ii) VAT claims up to six months before the relevant date.

  (iii) National insurance contributions for 12 months prior to the relevant date (for Class 1 or 2 social security contributions) or one year's assessment of Class 4 contributions before 5 April prior to the relevant date.

  (iv) Employees' arrears of wages or salary (including time or piece work and commission) for four months prior to the relevant date subject to an overall financial limit prescribed by delegated legislation (currently £800). These sums include sick pay, protective awards, and payments for time off work, such as on trade union work.

  (v) Accrued holiday remuneration.

(e) The ordinary unsecured creditors.

(f) Statutory interest which will be paid if a surplus remains after all previous claims have been paid. This interest is paid from the date of the order to the date of payment and the rate is the greater of the rate provided for in s.17 of the Judgments Act 1838 and the rate the bankrupt would have had to pay on the debt if he had not been made bankrupt.

(g) The postponed creditors such as the spouse of the bankrupt who has a provable debt as a result of a loan to the bankrupt spouse.

(h) The bankrupt receives any surplus.

Each class of creditor must be paid in full before the next class receives anything. If the assets are insufficient to meet the debts owed to the creditors of the class, they are paid rateably according to value.

22.7 Duration of the Bankruptcy and Discharge of the Bankrupt

22.7.1 DISCHARGE OF THE BANKRUPT

The Insolvency Act 1986, in relation to the majority of bankruptcies, provides for a bankrupt to be automatically discharged once the period of time specified by the Act has elapsed. In most circumstances this period is three years. The Act contains provisions which will prevent the 'automatic' discharge being available if the circumstances justify it.

22.7.2 EFFECT OF DISCHARGE

Once the bankrupt has been discharged, he is normally freed from the disqualifications suffered by undischarged bankrupts and from liability to meet his bankruptcy debts.

22.8 Individual Voluntary Arrangements

22.8.1 INTRODUCTION

While formal bankruptcy may be the appropriate method of dealing with many debtors who find themselves in financial difficulties, there will be certain cases where the debtor involved may be able to come to terms with his creditors without involving the full rigour of the bankruptcy procedure. Although deeds of arrangement entered into under the Deeds of Arrangement Act 1914 were intended to satisfy this particular need, that procedure is not entirely satisfactory since only the creditors who agree to the deed of arrangement are bound by its terms. The procedure under the 1914 Act has been little used and is not considered further in this book. Therefore, the Insolvency Act 1986 has introduced a new alternative method by which debtors can come to binding arrangements with their creditors. This allows debtors to propose a composition or scheme of arrangement to creditors. This is known as an individual voluntary arrangement, usually referred to in practice as an 'IVA'. The procedure for this is set out in Pt VIII of the Insolvency Act 1986.

22.8.2 INTERIM ORDER

22.8.2.1 Application by debtor

If a debtor in financial difficulties wishes to propose a voluntary arrangement to his creditors, he must first apply to the court, even if a petition for his bankruptcy has already been presented, for an interim order to be made. The debtor must have in place an insolvency practitioner who is willing to act in relation to the proposed voluntary arrangement. The latter is known as the 'nominee'.

22.8.2.2 Effect of interim orders

Once the interim order is made, no bankruptcy petition can be presented against the debtor and no other proceedings, execution or legal process can, without the leave of the court, be commenced or prosecuted against the debtor or his assets. (It should be noted that legislation has been proposed to allow a proposal to be made for a voluntary arrangement *without* first applying for an interim order. Obviously, in such a situation, the debtor would not have the benefit of the interim order.)

22.8.2.3 Period of interim order

The interim order is relatively short-lived since it will cease to have effect at the end of the period of 14 days beginning with the day after the order was made, although the court has power to extend the period.

22.8.3 PROCEDURE FOLLOWING THE MAKING OF THE INTERIM ORDER

22.8.3.1 Debtors to provide statements to nominee

After the order has been made the debtor must provide the nominee with a statement giving details of the proposed voluntary arrangement. He must also give a statement of his affairs, which will give details of his assets and liabilities. Failure to do so may result in the interim order being discharged.

22.8.3.2 Nominee's report to court

The nominee is required to report to the court, stating whether the voluntary arrangement has a reasonable prospect of being approved and implemented. In addition, he is required to state whether a meeting of creditors should be called to consider the proposed voluntary arrangements. Should the nominee fail to deliver the report to the court before the interim order expires, the debtor can apply to the court to have the order renewed or extended and the debtor may also apply to have the nominee replaced.

22.8.3.3 Discharge of interim order

If the nominee decides that a meeting of creditors should not be called and the court agrees, the interim order may be discharged.

22.8.4 CONSIDERATION OF THE DEBTOR'S PROPOSALS

If the nominee has submitted a report to the court recommending that a creditor's meeting be called to consider the debtor's proposals, subject to any directions made by the court, the nominee gives notice of the meeting (at the date, time and place specified in his report to the court) to all creditors of whom he is aware.

At the meeting the proposals will be considered and the proposals may be approved as proposed or with any changes thought appropriate.

22.8.5 EFFECT OF ACCEPTING THE PROPOSAL

Once the proposal is approved, all persons who had notice of the meeting and who were entitled to vote at the meeting (irrespective of whether they did so vote) are bound by the composition or scheme as if they were parties to it. Any creditor who would have been entitled to vote at the meeting, had they been given notice of it, will also be bound by the proposal.

Subject to any challenges within the 28-day period referred to in **22.8.6** below, once the proposal has been accepted, any interim order in force ceases to have effect and any bankruptcy petition which was stayed by the interim order is deemed to have been dismissed (subject to a court order to the contrary).

22.8.6 CHALLENGING THE DECISION OF THE CREDITORS' MEETING

22.8.6.1 Parties who may challenge

Once the creditors' meeting has reported its decision to the court, at any time during the 28 days commencing with the day the report is made to the court, that decision may be challenged by:

(a) the debtor;

(b) any person who was entitled to vote at the meeting;

(c) the nominee (or his replacement).

22.8.6.2 Grounds

The grounds of challenge are limited to the following:

(a) that the composition or scheme accepted by the meeting unfairly prejudices the interests of a creditor; and/or

(b) that there was a material irregularity at, or in relation to, the meeting.

22.8.6.3 Effect of challenge

If the court confirms the challenge, the approval of the meeting may be revoked or suspended. Alternatively, the court may order a further meeting to be held to consider any revised proposal or (if the challenge is based on 'material irregularity' in relation to the meeting) order that the meeting be held again to reconsider the proposal.

Having ordered a further meeting to be held, the court can extend or renew the interim order. However, if the court is satisfied that no revised proposal will be submitted by the debtor, the order to hold a further meeting will be revoked and the approval given at the original meeting will be revoked or suspended.

TWENTY THREE

COMPANY INSOLVENCY PROCEEDINGS

This chapter covers the following topics:

23.1 Introduction
23.2 Administration orders
23.3 Voluntary arrangements (sections 1 to 7)
23.4 Receivership
23.5 Liquidation or winding up
23.6 Liquidators
23.7 Collection and distribution of assets in liquidation
23.8 Order of entitlement to assets
23.9 Dissolution
23.10 Application to partnerships.

23.1 Introduction

All statute references in this and the following chapter are to the Insolvency Act 1986 except where otherwise stated.

In this chapter we shall deal with the procedures which are available when a company is insolvent and with the procedures which are designed to prevent insolvency where a company is having financial problems. In the final section of this chapter we shall look at the way in which insolvent partnerships can be subject to the same procedures as companies.

The law relating to these matters is now largely contained in the Insolvency Act 1986 together with the Insolvency Rules 1986. There are four principal procedures available where a company is insolvent or has financial problems:

23.1.1 ADMINISTRATION ORDER

This is a procedure which may be ordered by the court with a view to saving the business of the company (or part of it), or with a view to a more beneficial realisation of assets than could be achieved by winding up, or with a view to obtaining approval for a voluntary arrangement.

23.1.2 VOLUNTARY ARRANGEMENT UNDER THE INSOLVENCY ACT 1986

This procedure enables a variety of schemes to be implemented (with the agreement of the company and its creditors) either so as to avoid or to supplement other types of insolvency procedure.

COMPANY INSOLVENCY PROCEEDINGS

23.1.3 RECEIVERSHIP

A receiver is appointed by a lender who holds a charge over some or all of the company's assets. The main responsibility of the receiver is to take control of the company so as to pay off the appointing creditor. However, the law recognises that this may have a considerable and permanent effect on the company and its other creditors. Therefore various statutory powers are granted to the receiver and a number of obligations imposed on him.

23.1.4 LIQUIDATION (OR WINDING UP)

There are two types of liquidation: liquidation by the court (compulsory winding up) and voluntary liquidation. There are many procedural and other differences between these types of liquidation but each is designed to achieve the same thing, that is, the collection and distribution of all the company's assets. The effect of liquidation is that the company ceases to exist as a *commercial* entity. When the liquidation is over the company is 'dissolved', that is, it ceases to exist as a *legal* entity.

The administration procedure and liquidation by the court are initiated by petition. Applications to the court are required at various stages of the procedures for these remedies and also in relation to voluntary schemes, administrative receivership and voluntary winding up. The High Court has jurisdiction to deal with any such petition or application where the company is registered in England and Wales. This type of business is assigned to the Chancery Division. In addition the county court of the district in which the company's registered office is situated has concurrent jurisdiction where the company's paid-up share capital does not exceed £120,000.

23.2 Administration Orders

Administration is intended as an alternative to winding up. It is used principally in circumstances where a company is in difficulties but where something may be saved.

23.2.1 APPLICATION AND GROUNDS

23.2.1.1 Who may present a petition

A petition for the making of an administration order may be presented by the company, or its directors, or by a creditor or creditors (including any contingent or prospective creditor or creditors) or by any or all of those people together.

23.2.1.2 Grounds

The petitioner must show that the company is unable to pay its debts or is likely to become unable to pay its debts. The petitioner must swear an affidavit setting out the grounds for the petition. This may be supported by a report from an independent insolvency practitioner which sets out the practitioner's reasons for believing that at least one of the objectives can be achieved. If no such report is annexed to the petition, the petitioner must explain why none has been produced. In practice, a petition not supported by a report is unlikely to succeed except perhaps in cases of great urgency.

The circumstances in which a company is treated as being unable to pay its debts are the same as for compulsory winding up (see **23.5.2.1**). In addition to proving inability to pay debts the petitioner must also satisfy the court that the making of the administration order would be likely to achieve one or more of the following objectives:

COMPANY INSOLVENCY PROCEEDINGS

(a) the survival of the company, and the whole or any part of its undertaking as a going concern;

(b) the approval of a voluntary arrangement or a composition in satisfaction of the company's debts, or a compromise or arrangement between the company and some or all of its members under s. 425 CA 1985; or

(c) a more advantageous realisation of the company's assets than would be effected on a winding up.

23.2.2 CONSEQUENCES OF PETITION

23.2.2.1 Creates moratorium

The presentation of the petition for an administration order has an immediate and dramatic effect on the company. From the time when the petition is presented until the time when the court decides to make the order or to dismiss the petition a 'moratorium' is imposed on the company's debts. This means that creditors may not:

(a) take any steps to enforce any security over the company's property (this does not, however, prevent appointment of an *administrative receiver* — see **23.2.2.3**);

(b) repossess goods in the company's possession under a hire-purchase, conditional sale, chattel leasing or retention of title agreement;

(c) commence or continue proceedings, execution or other legal process against the company or its property (this includes forfeiting a lease by peaceable re-entry);

(d) levy distress against the company's property.

However, any of these things can be done with leave of the court. The object of these rules is to preserve the assets of the company so that if an order is made the administrator will have a better chance of saving the business.

23.2.2.2 Stay on winding up

During the period between the petition and the making of the order or the dismissal of the petition the company cannot be wound up. (A petition for winding up may, however, be presented — it will be considered only if the court dismisses the petition for administration.)

23.2.2.3 Effect on administrative receivership

Administration and administrative receivership are also mutually exclusive. Thus when a petition for an administration order is presented notice must be given to any person who has appointed or is entitled to appoint an administrative receiver (see **23.4.2** — broadly speaking a floating charge holder can make such an appointment). An administration order cannot be made if, by the time of the hearing, an administrative receiver has been appointed unless either the creditor who made the appointment consents or it is shown that his charge would be liable to be set aside under ss. 238, 239 or 245 (see **Chapter 24**).

23.2.3 DISCRETION OF THE COURT

The court has a discretion as to whether or not it will make an administration order. Very many companies are insolvent (unable to pay their debts) because of the 'balance sheet test' (that is, the value of the assets is less than the amount of the liabilities taking into account contingent and prospective liabilities). However, the court will exercise its discretion and

COMPANY INSOLVENCY PROCEEDINGS

refuse to make an administration order in cases where the company is viable even though technically insolvent.

23.2.4 CONSEQUENCES OF ADMINISTRATION ORDER

23.2.4.1 Administrator manages company's affairs

The administration order directs that the affairs, business and property of the company are to be managed by an administrator appointed by the court. The administrator must be a qualified insolvency practitioner.

23.2.4.2 Continuation of moratorium

While the administration order is in force the moratorium preventing creditors from enforcing their rights continues. The restrictions are the same as those following the petition (see **23.2.2**) save that the restrictions can be waived by the administrator as well as by the court. In addition, no appointment of an administrative receiver is possible while the order is in force. Together, these create a 'breathing space' during which the administrator can seek to achieve the statutory objectives for which he was appointed.

23.2.4.3 Effect on other insolvency procedures

Once the order is made any petition for the winding up of the company is dismissed and any administrative receiver vacates office. The administrator can also require any other receiver to vacate office.

23.2.5 THE ADMINISTRATION PROCESS

23.2.5.1 Powers and duties of the administrator

General

As we have already seen the administrator is appointed to run the company and its business with a view to saving the viable parts of the business or with a view to obtaining approval for a voluntary scheme or with a view to advantageous realisation of assets. The administrator is given very wide powers to achieve these things. He is given power to do 'all such things as may be necessary for the management of the affairs, business and property of the company' (s. 14(1)(a)) and specific powers listed in sch. 1. These include power to bring and defend proceedings, sell assets, borrow money, insure and appoint agents. In cases of difficulty, the administrator may apply to the court for directions.

Property subject to a floating charge

Section 15 gives the administrator power to deal with certain property of (or in the possession of) the company free from the claims of other persons. Section 15(1) allows the administrator to dispose of property which is subject to a floating charge as if the property were not subject to the floating charge. This provision applies also where the property is subject to a charge which was a floating charge when created even though it has since crystallised and thus turned into a fixed charge. Where property is disposed of by the administrator under s. 15(1), the holder of the floating charge (or former floating charge) is entitled to the same priority in respect of the property directly or indirectly representing the property disposed of as he would have had in respect of the property which was subject to the charge and which was disposed of by the administrator. Thus the position of the floating chargee is, in theory, as secure as it was before the administration order was made. However, the holder will have to wait for payment, possibly for a considerable time, and formidable problems may arise in trying to identify what property then is to be regarded as 'directly or indirectly representing the property disposed of'.

Fixed charge and other property

Section 15(2) allows the administrator to dispose of property which is subject to a fixed charge and of property in the possession of the company under a hire-purchase agreement, a conditional sale agreement, a chattel leasing agreement or a retention of title agreement. However, in this case the administrator can only dispose of the property with the agreement of the court which must be satisfied that the disposal is likely to promote the purpose for which the administration order was made. The court order must direct that the proceeds of sale (and any sum required to make good any difference between the proceeds and market value of the assets) shall be used to discharge the company's liability to the secured creditor or owner of the goods which have been disposed of as the case may be.

23.2.5.2 Statement of affairs

The administrator must require a statement of affairs to be prepared (s. 22). This will usually be required from the directors but the secretary, former directors, certain employees and former employees and the directors and certain employees of certain associated companies may also be required to make the statement. The statement must usually be prepared within 21 days but the administrator or court can extend this period. The statement must set out details of the company's assets, debts and liabilities, creditors and securities.

23.2.5.3 Proposals

Preparation

Because of the moratorium created by an administration order, the creditors of the company are forced to bear some of the risk inherent in the whole process of administration (that is the risk that, if the administration fails to save the business, the company will be in a weaker position when the administration ends than when it began). The creditors are, however, given a measure of control over the administration process. Section 23 requires the administrator to prepare proposals as to how he is going to achieve the purpose for which he was appointed. These proposals must be sent to the Registrar of Companies and to all creditors (so far as the administrator is aware of their addresses) within three months of the making of the order unless the court extends the period. Copies of the proposals must also either be sent to all the members or the members must be given an opportunity to ask for free copies.

Meeting of creditors

The administrator must hold a meeting of the creditors within three months of the order (unless the court extends the period) at which the proposals are considered. If the proposals are accepted by the creditors' meeting then the administrator must manage the company in accordance with the proposals. The creditors' meeting may propose modifications to the proposals but, as he is the person who will have to implement them, the administrator can reject such modifications.

If the creditors' meeting rejects the proposals the administrator must go back to the court. In such a case the court will usually discharge the administration order but it may also make any other order as it sees fit including a further administration order.

Revision of proposals

During the course of the administration the administrator may need to revise the proposals which have been accepted by the creditors. If he does so, and the revision appears to him to be substantial, then he must seek approval of the revision from a creditors' meeting (s. 25).

COMPANY INSOLVENCY PROCEEDINGS

23.2.5.4 Discharge of administration order

The administrator may apply to the court for discharge of the order at any time. He *must* make such an application when it appears to him that the purpose for which the order was made has been achieved or has become incapable of achievement, or when required to do so by a creditors' meeting.

23.2.6 ADMINISTRATION AND OTHER REMEDIES

23.2.6.1 Winding up

Administration is an alternative to winding up. An administration order cannot, therefore, be made once the company has gone into liquidation. This means that the passing of a winding up resolution by the company (see **23.5.3.1**) or the making of a winding up order (see **23.5.3.2**) preclude the making of an administration order. Similarly the making of an administration order prevents winding up.

23.2.6.2 Administrative receivership

Once an administration order has been made no appointment of an administrative receiver is possible. The rules give a creditor who can appoint an administrative receiver a right to veto administration but if he wishes to do so he must act quickly as the right to veto is lost if no appointment has been made by the time the petition for administration is heard.

23.3 Voluntary Arrangements (Sections 1 to 7)

23.3.1 PROPOSALS AND NOMINEE'S REPORT

The Insolvency Act 1986 seeks to promote agreement between a company in difficulties and its creditors. The directors or (where the company is being wound up) the liquidator or (where an administration order is in force) the administrator may make proposals to the company and its creditors. These proposals must, if they are to be put into effect under the Act, nominate a qualified insolvency practitioner to implement them. Where the nominee is not the liquidator or administrator, the person making the proposal (that is, the liquidator, administrator or directors) must submit details of the proposals and of the company's creditors, debts, liabilities and assets to the nominee. The nominee must then submit a report to the court stating whether or not he thinks that meetings of members and creditors should be called to consider the proposals.

23.3.2 CONTENT OF PROPOSALS

The proposals may be as simple or as complex as the situation of the company demands. In practical terms, the creditors are usually being offered something definite as an alternative to what they might obtain if the company was, for example, to be wound up. Examples of proposals which are commonly made may include one or more of the following:

(a) *Moratorium on repayment of debt*

Creditors are asked not to enforce debts for a specific period of time. The company may be unable to pay debts at present due to cash-flow problems but may expect to be able to pay them in the near future.

(b) *Composition of debt*

Creditors are offered a percentage of their debt in settlement. For example, they might be offered '65 pence in the pound': that is, 65 pence for every pound which the company owes them.

(c) *Debt for equity swap*

Major creditors may be offered the chance to swap their debt for shares in the company. From the company's point of view, the removal of the debt should ease cash-flow problems. The shares will usually give the creditors preferential rights which enable repayment through dividends as soon as profits are available. Such a proposal will often be combined with a fairly radical, general reorganisation of the company's affairs.

23.3.3 MEETINGS OF MEMBERS AND CREDITORS

Where the nominee recommends that meetings should be held he may call the meetings unless the court orders otherwise. Notice must be given to every creditor of whose claim and address the person calling the meeting is aware.

The meetings of members and creditors then consider the scheme, which they may reject, approve or approve with modifications. A simple majority is required at the members' meeting (members having the voting rights attached to their shares by the articles). The position is more complicated at the creditors' meeting but basically the net effect is that the resolution is only validly passed if approved:

(a) by at least three-quarters (by value) of the unsecured creditors; and

(b) by a simple majority (by value) of the unsecured creditors who are not connected with the company.

In relation to (a) only, secured creditors may count in the vote, but only to the extent of the value of their claim which they estimate will *not* be recovered under their security.

The result of the meetings must be reported to the court. The court can reject the scheme on grounds of unfair prejudice or material irregularity.

23.3.4 IMPLEMENTATION OF APPROVED SCHEME BY SUPERVISOR

Where both meetings approve a scheme the scheme becomes binding on all persons who had notice of the shareholders' or creditors' meeting and were entitled to vote at that meeting together with any creditors who would have been entitled to vote, had they been given notice of the meeting. However, unless he agrees, the scheme cannot affect a secured creditor's right to enforce his security nor a preferred creditor's preference.

Once approved, the scheme is implemented by the supervisor (who is the same person as the nominee unless the court or meetings decide otherwise).

23.3.5 RELATIONSHIP BETWEEN VOLUNTARY SCHEMES AND ADMINISTRATION

The proposal that a voluntary scheme should be implemented does not create a moratorium so that, unless and until the scheme is approved, any creditor can seek payment of his own debt (by court action, petition for winding up, repossession or any other lawful means available to him). Even when the scheme is approved it does not prevent secured creditors enforcing their security. A voluntary arrangement is, therefore, more likely to succeed if an application for administration is made first thus giving rise to the moratorium. The administrator may then be able to put together a satisfactory voluntary scheme which he can supervise.

23.3.6 MORATORIUM FOR SMALL COMPANIES

The Insolvency Act 2000 has caused the voluntary arrangement procedure to be amended for small companies (within the definition in s. 247 of the Companies Act 1985). The directors of these companies may now apply for a moratorium of up to 28 days to give them time to put their voluntary arrangement proposal to creditors. The moratorium is similar to that created on a petition for an administration order and will mean that creditors cannot take action against the company's assets during its term. The purpose behind the change in the legislation is to make the voluntary arrangement option more effective and thus attractive to companies in financial difficulties.

To obtain a moratorium, the directors must submit to the nominee the terms of their proposed voluntary arrangement together with a statement of the company's financial affairs. The nominee will then provide the directors with a statement indicating whether or not, in his opinion, the proposal has a reasonable prospect of approval. He will also indicate whether the company is likely to have sufficient funds available to it during the proposed moratorium to enable it to carry on its business, and whether meetings of the company and creditors should be summoned to consider the proposed voluntary arrangement. The directors must then file all the above documents, together with the nominee's consent to act and a statement that the company is eligible for a moratorium, with the court.

23.4 Receivership

23.4.1 NATURE OF RECEIVERSHIP

A receiver is a person who is appointed by or on behalf of a creditor to realise a security. His principal duty is to the appointing debenture holder. Receivers may be appointed by the debenture holder (provided that the debenture so provides) or by the court. In practice nearly all appointments are made by the debenture holder. The powers of the receiver are derived from the debenture under which he is appointed and certain sections of the Law of Property Act 1925. However, administrative receivers, as defined by the Insolvency Act 1986, have additional statutory powers.

23.4.2 ADMINISTRATIVE RECEIVERS — DEFINITION

Most receivers come within the definition of an 'administrative receiver' (s. 29(2)). The Insolvency Act 1986 imposes certain duties on and grants certain powers to administrative receivers which do not apply in the case of other receivers. Only a qualified insolvency practitioner can be appointed as an administrative receiver. An administrative receiver is:

(a) a receiver or manager of the whole (or substantially the whole) of a company's property appointed by or on behalf of the holders of any debentures of the company secured by a charge which, as created, was a floating charge, or by such a charge and one or more other securities; or

(b) a person who would be such a receiver or manager but for the appointment of some other person as the receiver of part of the company's property.

In practice, the person with a floating charge over the whole or substantially the whole of the company's property will usually be a bank. The bank is also likely to have fixed charges over land owned by the company and certain other assets (e.g., book debts) but these do not prevent it from appointing an administrative receiver.

23.4.3 ADMINISTRATIVE RECEIVERS — POWERS AND DUTIES

The administrative receiver, when appointed, effectively replaces the directors in the management of the company. His appointment is, therefore, a matter of great importance to the members, creditors and employees of the company. The law recognises this and so grants powers to and imposes obligations on an administrative receiver which make his position very similar to the position of an administrator. The administrative receiver is chosen by the debenture holder, not by the court, but can only be removed by the court.

23.4.3.1 General powers

An administrative receiver has all the powers conferred on him by the debenture under which he is appointed and also specific powers listed in the Insolvency Act 1986. The statutory powers include power to deal with the assets of the company, take or defend proceedings in its name and power to carry on the business of the company. These powers, listed in sch. 1, are the same as those granted to an administrator.

Disposal of property subject to prior charge

Section 43 gives an administrative receiver power to go to court to obtain an order for the sale of assets free from any security with priority over the debenture under which he was appointed. The court may only authorise the administrative receiver to dispose of such property if it is likely to promote a more advantageous realisation of the company's assets. The court might, for example, authorise such a disposal so as to enable the receiver to sell the business of the company as a going concern. The proceeds of disposal (plus any difference between those proceeds and market value) must be paid to the person who was entitled to the security.

23.4.3.2 Legal position

The administrative receiver is deemed to be the agent of the company (s. 44). Any contract which he makes is, therefore, binding on the company. The agency, however, ends when the company goes into liquidation. Section 44 also makes the administrative receiver personally liable on any contract which he himself makes and on any contract of employment which he 'adopts'. Following the cases of *Paramount Airways* [1994] BCC 172 and *Leyland DAF* and *Ferranti* [1994] BCC 658, an employee's contract of employment is 'adopted' if he is continued in employment for more than 14 days after the appointment of the administrative receiver (or administrator in the case of administration). The administrative receiver is entitled to an indemnity against personal liability out of the assets of the company and, if the debenture so provides, will have an indemnity from his appointor.

23.4.3.3 Duty to pay preferential creditors

The primary duty of any receiver is to realise the security of the debenture holder who appointed him. A receiver appointed on behalf of a floating charge holder (whether or not he is an administrative receiver as defined) is, however, under a duty to pay preferential creditors (see **23.8**) in priority to the debt secured by the floating charge.

23.4.3.4 Investigation and report into company's affairs

An administrative receiver is entitled to a statement of affairs from the directors (or in certain cases other officials) of the company. Within three months of his appointment (or longer if the court so directs) he must make a report which he must send to the Registrar of Companies and to creditors.

The report must give details of the events leading to the appointment of the receiver, his dealings with the property of the company, his payments to the creditor who appointed him and to preferential creditors and an assessment of what will be available (if anything) to ordinary creditors.

23.4.4 CHOICE OF REMEDY

23.4.4.1 Position of floating chargeholder

A bank or other creditor with a floating charge will often be faced with a choice if its customer gets into difficulty. It may go to court to seek an administration order, or it may appoint its own administrative receiver, or it may seek winding up. As we have already seen (at **23.2.6.2**) the debenture holder loses the right to appoint an administrative receiver once an administrator has been appointed but, until that time, can effectively veto administration by appointing an administrative receiver.

COMPANY INSOLVENCY PROCEEDINGS

23.4.4.2 Comparison of administration and administrative receivership

Administration and administrative receivership are in many ways very similar but are different from each other in the following principal respects:

(a) The administrative receiver is chosen by the debenture holder, the administrator is appointed by the court.

(b) The administration procedure leads to a moratorium, administrative receivership does not.

(c) Administration blocks winding up petitions by other creditors.

(d) In administration certain transactions may be set aside (see **Chapter 24**).

(e) In administration owners of goods in the company's possession under hire-purchase and retention of title agreements cannot repossess without leave of the administrator or court.

23.5 Liquidation or Winding Up

23.5.1 TYPES OF WINDING UP

There are two types of winding up: compulsory liquidation and voluntary liquidation. Compulsory liquidation is initiated by petition to the court. Voluntary liquidation is initiated by a decision of the members of the company. Both types of winding up are designed to bring the existence of the company to an end and to distribute its assets to those entitled to them.

23.5.2 COMPULSORY WINDING UP

23.5.2.1 Grounds

Compulsory liquidation begins with a petition to the court (Chancery Division or, in some cases, county court — see **23.1.4** above). A petition can be presented on a number of grounds. By far the most common ground is that the company is unable to pay its debts (defined in s. 123). A company is treated as being unable to pay its debts if:

(a) a demand for payment, in the prescribed form (a 'statutory demand'), for more than £750 (this figure may be changed from time to time by regulations) has been left at the company's registered office and the company has neglected to pay the debt, or to secure or compound for it (that is, agree to a reasonable compromise) to the reasonable satisfaction of the creditor for three weeks; or

(b) execution or other process issued on a judgment, decree or court order is returned unsatisfied; or

(c) it is proved that the company is actually unable to pay taking into account contingent and prospective liabilities; or

(d) it is proved that the value of the company's assets is less than the amount of its liabilities taking into account contingent and prospective liabilities.

Apart from inability to pay debts there are other grounds on which a company may be wound up. These are, however, seldom resorted to and are not considered in this book save that the 'just and equitable' ground is considered briefly in **Chapter 9**.

23.5.2.2 Locus standi

A petition for compulsory winding up may be presented by the company itself, any creditor or creditors (including contingent or prospective creditors), any contributory or contributories (the term 'contributory' includes the members of the company and certain former members) and, in very limited circumstances, by the Department of Trade and Industry. In practice, the overwhelming majority of petitions are presented by creditors.

23.5.2.3 Court's discretion to refuse order

Even where a creditor has proved grounds for winding up, the court has a discretion to refuse to make an order winding up the company. An order will normally be refused where:

(a) The petitioning creditor (together with any supporting creditors) is owed £750 or less. This is by analogy with the rule whereby a statutory demand for more than £750 can be used as proof of inability to pay debts.

(b) The majority by value of the creditors oppose the winding up of the company.

23.5.3 VOLUNTARY WINDING UP

23.5.3.1 Commencement

By s. 84 a company can be wound up voluntarily if:

(a) a special resolution to wind up is passed; or

(b) an extraordinary resolution is passed to the effect that the company should be wound up as it cannot continue in business because of its debts (that is, the company is, in effect, insolvent).

The winding up commences from the date of passing the appropriate resolution. A notice of the resolution must appear in the *London Gazette* within 14 days of its being passed.

23.5.3.2 Types of voluntary winding up

There are two types of voluntary liquidation; a members' voluntary winding up and a creditors' voluntary winding up.

Members' voluntary winding up

This form of liquidation is utilised if the company is solvent. Within the five weeks immediately preceding the date of the resolution (or on that date but before the resolution is actually passed) the directors (or the majority of them if more than two) make a statutory declaration, setting out the company's assets and liabilities, and stating that they have made a full enquiry into the company's affairs and are of the opinion that the company will be able to pay its debts in full within 12 months of the commencement of the winding up. The declaration must be delivered to the registrar within 15 days after the day the resolution was passed.

Creditors' voluntary winding up

If no such 'declaration of solvency' is filed, the winding up is a creditors' winding up. A meeting of the creditors must be called for a day not later than the 14th day after the day on which is held the meeting at which the members pass the winding-up resolution. Notice of the meeting must be posted to the creditors at least seven days before the creditors' meeting and the meeting must also be advertised in the *Gazette* and at least two newspapers.

Conversion from members' to creditors' voluntary winding up

During the course of a members' voluntary winding up, it may become clear that the company will be unable to pay its debts within 12 months of commencement of the winding up. If this happens the liquidator must report the fact to the creditors, call a creditors' meeting and convert the liquidation into a creditors' voluntary winding up.

23.6 Liquidators

For all forms of liquidation, any liquidator appointed must be a qualified insolvency practitioner.

23.6.1 COMPULSORY LIQUIDATION

When a winding-up order is made, the official receiver of the court becomes the liquidator of the company and continues in office until someone else is appointed (s. 136(2)). The official receiver may summon meetings of creditors and contributories with a view to the appointment of a liquidator. He must either do so or give notice that he intends not to do so within 12 weeks of the winding up order and may be required to call such meetings by one-quarter (by value) of the creditors.

Where meetings of creditors and contributories are held, each meeting may nominate a liquidator. If the same person is nominated by each meeting, he becomes the liquidator. If different people are nominated, the creditors' nominee takes office unless a creditor or contributory successfully applies to the court for the appointment of the contributories' nominee (either alone or jointly with the creditors' nominee) or of some other person.

23.6.2 CREDITORS' VOLUNTARY WINDING UP

As we have already seen, in a creditors' winding up a meeting of creditors must be held within 14 days of the meeting (of the members) at which the winding-up resolution was passed. The creditors may nominate a liquidator at their meeting. He will then become liquidator of the company but any director, member or creditor may apply to the court for the appointment of the members' nominee (either alone or jointly with the creditors' nominee) or of some other person.

The members will often have appointed a liquidator at the meeting at which the resolution for creditors' winding up was passed. Such a liquidator is entitled to act until the creditors' meeting is held but during that period his powers are restricted to collecting the company's property, disposing of perishable goods or other goods which may decline in value and taking other steps to protect the company's assets.

23.6.3 MEMBERS' VOLUNTARY WINDING UP

The liquidator is appointed by the members in general meeting.

23.6.4 FUNCTIONS OF LIQUIDATORS

The function of the liquidator of a company is to collect in the assets of the company and to pay their value to those creditors who are entitled according to the statutory order for payment (see **23.8**). If there is anything left after all creditors have been paid their debts and interest, the surplus goes to the members. If there are two or more classes of shares some members may have priority over others in claiming the surplus.

Sections 165 and 167 give liquidators extensive powers to assist them in performing their functions. These powers include:

(a) Power to pay any class of creditors in full.

(b) Power to enter into a compromise or arrangement with creditors (this can be made binding without the agreement of all the creditors in certain cases provided that the voluntary arrangements procedure (**23.3**) is used).

(c) Power to compromise claims to which the company is entitled.

(The liquidator can only exercise the above powers with the sanction of an extraordinary resolution in the case of members' winding up, of the court, a committee of creditors or creditors' meeting in the case of creditors' winding up and of the court or committee in the case of compulsory winding up.)

(d) Power to bring or defend legal proceedings.

(e) Power to carry on the company's business for the purpose of beneficial winding up.

(Sanction is required in the case of compulsory winding up only.)

(f) Power to sell the company's property.

(g) Power to execute documents (including deeds).

(h) Power to borrow on the security of the company's assets.

(i) Power to act through agents.

(j) Power to do 'all such other things as may be necessary for winding up the company's affairs and distributing its assets'.

(No sanction is required for items (f) to (j) in any type of winding up.)

23.6.5 PROCEEDINGS AGAINST THE COMPANY

It would obviously be unfair if one creditor could start an action after the liquidation had begun and so obtain priority over the other creditors. Therefore, once an order for compulsory winding up has been made, no action can be started or proceeded with unless the leave of the court is obtained (s. 130). In addition, at any time between presentation of the petition and the making of the order, the company, or any creditor or contributory, can apply to have any action pending against the company stayed (s.126). Furthermore, any execution, attachment, sequestration or distress started after the commencement of a compulsory liquidation is void. However, if the attachment or execution was begun before presentation of the petition, it can only be avoided by the liquidator if it was completed after commencement of the liquidation. This last provision also applies to voluntary liquidations, the operative date being the date the resolution to wind up the company was passed.

With regard to voluntary liquidations, the liquidator, any creditor or member, may apply to the court to have actions stayed. Such a stay is not granted automatically although, if the action is begun after the date of passing the resolution to wind up an insolvent company, it will normally be granted.

COMPANY INSOLVENCY PROCEEDINGS

23.7 Collection and Distribution of Assets in Liquidation

23.7.1 PROPERTY OF THE COMPANY

23.7.1.1 Power to sell or charge

The liquidator has power to sell or mortgage the property and to satisfy the claims of the various people entitled in the company's liquidation (see **23.6.4**).

23.7.1.2 Power to disclaim

An important power of the liquidator in relation to the company's property is the right of disclaimer given by s. 178. The section gives the liquidator power to disclaim any of the company's property which consists of unprofitable contracts, or other property that is unsaleable or not readily saleable.

23.7.2 ASSETS IN THE HANDS OF THE COMPANY

23.7.2.1 Assets held on trust

The creditors of an insolvent company are entitled to payment from its assets. They are not entitled to any assets of which the company is the legal owner but which it holds on trust for a third party. This has been held to apply in certain cases where a company holds cash for its customers. In *Re Kayford Ltd* [1975] 1 All ER 604, the company put money received from mail order customers into a special trust account from which it only made withdrawals when goods were delivered to the customers. When the company went into liquidation it was held that the money in the account belonged to the customers whose orders had not been fulfilled and so was not available to the liquidator.

23.7.2.2 Assets subject to retention of title

Many suppliers of goods supply goods under contracts which contain retention of title clauses. These are clauses which state that the vendor retains title to the goods supplied until the purchaser pays for them. Such clauses have been considered in a number of reported cases (the leading case is *Aluminium Industrie Vaasen BV* v *Romalpa Aluminium* [1976] 2 All ER 552). Their effect varies depending on the exact wording which is used and on the circumstances of the case. A straightforward reservation of title clause is effective in ensuring that the vendor, not the liquidator, is entitled to the goods (or the proceeds of their further sale) if the company becomes insolvent. However, clauses which have tried to extend the unpaid vendor's rights (for example, by purportedly transferring them to newly manufactured goods only partly consisting of the goods which he originally supplied) have generally failed. (For the powers of an administrator to dispose of goods despite a retention of title clause see **23.2.5.1**.)

23.8 Order of Entitlement to Assets

The principal duty of the liquidator of a company is to distribute the assets to those entitled. In a large majority of cases there will be insufficient funds available to pay all the creditors in full. There is, therefore, an order in which the assets must be paid to the creditors.

23.8.1 CREDITORS WITH FIXED CHARGES

Creditors with fixed charges are entitled to payment out of the assets which are charged to them before those assets are used for any other purpose. As between creditors with fixed charges over the same assets priority is governed by registration under s. 395 CA 1985 (but remember that a fixed charge gives priority over a floating charge, even though the latter is created and registered first, unless the floating charge prohibited the creation of later fixed charges ranking in priority to it and the fixed chargee had notice of this prohibition when he took the charge).

If the security of a fixed charge is inadequate (that is, the value of the charged assets is less than the amount of the debt), the chargee may claim the balance of the debt as an ordinary creditor (or under any valid floating charge in its favour). If the debt is oversecured (that is, the value of the charged assets is more than the amount of the debt), the chargee will be paid in full and the balance will be available for other creditors.

It should be noted that the costs of realising fixed charge assets should be paid out of the amounts realised from the sale of such assets.

23.8.2 COSTS OF WINDING UP

Costs of winding up, including liquidators' fees and expenses, are paid in full before any other creditors (except those with fixed charges who are paid first to the extent of their security).

(Remember, following **23.8.1** above, that the costs of realising fixed charge asset should be paid from the proceeds of such assets. Therefore, there will be an apportionment of costs between fixed and floating charge assets in those cases where both types of charge have been taken.)

23.8.3 PREFERENTIAL CREDITORS

After payment of costs and expenses the next category of creditor is the preferred creditor. Preferred debts are:

(a) Sums owed to the Inland Revenue for PAYE deducted from employees' wages in the 12 months before the relevant date.

(b) VAT (and certain other sums due to Customs and Excise) referable to the six-month period before the relevant date.

(c) Certain social security contributions and contributions to occupational pension schemes.

(d) Wages owed to an employee in respect of the four months before the relevant date up to a maximum of £800 per employee (this figure may be varied from time to time by statutory instrument). Certain categories of holiday pay are also preferential.

(e) Money lent to an employer so as to enable it to pay debts in category (iv) above and which was in fact used for that purpose. (Thus a bank is a preferential creditor if it allows an employer to overdraw a 'wages account' so as to keep on the workforce in the four months before the relevant date.)

The 'relevant date' is usually the date of the winding-up resolution or order (as applicable) or date of appointment of a receiver.

Preferred creditors (to the extent of their preference) are entitled to payment in full before ordinary creditors or holders of floating charges receive any payment. If the assets are insufficient to pay the preferred creditors in full they rank equally *inter se* and so each is paid the same proportion of the preferred debt.

COMPANY INSOLVENCY PROCEEDINGS

23.8.4 CREDITORS WITH FLOATING CHARGES

Floating chargees rank after preferred creditors but, to the extent of their security, before ordinary creditors. Priority is determined by date of registration where there are two or more floating charges over the same property.

23.8.5 ORDINARY CREDITORS

Ordinary creditors rank after all preferred creditors and secured creditors. They rank equally *inter se*.

23.8.6 INTEREST ON DEBTS

Once all creditors have been paid in full any surplus is first used to pay interest on debts from the date of liquidation. This interest is paid to all creditors equally regardless of whether their debts ranked equally for payment.

23.8.7 SHAREHOLDERS

Any surplus after payment of debts and interest goes to the members according to the rights attached to their shares.

23.9 Dissolution

Once winding up is complete the company may be dissolved. This is achieved in the following ways:

(a) In compulsory liquidation the liquidator gives notice to the Registrar of Companies that he has completed the winding up. The company is then automatically dissolved three months later.

(b) In voluntary winding up the liquidator holds a final meeting and files certain returns with the Registrar of Companies. The company is then automatically dissolved after three months.

(c) The Registrar may dissolve a company by striking it off the register in certain circumstances where the company has ceased to trade.

23.10 Application to Partnerships

23.10.1 INTRODUCTION

Care must be taken to define the precise nature of insolvency in relation to a partnership. It is possible for an individual partner to be bankrupt without the partnership being insolvent. Equally, it is possible for a partnership to be insolvent without any of the partners being bankrupt. Finally, a situation could exist where a partnership was insolvent *and* some or all of its partners bankrupt. A distinction must be maintained between an insolvent partnership and bankrupt partners since applicable procedures and the rights of the creditors of each will vary according to which you are dealing with. The provisions of the Insolvency Act 1986 relating to bankruptcy (see **Chapter 22**) will apply to individual bankrupt partners. In the case of an insolvent partnership, specific provisions of the Insolvency Act 1986 which apply to companies can also be applied to a partnership, as a result of the Insolvent Partnerships Order 1994.

23.10.2 INSOLVENT PARTNERSHIPS ORDER 1994

23.10.2.1 Winding up as an unregistered company

The Insolvent Partnerships Order 1994 (the 'Order') provides that an insolvent partnership may be wound up as an unregistered company under the Insolvency Act. A petition may be brought by a partner or a creditor. If it is thought that debts will not be met from the assets of the firm, the Order allows bankruptcy petitions against individual partners to be brought in conjunction with the petition to wind up the partnership.

23.10.2.2 Priority of creditors on a winding up of a partnership

Under the Order, priorities operate as in the case of an insolvent company, with preferred and secured creditors having priority over ordinary creditors. However, the situation becomes more complex where a partnership is being wound up and bankruptcy petitions are being brought against individual partners. In this situation, there are effectively two sets of creditors, those of the partnership and those of the individual partners. The Order provides for the following priorities in such a situation:

(a) Partnership creditors must first seek to satisfy their claims from the partnership property.

(b) Creditors of individual partners must first look to the personal assets of those individuals.

(c) Should there be insufficient partnership assets, partnership creditors may seek to satisfy their claims from the personal assets of the individual partners. In such a situation, their claims are apportioned amongst the individual partners and *rank equally* with those of the creditors of those individual partners.

(d) Should creditors of individual partners find that those partners have insufficient assets to meet their claims, they may look to the partnership property. However, they can only do so *after* all the claims of partnership creditors have been met.

23.10.2.3 Disqualification

The Order applies certain provisions of the Company Directors Disqualification Act 1986 (see **8.4.2**) to partners of an insolvent partnership. A court may therefore, following a petition of the Secretary of State for Trade and Industry, find that a partner's conduct was such as to make him unfit to be concerned in the management of a company. If this is the case, the partner can be disqualified for a period of between two and fifteen years from being involved in the management *of a company*. Such disqualification does *not* prevent him becoming involved in another partnership.

23.10.2.4 Administration and voluntary arrangements

The Order also provides that partnerships may be made the subject of an administration order or enter into a voluntary arrangement with their creditors.

TWENTY FOUR

LIABILITIES ARISING FROM INSOLVENCY

This chapter covers the following topics:

24.1 Wrongful trading
24.2 Transactions at an undervalue and preferences
24.3 Transactions defrauding creditors
24.4 Floating charges.

In this chapter we will look at a number of rules which enable insolvency practitioners to claim assets which are not held by the insolvent company itself. You should note that the ability to take action under some of these rules is limited only to a liquidator, or a liquidator or administrator.

24.1 Wrongful Trading

Under s. 214, the directors of a company which is being wound up may be made liable, by the court, to contribute to the assets of the company if they are found to be guilty of wrongful trading.

24.1.1 GROUNDS

A person is guilty of wrongful trading where:

(a) the company goes into insolvent liquidation;

(b) that person knew or ought to have concluded (at some time before the commencement of winding up) that there was no reasonable prospect that the company would avoid going into insolvent liquidation; and

(c) that person was a director of the company at that time.

24.1.2 DEFENCE

A defence is available to a director who shows that he took *every* step with a view to minimising the potential loss to the company's creditors as he ought to have taken. However, in judging whether this defence is available, the court applies a combined objective and subjective test in examining the knowledge and actions of the director. They are taken as being those of a reasonably diligent person having both:

LIABILITIES ARISING FROM INSOLVENCY

(a) the general knowledge, skill and experience that may reasonably be expected of a person carrying out the same functions as are carried out by the director in relation to the company; and

(b) the general knowledge, skill and experience that that director has.

The steps which a director must take to avoid liability for wrongful trading will vary depending on the circumstances of the case.

24.2 Transactions at an Undervalue and Preferences

Certain transactions which a company has entered into may be set aside on the ground that they are transactions at an undervalue or preferences. An application to the court by the liquidator is required for such transactions to be set aside. (The same rules apply where an administration order has been made save that the application is then made by the administrator.)

24.2.1 TRANSACTION AT AN UNDERVALUE

A transaction at an undervalue (s. 238) is a transaction where the company makes a gift to any person and receives either no consideration or consideration worth significantly less than the consideration provided by the company. However, a transaction cannot be set aside if it was entered into in good faith for the purpose of carrying on the company's business and at a time when there were reasonable grounds for believing that the transaction would benefit the company. For this reason a transaction cannot be set aside when the company sells stock or other assets at a reduced price so as to overcome cash flow problems.

24.2.2 PREFERENCE

A preference (s. 239) is given if the company does anything or suffers anything to be done which puts a creditor, or a surety or guarantor of a debt of the company, into a better position on an insolvent liquidation than he would have been in if that thing had not been done. Examples of preferences include payment in full of a debt to a particular creditor who would only have received partial payment on winding up or the giving of security to a creditor. A transaction cannot be set aside as a preference unless the company was influenced in deciding to give the preference to a person by a desire to put that person into a better position on liquidation than he would have been in if it had not been done. Such a desire is presumed where the preference was given to a connected person (defined in s. 249), which includes any director of the company. (This presumption is rebuttable: *Re Fairway Magazines* [1993] BCLC 643.) Where payment was made or security was given to a creditor because he was threatening proceedings or otherwise insisting on payment he will usually be able to show that there was no desire to put him in a better position on liquidation. This will be on the grounds that the company was merely responding to genuine commercial pressure.

24.2.3 'RELEVANT TIME' REQUIREMENT

Undervalue transactions and preferences can only be set aside if they were entered into at a 'relevant time', that is, when both of the following requirements are satisfied:

(a) in the case of a transaction at an undervalue, the transaction takes place within two years before commencement of winding up or presentation of the petition for administration or, in the case of a preference, within six months before that date (unless the preference was made to a connected person in which case the period is extended to two years); and

(b) in the case of either an undervalue or preference, the company is insolvent at the time of the transaction or becomes insolvent as a result of the transaction. Where a transaction at an undervalue has been entered into with a connected person, insolvency is presumed unless it can be disproved.

24.2.4 COURT CAN MAKE ORDER AS IT SEES FIT

Where it is shown that a transaction can be set aside as a transaction at an undervalue or preference the court can make such order as it sees fit for restoring the position to what it would have been if the transaction had not been entered into. This could include, for example, ordering the person who entered into the transaction or who received the preference to return property or its value to the company. The position of a bona fide purchaser for value is, however, protected.

24.3 Transactions Defrauding Creditors

Sections 423–425 contain further provisions by which transactions at an undervalue can be set aside. The application of these is not restricted to liquidation or administration and the undervalue transaction can be set aside whenever it was made. However, the person who applies to the court to have the transaction set aside must show that the company in entering into the transaction did so with the purpose of putting assets beyond the reach of that person.

24.4 Floating Charges

Under s. 245, a floating charge is prima facie invalid if:

(a) it was made within 12 months before the presentation of a successful petition for winding up or for an administration order or before the passing of a winding-up resolution; and

(b) it was made at a time when the company was unable to pay its debts or became unable to do so as a result of the charge.

Where the company has created a floating charge in favour of a connected person the charge is prima facie invalid if it was made within *two* years before the petition or resolution. The charge is prima facie invalid in such a case even if the company was (and remained) solvent when the charge was created.

A floating charge created within the time-limits (and so prima facie invalid) is, however, valid to the extent of:

(a) consideration for the charge consisting of money paid or goods and services supplied to the company at or after the creation of the charge; and

(b) consideration consisting of discharge or reduction of any debt of the company at or after the creation of the charge; and

(c) interest on (a) and (b) above.

Section 245 is designed to prevent a company benefiting a creditor by giving a charge for existing debt. The exceptions are designed to ensure that a company may still give security in order to obtain money or supplies even though in some difficulty. This should not in principle cause any harm to existing creditors.

SPECIAL TOPICS

TWENTY FIVE

THE PARTNERSHIP AGREEMENT

This chapter covers the following topics:

25.1 Introduction
25.2 Is a written partnership agreement necessary?
25.3 The clauses of the partnership agreement
25.4 Issues for an incoming partner.

25.1 Introduction

In this chapter we will look at the provisions which should be considered for inclusion in a partnership agreement. Much of the contents of a partnership agreement will address issues raised by the provisions of the Partnership Act 1890 which we considered in **Chapters 1–5**, or which may be relevant to the tax provisions applicable to partnership which we considered in **Chapters 13, 14 and 18**. Those detailed provisions should be borne in mind when reading this chapter.

Before we look at the possible contents of a partnership agreement, we will consider whether a formal, written agreement is necessary at all and at the end of the chapter we have included a section dealing with the points which a prospective new partner might wish to consider before putting his signature to a partnership agreement.

25.2 Is a Written Partnership Agreement Necessary?

A written agreement is not required for the formation of a partnership. This contrasts with the position of a company where the memorandum and articles, which have contractual effect under s. 14 CA 1985, must not only be in writing but must also be registered with the Registrar of Companies.

In practice, many partnerships decide that the agreement between the partners, as to how the business is to be regulated, should be in the form of a written agreement. Such an agreement is often called a partnership agreement, a partnership deed or articles of partnership.

The draftsman of a partnership agreement should bear in mind that many provisions of the Partnership Act 1890 apply to regulate the relationship of the partners except to the extent that there is contrary agreement. However well intentioned and however well drafted such

THE PARTNERSHIP AGREEMENT

legislation is, it is unlikely that it will entirely coincide with the wishes of a particular group of businessmen setting up a partnership.

The draftsman's task in drafting a partnership agreement is more onerous than his task in drafting articles of association for a company. In the case of a company a 'model' set of articles (Table A) is provided, which will suit the needs of most companies with comparatively minor alterations. The provisions of the Partnership Act are both more out of date and less comprehensive than those of Table A. The nature of a partnership agreement must, of course, depend upon the circumstances but we have set out in the next paragraph the most important matters which need to be considered.

25.3 The Clauses of the Partnership Agreement

25.3.1 THE PARTIES

The parties to the agreement will be the partners, old and new.

25.3.2 THE COMMENCEMENT DATE AND TERM OF THE PARTNERSHIP

While most partnerships will be partnerships 'at will' (and so can last indefinitely subject to notice to dissolve the partnership being given), it is possible to specify the length of the partnership's 'life'. Although the date the partnership agreement was entered into can determine the commencement of the partnership (which could be a newly constituted partnership following the retirement or admission of partners), partnership agreements often include a term stating the date on which the partnership commenced.

25.3.3 THE NATURE OF THE PARTNERSHIP'S BUSINESS

The ultra vires rule does not apply to a partnership. The business should, however, be specified so that a partner who objects to what is being done by way of new types of business can insist on the agreement being followed. Unless the partnership agreement provides to the contrary, the clause specifying what business is to be carried on can only be altered with the unanimous agreement of the partners (s. 24(8) PA 1890). This clause may also specify where the partnership is to carry on business.

25.3.4 THE PARTNERSHIP NAME

The business name of the partnership should be specified. The requirements as to approval for and publicity of business names were dealt with in **1.7**.

25.3.5 THE INCOME OF THE PARTNERSHIP

If the partnership agreement is silent on the point, the partners will share the income (and liabilities) of the partnership equally. Even if this is in accord with the partners' wishes, it is best to state specifically the way in which the partnership's profits will be shared. However, in many partnerships, this simple position is not what the partners require. The share of profits between the partners may be unequal to reflect differing levels of contributions of capital, or differing levels of involvement in the partnership's business. Some partnerships may choose to build a mechanism into their partnership agreements for regular reviews of the profit sharing ratios to take into account the relative achievements of the partners. Other partnerships adopt a 'lock step' arrangement by which a partner's share of the profits may increase by a fixed amount annually over a period of years. If the partners have agreed among themselves that some or all of them should receive 'interest' on capital or 'salary' (see **13.5**), these arrangements should be set out in the partnership agreement. However, care should be taken to ensure if a 'salary' is paid to the partner that the Revenue cannot argue that the recipient was, in reality, an employee rather than a full equity partner (if the latter is what the partners were trying to achieve).

25.3.6 THE CAPITAL OF THE PARTNERSHIP

A clause (or group of clauses) should be included dealing with the financial relationships between the partners. This should state what investment each partner is to make in the business, how each partner will satisfy his obligation to contribute capital (for example, whether in cash or assets) and over what period (if the capital contribution is not to be made in full on admission to the partnership). Although it may be difficult to specify the circumstances, it is worth giving thought to the circumstances in which further capital might have to be introduced. The reverse of these provisions is what should happen to the capital when the partnership is dissolved or a partner retires. What are the arrangements for a partner to withdraw capital and how is the goodwill of the business to be dealt with when a partner leaves?

25.3.7 THE PROPERTY OF THE PARTNERSHIP

The partnership agreement should include provisions specifying which property is to be regarded as partnership property and which is to remain the property of individual partners.

25.3.8 THE MANAGEMENT OF THE PARTNERSHIP

Small partnerships of two or three people will usually be run by the partners (perhaps in conjunction with a small number of employees) and each partner will have an equal say in management. In a large partnership (especially a professional partnership where there may be dozens of partners), a more complex management structure may be considered desirable and the structure should be specified. In the absence of contrary agreement all partners have an equal say in management. Among the more mundane, but very vital, matters which should be considered under this heading are questions such as where will the partnership maintain its bank account, who should be entitled to sign cheques for the partnership, who will allocate work to the employees, what authority is each partner to have in relation to buying stock, paying bills and so on. In most cases, the clause dealing with management of the partnership should be stated in general terms. It is better, for example, to say that junior partners are to have such functions as are assigned to them by the managing or senior partners than to list in minute detail what they are to be authorised to do.

25.3.9 THE EFFECT OF PROLONGED ABSENCE

It is now common to find included in partnership agreement clauses dealing with the consequences for a partner who is absent from the business for a prolonged period. This may be through illness, maternity leave or compassionate leave. The nature of the provisions will be determined by the necessity for the partners to balance the needs of the business with supporting their fellow partner. However, these provisions often mirror corresponding provisions found in employment contracts (so that a partner may be permitted to be away from the partnership's business for six months due to illness before he can be expelled, or the partnership agreement may provide maternity leave provisions similar to the statutory provisions which employees enjoy).

25.3.10 RESTRICTIONS

Terms may be included dealing with the partners' obligations to the firm. It is quite common, for example, to provide that the partners are to give their whole time to the business of the firm or to provide that they are only to take up other businesses with the approval of their partners. Consideration should also be given to the inclusion of a clause preventing competition with the firm during the lifetime of the partnership (even if the partners are not full time), although such competition would in any case normally be a breach of the partners' duty of good faith. Similarly, it is often desirable to include a restrictive covenant to prevent competition with the firm by a partner after he has left the firm. Such a term must be reasonable otherwise it may be declared void as being a term in unreasonable restraint of trade. The partners may also decide to place specific restrictions on the activities of particular partners in relation to the running of the business. For example, a partnership agreement could prevent an individual partner from charging or selling any of the partnership's assets.

25.3.11 PARTNERSHIP DISPUTES

It is sensible to anticipate that problems may arise within the partnership and so provide for how disputes should be resolved. Commonly, clauses dealing with disputes require the partners to refer the dispute (whatever subject matter of the dispute may be) to an independent arbitrator. This approach may lead to the resolution of the dispute and thus avoid the dissolution of the partnership.

25.3.12 DISSOLUTION, DEATH, RETIREMENT AND ADMISSION OF PARTNERS

It is sensible to set out the circumstances in which the partnership will be dissolved or in which a partner can be expelled from the partnership. If the partnership comes to an end, tax liabilities can arise (see **Chapter 18**) and the partnership agreement should include a provision as to whether the firm should set aside a proportion of each partner's profit share to provide a fund to discharge any tax liability which might arise on a 'cessation'. It will be remembered from **Chapter 18** that it is possible to make an election under s. 113 ICTA 1988 for the partnership to be taxed on a continuing basis despite a change in the make-up of the partnership (which would normally give rise to a 'cessation'). As a result, firstly, it is common to find in partnership agreements an obligation imposed on outgoing partners (or their personal representatives if appropriate) to enter into the s. 113 election if requested. Any outgoing partner, if he is retiring, will be concerned to secure an income during his retirement. While the partner can create a fund from which a pension can be paid during his years as a partner, many partnerships provide annuity or consultancy arrangements for former partners. The terms of such arrangements should be set out in the partnership agreement. Secondly, since the election for assessment on the continuing basis can mean that an incoming partner can be taxed on a share of profits in excess of the amount he actually receives, it is also common for the incoming partner to be indemnified by the existing partners for any extra tax he suffers as a result. The agreement should specify how new partners are to be admitted to the partnership. In the absence of agreement to the contrary, new partners may only be admitted with the unanimous consent of the existing partners (s. 24(7) PA 1890).

25.4 Issues for an Incoming Partner

We have seen the legal consequences of admission to a partnership in **Chapter 3** and the tax consequences of admission in **Chapter 18**. However, before accepting the offer of a partnership, a prospective partner needs to consider whether the partnership's business, management and finances are such as to justify the risk of taking on unlimited liability with his future fellow partners.

The partnership agreement will be a useful source of information about the way the partnership's affairs are handled but the agreement will be, by no means, the only document the prospective partner will want to examine. Other documents will include previous years' signed accounts, as well as previous years' budgets and management accounts (which will show whether the business has suffered an unexpected shortfall in income or cost overruns which will need to be explained). The prospective partner should try to anticipate any future financial problems the partnership may face by investigating whether there are any contingent liabilities, whether the firm's insurance cover is adequate, and what steps the firm is taking to make provision for bad debts. Perhaps the most significant protection against problems in the future would be if the firm has a carefully thought out, effective business strategy and the prospective partner will need to satisfy himself that he considers the strategy to be appropriate given the firm's position in its particular market place.

TWENTY SIX

THE ARTICLES OF A PRIVATE COMPANY

This chapter covers the following topics:

26.1 Table A
26.2 Provisions concerning shares and membership
26.3 Provisions concerning meetings of shareholders
26.4 Provisions concerning directors
26.5 Alteration of articles.

In this chapter we will look at the articles of a private company. We saw in **Chapter 7** that all companies are required to have articles of association and that these articles define the relationships within the company. We also saw that a company can either adopt Table A as its articles or have articles drafted for the company. Table A is a model set of articles contained in the Companies (Tables A to F) Regulations 1985 as amended.

In this chapter we will look at some of the major terms which it may be desirable to include in the articles of a private company. We will also look at the methods by which the articles of a company can be altered and any restrictions thereon.

26.1 Table A

Most companies will find it advantageous to use Table A as the basis of their articles. The main advantage of doing so is that a great deal of work in drafting will be saved. Furthermore, although Table A has been amended over the years, much of it has been in use for many decades. As a result of this most of the problems in interpretation which might arise have been ironed out (often by decisions of the courts). However careful a draftsman is in preparing new articles which do not follow Table A as a precedent, there are bound to be difficulties of interpretation. Table A also has the advantage of providing a set of articles which have been used by very many companies. This means that any difficulties of application of the provisions have been resolved (ultimately by amendments to Table A).

Many small companies have as their articles Table A in toto, either because of the ease and cheapness of doing so or because they have not been advised to the contrary. Certainly, most companies could use Table A as a starting point. However, one of the drawbacks of Table A is that it attempts to be a 'universal' set of articles for any size and type of company. Because of this, it may be overly-complex or overly-procedural in certain instances. Also, it may not fulfil the specific wishes of a company. As such, most of this chapter will be concerned with preferable or suitable amendments to Table A.

THE ARTICLES OF A PRIVATE COMPANY

The first time when these amendments should be considered is when the company is formed. At that stage the draftsman of the articles should discuss the needs of this particular company with those who wish to have the company formed and should suggest possible amendments to Table A. Future problems should be anticipated as far as possible at this stage. For example, will the suggested articles be suitable if the company grows in the future?

The articles should also be kept under review as they may need to be changed from time to time. It may also be appropriate to consider amending the articles if a new Table A is introduced. If a company adopts Table A as its articles it will get the Table A which is in force at the time of its incorporation. Its articles will not be automatically amended when a new Table A is introduced.

26.2 Provisions Concerning Shares and Membership

26.2.1 SHARE CAPITAL

The first part of Table A deals with shares and membership of the company. It provides for the creation of different classes of shares (arts. 2 and 3). There are also provisions which deal with partly paid shares and the company's lien for amounts unpaid on shares (i.e., if shares are issued without being paid for in full the company has a lien (a charge) over the shares to secure payment for them). There are now relatively few cases where shares are issued by private companies without payment in full at the time of issue so that these provisions are unlikely to need amendment. You will sometimes see an extension to the lien so that it applies to any money that the shareholder owes to the company and to any shares whether fully paid or not.

26.2.2 ISSUE OF SHARES

Table A does not give the directors authority to issue shares. (Remember even if such a provision is included in the articles it can only last for five years from the date of incorporation of the company; see **10.2.4**.) It may be considered desirable to include such power in the articles of a newly formed company so that a meeting of members is not needed for the issue of shares when the company is newly formed.

If there are no provisions in the articles, any issue of shares for cash has to be offered to the existing members pro rata (see **10.2.4**). Those drafting the articles should consider whether this is appropriate. A number of amendments is possible and the following, in particular might be considered:

(a) A provision which disapplies these pre-emption rights so as to allow the shares to be issued to non-shareholders or other than pro rata (provided the directors are authorised to issue shares under s. 80).

(b) Alternatively it may be decided that pre-emption rights of the existing members to take shares only when issued for cash are insufficient. In this case the provisions of Table A could be amended to say that the shares are to be offered to the existing members in all cases whether or not the directors' primary intention is to issue the shares to outsiders for a non-cash consideration.

26.2.3 TRANSFER OF SHARES

Transfer of shares is dealt with in articles 23–28. A shareholder is free to transfer his shares to anyone in most cases. The directors have power to refuse only if the shares are not fully paid or the company has a lien on them (the company will only have a lien if the shares have not been fully paid for unless there have been other amendments to Table A).

In the case of many private companies it is considered appropriate that a shareholder should not be free to transfer his shares to anyone he chooses. The reason for this is that if an existing shareholder is free to transfer to anyone he is, in effect, in a position to decide who his fellow-shareholders' future associates should be. There is a considerable range of possibilities as far as restrictions are concerned. We will consider the most common and most important of them.

26.2.3.1 A simple restriction giving the directors power to refuse to register a transfer

This type of restriction is very common (indeed it was included in Table A at one time). It allows the directors to refuse to register any transfer of shares. Notice that with this type of provision a majority vote of the directors is needed to refuse to register the transfer. If the directors are equally divided and there is no casting vote (as to which see **8.1**) the transferee will become entitled to be registered. Notice also that if the directors have not refused registration within two months of the application for registration, the transferee again effectively becomes entitled to be registered (Companies Act 1985, s. 185).

If a restriction of this type is considered desirable, the article should say that the directors need not give any reason for their refusal to register the transfer.

Sometimes the article says that the directors may refuse to register if they disapprove of the transferee. This wording is undesirable as the directors may wish to refuse registration for other reasons.

The power of the directors to refuse to register a transfer does not prevent the existing shareholder from selling his shares or giving them away; it simply prevents the transferee from becoming the legal owner of the shares. If the registration is refused then the existing shareholder holds the shares on trust for the purchaser or donee who becomes the equitable owner of the shares. Quite what the relationship between the two parties will then be is uncertain. However, this is obviously an undesirable situation for the transferee to be in (especially if a considerable amount of money has been paid for the shares). Therefore, every effort should be made by the solicitor of the transferee to ascertain that there will be no such problems.

26.2.3.2 A requirement that a member who wishes to sell should first offer the shares to the existing members pro rata

This type of right is usually called a pre-emption right. It should not be confused with the statutory pre-emption right which arises on the issue of new shares for a cash consideration (and which was referred to above). Neither the Companies Act 1985 nor Table A impose any pre-emption rights where a shareholder wishes to transfer shares.

In its simplest form a pre-emption right which applies on transfer will provide that if a shareholder wishes to transfer his shares, he must first offer them to some or all of the existing shareholders, either in all circumstances or in some specified circumstances. The details of such clauses vary very considerably. An attempt is usually made to be fair to both the shareholder who wishes to transfer his shares and to those who may wish to buy.

In drafting such a clause, the following are among the matters which should be considered:

(a) Are all the other shareholders to be entitled to buy some of the shares? (The right could be restricted for example, to the directors or to shareholders of the same class.)

(b) Are the shares to be offered to those entitled according to the proportion of shares which they own? (This is by far the most likely arrangement.)

THE ARTICLES OF A PRIVATE COMPANY

(c) If a shareholder does not wish to buy, then what is to happen to the proportion of the shares which he could have bought? (In such a case the article could provide for a second round of offers to those shareholders who did take up the initial offer, or it could allow the selling shareholder to sell to whoever he chooses once the initial offer has been rejected.)

(d) How is the price to be fixed? (It is important that there should be a mechanism, otherwise the shareholder who wishes to sell to an outsider could circumvent the pre-emption procedure by offering to sell at an excessive price. The article may require an independent valuation by a specially appointed accountant, may provide for valuation by the company's own auditor or may fix the price in some arbitrary way.)

(e) Are there to be time limits? (There should be, otherwise the procedure will be unfair to the shareholder who wishes to sell as the others will be able to cause him delay.)

(f) Are there to be any safeguards in case the selling shareholder refuses to make the offer? (A common provision is to say that the directors are his agents and so can make the offer on his behalf.)

26.2.3.3 Variations on the above two articles

Within the range of absolute refusal of a transfer to pre-emption rights for existing members are many hybrid transfer articles. Some examples are:

(a) complete freedom to transfer, so long as to a family member or another shareholder, otherwise the directors may refuse to register the transfer;

(b) complete freedom to transfer, subject to specifically-defined exceptions, such as transferees who are not based in the UK or corporate transferees.

26.3 Provisions Concerning Meetings of Shareholders

Table A makes provision for company meetings which are likely to be satisfactory in most cases. However, it may be considered appropriate to remove the chairman's casting vote (art. 50). It may also be considered unnecessary to require 21 clear days' notice of a meeting at which a director is to be appointed (art. 38). However, if it is decided to remove this requirement, then the procedure for giving notice of the intention to propose the appointment of a director (which is contained in art. 76) should also be simplified (see **26.4.3** below).

26.4 Provisions Concerning Directors

26.4.1 RETIREMENT BY ROTATION

Table A (arts. 73ff) makes elaborate provision for directors to retire by rotation (one third of the board retires each year in most circumstances). Such provisions are unnecessary in the case of a private company and it may be desirable to remove them (especially if it is contemplated that an elective resolution will be passed to dispense with the need to hold annual general meetings).

26.4.2 RESTRICTIONS ON VOTING

Table A also contains a provision (art. 94) which prevents directors from voting at board meetings on anything in which they have a personal interest. If a director is so prevented, he also cannot count in the quorum (art. 95). Although such a provision may have beneficial consequences as far as prevention of fraud is concerned, it is usual to remove this provision in the case of a small private company. If art. 94 is not amended or removed, then it may be difficult to transact business in certain cases as there may not be enough directors qualified to vote who can constitute a quorum at the meeting.

26.4.3 APPOINTMENT OF DIRECTORS

Table A contains two methods for appointing directors; either by ordinary resolution (art. 78) or by a board decision (art. 79). Both these methods involve Byzantine notice procedures contained in arts 76 and 77. It is wise to consider ways of simplifying these.

26.4.4 REMOVAL OF DIRECTORS

The members of the company have power to remove a director from office by ordinary resolution (see Companies Act 1985 s. 303 and **8.3.2**). It may be considered appropriate to include in the articles a *Bushell* v *Faith* clause. This is a clause which says that if a director's removal from office is proposed he has weighted voting rights which effectively give him the power to defeat the resolution for his removal.

Whilst a *Bushell* v *Faith* clause is acceptable to protect a director, any attempt to deprive the shareholders of their rights under s. 303 is not, so any attempts to provide the shareholders with 'alternative' methods of removal in the articles must be treated with caution. However, it is acceptable to allow the board to decide about the removal of a director. The mechanism commonly employed is to state that a director must resign if requested by all other directors to do so. (See also **8.4**.)

26.5 Alteration of Articles

26.5.1 POWER TO ALTER

Section 9 CA 1985 gives a company power to alter its articles by special resolution. The power of alteration is expressed to be 'subject to the provisions of this Act' — all this really means is that the altered articles may not conflict with other parts of the legislation (so that, for example, they cannot deprive the shareholders of a right to remove directors from office under s. 303 CA 1985). Also, an alteration requiring the members to buy more shares or otherwise invest more money is void as against persons who were members at the time of the alteration (s. 16 CA 1985).

The articles of a company may not be made unalterable. A clause in the articles which purports to prevent the shareholders from altering the articles is invalid. However, a contract between shareholders as to how they will vote on a resolution to alter the articles is not void (*Russell* v *Northern Bank Development Corporation* [1992] 1 WLR 588).

The memorandum of association is regarded as being of greater authority than the articles, so that an article (whether included on incorporation or later) which contradicts the memorandum is invalid.

26.5.2 REGISTRATION

Once the special resolution altering the articles has been passed, the resolution and a printed copy of the amended articles must be sent to the Registrar within 15 days. The Registrar officially notifies his receipt of these documents and the company cannot rely on the changes as against other persons who did not know of such changes until he has done so under the same rules as for change of name and alteration of objects. The company must ensure that copies of the altered articles are available, so that the directors and secretary may consult them and in case any member exercises his statutory right to a copy of the articles (s. 19 CA 1985).

THE ARTICLES OF A PRIVATE COMPANY

26.5.3 ALTERATION TO BE FOR THE BENEFIT OF THE COMPANY

26.5.3.1 Shareholders may decide for themselves

There are no provisions in the Companies Act giving shareholders, or any particular proportion of the shareholders, power to challenge the validity of an alteration to the articles. However, the courts have held that an alteration is invalid if it is not 'bona fide in the interests of the company as a whole' (per Lord Lindley MR in *Allen v Gold Reefs of West Africa Ltd* [1900] 1 Ch 656). The test is very much easier to state than to apply to the facts of particular cases. As we have already seen in relation to the rule in *Foss v Harbottle* (see **9.6**), the court is very reluctant to interfere with business decisions merely because some of the shareholders object to what has been decided.

The court will normally regard an alteration as being in the interests of the company if the majority of the shareholders are in favour of the alteration (as they must be since a special resolution will have been passed before any question as to the validity of the alteration can arise). Thus in *Allen v Gold Reefs of West Africa Ltd* the articles contained a provision imposing a lien on partly paid shares. One shareholder owed money to the company and the articles were altered to impose a lien on fully paid shares as well as on partly paid shares. The court regarded the fact that one (and only one) shareholder was indebted to the company at the time of alteration as something exciting suspicion as to the bona fides of the company, but nevertheless came to the conclusion that the alteration was in the interests of the company as a whole. Clearly it is in the interests of a company that it should have security for money due to it and no discrimination against particular members was expressed in the altered articles.

Shuttleworth v *Cox Brothers and Co. (Maidenhead) Ltd* [1927] 2 KB 9, is perhaps a stronger illustration. The majority of the directors suspected that one of the board had been guilty of misconduct but they had insufficient proof of any grounds giving a right to dismiss him. They therefore altered the articles to say that any director would cease to hold office if requested to resign by the majority of the directors. The test applied by the court was whether any reasonable man could come to the conclusion that the alteration was in the interests of the company. If it was open to a reasonable man to come to that conclusion, the alteration would only be invalid on proof of actual bad faith. The court was satisfied that a reasonable man could come to the conclusion that the alteration was in the interests of the company and so, since the plaintiff could not prove actual bad faith, the alteration was held to be valid.

26.5.3.2 Discrimination

The courts have recognised that an alteration to the articles cannot be in the interests of the company as a whole if it discriminates against some members, however few. At first sight this seems strange in view of the two cases mentioned above, both of which appear to involve actual discrimination against a particular shareholder. However, on closer analysis neither of those cases involved any discrimination. In *Allen v Gold Reefs of West Africa* the lien applied, potentially, to all the fully paid shares whoever owned them, so that it might apply to any shareholder at some time. Similarly in *Shuttleworth* v *Cox* the new article potentially applied to any shareholder who became a director and who fell into disfavour with the rest of the board. A good illustration of the type of case where an alteration *is* discriminatory and so void is given by the Australian case, *Australian Fixed Trust Proprietary Ltd* v *Clyde Industries Ltd* (1959) SR (NSW) 33. In that case the articles were altered so as to require shareholders who were unit trust managers to obtain the approval of the majority of their unit-holders before exercising the voting rights attached to their shares. This clearly discriminated against shareholders who happened to be unit trust managers and so was void.

The narrowness of the distinction between cases which are, and cases which are not, discriminatory is well illustrated by the cases of *Sidebottom* v *Kershaw, Leese and Co. Ltd* [1920] 1 Ch 154, and *Brown* v *Abrasive Wheel Company* [1919] 1 Ch 290. In *Sidebottom* v *Kershaw, Leese* the articles were altered so as to give the directors power to direct a shareholder who was concerned with a competing business to transfer his shares. This was held to be a valid alteration. The company could properly come to the conclusion that it was in its interests that competitors be excluded from membership and there was no discrimination based on the number of shares owned. In *Brown* v *Abrasive Wheel Co.* the articles were altered to give 90% of the shareholders power to require the minority shareholders to sell their shares. In fact, the majority shareholders (who owned 98% of the shares) had good commercial reasons for wanting the alteration, but nevertheless the court held that the alteration was invalid. Although it was bona fide in the interests of 98% of the present shareholders it was not in the interests of the other 2%, nor nor was it necessarily in the interests of future shareholders and so it was discriminatory.

26.5.3.3 Conclusion in the common law

The two basic rules which seem to have evolved from the cases are:

(a) The members may generally decide themselves whether an alteration is bona fide in the interests of the company as a whole.

(b) The court will interfere with their decision where the members could not properly come to that decision because it discriminates between groups of members.

26.5.3.4 Section 459 Companies Act 1985

It should be remembered that much of the usefulness of the common law has been superseded by the above section. The alteration of articles to the prejudice of some part of the members will be good grounds under which to bring an action under s. 459. However, if the alteration affects directors as opposed to shareholders (as in the *Shuttleworth* case), the common law is still of relevance.

26.5.3.5 Class rights

Sections 125–129 Companies Act 1985 deal with class rights i.e., different rights attaching to different shares. The basic rule is that any proposed amendment to any class rights must be approved either:

(a) in writing by three-quarters of the shareholders in the relevant class; or

(b) by an extraordinary resolution at a separate meeting of the class of shareholders in question.

Any proposed amendment to the articles which affects such class rights must first receive such approval as well as be approved itself by special resolution of the company as a whole.

TWENTY SEVEN

A DEBENTURE DOCUMENT

This chapter covers the following topics:

27.1 Introduction
27.2 Terms relating to repayment and interest
27.3 Terms relating to security
27.4 Clauses designed to give the lender further protection.

27.1 Introduction

In this chapter we will look briefly at some of the terms which might be found in a debenture document. Before reading this chapter you will find it useful to read **Chapter 10** again.

Debentures vary enormously. In this chapter we will be looking at one type of debenture only, that is, a debenture which is given by a company in return for a loan by a bank. This type of debenture will contain different provisions from a debenture which is designed to secure a long term loan from people who want to invest money in a company but who prefer a fixed return rather than the possibility of a variable dividend which would be produced by an issue of shares.

A debenture is likely to contain clauses dealing with the following matters:

(a) the amount of the loan (which may be fixed or variable);

(b) a promise by the company that it will repay the loan on a fixed date and/or on the happening of certain events;

(c) a promise by the company that it will pay interest at a fixed or variable rate;

(d) a charge or charges over some or all of the company's assets, this may include floating as well as fixed charges;

(e) clauses designed to protect the position of the lender (e.g., by giving the lender power to appoint a receiver).

In the rest of this chapter we have given examples of the sort of clauses which may be found in debentures of this type. They are not taken from the debenture of any particular bank. They are provided for the purposes of illustration only so that students may get an idea of what the different clauses in the debenture are for. In practice those who draft debentures for banks

A DEBENTURE DOCUMENT

will (quite rightly) wish to cover every possible contingency in their debentures. The clauses which they draft are, therefore, usually much fuller than the illustrations given below.

27.2 Terms Relating to Repayment and Interest

The debenture will include a promise by the company that it will repay to the bank the amount which is lent to it. Frequently the debenture will relate to any money which the company owes to the bank. In this case the debenture is mainly designed to secure the repayment of an overdraft by the company. The repayment clause will then refer to something along the lines of 'all monies or other liabilities actual or contingent now or in the future owed by the company to the bank on any account or for which the company may for any reason be or become liable to the bank now or in the future'. Usually provision is made for payment 'on demand', i.e., as soon as the bank asks for it.

If none of the money secured by the debenture consists of a long term loan (so that the sums secured all relate to variable amounts such as overdraft, interest and bank charges) there will often be a promise to pay a fixed small amount. The clause might, for example, include a term under which the company 'covenants to pay to the bank the sum of one pound (£1) on demand'. Such a provision ensures that the agreement between the company and the bank is not discharged if the company temporarily pays off its overdraft so that the bank temporarily is owed nothing.

There will be a promise to pay interest. In the case of the type of loan we are considering (i.e., a loan by a bank) this will usually be a promise to pay a variable rate of interest on any money outstanding from time to time. This clause could refer to a particular way in which interest is to be calculated (e.g., that it should be a certain number of percentage points above the bank's base rate from time to time). However, the more usual provision is to say that the interest is to be calculated 'in accordance with the bank's usual practice'. Provision may also be made for the rate to be agreed between the parties if possible. Such provisions might at first sight seem rather vague. However, the practice of banks in relation to various classes of loans can be determined objectively if it becomes necessary to do so. The bank is also protected by the fact that if the company does not pay the interest which it is asked to pay, the bank can always call in the whole loan. The company also has the right to redeem the loan by paying the bank, if it can afford to do so.

27.3 Terms Relating to Security

It is possible to have an unsecured debenture. However, the type of bank debenture which we are examining in this chapter is pointless unless security is given by the borrowing company to the bank. Before it will lend or allow an overdraft the bank will wish to be satisfied that the company is and is likely to remain solvent. Before it will lend or allow an overdraft the bank will also wish (in most cases) to be satisfied that the company's assets are sufficient security for the loan. This will require the bank to consider two matters:

(a) what is the value of the assets offered as security?

(b) is the company free to give security over the assets?

Valuation is a question of fact. As far as security is concerned the bank will wish to know what other charges the company has already created over its assets. This information will be available from a company search (see the requirements as to registration in **Chapter 10** and as to searches in **Chapter 29**).

27.3.1 FIXED CHARGES

The first type of security which the bank will wish to consider is fixed charges over the valuable assets of the company. A fixed charge in the form of a legal mortgage of any land which the company may own, is likely to be viewed as the best security which the bank can take in most cases. It is usual for the debenture to give such a charge to the bank over the land owned by the company at the date of the mortgage. This charge will be supplemented by a charge over later acquired land (freehold and leasehold) which the company may acquire. This charge will be an equitable charge as a legal mortgage of land to be acquired in the future is not possible. The debenture will often also say that the bank can insist on the company executing a legal mortgage of any future acquired land once it is acquired and that the title deeds are to be deposited with the bank in the mean time. For most purposes a specific equitable charge is as good as a legal mortgage so this adds little to the bank's security.

The debenture will also usually provide for security by way of fixed charge over any shares which the company owns in other companies.

The debenture will also frequently contain a fixed charge over the company's goodwill. This is not necessarily a very valuable security as the goodwill is itself often of rather questionable value especially as the security is only likely to be enforced if the company is in financial difficulties.

Modern debentures often contain a fixed charge over 'the book debts and other debts of the company'. Book debts are the sums owed to the company by, for example, its customers. In effect the fixed charge over book debts says that the bank is entitled to collect the money due to the company in order to discharge the company's own debt to the bank. The law recognises that such a charge is possible but there are technical problems with regarding the charge as a fixed charge as the company is usually free to deal with its book debts as it wishes. The debenture will, therefore, provide that when payment of the debts is received by the company the money must be paid into the company's account at the bank and that the company is not to be free to assign or otherwise deal with its debts.

In *Re New Bullas Trading* [1994] BCC 36 a charge was expressed to be a fixed charge over book debts and gave the lender power to give directions as to how the debts were to be dealt with. No such directions had in fact been given. Notwithstanding this, the Court of Appeal stated that the uncollected book debts of the company were subject to a fixed charge. Proceeds of book debts were held to be subject to a floating charge. While the decision lends support to the proposition that a fixed charge can operate over book debts, there remains much debate on the subject.

The mortgage will require the company to insure the property and to keep it in a good state of repair.

27.3.2 FLOATING CHARGES

As we saw in **Chapter 10** a company can create a floating charge over any of its assets. This is a charge which allows the company to deal with the assets even though they are the subject of the charge. This has the benefit of giving the company flexibility while at the same time giving the bank some sort of security. The problem from the bank's point of view is that the charge is of uncertain value until the security crystallises. In order to reduce this problem it is usual to provide that the company is not free to sell the whole of its undertaking without the consent of the bank. There will also be provision stating that the bank can give notice of crystallisation. This is a clause which says that the bank may 'give notice to the company converting the floating security into a fixed charge in relation to any assets specified in the notice'.

A DEBENTURE DOCUMENT

The company will normally be prohibited from creating any later charge ranking in priority to the floating charge. Such a provision is necessary as without it the company is free to charge the floating charge assets by way of specific charge. This does not invalidate the floating charge but clearly if the assets are now subject to a fixed charge which will take priority, the value of the floating charge as a security is greatly reduced.

Often the security document will prohibit the company from creating *any* other interest in the charged property, without first obtaining the permission of the bank. Such a provision is known as a 'negative pledge'. While a later floating charge over assets of a company would not rank ahead of a bank's earlier floating charge, it might allow the later chargee to appoint an administrative receiver over the company's assets thus removing an element of control from the bank. The negative pledge aims to prevent such a situation arising.

The company will usually also be required to insure the floating charge property.

27.4 Clauses Designed to Give the Lender Further Protection

27.4.1 PERSONAL GUARANTEES

If the bank is not satisfied with the security which the company can provide, it may well require personal guarantees from the directors of the company in addition to the security given by the company.

27.4.2 APPOINTMENT OF A RECEIVER

One of the clauses which will be contained in the debenture will allow the bank to appoint a receiver. Where the debenture includes a floating charge the receiver will normally satisfy the definition of an administrative receiver and so will have all the powers of such a receiver (see **Chapter 23** for the powers and duties of an administrative receiver). The function of the receiver is to realise assets for the bank, pay them off and then return the company to the directors. In practice the company may well be wound up after the receivership as the receiver will have withdrawn many of the assets of the company. The powers and duties of a receiver are dealt with in **Chapter 23**.

Debentures vary somewhat as to the circumstances in which a receiver may be appointed. The following are likely to be among those which are included:

(a) The bank demands payment of the principal, interest or any other obligation of the company and the company fails to pay within a specified period of time (usually this will be a small number of days).

(b) A petition for an administration order is presented. As we saw in **Chapter 23** the power to appoint an administrative receiver is lost if an administration order is made. However, a person with power to appoint an administrative receiver has power to veto an administration order by appointing an administrative receiver in most circumstances.

TWENTY EIGHT

SHAREHOLDERS' AGREEMENTS

This chapter covers the following topics:

28.1 Introduction
28.2 The advantages of a shareholders' agreement
28.3 Drafting a shareholders' agreement
28.4 Legal limits on the use of shareholders' agreements
28.5 Enforcing the agreement.

28.1 Introduction

In this chapter we will look at shareholders' agreements. These are agreements between shareholders about how their company should be run. The company is also sometimes joined as a party in the agreement so that it too will be bound by the terms (the company cannot, however, override its statutory powers in this way). In particular they are likely to contain terms under which the shareholders agree how they will vote on various issues which may be raised at company meetings. For example, each shareholder might agree to support the re-election of the other shareholders as directors.

Shareholders' agreements are only likely to be effective in the case of companies with a small number of shareholders. If an agreement about how members will vote is to be effective it must usually be made by at least enough members of the company to ensure that a majority of the votes at any meeting will be cast in accordance with the agreement. If there are many members it will be difficult to get a large number of them to enter into a contract. Remember also that the contract (like any other contract) is only enforceable by and against those who are parties to it, so the effectiveness of the agreement is much reduced if a large number of members are not party to it.

28.2 The Advantages of a Shareholders' Agreement

28.2.1 SECRECY

The agreement, unlike the articles, is not open to inspection by the public.

28.2.2 PROTECTION OF INTERESTS

A shareholders' agreement can protect the interests of some of the members in ways which cannot be easily achieved by the articles. In particular, unless the company provides for

SHAREHOLDERS' AGREEMENTS

different classes of shares, all the shareholders have to be treated alike. If this is not what is desired then it may be much simpler to give one shareholder exceptional rights in a shareholders' agreement. For example, it may be intended that one person (perhaps the founder of the company) should remain a director throughout his life. This is quite difficult to achieve in the articles because the shareholders have a statutory right to remove a director from office. Added voting rights may effectively give a director an invulnerable position (see, for example, *Bushell* v *Faith* at **8.3.2.4**) but these rights will be attached to the shares and so will pass to the director's successors in title unless very cumbersome arrangements are made. A shareholders' agreement can achieve this very simply if the shareholders agree to vote for X each time his re-election as a director is in issue and to vote against any resolution to remove him from office.

28.2.3 DIFFICULTIES OF ENFORCING ARTICLES

Although the articles of a company are deemed to be a contract between the company and its members, many cases have decided that this does not mean that each individual member is entitled to enforce compliance with every term of the articles. Generally only those terms which relate to the membership rights of the shareholder can be enforced. If the terms are included in a shareholders' agreement then any party to the agreement can enforce it in full. Furthermore a shareholders' agreement can be enforced simply by means of an action by one shareholder against another. If a shareholder seeks to enforce a term in the articles he will normally have to sue in a representative capacity.

28.2.4 VETO

A shareholders' agreement may give each individual party to it a veto over any proposal which is contrary to the terms of the agreement. In this way a shareholder may be protected even though he only has a small number of shares. However, such agreements should not be lightly entered into. Each shareholder will wish to have a veto against any decisions which he thinks are inappropriate, but he should remember that the other parties will also have the same veto powers (unless he is able to negotiate them for himself alone).

28.3 Drafting a Shareholders' Agreement

The uses to which shareholders' agreements are put and consequently the clauses which are included in them vary greatly depending on the circumstances which lead to the particular agreement. In this paragraph we will examine some of the main types of provision which may be included.

28.3.1 APPOINTMENT OF DIRECTORS AND SERVICE CONTRACTS

The agreement will frequently require all the parties to the agreement to vote in favour of any resolution which reappoints any of them to be a director of the company. It should then also include a term requiring each party to the agreement to vote against any resolution for the removal of any of the parties from the office of director. If it is decided to include such terms, then it may also be appropriate to consider whether there should be any time limit; for example, it might be for a fixed period of time, or it might only apply until each director reaches a specified age.

This clause might also provide for remuneration of the directors and approval of their service contracts for specified or indefinite periods exceeding five years.

28.3.2 APPROVAL FOR POLICY DECISIONS

The articles of almost all companies including those (the vast majority) which use Table A as the basis of their articles, provide that business decisions are to be taken by the directors. It

SHAREHOLDERS' AGREEMENTS

would usually be quite inappropriate for articles to provide that the shareholders are to have power to run the company's business. However, if there are particular issues which the shareholders have agreed to as matters of policy, these could be included in a shareholders' agreement. The agreement might, for example, require the agreement of the parties before any new ventures could be undertaken by the company, or before the company could expand the area of its operation. This would be reinforced by an agreement that the parties would vote against any attempt to circumvent such an agreement, and would take whatever steps they could to prevent these things from happening without such approval.

28.3.3 ISSUE OF SHARES AND PROTECTION OF VOTING RIGHTS

One of the main purposes for which a shareholders' agreement may be used is to protect the shareholders from 'watering' of their interests. This occurs where new shares are issued and a shareholder does not get some of the shares. For example if a shareholder now has 40 per cent of the 1,000 shares which have been issued, he has enough shares to block a special resolution. If a further 1,000 shares were issued and he got none of them then his interest would be reduced to 20 per cent and so (unless the voting rights were changed) he would lose the power to block a special resolution. To prevent this from happening pre-emption rights may be included in the shareholders' agreement.

The considerations here are similar to those in relation to pre-emption rights contained in the articles of a company which we considered in **Chapter 26** (and remember that there are also statutory pre-emption rights in limited circumstances; see **10.2.4**). In some cases it may be more appropriate to include pre-emption rights in a shareholders' agreement. This would be so, for example, if the shareholders wished to keep the existence of the pre-emption rights secret or if they were to apply only to some of the shareholders.

An issue of debentures or other borrowing by the company will not affect the powers of the shareholders to vote in respect of their shares. However, the effect of borrowing will be to reduce the amount of profit available for potential dividend payments to the shareholders. It may, therefore, be appropriate for the clause to require the approval of the parties for borrowing above a certain figure.

A clause in a shareholders' agreement could be drafted so as to require approval of the parties to the agreement for any issue of shares or other reorganisation of capital. This would go further than a simple pre-emption right as it would effectively give the parties a right to veto issue of shares, not just a right to insist on taking some of the shares themselves. Alternatively the clause could provide that the existing shareholders would be bound to make further investment in certain circumstances specified in the clause. Obviously a shareholder should not undertake such an obligation lightly in case he does not have the resources to meet his obligation when it arises.

28.3.4 WITHDRAWAL FROM THE COMPANY

One of the principal features of company law is that a shareholder (unlike a partner in a partnership) is not normally allowed to withdraw his investment. This is the idea of maintenance of capital which we saw in **Chapter 10** (we also saw the limited exceptions in **Chapter 11** under which a company can redeem or buy back its own shares). A shareholders' agreement can be used to allow a shareholder an opportunity to leave the company and to take out his capital. For example, the agreement will often include a clause requiring a shareholder to offer his shares to the other members pro rata if he wishes to sell. As in the case of a pre-emption right on transfer contained in the articles (see **Chapter 26**), this clause will contain valuation provisions which will be designed to ensure fairness to both the selling member and the buying member.

SHAREHOLDERS' AGREEMENTS

A simple pre-emption right will not, however, ensure that the shareholder can sell his shares. He must offer them to the other members but they may not wish to buy. In this case the member is unlikely to be able to sell to an outsider, as there is likely to be a restriction on the right to transfer either in the articles or in the shareholders' agreement. It is possible to include a term whereby the shareholder who wishes to get out of the company has a right to insist that the other members of the company will buy his shares. Such a clause should only be entered into if the finances of the potential purchasers are likely to be strong enough to be able to comply with the agreement.

28.3.5 PAYMENT OF DIVIDENDS

Although it is not likely to be one of the commonest clauses to be found in a shareholders' agreement, it is possible to include a term which will either require the payment of dividends or which will restrict the payment of dividends. A clause which purported to require payment of dividends other than out of accumulated realised profits (after deduction of accumulated realised losses) would be unenforceable as such payments would be illegal.

28.3.6 RESTRICTIVE COVENANTS

Restrictive covenants may be included in a shareholders' agreement. This sort of term might be appropriate where a shareholder has brought particular expertise to the company and the other shareholders wish to preserve that expertise for the company. If such a clause is included it is likely also to appear in any service contract which the shareholder has with the company (for example where he is a director as well as a shareholder). Restrictive covenants are void on grounds of public policy unless they are reasonable in area and time.

28.3.7 AN ARBITRATION CLAUSE

Like many commercial agreements the shareholders' agreement will often include an arbitration clause so that any disputes which arise out of it can be resolved without the need for action in the courts.

28.4 Legal Limits on the use of Shareholders' Agreements

28.4.1 POWER TO ALTER THE ARTICLES

A company has a statutory power to alter its articles by special resolution. A shareholders' agreement cannot take this right away. However, it can provide that members are personally in breach of contract if they vote in favour of an alteration which is contrary to the terms of the agreement: see for example, *Russell* v *Northern Bank Development Corporation* [1992] 1 WLR 588.

28.4.2 DIRECTORS' DUTIES

The directors of a company have a fiduciary duty to the company. A shareholders' agreement could not lawfully permit the directors to breach this fiduciary duty. Furthermore directors have a number of duties which are of a public nature (particularly in relation to insolvent companies). A shareholders' agreement could not authorise or direct the directors as to how they are to perform their functions. For example, a director would be liable for failure to make statutory returns to the Registrar of Companies even if his shareholders' agreement purported to require this. Similarly a director could not absolve himself from liability for wrongful trading on the basis of a shareholders' agreement.

28.5 Enforcing the Agreement

A shareholders' agreement is a contract. Each party provides consideration by agreeing to abide by the terms of the agreement. It follows from this that if the agreement is broken, the other parties can claim damages. The agreement can also be enforced by an injunction which requires a shareholder who is a party to it not to vote in a way contrary to the terms of the agreement. It may also be enforced by a positive injunction requiring a shareholder who is a party to it to vote in accordance with its provisions.

TWENTY NINE

COMPANY SEARCHES AND COMPANY ACCOUNTS

This chapter covers the following topics:

29.1 Introduction
29.2 Official notification
29.3 Company searches
29.4 The duty to submit accounts
29.5 Small and medium sized companies
29.6 Profit and loss account
29.7 Balance sheet
29.8 Format of accounts
29.9 Interpretation of accounts
29.10 Solvency
29.11 Profitability.

29.1 Introduction

One of the core concepts of company law is that information about a company, its 'constitution' and financial status should be made available to the public. The purpose of this policy of 'openness' is to enable anyone interested in the affairs of a company (whether they are current or prospective shareholders in the company or its creditors) to have access to the information they need to make an informed judgment on the company's financial affairs and the abilities of the company's management. They will also be able to determine whether the company and its directors have the necessary authority and powers to enter into the transaction which, for example, a third party creditor may be considering. In any transaction involving a company, it is prudent to carry out relevant searches to obtain all necessary information *and* to obtain confirmation from the company that such information is up to date and correct.

Information is made available by the company:

(a) keeping at its registered office records and registers available for inspection by its members and the public;

(b) disclosing financial information to its members through the annual directors' report and annual audited accounts;

(c) delivering to the Registrar of Companies documents which the Registrar in turn makes available to the public for inspection; and

COMPANY SEARCHES AND COMPANY ACCOUNTS

(d) the publication of certain information about the company in the *London Gazette*.

In this chapter, we will look at the information which will be made public in the *London Gazette* as well as the information which can be found through making a search at the Companies' Registry. At the end of the chapter, we will look at the rules with which the company must comply in relation to its account, as well as giving some guidance on how to interpret the published accounts of a company.

29.2 Official Notification

Section 711 CA 1985 requires the Registrar of Companies to advertise the issue by him or receipt by him (as the case may be) of certain documents in the *London Gazette*. This is called official notification and applies to the following in relation to any company.

(a) the issue of any certificate of incorporation;

(b) the receipt of any document making or evidencing an alteration to the memorandum or articles;

(c) the receipt of a notification of any change of directors;

(d) the receipt of the company's accounts;

(e) the receipt of a notification of the change of the address of the company's registered office;

(f) the receipt of a copy of a winding up order;

(g) the receipt of a copy of a dissolution order after winding up;

(h) the receipt of a return by the liquidator following a final meeting; or

(i) the receipt of certain other documents in relation to public companies only.

In the case of the making of a winding up order, alteration to the memorandum and articles, or a change in the directors, the company cannot rely on the happening of the event against another person until the notice is put in the *Gazette* unless the other person actually knew about it. The company cannot rely on the event for 15 days after it is put in the *Gazette* if the other person is unavoidably prevented from knowing about the event. The same rule applies to a change in the address of the registered office as regards service of any document on the company (i.e., service is effective at the old registered office until the change is gazetted), and also to the appointment of a liquidator in a voluntary winding up (in this case, the notice is put in the *Gazette* by the liquidator, not by the Registrar).

In addition to the file kept by the Registrar, certain information about a company is available for inspection at the company's registered office (see **7.7.3**).

29.3 Company Searches

29.3.1 GENERAL

While information about a company can be obtained from advertisements in the *London Gazette* or from inspecting the records and registers maintained by the company at its registered office, a great deal of information about a company can be discovered from making a search at the Companies' Registry. The Registrar of Companies keeps copies of the information supplied to him by the company and this is available for public inspection. In this

COMPANY SEARCHES AND COMPANY ACCOUNTS

section of the chapter we will look at the information which a company must supply to the Registrar and then look at the procedure for making a company search.

29.3.2 THE INFORMATION AVAILABLE FOR INSPECTION

The information available for inspection at the Companies' Registry includes the following:

(a) the company's memorandum and articles of association (changes to be registered within 15 days of relevant company resolution);

(b) particulars of directors and secretary (giving details both of the original directors and secretary as well as subsequent changes);

(c) particulars of the issue of shares;

(d) particulars of (most) charges (within 21 days of the charge being given);

(e) particulars of all special, elective and extraordinary resolutions (copy resolutions to be delivered within 15 days);

(f) the notice of the accounting reference date;

(g) the notice of any increase of capital (within 15 days of the change);

(h) resolutions under s. 80 CA 1985 (copy resolutions to be delivered within 15 days);

(i) particulars of the address of the registered office (both the first address and subsequent changes);

(j) the annual return; and

(k) the accounts.

Of this list, the last two items merit further consideration (see **29.4** for the rules relating to the accounts which the company must file). So far as the 'annual return' is concerned, s. 363 CA 1985 requires every company to make an annual return to the Registrar on Form 363 once in every year (a fee of £15 is payable). The company is required to file returns signed by a director or the secretary made up to the company's return date which must be within 12 months of the date of the previous return or, in the case of a new company, the date of incorporation. The return must be filed with the Registrar within 28 days of the return date. The return must set out details of:

(a) the address of the registered office of the company;

(b) the company's principal business activities;

(c) the location of the register of members if it is not kept at the registered office;

(d) the location of the company's register of debenture holders if it is not kept at the company's registered office;

(e) the company's type (that is to say, public limited company, private company limited by shares or whatever);

(f) the name and address of the company secretary;

(g) the name and address of every director plus nationality, date of birth, business occupation and the particulars required for the register of directors;

(h) details of the company's issued share capital (stating for each class of share, the nature of the class and the total number and aggregate number of issued shares of that class as at the date of the return);

(i) names and addresses of the members of the company on the date on which the return is made up plus the persons who have ceased to be members since the last return;

(j) details of the shares held by member; and

(k) a statement that the company has elected to dispense with the holding of annual general meetings, or with the laying of accounts in general meetings, if it has.

The Registrar of Companies will not keep documents in relation to a company at the Registry indefinitely. At any time after the expiration of two years from the date of the dissolution of any company, the Registrar may direct that any records in his custody relating to that company be removed to the Public Record Office. Furthermore, the Registrar is only obliged to keep originals of documents for 10 years. Once that period has expired, the documents may be destroyed.

29.3.3 THE PROCEDURE FOR MAKING A COMPANY SEARCH

The wide range of information which companies are required to file with the Registrar of Companies is filed by the Registrar by reference to each company's unique company number. With the company's current name or registration number (and on payment of the relevant fee), it is possible to obtain a copy of the company's file. To do this, a company search can be carried out in person, by post, telephone or via Companies House Direct, a web-based on-line service. Full details of the latter, together with information on all Companies House services, can be obtained at *http://www.companieshouse.gov.uk*. The on-line service provides free access to certain general company information, including an index of all registered companies. More specific information and company documents can be downloaded on payment of the relevant fees. While Companies House can supply hard copies of company documentation on request, the traditional manner by which company information is supplied is via a set of microfiches. These contain, in date order, all the information which the company has filed with the Registrar. The number of pages can be considerable in the case of long-established companies.

29.3.4 FAILURE TO FILE RETURNS

The effectiveness of the system requiring companies to make information about themselves public depends on the companies making the information available whether in their own records and registers or by filing the information with the Registrar of Companies. Section 713 CA 1985 enables the court to make an order directing a company and its officers to provide information when they are in default. The application to the court can be made by a member of the company, a creditor of the company or by the registrar of companies. Failure to comply with an order under s. 713 can lead to the company and its officers being charged with contempt of court and so subject to a fine and imprisonment. Furthermore, under s. 652 CA 1985, the Registrar of Companies can strike from the register the name of the company in default in relation to delivering information, but only if the Registrar has reasonable cause to believe that the company is not carrying on business or is not in operation.

29.4 The Duty to Submit Accounts

Limited companies are required, by law, to prepare a set of 'final accounts'. These consist of a profit and loss account and a balance sheet. The accounts will usually be prepared by accountants, but the duty to ensure that they are prepared is placed on the directors of the company by s. 266 CA 1985. Once they have been prepared the final accounts are laid before the company in general meeting (s. 241). This means that a general meeting of the company will be held at which the accounts will be placed before the shareholders for their consideration. This meeting is called the accounts meeting. It may be either the annual general meeting of the company or an extraordinary general meeting. However, the company can dispense with the need to hold an accounts meeting if it passes an elective resolution to that effect.

In addition to presenting the accounts to the shareholders at a general meeting, the company is also required to send copies of the accounts to the shareholders (if an accounts meeting is held this must be done before the meeting). This must be done within seven months after the end of the company's financial year in the case of a public company and within ten months in the case of a private company.

(The Companies (Summary Financial Statement) Regulations 1992 (SI 1992 No. 3075) permit a public company whose shares are listed on the Stock Exchange to send out a summary financial statement to a member, rather than full accounts, provided specified requirements are satisfied. The details of these requirements are beyond the scope of this Guide.)

Subject to what is said below about small and medium sized companies, all companies must also send copies of their accounts to the Registrar of Companies. Failure to deliver accounts on time leads to an automatic penalty. These accounts are then a matter of public record and anyone who pays to do a company search will get a microfiche copy of the accounts (s. 241(3)).

29.5 Small and Medium Sized Companies

If a private company comes within the definition of a small or medium sized company for a particular financial year, its duty to deliver accounts to the Registrar of Companies is modified. A company is small if at least two of the following criteria are satisfied:

(a) the company's turnover does not exceed £2,800,000;

(b) its balance sheet total does not exceed £1,400,000;

(c) the average number of employees does not exceed 50 people.

A small company does not need to submit a profit and loss account and the information required in its balance sheet is reduced.

A medium sized company is one which satisfies at least two of the following criteria:

(a) its turnover does not exceed £11,200,000;

(b) its balance sheet total does not exceed £5,600,000;

(c) the average number of employees does not exceed 250.

A medium sized company must submit both a balance sheet and a profit and loss account, but the profit and loss account is in an abbreviated form.

In the above definitions 'turnover' broadly speaking means the sums earned by the company in selling goods or services before deducting expenses. The balance sheet total is broadly speaking the value of the company's assets without deducting any liabilities except short term liabilities.

The exemptions from reporting available to small and medium sized companies mean that they can keep their affairs secret from the public to a greater extent than public companies, or companies which do not satisfy these definitions. However, small and medium sized companies are not exempt from the requirement to produce full accounts nor from the requirement to present the accounts to their own shareholders. The duty to have the accounts independently audited remains but the auditors need not make a full report.

29.6 Profit and Loss Account

A profit and loss account is an account which shows what income the company has received in a particular period of time and what expenses have been incurred by the company in producing that income. Once the expenses are deducted from the income the resulting figure is a profit (or a loss if the expenses are more than the income). The profit and loss account is strictly speaking only designed to show income profits. If a company makes a capital profit (for example, if it sells its factory for a profit) this may be shown as an addition to the profit and loss account. It will then usually be labelled as an 'exceptional item' as opposed to the ordinary income profit.

Profit and loss accounts are almost always prepared for 12 month periods (the company may wish to produce forecasts or full accounts for its own internal purposes on a more regular basis). The period covered by the accounts ends with the accounting reference date which the company can choose for itself (see **7.11**). Companies are not required to prepare accounts for a calendar year (although some companies do choose 31 December as their accounting reference date in which case the accounts will be for a calendar year).

A very simple traditional profit and loss account might look like the following:

XYZ Ltd
Profit and Loss Account
Year ending 31 March 2000

	£	£
INCOME		
Sales		200,000
Opening stock	80,000	
Purchases	90,000	
	170,000	
Less closing stock	70,000	
		100,000
Gross profit from sales		100,000
Interest received		8,000
		108,000
EXPENDITURE		
Wages	55,000	
Miscellaneous	10,000	
		65,000
PROFIT BEFORE TAX		43,000
DEDUCT TAX		12,000
TRANSFERRED TO RESERVE		31,000

Notice the following points in relation to it:

(a) The account is divided into three parts. The first shows the income of the business. The second shows the expenditure which is incurred in earning that income and the third shows what has happened to the income (this third part is strictly speaking the appropriation section rather than part of the profit and loss account itself. If any dividends were paid they would be shown as a deduction in this section).

(b) In the income section the opening and closing stock are shown. Unless stock is taken into account it is impossible to work out the profit. If a company has a storeroom full of goods left over from last year which it sells this year, it cannot calculate its profit unless it takes into account the fact that it paid for that stock.

(c) The figure which is labelled transferred to reserve is what is left of the profit after the tax has been paid. It is in effect profit which has been retained in the business. An explanation of the term 'reserve' in this context is given in **29.7**.

29.7 Balance Sheet

A balance sheet shows the assets and liabilities of the company. An asset is something of value or potential value. The factory which a company owns is an asset, so is any money which it has in the bank. Sometimes the balance sheet will also show much more intangible things such as goodwill. Goodwill is the difference between the real assets of a company and its overall value to a purchaser. For example, a company running a business in a shop might own the following assets:

	£
The shop	100,000
Fixtures (shelves etc.)	10,000
Stock (the goods for sale)	5,000
Cash	2,000

If the company decided to sell the business it would be likely to want more than £117,000 for it. The real value of the business includes the fact that it has a loyal group of customers, or it is situated in a good location for running this type of business (or both). The difference between the assets value and what the shop could be sold for is the goodwill of the business.

The liabilities part of the balance sheet includes liabilities due to outsiders (such as bills owed by the shop), money owed to the bank or other lenders. The money which would be paid to the shareholders if the company were wound up is also shown as a liability because, at least in theory, it will be paid out to the shareholders one day.

A simple traditional balance sheet might look like this:

COMPANY SEARCHES AND COMPANY ACCOUNTS

Balance Sheet of XYZ Ltd
31 March 2000

	£	£
FIXED ASSETS		
Premises		400,000
Fixtures		10,000
		410,000
CURRENT ASSETS		
Stock (goods for sale and/or materials)	5,000	
Cash	2,000	
	7,000	
LESS CURRENT LIABILITIES		
Electricity bill	4,500	
		2,500
		412,500
CAPITAL		
Share capital		200,000
Share premium account		160,000
Bank loan		10,000
Reserves		42,500
		412,500

Notice the following points in relation to it:

(a) The totals balance, i.e., the net assets of the company equal its capital. This happens because of the 'double entry' system used to record transactions in the company's books. A simple example of this is where share capital is contributed to a company. If someone buys shares for £100 at par value, this would be represented in a balance sheet by two entries. The company would have £100 in cash, a current asset; and it would have capital of £100 (a liability to the shareholder). Extrapolating this, a company's net assets will always reflect its capital, as is seen here. They can effectively be seen as the way in which a company has employed its capital in its business.

(b) A distinction is made between fixed assets and current assets. Fixed assets are assets which are likely to be held by the company for a considerable period of time. Current assets are those which are likely to be used up by the company in the course of its business.

(c) Current liabilities (that is sums owed by the company which are likely to be paid within a year) are shown as a deduction from current assets. They are accordingly not in the same part of the account as the long term liabilities.

(d) The second half of the balance sheet is labelled 'capital'. Although in common parlance the word capital often means money or wealth, to an accountant it is a liability which is owed to someone with a proprietary or other long term interest in the business. The money owed to the bank is included in capital on the assumption that it is a long term loan and so is something like an investment in the business. If the same money was owed to the bank on an overdraft it would be shown as a short term liability like the electricity bill.

(e) The other sums shown under the heading of capital are all sums due to the shareholders of the company. The share capital is the liability which arises from the fact that the shareholders paid the nominal value of their shares to the company at some time in the past. The share premium is the liability which arises from the fact that when the shares were issued the shareholders paid more than the nominal value for them. The difference between these two sums is theoretical only. Remember that a company cannot generally return the sums invested by the shareholders until the company is wound up.

(f) The item referred to as reserves is in a way a balancing item. If the company was wound up its assets would realise £417,000. This would be used to pay the bank and the outstanding bill. This would then leave £402,500 for the shareholders. They would be repaid their original investment of £360,000 (shown in share capital and share premium). This would then leave £42,500. The reserve is in effect a liability owed to shareholders which results from the fact that the company has made profits over the years.

(g) The balance sheet is dated 31 March. Businesses constantly acquire and dispose of assets, pay bills and incur new liabilities. A balance sheet is, therefore, always relevant to a particular moment in time, not to the whole of a period of time (in which respect contrast the profit and loss account).

(h) The company has a surplus of short term assets over short term liabilities. The resulting surplus is called net current assets (confusingly it is also often called 'working capital' even though it is an asset). This figure is particularly important as it is a strong indication of the solvency of the company.

29.8 Format of Accounts

Schedule 4 to the Companies Act 1985 contains formats for both profit and loss accounts and balance sheets. These are templates which all companies must choose from in presenting their accounts for each financial year. They set out the order in which all the different items in the accounts must appear. For the purposes of illustration we have not adhered exactly to any of the formats in the very brief examples given above.

Companies' published accounts are often difficult for beginners to follow because much of the information is given in the form of notes. Indeed the published profit and loss account is likely to contain very little information about the company's income and expenditure unless close attention is paid to the notes as well as to the account itself.

29.9 Interpretation of Accounts

29.9.1 INTRODUCTION

In this paragraph we will look at some ideas about interpretation of accounts. Interpretation is a process whereby information is extracted from the accounts for two main purposes:

(a) to assess the company's present financial position in relation to profitability and solvency;

(b) to predict the future prospects of the company.

Neither of these processes is an exact science. Interpretation of accounts will not always produce a 'right answer' but rather an opinion about the company.

COMPANY SEARCHES AND COMPANY ACCOUNTS

29.9.2 REASONS FOR INTERPRETATION AND SOURCES OF INFORMATION

Interpretation of accounts is likely to be undertaken by or for a variety of people for a variety of reasons. In particular the management of the company may wish to know how efficient the business is. Investors or potential investors in a quoted company will want to know whether the company is over or under valued (in their opinion) at the present price of the shares. Creditors will be particularly concerned to investigate the company's solvency.

The most obvious source of information about the accounts of the company is the published accounts of the company. It should be noted, however, that these accounts will not provide as much information as the interpreter might ideally like. The management of the company will have more detailed accounts than the published accounts in the form of what are usually called management accounts. These are not available to the public (not even to the shareholders) as a matter of right, but sometimes the management may be willing to show them to others such as potential lenders or purchasers of the business.

If the information which is available to the particular investigator is limited to published accounts, then he will usually do well to look at the accounts for several years. In interpreting the performance of a business the trend over a period of time is very important. Past results are not necessarily a guide to the future, but nevertheless they may give some indication of the likely progress of the company in the future. An investor, for example, is likely to be more interested in a company which shows a long record of growth than one which has been merely holding its own.

29.9.3 WHAT ARE THE LIMITS INHERENT IN ACCOUNTS?

The most obvious limit is the possibility of outright fraud. If the accounts are a work of fiction they will tell you nothing useful. The process of auditing accounts ensures that fraud is unusual.

Published accounts are produced once a year and, as we have seen, may be submitted to the Registrar up to seven months after the end of the accounting period (ten months if the company is private). This means that the accounts may be quite considerably out of date. The balance sheet date should be checked both to see how out of date the accounts are and also to see how typical that date might be. The balance sheet of a resort hotel business may tell a very different story if it is drawn up just after the end of the season (when there will be an unusually large amount of cash or an unusually small overdraft), than if it is produced at the end of the winter.

The notes to the accounts should be examined carefully to see what the company's policy is in relation to valuation of assets. In particular, have the fixed assets been revalued recently so that the figures approximate to market value? If not, then the fixed assets may be shown at historic cost (i.e., what was paid for them) in which case they, and so the company, may be worth much more than shown.

Another important factor to look for is how debtors have been dealt with in the accounts. The figure described as debtors shows the amount of money owed to the company. Almost all businesses suffer some degree of bad debts. That is, some of the people who owe them money cannot or will not pay what they owe to the company. Bad debts and an estimate of potential bad debts ('provision for bad debts') should be deducted in computing the profits, and from the current assets of the company, otherwise the accounts will be misleading.

Often the accounts will include some special feature which is relevant to the accounts in a particular year only. These are usually called exceptional items. For example, in a particular year a company may have sold a fixed asset or issued shares. In both of these cases it will have received a large amount of cash. If it has not yet spent the cash then the net current assets figure may be unusually high. Will the company still have enough cash to pay its creditors if it replaces the fixed asset which it sold?

29.10 Solvency

A company is solvent if it is able to pay its debts as they fall due. It is important to realise that solvency is not the same thing as profitability. A company may make profits and yet be insolvent. For example, the profits may arise from the fact that the company has supplied goods or services for which it has not yet been paid. This company will be insolvent if it has to pay its own creditors before it collects from its debtors. Similarly a company may be unprofitable and yet solvent for a very long time. For example, a company may be making losses and yet can keep itself going by selling fixed assets.

In judging the solvency of a company it is desirable to work out certain solvency ratios. These are calculations made from the information given in the accounts.

The first of the ratios is the 'current ratio': this is a test of the company's liquidity. Liquidity is the ability of a company to pay its debts in the short term. The current ratio is the ratio of current assets to current liabilities. In the example in **29.7**, the current assets were £7,000 and the current liabilities were £4,500. This gives a ratio of 7:4.5 or 1.55:1. This would generally be regarded as a satisfactory figure as it means that for every pound which the company will have to pay in the short term, it has, or will soon receive, £1.55. However, this does assume that the stock will be easy to sell at the value shown in the balance sheet (in the case of stock the value will normally be the lower of purchase price or current value).

Because stock cannot always be sold in a hurry the liquidity ratio (also known as the acid test) is often preferred to the current ratio. This compares liquid assets (i.e., cash and things as good as cash) with current liabilities. Applying this ratio to our figures we get a ratio of 2:4.5 or .44:1. This is much less satisfactory. It means that for every pound that the company will have to pay, it only has ready access to 44p. This is not necessarily as dangerous as it may seem at first sight, however. If the company can rely on selling a lot of stock quickly it will be able to pay the electricity bill. Similarly the company may have an arrangement with its bank for an overdraft which will see it through the temporary crisis of the payment of the electricity bill.

A company which is in the position of the one illustrated here is in danger of overtrading. This occurs where the company has insufficient working capital (i.e., net current assets). As it pays its bills it may be unable to replace its stock which obviously means that it cannot continue to be profitable and solvent in the future. The solution to this problem may be for the company to acquire more working capital, either by retaining more profits in the business, by acquiring further investment or by increasing the size of its long term borrowing (the last of these is likely to be a real possibility in view of the large amount of fixed assets and the small amount of borrowing). The fact that not all companies can in practice do any of these things is the reason for a very high proportion of business failures.

29.11 Profitability

The bottom line profit figure is found in the profit and loss account. In our example the profit is £43,000 before tax and £31,000 after. The proprietor of the business will want to know whether this figure is satisfactory or not. There is no simple answer to this, not least because different people have different expectations and so are more or less easily satisfied. The most important step to take may be to compare with previous years and to compare with other similar business (this is more easily done with large companies as the published accounts of small and medium sized companies give much less information). However, ratios can help here as with solvency.

COMPANY SEARCHES AND COMPANY ACCOUNTS

29.11.1 INVESTMENT

An investor or potential investor will be interested in the whole of the company's financial situation. He will be particularly interested in what return on capital he can expect (i.e., in how much income will be generated by his investment). One simple calculation which may assist in judging this is the 'return on capital employed'. This is the net profit (before tax, dividends and any interest paid) expressed as a percentage of the company capital (including debentures and other long term loans), in our example this is $43,000/412,500 \times 100 = 10.42\%$. This figure should be judged against previous year's profits and is possible against other similar companies. If the shareholders are also directors of the company, they might wish to treat any directors' fees as part of the return on capital if they exceed what the directors regard as a fair return for their labour.

An alternative to the return on capital calculation is to calculate earnings per share. In our example assume that there are 10,000 shares, the earnings per share would then be $31,000/10,000 = £3.1$ per share (it is usual to deduct tax in this calculation). This information is often given in relation to companies quoted on the stock exchange. Similarly in relation to such companies a price/earnings (or P/E) ratio can be calculated. This compares the market price of the share (on the stock exchange) with the earnings per share. A high P/E ratio shows that the stock market has confidence in the company as its shares are valuable despite low earnings. It is not possible to calculate a P/E ratio for a private or unquoted public company as there is no market price for their shares.

29.11.2 EFFICIENCY RATIOS

These are ratios which are mainly calculated so that the management of the company and other interested parties can calculate how efficient the profit making process of the company is. The return on capital employed (see **29.11.1**) is a good indicator of the company's general efficiency in making money.

Another useful ratio is the net profit percentage. This expresses trading profit (before deduction of tax and interest payments) as a percentage of sales. In our example this is $43,000/200,000 \times 100 = 21.5\%$. This should be compared with other businesses and with previous years. Whether 21.5% is a good profit margin depends on the nature of the business in question.

THIRTY

SALE OF A BUSINESS TO A COMPANY

This chapter covers the following topics:

30.1 Introduction
30.2 Income tax
30.3 Capital gains tax
30.4 VAT
30.5 Stamp duty
30.6 Subsidiary matters.

30.1 Introduction

A sole trader or partnership may decide, for a variety of reasons, to incorporate the business. If this step is taken, although the business will remain unchanged, the incorporation will give rise to a number of tax and other problems. In this chapter we will consider these problems and how they can be avoided, or at least mitigated. As we shall see, the tax rules are the most important in this area, since if they are not appreciated the payment of an unexpected tax bill can cause very serious cash flow problems. As an aid to understanding these problems, it is helpful to bear in mind that when the trader (which for these purposes includes partnerships) incorporates the business, it is transferred to a separate legal entity, the company. This means that the trader ceases to trade as an unincorporated business and disposes of the business and its assets to the company. The fact that the former proprietor or proprietors own the company and operate the business in exactly the same way as before is immaterial since the members of the company are distinct legal entities (*Salomon* v *A. Salomon & Co. Ltd* [1897] AC 22).

It may therefore come as a surprise to many traders who incorporate their businesses to discover that incorporation can lead to the payment of income tax, capital gains tax and stamp duty. In this chapter these tax liabilities will be considered in turn.

30.2 Income Tax

30.2.1 THE CLOSING YEAR RULES

Of the possible tax liabilities which can arise, the one which may cause the most difficulties, if it is not provided for, is the liability to income tax. Transferring the business to the company means that the unincorporated trader has permanently stopped trading, with the result that the closing years rules of assessment set out in s. 63 ICTA 1988 will apply. (See **13.3.2.3** for an explanation of the closing year rules.)

SALE OF A BUSINESS TO A COMPANY

30.2.2 LOSS RELIEF

If a loss is made in the final 12 months' trading, it can be carried across against income from another source under s. 380 ICTA 1988, and any unabsorbed loss carried back and set against the profits of the three tax years immediately preceding the year of incorporation, taking later years before earlier ones (s. 388 ICTA 1988). If, having made use of both provisions, there is still an unabsorbed loss, it cannot be used by the company. However, s. 386 permits the former proprietors, provided they sold the business in exchange wholly or mainly for shares in the new company, to set the remaining loss against income received from the company while they continue to own the shares. They must reduce earned income (such as directors' fees) before investment income (such as dividends).

Although it may appear strange that a loss-making business should be incorporated there may be sound reasons for doing so. For example, the business may be entering a temporary period of recession and the trader may want to protect himself from personal liability for future debts, or the loss may have been deliberately created by claiming capital allowances in respect of items of plant and machinery bought shortly before incorporation.

30.2.3 CAPITAL ALLOWANCES

Whether or not the purchase of an item attracting capital allowances has created the final year loss, the trader's capital allowance position is the remaining income tax point which needs to be considered. The rules relating to capital allowances have already been considered (see **Chapter 17**). The important point to be considered in the context of incorporating a trader's business, is that the transfer to the company, even if the purchase price is to be paid in shares, will be a disposal. If the capital allowances already claimed exceed the amount by which the assets have actually depreciated in value, the Revenue have a right to levy a balancing charge under Schedule D Case VI. This means the Revenue recovers the tax lost as a result of the over-deduction of allowances. Thus there can be another additional income tax bill arising on the incorporation. However, it is possible to ensure that the transfer of plant and machinery is not to be regarded as a discontinuance of the trade for the purposes of capital allowances provided:

(a) the trader and persons connected with him (which includes partners) are the majority shareholders in the new company; and

(b) an election is made to the effect that if there is no discontinuance, there is no disposal and the balancing charge does not arise. The result is that the new company takes over the trader's capital allowance position and makes the appropriate claims for writing-down allowances in respect of the, as yet, unallowed expenditure.

30.3 Capital Gains Tax

30.3.1 THE DISPOSAL

The incorporation of the old business not only means there is a discontinuance for income tax purposes, but that there is also a disposal for CGT purposes. This disposal arises because the business, its assets and connections (i.e., goodwill) are being *sold* to the company in exchange for shares. This is a chargeable disposal within the Taxation of Chargeable Gains Act (TCGA) 1992 and the trader will be liable for any gain that is realised.

The gain is calculated in the normal way by deducting the allowable expenditure from the market value of the assets transferred. Allowable expenditure includes the expenses incurred in acquiring, improving and disposing of the assets. Any indexation allowance which is available is also deducted. This liability cannot be avoided by the company issuing shares of a purely nominal value in exchange for the assets, as the Revenue have a right to substitute the market value of the assets in such circumstances. This gain could be considerable, especially if the business is successful and was set up several years previously. However, a number of reliefs operate in these circumstances which will be looked at in turn. (It should be noted that, with the introduction of the tapering relief on chargeable gains from 6 April 1998, not all of the chargeable gain will be taxable in any event — see **14.2.7**.)

A business owner has essentially three options as to how his capital gains tax situation is managed on an incorporation:

(a) Transfer the entire undertaking as a going concern in return for shares in the new company and claim roll-over relief.

(b) Transfer certain assets for full value and pay the tax on those and keep other assets and allow the company to use such retained assets.

(c) Transfer certain assets either for nil consideration or at an undervalue and claim hold-over relief in respect of those and keep other assets and allow the company to use such retained assets.

Option (b) requires no explanation as it does not involve a specific relief, but options (a) and (c) will be looked at in turn.

30.3.2 RELIEF UNDER s. 162 TCGA 1992

30.3.2.1 The basic rule

Section 162 TCGA 1992 applies where a person (not being a company) 'transfers to a company a business as a going concern, together with the whole assets of the business, or together with the whole of those assets other than cash, and the business is transferred wholly or partly in exchange for shares issued by the company to the person transferring the business'. The section permits a deduction to be made from the gain arising when the business and its assets are disposed of. Section 162(4) provides that this deduction is the gain reduced by the fraction A/B, where A is the 'cost of the new assets' (that is, the value of the shares issued to the former owner), and B is the whole of the consideration received by the former owner in exchange for the business. Thus, if the former owner transfers a business with assets worth £100,000 to the new company and receives £90,000 worth of shares and £10,000 worth of debentures in exchange, his gain will be reduced by the fraction £90,000/(£90,000 + £10,000), i.e., 9/10ths. This means that the former owner only pays tax on 1/10th of the gain realised on the disposal of the business; the remaining 9/10ths are, however, taxable when he disposes of the shares at some time in the future. If he only receives shares, the whole of the tax liability on the gain would be postponed in this way, or 'rolled-over' as the Act describes it.

It should be noted that the relief only applies to the former owner and his tax liability. The company's acquisition price of the assets will be their full market value at the date of the disposal.

30.3.2.2 The assets transferred to the company

Although these rules may appear complex at first sight, two simple requirements can be extracted from them. First, to claim the relief at all, the whole of the assets of the business (other than cash) at the date of incorporation must be transferred to the company, and secondly, the relief may only be claimed in full if the consideration received was entirely in the form of shares. Provided these conditions are satisfied, the effect of s. 162 is that the former owner acquires the shares at a value equal to his original acquisition price of the assets that have just been transferred to the company, so tax is only paid when they are later sold or

SALE OF A BUSINESS TO A COMPANY

given away (by which time he may qualify for retirement relief or taper relief). Since s. 162 relief can be obtained so easily by following these rules, it may seem strange that a number of traders choose not to take advantage of the relief and actually retain ownership of certain assets which they subsequently allow the new company to use (whilst still transferring the bulk of the business assets to the new company). There is, however, a good reason for this which is to avoid the 'double capital gains tax charge', which is a problem where companies own appreciating assets, such as land or buildings. If a company owns such an asset and disposes of it realising a gain, the company will pay corporation tax on that gain. The post-tax gain will then increase the value of the company's assets, which in turn has the effect of increasing the value of the shares. This will result in the shareholder making an increased gain, and so paying more capital gains tax, on a later disposal of the shares. Retaining the asset in the former owner's hands ensures that there is only one capital gains tax charge if the asset is disposed of. It may also produce a stamp duty saving (see **30.6.5**).

30.3.2.3 Method of payment for assets

Even if the Revenue is convinced that all the assets comprised in the business have been transferred, the relief can only be claimed in full if the company 'pays' for the assets in shares. As has already been explained, if the consideration is wholly or partly in debentures and/or cash the roll-over relief is wholly or partly denied to the former owner.

It is much more common, however, for the former owner to be paid in shares and debentures (the reason being that, as a shell, the company will have no cash with which to make the purchase). Debentures have advantages for both the holder (in the form of security of both capital and income) and the company (in the form of a pre-tax deduction in respect of the interest payments), and these advantages may compensate the former owner for partial loss of capital gains tax relief. It should be remembered that receiving part of the consideration in debentures means a proportionate part of the gain is taxable, but this taxable gain could be reduced or wiped out by the annual exemption and any indexation allowance or taper relief which may have accrued. This has the attraction of reducing any future taxable gain and also of ensuring that the owner does not lose the benefit of the annual exemption for the year of incorporation.

30.3.3 RELIEF FOR GIFTS OF BUSINESS ASSETS (s. 165 TCGA 1992)

Section 165 gives 'hold-over' relief where an asset used by the trader in his trade, profession or vocation is transferred to a company, provided the transaction is not a bargain at arm's length. This means that if the asset is 'sold' at an under-value, or even given to the company, the trader and the company can elect that the company acquires the asset for a consideration equal to the trader's acquisition cost (if there is an outright gift) or the sale price (if there is a sale at an under-value). The effect of the relief is to postpone the payment of tax until the asset is disposed of, when the *company* will be liable to pay the tax, not the trader.

In contrast to the relief under s. 162 TCGA 1992, this relief operates even if not all assets are transferred simultaneously. It does have, therefore, the advantage of flexibility.

30.3.4 TO RETAIN OR NOT TO RETAIN

It will be seen that there is no simple answer to the question of whether or not to retain assets. However, a number of matters can be borne in mind.

(a) The choice to retain an asset will result in the denial of relief under s. 162 TCGA 1992. The other possible relief under s. 165 TCGA 1992 will, however, still be available for other assets which are transferred. It should be remembered that this relief, in effect, puts the gain into the hands of the company.

(b) If the proprietor in question is quite young, then retirement relief is not an immediate issue, especially as the relief will cease to exist from 6 April 2003.

(c) If the intention is that an appreciating asset is to be disposed of in the near future and replaced, then either the proprietor or the company may still be entitled to roll-over relief under s. 152 TCGA 1992.

(d) If the intention is that an appreciating asset is to be disposed and *not* replaced, then which party is to realise the gain requires careful consideration. First, if the proprietor is a higher rate taxpayer, the gain in his or her hands will be charged at 40%. The company will pay tax at 30%, or possibly less. It should also be remembered that companies do not benefit from taper relief, but, instead, are subject to the established rules on indexation allowance. As a rule of thumb, indexation allowance generally will be more generous than taper relief in respect of assets with a high base cost. Therefore, the use of either s. 162 or s. 165 to first put the asset into the hands of the company may produce an immediate benefit. If, however, the proprietor has accumulated capital losses or could realise the same, it may be sensible for him or her to realise the gain.

(e) The prospect of a double charge to tax may be more imagined than real, especially if the intention is that the proprietor will retain the shares for several years. Also, to substitute a single asset for a number of shares provides greater scope for tax planning as an asset will normally have to be sold in toto, whereas fractions of a shareholding can be disposed of over a period of time. Therefore, the use of s. 162 relief may produce a number of benefits in this regard.

(f) Taper relief will become increasingly important as a determining factor. If at the time of incorporation the business owner has acquired a good proportion of the relief, it may be best simply to realise any gains at that stage and claim the relief. This is particularly so when one considers that if the s. 162 relief is used, the length of ownership of the transferred assets will be irrelevant for calculating taper relief on any subsequent disposal of the shares taken. Therefore, if the owner has acquired, for example, eight years of taper relief at the time of incorporation, this will be lost.

(g) Stamp duty will play an important part in the decision. The retention of assets or their transfer for nil consideration, so as to claim s. 165 relief, will ease the stamp duty burden. However, a balance has to be struck between this and capital gains tax to ensure the best saving for the owner. Stamp duty is looked at in detail below.

30.4 VAT

If the trader is registered for VAT, VAT may be chargeable on the transfer of the assets unless the business is transferred as a going concern (s. 33 Value Added Tax Act 1983).

30.5 Stamp Duty

30.5.1 INTRODUCTION

So far we have considered the tax liabilities of the trader personally; now we will consider the liabilities of the company to stamp duty. When a business is incorporated sufficient provision must be made to enable the company to meet this liability as it falls on the transferee of an asset. In this section we do not intend to consider the duty in great detail, but will look at the particular points relevant on the incorporation of an existing business.

SALE OF A BUSINESS TO A COMPANY

It should be understood at the outset that the following discussion is limited to stamp duty on items of property other than shares. (Stamp duty on a share transfer is discussed at **11.2.4**.)

30.5.2 THE CHARGE TO TAX AND s. 59 OF THE STAMP ACT 1891

When dealing with stamp duty it is necessary to decide whether the assets transferred attract the duty at all, whether duty is paid on the contract or the conveyance, and finally, what the rate of duty should be.

Stamp duty is only payable if a transaction is evidenced by written instrument. Thus, oral contracts do not attract the duty, neither do transactions where ownership of the asset passes by delivery. Where a written instrument is used, stamp duty is payable, by s. 54 of the Stamp Act 1891, on the conveyance on sale but not on a mere contract to convey. Since a binding contract transfers the equitable title, if a purchaser is satisfied with the equitable title, it is prima facie possible to avoid stamp duty by never executing the conveyance. Normally a purchaser will not be satisfied with such title, but where a business is being incorporated, the new company may be prepared to accept this. To prevent the loss of revenue that would result from this situation, s. 59(1) of the Stamp Act 1891 provides that the purchaser shall pay duty on the contract for the sale of any equitable interest or interest in any property or for the sale of any estate or interest in any property, except (*inter alia*) land, goods, wares or merchandise, or marketable securities or any ship or vessel, as if it were an actual conveyance on sale of the estate, interest, or property contracted or agreed to be sold.

The effect of the section is to levy duty on any contract to sell many of the assets that are likely to be transferred when incorporating an existing business (for example, goodwill, book debts, patents, 'know-how', the benefit of pending contracts, tenants' fixtures on *leasehold* property, *equitable* interests in freehold property and cash on deposit). If there is a subsequent conveyance no further duty is payable on that conveyance but if the duty was not paid on the contract no penalty becomes payable (other than one for late stamping), provided a conveyance or transfer is presented for stamping within six months of its execution (or within such longer period as the Commissioners of Inland Revenue may think reasonable in the circumstances of the case).

30.5.3 TREATMENT OF ITEMS OUTSIDE THE s. 59 CHARGE

Of the items excepted by s. 59, those falling into the category 'goods, wares or merchandise' are totally exempt from the charge provided title in them passes by delivery. This will be so in relation to stock-in-trade, plant and machinery, cash in hand and cash in a current bank account, but only if they are not specifically dealt with in the later conveyance (s. 34(4) Finance Act 1958). With regard to the cash, the exemption only applies to cash in hand or in a current account, since the Revenue regards such money as not being 'property' within the meaning of s. 59(1). However, cash on deposit is a debt to the customer by the bank (*Foley* v *Hill* (1848) 2 HL 28) and so is caught by the section.

Where a legal estate in land (which includes fixtures on freehold property), marketable securities or ships is transferred, duty is paid, but on the conveyance or transfer, if there is one, and not the contract, so that it is theoretically possible to avoid stamp duty in respect of these items, although in practice a conveyance will normally be required.

Once the items that are subject to the duty have been valued, all the values are aggregated to calculate the rate of duty that is payable. If the business has liabilities that the new company is taking over, s. 57 of the Stamp Act 1891 requires duty to be paid on the total value of the dutiable assets being transferred without the deduction of the liabilities. This is because the agreement to pay the debts is part of the consideration given in exchange for receiving the assets (one practical point, unrelated to stamp duty, is that in such a case the agreement of the creditor will have to be obtained).

30.5.4 THE STAMP DUTY RATES

The amount of stamp duty payable is ad valorem, that is based on the value of dutiable assets transferred. The rate increases as the value increases. However, if the value of dutiable assets does not exceed £60,000, no stamp duty is payable.

Value of assets	Rate
Up to £250,000	1%
£250,001–500,000	3%
In excess of £500,000	4%

To claim the exemption from stamp duty and to claim the different bands of duty, the instrument must contain a certificate of value confirming the value of the dutiable items transferred. However, if the value of the assets exceeds £500,000, the certificate becomes irrelevant. If such a certificate is omitted from the document, it will bear duty at the top rate irrespective of the actual value of the assets. It is, therefore, a crucial clause. The usual wording for the certificate is:

> It is hereby certified that the transaction hereby effected does not form part of a larger transaction or of a series of transactions in respect of which the amount or value or the aggregate amount or value of the consideration exceeds £[insert consideration paid].

It is important to note that the certificate of value relates to the total value passing under the transaction as a whole, so that where some assets pass under the contract and others under a conveyance, the values of property passing under both the contract and the conveyance must be aggregated. The calculation of the duty paid on the contract is made by apportioning the total consideration on the form 'Stamps 22'. This form must be submitted to the Stamp Office along with the relevant documentation which is to be stamped.

30.5.5 SAVING STAMP DUTY

Stamp duty can be saved in two ways: either by not transferring dutiable items to the company, or by converting ones that attract the duty into ones that do not. Thus the trader can retain book debts to provide a source of money to meet his additional income tax liability or to pay his existing trade creditors. Another possible way of saving stamp duty is to transfer cash on deposit into a current account. This need only be done for the day of the transfer.

30.6 Subsidiary Matters

The tax matters already dealt with will, of course, be important to the former owner but there are a number of other points that must not be overlooked.

30.6.1 THE TRANSFER AND EMPLOYMENT LAW

The general rule used to be that the transfer of the business terminated the contracts of employment of all the employees and, if common law and statutory claims against the business owner were to be avoided, the employees had to be notified of the transfer and offered employment with the new company on the same, or suitable, terms before the transfer took place. However, as a result of the Transfer of Undertakings (Protection of Employment) Regulations 1981 (SI 1981 No. 1794), this is no longer the case, since regulation 5(1) provides that a 'relevant transfer' shall not terminate a person's contract of employment and the contract shall have the effect after the transfer as if it had originally been made between the employee and the transferee. (A 'relevant transfer' is defined in regulation 3(1) as being 'a transfer from one person to another of an undertaking situated immediately before the transfer in the United Kingdom or of a part of one which is so situated'.) Thus, if a business is transferred to a company, the employees are treated as if their contracts had originally been made with the new company, which takes over all the trader's rights, powers, duties and liabilities under the employment contracts. Therefore, the employee's period of continuous employment is preserved, as are any pre-existing rights against the old employer for breach of contract or duty. As a result, the new employer could be faced with liability for a constructive dismissal arising from the old employer's breach, for example, and should obtain suitable indemnities.

While these regulations do not prevent an employee bringing a claim against the trader if there is a substantial change made in his working conditions, no action can be brought simply because the identity of the employer has changed, unless the employee shows the change to be significant and to his detriment.

Regulation 5 does not enable the fact of the transfer to be kept from the employees. Regulation 10 imposes an obligation on the transferor to inform and consult with trade union representatives.

30.6.2 THE TRANSFER AND COMPANY LAW

In addition to the matters that always arise on the formation of a new company, one special problem particularly relevant to this kind of transfer must be considered. On the assumption that the transferor of the business will be a director of the new company, the consent of the members in general meeting will almost certainly be needed to the purchase by the company of the assets. Section 320 CA 1985 requires such consent to be obtained if a director sells to (or buys from) the company a non-cash asset or assets of the 'requisite value', which means assets worth £100,000 or representing at least 10% of the company's assets (subject to a minimum value of £2,000). If the consent is not obtained, the transaction is voidable at the instance of the company and the director will have to account to the company for any profit made and indemnify it for any loss or damages arising. In order to obtain the necessary consent, a general meeting of the company will have to be held immediately after incorporation and before the transfer takes place.

Furthermore, the transferor must make sure that the new company's name appears on all letters, cheques and order forms as required by s. 348 CA 1985, and that the letters have printed on them the information required by ss. 305 and 351 CA 1985.

30.6.3 THE TRANSFER AND OTHER MISCELLANEOUS MATTERS

Further practical points to be dealt with include:

(a) The local inspector of taxes must be notified that there is a new employer for PAYE purposes as well as there being a new company liable to corporation tax.

(b) If the business's turnover exceeds the threshold for VAT registration, its VAT registration must be cancelled and the company must apply to have itself registered. In order to ensure there is no gap in the VAT registration it is advisable to cancel the old one after the company's registration has been confirmed.

(c) The consent of a landlord to the assignment of a lease must be obtained. If the new company is taking over responsibility for hire-purchase contracts, the consent of the finance house must be obtained.

(d) The former owner can bring his personal liability to existing creditors to an end by entering into a contract of 'novation'. However, the consent of the creditors is required. As a counterpoint to this, the owner may still be asked to guarantee liabilities which have been assumed by the new company, for example, indebtedness to a bank and those under a lease.

(e) The company must take out appropriate insurance cover and have any vehicles transferred into its own name.

THIRTY ONE

CHOICE OF BUSINESS MEDIUM

This chapter covers the following topics:

31.1 Introduction
31.2 Risk of capital
31.3 Expense
31.4 Management
31.5 Publicity
31.6 Taxation — trading profits
31.7 Interest relief
31.8 Capital gains
31.9 Inheritance tax
31.10 Pensions and social security
31.11 Conclusion.

31.1 Introduction

The purpose of this chapter is to make a comparison between companies, on the one hand, and partnerships or sole traders on the other, with a view to explaining the various factors which ought to be taken into account when a choice is made between the two business media.

Once these comparisons are understood, **Chapter 34** should then be considered to understand how the further possible choice of a limited liability partnership should be assessed. As limited liability partnerships fall somewhere between companies and partnerships, it is essential that either side of the spectrum of choice is considered first.

The choice will first be made when a new business is set up, but should be kept under review as circumstances (and the law) change. For the sake of clarity, the differences between companies and partnerships are considered under various headings. It is important to realise that in making a choice each factor should be taken into account. In particular cases one factor may outweigh all the others, but generally each medium has some advantages and some disadvantages so that often the choice will be a difficult one.

31.2 Risk of Capital

All business involves a risk of capital. The degree of risk obviously varies considerably depending on the nature of the business, the economic climate and the skill of the people

CHOICE OF BUSINESS MEDIUM

running the business. The amount of capital which is at risk also varies considerably — some types of business require a great deal of capital, others very little.

One advantage of a company over a partnership is that a company can be formed with limited liability. This means that the shareholders must contribute the amount unpaid on their shares, but no more, if the company goes into liquidation when it is insolvent. In the vast majority of cases the shares will be fully paid, so that no contribution towards the company's debts has to be made. However, the shareholders will lose their shares when the company fails so that, realistically, the limit to their liability is what they have invested in the company. A shareholder who is also a director will also lose his livelihood. A director (including a shadow director) may also become personally liable in certain circumstances when the company is wound up (see **Chapter 23**).

If a partnership becomes insolvent, each of the partners is jointly and severally liable for all the debts of the partnership. This means that he stands to lose not only what he has invested in the business but also any other property which he owns. The liability of partners is, therefore, unlimited in amount. The partnership agreement may make provision as to how losses are to be shared between the partners but this does not prevent creditors claiming in full from a rich partner whose poor partners are unable to pay their share of the loss.

It should be noted that the proposed introduction of a new type of business medium, the limited liability partnership, may affect the above explanations. However, at the time of writing, details of the full consequences of such a change to the law are sketchy. The reader must, therefore, track the progress of the proposed legislation in this area.

At first sight limited liability would seem to be an enormous advantage to the proprietors of a business in every case. However, there are at least two circumstances where limited liability is not very significant:

(a) *Where there is little risk of substantial loss of capital*

The clearest example of this is a business involving the giving of advice, such as a consultancy. The proprietor expects to make profits by providing expertise in return for payment; comparatively little is required in the way of capital expenditure on equipment and the running costs of the business will be small. In many cases the biggest potential loss will be claims for damages if bad advice is given to clients and this can be covered by insurance.

(b) *Where the proprietor risks everything he owns in the business*

If the proprietor's only assets are what he has invested in the business, he will effectively lose everything when the business fails whether it is a company or partnership. (This is, of course, only true while all the capital remains in the business, so that limited liability will become relevant once the proprietor starts to take profits out of the business on a large scale.)

Limited liability afforded by incorporating a business can sometimes be made illusory by the directors of the company having to give guarantees. Many businesses rely on borrowed money. A bank lending to a small company will often require a personal guarantee from the directors or shareholders, so that if the company cannot repay the loan the bank has further security. Guarantees may also be required from the landlord of any premises which a company may lease. These will primarily be in respect of the company's obligations to pay rent, but may also cover performance obligations, such as those requiring a tenant to keep the property in good repair.

Limited liability is most significant (and can realistically be achieved) where there is a substantial risk of loss of capital invested and the proprietor (or one of the proprietors) has private wealth not invested in the business. In such cases limited liability may be so desirable that it far outweighs any other consideration and, therefore, the business must be run as a company.

31.3 Expense

Certain expenses must inevitably be incurred when a company is formed. These include the Registrar's fee on incorporation and the cost of preparing the memorandum and articles. If a partnership is formed these expenses need not be incurred since there are no registration requirements. However, in most cases the partners will want a properly drawn up partnership agreement and will wish to instruct a solicitor to draw it up for them.

It is difficult to make any general comparison between costs of formation, since they will depend largely on the complexity of the proposed memorandum and articles or partnership agreement. The legal fees payable for formation are about the same in both cases where the documents have to be drafted by a solicitor. Where a company is bought 'off-the-peg' from a law stationer the costs are likely to be in the region of £100 (including the Registrar's fee), which is likely to be less than the cost of drawing up a partnership agreement of similar complexity.

In addition to legal advice, the proprietors of a new business will often wish to seek advice from accountants. Again, the amount payable for the advice will depend on the complexity of the advice given rather than the business medium used. Similarly, certain printing costs will be incurred for business letter paper. These expenses are only *necessary* in the case of a company (which must comply with the provisions of the Companies Act relating to the name, number and address of the company), but in the case of a partnership printed letter paper will normally be used even though it is not required by law.

With both media, formation expenses are likely to be fairly substantial (for a small business, hundreds rather than thousands of pounds) but are unlikely to influence the *choice* of business medium.

After formation the major administrative costs of a business will again depend on the complexity of the business. However, in respect of accounts a company is at a disadvantage when compared with a partnership. All types of business will wish to keep accounts and prepare final accounts annually. Nearly all businesses will wish to pay a qualified accountant to draw up these accounts (if only so as to make sure that advantage is taken of tax reliefs and exemptions). A company, however, must draw up the accounts in a particular way. This means that the accounts must in some respects show more information than the accounts of a partnership and for a small business this may involve considerable extra cost. (It should be remembered that the partial exemption of 'small' companies from accounting requirements applies only to the published accounts — full accounts must be prepared for the members.) Furthermore, once the accounts have been produced they must be audited by an independent qualified accountant. This means that a company must incur two lots of accountants' fees annually, whereas a partnership need only incur one.

A company is also required to prepare an annual return and to pay a fee on filing it with the Registrar. The Companies Act also requires many other returns to be filed from time to time (e.g., particulars of directors, charges and address of registered office); although fees are not payable on the filing of these returns, their preparation will add to the running costs of the business if it is a company. Many company directors will not feel able to deal with these matters themselves and so will have to hire a qualified company secretary or take legal advice.

CHOICE OF BUSINESS MEDIUM

The running costs of a company will be more than those of a partnership although the difference is not likely to be great enough to be significant except in the case of small businesses.

31.4 Management

The Companies Act lays down certain rules as to the management structure of companies. A company is, for example, required to have at least one director and a secretary. Certain obligations are imposed on these officials in relation to filing returns. However, a company is entitled to lay down in its articles rules as to management of whatever type it chooses. A partnership may also establish its own rules for management of the business. The Partnership Act 1890 lays down certain presumptions (e.g., that, in the absence of contrary agreement, decisions are taken by a majority vote of the partners except in a limited number of cases where unanimity is required). The partners are free to vary these presumptions by agreement or by a course of dealings. Both types of business medium are, therefore, entitled to choose a management structure which is suitable for the particular case.

31.4.1 INTERNAL FLEXIBILITY

After a suitable management structure has been chosen it may need to be changed because of changed circumstances. In the case of a company, changes to the articles require a special resolution (i.e., a 75% majority of the shareholders). However, many changes of management structure can be made without a change in the articles. Thus if the articles are in the usual form, the maximum number of directors can be increased and new appointments can be made to the board by an ordinary resolution (simple majority of shareholders) and a managing director can be appointed by the board. The board may also decide on its own procedures for taking decisions and may delegate decision making powers as and when necessary. If it is considered that the structure is too flexible, the articles may provide for special resolutions in circumstances where an ordinary resolution would otherwise be sufficient (except in the case of removal of directors from office, where an ordinary resolution is always sufficient (s. 303 CA 1985)). The articles may also restrict the powers of the board and require the approval of the members in general meeting for major decisions. An extreme degree of inflexibility can be achieved, if desired, by including in the memorandum provisions which could have been included in the articles and by making these provisions unalterable.

In the case of a partnership, the agreement between the partners can be altered. This normally requires the approval of all the partners so that the 'constitution' of a partnership is more rigid than that of a company. However, if, when the partnership agreement is drawn up, it is decided that a greater degree of flexibility is required, the agreement can provide for alteration by a majority (without unanimous agreement), either in general or in particular cases.

It is, therefore, possible for either business medium to have a very flexible or a very rigid management structure, as the proprietors wish.

31.4.2 SECURITY OF TENURE

Just as the profits of a partnership are divided between the partners so, in the case of most small companies, the profits will be divided between the directors. Security of tenure as a partner or director is, therefore, of vital concern to the proprietors of a business.

A director is always subject to removal by an ordinary resolution of the members. However, a director who has the majority of votes (or a majority of votes on a resolution for his removal — see *Bushell* v *Faith* [1970] AC 1099, at **8.4.1.4**) is effectively irremovable. A director who does not have a majority of votes but who has a service agreement may be entitled to substantial compensation if removed from office, and so to that extent may be protected.

In the case of a partnership, removal of a partner will, subject to contrary agreement, involve the dissolution of the partnership. At first sight this would seem to put a partner in a stronger position than a director. However, in practice, this is not necessarily so. In some cases it will be possible for some of the partners to get rid of one of their colleagues and then set up a 'new' business after the dissolution, which will in effect be a continuation of the old business. This will be possible particularly if those who remain own the premises where the business is carried on. The position of a junior partner is not, therefore, necessarily stronger than that of a director who is not in control of the company.

The practical reality of the situation is that if a director or partner is vital to the business he cannot be removed without bringing the business to an end. However, where a director or partner is really no more than a senior employee, he can be removed on payment of any compensation provided for in his service contract or in the partnership agreement. A director, but not a partner, may also be entitled to compensation for unfair dismissal or redundancy.

31.4.3 SUCCESSION TO THE BUSINESS

The articles of a company may restrict the right to transfer shares, thus preventing a shareholder from selling out or giving away shares to anyone he pleases. Such restrictions may be coupled with pre-emption rights given to the other shareholders. Alternatively, shares may be freely transferable. It is, therefore, possible to make provision for succession in advance, provided that sufficient thought is given to the problem at the time when the articles are drafted. Similarly, a partnership agreement may make provision for bringing in new partners and for payment to the existing partners on leaving. If no other provision is made, unanimity is required for the admission of a new partner. Since the partners have to be able to work together in running the business, it is unlikely that they would be willing to allow admission of new partners without such agreement.

It is, therefore, possible to lay down rules for succession with either type of business medium. In practical terms the problem of succession is one which can only be solved if suitable purchasers can be found or if suitable donees willing to carry on the business are available. It is generally easier to achieve succession in the case of a company, since the sale of a majority shareholding passes control to the purchaser. The majority shareholder will usually be free to sell out since he is in control of the board who will, therefore, approve any transfer of his shares unless there are any pre-emption rights.

31.4.4 LEGAL STATUS OF BUSINESS MEDIA

There are a number of ways in which the legal status of a company differs from that of a partnership, for example:

(a) A company is a separate legal person whereas a partnership is not.

(b) Only companies can create floating charges.

(c) A company is bound by the ultra vires doctrine (to the extent provided by s. 35 CA 1985) whereas a partnership is not, so that a partnership is free to change the nature of its business (unanimous agreement of the partners is required but outsiders will not be affected by the absence of such agreement).

(d) An unlimited number of persons may be members of a company at any time whereas partnerships (other than in certain professions) are limited to 20 members.

None of these differences is likely to affect the choice of business medium in most cases.

CHOICE OF BUSINESS MEDIUM

31.5 Publicity

A company is required to make a considerable amount of information, including annual accounts, available to the public. A partnership is not required to make such information available. A desire to keep the affairs of the business secret may influence some businessmen to prefer a partnership to a company, but it is not likely to be a major factor in most cases, especially since the partners will, in practice, be required to show their accounts to any prospective lender.

31.6 Taxation — Trading Profits

31.6.1 COMPANIES

The reader is advised to have read **Chapters 13–18** before reading the rest of this section. A company has a choice as to how to use its profits — they may be used to pay dividends, interest, or directors' fees, or they may be retained in the business. Each of these four possibilities has different tax consequences. Generally speaking, the payment of directors' fees is the most tax-efficient use of profits, and for a small private company most of the profits will normally be used for this purpose for non-tax reasons anyway. This is because the directors must be compensated for the work that they do for the business and often little profit will be left over for other purposes.

Where profits are sufficiently large, however, a company can be used as a means of tax planning by deciding to retain profits or pay dividends. Retained profits are liable to corporation tax at 20% or 30% (depending on the size of the profit). The rate can be kept down to 20% if sufficient is paid in directors' fees to keep the profits below the threshold for the higher rate of corporation tax. This rate of tax may be somewhat less than the shareholder's rate of income tax (which may be 40%). However, the future consequences of capital taxes must also be taken into account. The accumulated profits will be reflected in the value of the shares in the company so that on a disposal of shares CGT and/or IHT may be payable, thus reducing the effectiveness of the income tax saving resulting from retention of the profits.

From 1 April 2000, there is a new starting rate of 10% corporation tax for taxable profits up to £10,000. Profits of between £10,000 and £50,000 are taxed at a marginal rate. (See **Chapter 15** for more details.) This means that it is cheaper to retain profits in a corporate structure than in an unincorporated one (subject to what was mentioned above about the retention of profits exacerbating the double tax charge).

A decision to pay dividends may be taken for non-tax reasons, since it is the only way to provide a shareholder who is not also a director with a return on his investment. However, a dividend may be tax-inefficient in the case of a company where profits are high.

31.6.2 PARTNERSHIPS

A partnership offers less scope for tax planning in relation to income profits than a company. All the income profits are taxed as income of the partners whether they are actually paid to them or are retained in the business (unless a capital allowance is available). To the extent that profits are withdrawn from the business a partner is in the same position as a director receiving directors' fees — both pay income tax on the sums that are received.

It used to be the case that the preceding year basis for partnerships was an incentive against forming a company on the start up of a business venture. However, because of the change to the system, any new business will now be immediately taxed on a current year basis. However, it should still be borne in mind that a payment of a salary to a director will suffer an immediate deduction for tax under the PAYE system, whereas drawings by a partner will not.

To the extent that profits are retained in the business, a partner pays the same tax as if the profits had been withdrawn. This will be an advantage when compared with a company where the partner's rate of tax is less than the rate of corporation tax, and a disadvantage when it is more.

31.6.3 CONCLUSION

It is, unfortunately, not possible to come to any general conclusions about which business medium is the more suitable from the point of view of income taxation. Probably in most circumstances there is now little to choose between the two. This is partly the result of the fact that relatively small differences now exist between the rates of tax applying to individuals and companies. In any case, in most businesses, substantially all the profits will be used to pay directors' fees or will be withdrawn by the partners. Where profits are sufficiently large that there is a real possibility of tax planning, the greater flexibility provided by the system of company taxation may be advantageous.

31.7 Interest Relief

A payment of interest by an individual must generally be paid out of taxed income. However, in some cases interest paid may be deducted from income before it is assessed to tax as a 'charge on income' (so that tax relief is available on the interest payment). This relief is available where money is borrowed to buy an interest in a partnership. Relief is also available where money is borrowed to buy shares in a close company provided that either:

(a) the shares give the borrower a 'material interest' (i.e., more than 5% of ordinary share capital or a right to more than 5% of the income); or

(b) the borrower owns some shares and, from the time when he used the loan until the time when the interest was paid, he was working for the greater part of his time in the management or conduct of the company.

31.8 Capital Gains

A company pays corporation tax at the rate of 20% or 30% of any capital gain which it makes. The disposal of assets by a partnership gives rise to tax at the appropriate rate or rates of the partners (which is likely to be 20% or 40%). However, a company and its proprietors suffer two disadvantages in respect of capital gains. Firstly, the profit made on the disposal of a capital asset (after payment of tax) will be reflected in the value of the shares in the company and further capital gains tax will be payable on disposal of those shares. For example, an asset is purchased for £10,000 and sold for £20,000. Tax of (say) £2,500 will be paid, leaving a net profit of £7,500. This profit will be reflected in the value of the shares so that if they are disposed of, a further gain of £7,500 will be taxed. Secondly, a company is not entitled to an annual exemption, whereas in the case of a partnership each partner is entitled to an annual exemption for the first £7,100 worth of gains during each tax year.

Whilst taper relief is available to individuals, companies' capital gains are still calculated according to the previous rules involving the indexation allowance. This can lead to some nice issues about whether or not one system will result in a more generous treatment of gains than another. Certainly one downside of taper relief is that it is calculated in respect of complete years of ownership, whereas indexation effectively takes into account monthly periods of ownership.

CHOICE OF BUSINESS MEDIUM

31.9 Inheritance Tax

31.9.1 CLOSE COMPANIES AND ANTI-AVOIDANCE

A company cannot normally be used as a means of avoiding IHT, since gifts by a close company are attributed to the shareholders in the company (s. 94 IHTA 1984). Nearly all small companies come within the definition of a close company. Similarly, gifts of partnership assets will be liable to tax as gifts of the individual partners. Inheritance tax is, therefore, generally a neutral factor in the choice of business medium.

31.9.2 BUSINESS PROPERTY RELIEF

Prior to 6 April 1996 one potential taxation disadvantage of incorporation was that *any* partnership share would attract 100% business property relief on its subsequent transfer but a shareholding of less than 25% would only attract 50% relief. After this date the situation changed and along with it this curious distinction. Any shareholding in a private company will attract 100% business property relief (see **14.6.6**).

There is, however, still a difference in the relief given where an asset is owned by an individual partner or shareholder but used by the partnership or company. A partner whose private property is used by his partnership is entitled to relief of 50% when he gives the property away. Similar relief is available to a shareholder but only if he owns shares which give control of the company.

31.10 Pensions and Social Security

There are a number of ways in which businessmen may provide for their retirement. The most favourable method from the tax point of view is an 'exempt approved occupational pension scheme'. Such a scheme affords generous tax relief on contributions by both employers and employees and further relief from capital taxes to the managers of the scheme. Its purpose is to provide a pension and, in some cases, a lump sum on retirement. Such schemes are not available to the self-employed (such as partners). Partners are able to get the relief by means of a personal pension. Contributions are deductible from taxable income up to a certain percentage of relevant earnings depending on the age of the contributor. However, the relief is limited to the appropriate percentage of £90,600 in the case of partners whose income exceeds this figure.

Social security also operates differently in respect of employees and the self-employed. Contributions must be made by both employer and employee in respect of an employed person; a self-employed person must contribute at a rate higher than the employee's contribution but lower than the employer's and employee's contributions combined. The benefits to which an employed person is entitled are correspondingly higher than those to which a self-employed person is entitled. The overall effect of the differences between the two schemes is controversial but many consider that the self-employed are at a disadvantage.

31.11 Raising Finance

Whilst there are numerous partnerships which have bank borrowings, as a general rule companies are treated as a more attractive proposition as borrowers, because of their ability to grant floating charges, which in turn gives the lender greater security and the ability to appoint an administrative receiver over the business of a borrower.

A corporate structure also makes the introduction of new investment capital easier. An investor in a partnership will ideally have to be made a partner, if he or she is to own a stake in the business. This can be disruptive for the existing management structure of the partners and also has the downside for the investor in that henceforth he or she will have unlimited liability for the debts of the partnership. Taking on a new shareholder in a company can have no disruptive influence on its management, since the roles of shareholder and director can be kept separate, and the investor only stands to lose the value of the investment and nothing further. Also, an equity investor in a company has greater flexibility in their exit from such an investment, in that they can sell all or part of their shareholding to existing shareholders, third parties (subject to any terms of pre-emption in the articles of association) or back to the company itself. With a partnership share the only truly feasible exit is to sell it in its entirety to existing partners.

An investor can, of course, simply lend money to a partnership. However, there will be no capital growth in such investment, as there would be with becoming a partner and taking a partnership share. A shareholding, particularly if it has voting rights, will normally always have the possibility of capital growth.

31.12 Conclusion

It is not possible to lay down any hard and fast rule as to which business medium is the more beneficial since there are too many variables. In a significant number of cases the desirability of limited liability will indicate company formation as the only real possibility. Where limited liability is not of great importance, the tax factors will be more significant. Generally speaking, a company will be more likely to be required where profits are large and a partnership where they are small, but really the only sound advice is that each case must be determined according to the particular circumstances and the particular wishes of the partners of the business.

THIRTY TWO

PUBLIC COMPANIES

This chapter covers the following topics:

32.1   Introduction
32.2   The distinguishing features of a public company
32.3   Seeking and maintaining a listing.

32.1   Introduction

Under s. 1(2) of the Companies Act 1985 it is possible to create three different types of company:

(a)   a company limited by shares;

(b)   a company limited by guarantee; and

(c)   an unlimited company.

We considered the key elements of these three different types of company in **6.5**. It is possible to incorporate all three types of company as a 'private company' but only companies limited by shares can be 'public companies'. We considered in outline the key differences between public and private companies in **6.6.2**.

Throughout the rest of the book we have not drawn any distinction between public and private companies as the majority of the rules to which companies are subject apply to both types of company limited by shares. However, the differences between the two types of company are important and we will consider them in this chapter. In addition, we will look briefly at the rules for re-registering a private company as a public company and vice versa, as well as the procedure by which a public company can gain a listing and have its shares traded on the Stock Exchange.

Although the most well known companies in the country will (with very few exceptions) be public companies with a listing, in terms of numbers they represent a tiny minority of the total number of companies registered at the Companies' Registry. Furthermore, being a public company does not necessarily mean the company is listed as it is possible to be an unlisted public company.

PUBLIC COMPANIES

32.2 The Distinguishing Features of a Public Company

32.2.1 DEFINITION

A public company is defined by s. 1 CA 1985 as:

A company limited by shares ... being a company:

(a) the memorandum of which states that the company is to be a public company; and

(b) in relation to which the provisions of [the Companies Act] as to the registration or re-registration of a company as a public company had been complied with ...

32.2.2 THE DIFFERENCES BETWEEN PUBLIC AND PRIVATE COMPANIES

These were outlined in 6.6. For the sake of completeness, these differences are repeated here but with some additional detail.

32.2.2.1 Name

The name of a public company must end with the words 'Public Limited Company' or its equivalent. Equivalent for this purpose includes 'PLC' (although there is no requirement that these letters be capitalised) and, for Welsh companies, Cwmni Cyfyngedig Cyhoeddus (or CCC). The company will be a Welsh company if the company states in its memorandum that its registered office is to be in Wales.

32.2.2.2 The company's memorandum

The memorandum which the company registers with the Companies' Registry must be in the form specified for a public company by the Companies (Tables A to F) Regulations 1985, or be as close to that form as is possible in the circumstances. If the company is to be a public company limited by shares, the form with which it has to comply is contained in Table F. The main difference between the form of memorandum specified for public companies and for private companies is that the form for a public company requires its memorandum to include an additional clause stating that the company is to be a public company.

32.2.2.3 The nominal value of the share capital

The nominal value of the public company's allotted share capital must not be less than the 'authorised minimum' which is currently £50,000 (although this figure can be changed by Statutory Instrument). When a public company allots shares, while it can make a part call when seeking payment, it is under an obligation to ensure that at least 25% of the nominal value of the shares (plus the whole amount of any premium on the shares) is paid on allotment. It will be recalled from 6.6.2 that a private company can issue shares without requiring any immediate payment for them (i.e., they can be issued 'nil paid').

32.2.2.4 Number of members and officers

Public companies, like private companies, need only two members (in the past they needed seven members) but public companies must have at least two directors whereas private companies need have only one. The company secretary of a public company must be qualified to act as such (s. 282 CA 1985).

32.2.2.5 The issue of shares or debentures

The principal advantage which a public company had over a private company used to be that public companies could offer shares or debentures to the public (for cash or other consideration) and to allot those shares or debentures with a view to them being offered for sale to the public (s. 81 CA 1985). Offers of shares to the public are governed by Part IV of the Financial Services Act 1986 and the Public Offers of Securities Regulations 1995 (SI 1995 No. 1537). These require the issue of a prospectus in any case where shares are to be 'offered to the public' within the terms of the legislation.

32.2.2.6 Registration requirements

Subject to the points on the contents of the documents set out above, the procedure followed and documents required to register a public company are the same as for a private company. Once the Registrar of Companies is satisfied that the documents comply with the registration requirements, a certificate of incorporation will be issued. However, before the public company can do business or borrow money, the company must obtain from the Registrar a further certificate which will only be issued if the Registrar is satisfied that the company's share capital is adequate. The procedure which the company must go through to get this additional certificate involves a director or the company secretary filing a statutory declaration (on Form 117) with the Registrar. The declaration will state that the nominal value of the company's allotted share capital is at least equal to the authorised minimum (of £50,000). The company must also supply on Form 117 details of:

(a) the amount paid up on the allotted share capital (which must exceed the minimum referred to in **32.2.2.3**);

(b) the amount of the preliminary expenses and details of who will meet them; and

(c) any amount or benefit paid to the company's promoters.

A company which does not obtain this additional certificate before it commences business can face some severe consequences. If the company fails to meet its obligations in connection with a transaction entered into at a time when it does not have the additional certificate, the directors will be jointly and severally liable to indemnify the other parties to the transaction for any loss. Furthermore, both the company and its offices will be liable to a fine and if the company fails to obtain this certificate within one year of its registration, the court can wind the company up (s. 122 Insolvency Act 1986).

32.2.3 SPECIAL RULES APPLICABLE TO PUBLIC COMPANIES

We saw in **32.2.2.5** that a public company can solicit investment in itself from the public. This can give the company a much wider source of potential investors than is the case with the private company but, in order to protect the public, public companies are subject to a number of restrictions which do not apply to private companies. We will consider them in this section.

32.2.3.1 Payment for share capital

(a) The original subscribers to a public company's memorandum are required to pay cash for their shares.

(b) At least 25% of the nominal value and the whole of any premium on shares in a public company must be paid on allotment.

(c) A public company cannot accept an undertaking to do work or perform services as consideration for the allotment of shares.

(d) A public company can accept the transfer of assets to the company as full or part (subject to the 25% limit) payment for the allotment of shares but any undertaking to transfer those assets to the company must be performed within five years of the

PUBLIC COMPANIES

allotment. In addition, the company must take steps to satisfy itself that the value of the assets transferred to the company is accurate by obtaining an expert's valuation and report.

32.2.3.2 Pre-emption rights on the allotment of shares

A public company, unlike a private company, cannot exclude the statutory pre-emption rights (set out in ss. 89–96 CA 1985) by a provision in its memorandum or articles. However, a public company (like a private company) can prevent the pre-emption rights applying by giving the directors the authority to allot shares in accordance with s. 80 CA 1985.

32.2.3.3 Maintenance of capital

The directors of a public company are under an obligation to convene an extraordinary general meeting (EGM) if the company's net assets are 50% or less of its called up share capital. The meeting must be convened within 28 days of one of the directors becoming aware of this fact and it must be held within 56 days. Obviously, the purpose of the meeting is for the problem to be considered but the governing provision (s. 142 CA 1985) does not require the directors to take any definite steps to remedy the position.

32.2.3.4 Purchase by a public company of its own shares

Public companies, like private companies, can buy back their own shares and issue redeemable shares. However, public companies cannot (unlike private companies) use capital to purchase or redeem shares; a public company can only use its profits for these purposes. (In addition, the tax rules which, if the various conditions are complied with, allow the shareholder whose shares have been bought by the company to treat the purchase as a disposal for capital gains tax purposes, rather than the receipt of a distribution attracting income tax liability, only apply to the shares in *unquoted* companies. It should, however, be remembered that a public company will not necessarily have a listing on the Stock Exchange.)

32.2.3.5 Financial assistance for the acquisition of shares and loans to directors

The rules prohibiting companies from providing financial assistance for the purchase of their own shares are more stringent in the case of public companies than in the case of private companies (see ss. 151 and 155–158 CA 1985). Similarly, the rules dealing with loans to directors are more stringent in the case of loans to directors of public companies (see s. 330 CA 1985).

32.2.3.6 Distribution of profits

In addition to the general rules restricting the funds from which companies can make distributions, public companies are only permitted to make a distribution if their net assets are not, as a result of the distribution, reduced below the combined total of their called up share capital and 'undistributable reserves'.

32.2.3.7 Accounting requirements

The provisions which permit 'small' and 'medium sized' companies to file less detailed accounts with the Registrar of Companies do not apply to public companies. They also cannot qualify as 'dormant' companies (which would lead them to be able to dispense with auditors). As we explained at **29.4**, the Companies (Summary Financial Statement) Regulations 1992 (SI 1992 No. 3075) permit a public company whose shares are listed on the Stock Exchange to send out a summary financial statement to a member, rather than full accounts, provided specified requirements are satisfied. The details of these requirements are beyond the scope of this Guide.

32.2.3.8 Age of directors

A public company may not appoint a person aged 70 or more to be a director unless the appointment is approved by the company in general meeting, following special notice (giving the age of the director) of such resolution. When a director of a public company reaches the age of 70, he must retire unless the company in general meeting votes to retain him. Again, special notice must be given of any such resolution. These provisions are contained in s. 293 CA 1985.

32.2.3.9 Written resolutions

Section 381A Companies Act 1985, under which the members of private companies can take decisions by written resolutions rather than passing resolutions at general meetings, does not apply to public companies.

32.2.4 RE-REGISTRATION OF A PRIVATE COMPANY TO A PUBLIC COMPANY AND VICE VERSA

Given the various special rules to which public companies are subject, promoters of a company are unlikely to want to incorporate the company as a public company unless they intend to issue securities in the company to the public within the foreseeable future. However, many companies start life as private companies and are then converted into public companies so that they can be listed and have their shares traded on the Stock Exchange. The reasons why a company might do this are explained in **32.3.2**. Equally, although perhaps less frequently, the shareholders and/or directors of a public company may decide to convert the company into a private company. They may do so for a variety of reasons, for example, where they have decided that the company's securities should no longer be available to the public.

32.2.4.1 Re-registration of a private company to a public company

The procedure which the private company will have to go through in order to re-register as a public company is set out in ss. 42–47 CA 1985. The company cannot be re-registered unless it satisfies the various requirements in relation to share capital to which public companies are subject. These were referred to in **32.2.2** and **32.2.3** and include the requirement that the company's allotted share capital must not be less than the authorised minimum of, currently, £50,000 and that not less than 25% of the nominal value of shares allotted plus the whole of the new premium on the shares must be paid up.

Provided the requirements with regard to share capital are satisfied, the company must pass a special or written resolution (a copy of which must be sent to the Registrar of Companies within 15 days of it being passed) which:

(a) states that the company should be re-registered as a public company;

(b) alters the company's memorandum by adding a clause stating that the company is to be a public company and making other consequential amendments to the memorandum (for example, changing the company's name to show that it is a 'public limited company'); and

(c) alters the company's articles to meet the company's new circumstances (by, for example, removing restrictions on transferability).

Once the resolution has been passed, a director or the company secretary must sign the application for re-registration and submit it to the Registrar of Companies with:

(a) a printed copy of the company's memorandum and articles in their altered form;

PUBLIC COMPANIES

(b) a copy of a statement in writing by the company's auditors confirming that the company's net assets are not less than the combined total of its called up share capital and distributable reserves (this written statement should relate to a balance sheet prepared for a date not more than seven months before the date the company has made its application for re-registration);

(c) a copy of the balance sheet on which the auditors based their written statement referred to in (b) above together with an unqualified report on the balance sheet by the company's auditors;

(d) certain reports and statutory declarations where shares have been allotted for non-cash consideration since the date of the balance sheet; and

(e) a fee of £20 (or £100 if same-day registration is required).

Once the Registrar of Companies is satisfied with these papers, a certificate will be issued confirming that the company has been re-registered as a public limited company.

32.2.4.2 Re-registration of a public company as a private company

It is easier for a public company to be re-registered as a private company than the other way round. A company must pass a special resolution by which it:

(a) resolves to re-register as a private company;

(b) removes the words 'public limited company' (or their equivalent) from its name and replaces them with 'limited'; and

(c) makes any other alterations to the memorandum and articles of the company to suit its new circumstances.

The special resolution must be filed within 15 days will normally be filed with the application (on Form 53) signed by a director or the company secretary seeking the re-registration (which will be accompanied by a printed copy of the altered memorandum and articles).

One consequence of a public company re-registering as a private company is that its securities may be less easily transferred. Therefore, protection has to be given to minority shareholders in case they object to this change in the status of the company. In any event, the Registrar of Companies will not normally issue a certificate confirming the re-registration until 28 days after the passing of the special resolution. This ties in with the provisions contained in CA 1985 giving minority shareholders a right to apply to the court within the 28 day period to have the resolution cancelled. Such an application for cancellation can only be made by (in the case of shareholders in companies limited by shares):

(a) shareholders holding not less than 5% of the nominal value of the company's issued share capital (or for any class of the share capital, if there is more than one); or

(b) not less than 50 of the company's members.

The application for cancellation can only be made by a person who has not consented to or voted in favour of the resolution and the court can make an order either cancelling or confirming the resolution on such terms and conditions as it thinks fit (which could, for example, include ordering that the company should buy the shares of the dissentient member or members).

Re-registering a private company as a public company is always a voluntary act. However, in two circumstances, a public company can be compulsorily re-registered as a private company:

(a) If the court makes an order confirming a reduction of capital of a public company which results in the nominal value of the company's allotted share capital falling below the authorised minimum (currently £50,000) the company ceases to be a public company. In these circumstances, the court can make an order to the effect that the company will be re-registered as a private company (making consequential amendments to the memorandum and articles of the company) which will avoid the necessity for the company to pass a special resolution to re-register.

(b) The cancellation by a public company of shares will lead to the company having to apply to be re-registered as a private company if the cancellation reduces the company's allotted share capital below the authorised minimum (currently £50,000).

32.3 Seeking and Maintaining a Listing

32.3.1 INTRODUCTION

In this section we will look in outline at the advantages and disadvantages of obtaining a listing and the requirements for seeking and maintaining that listing. It is not our intention to go into this area in detail, we will merely outline the key issues. We have used the expression 'a listing' as a generic expression for obtaining a listing of a company with the UK Listing Authority ('UKLA') and having its shares admitted to trading on the Stock Exchange.

32.3.2 THE ADVANTAGES AND DISADVANTAGES OF A LISTING

It will take a great deal of time by the officers of the company (and their advisers) to seek and maintain a listing which is, therefore, an expensive exercise. While there may be a number of advantages to the company in being listed, the company will have to accept the imposition of restrictions over and above those imposed on it by the Companies Acts and other legislation which affects listed companies. The key to understanding the need for these restrictions to be imposed is to appreciate that the principal advantage to a company of being listed is that its shares are more easily marketed. Therefore, the company has the obligation to make public information relating to its current performance and future prospects. This will give the company's current and potential future shareholders adequate information on which to base their decisions on how to deal in the company's shares.

While improved marketability (in the sense that all the shares, including minority holdings, will be freely tradable on a market which is open to a wide range of potential investors) is the principal advantage of the company being listed, it is not the only advantage. The mere fact of being a listed company may improve the status of the company within the market in which it operates. Having quoted shares may open to the company a future source of finance in the sense that it can issue new shares to raise additional funds rather than incur the expense of borrowing money from a bank (although the issue of new shares will itself give rise to some expense). Should the company wish to grow by means of acquisitions, it may find that its ability to offer its quoted shares as full or part payment of the purchase price for the company it is acquiring is an attractive and cost efficient alternative to borrowing money or using its own cash reserves.

While a listing can be attractive to an acquisitive company, it can also create problems for a company which could be the target of a take-over itself. Such a company could find that a potential bidder is able to acquire a stake in it through the open market, although there are a number of mechanisms in place to ensure that a company is aware if it is the target for a potential bid. Another potential disadvantage, particularly if the company seeking the listing

PUBLIC COMPANIES

has traditionally been run by a small group of directors/shareholders, is that they will find their activities become the subject of much closer scrutiny by both their shareholders and other interested parties (both potential investors and the press) following the listing. Since the price of a company's shares will depend on the market's view of their value, the price can fluctuate, sometimes dramatically, in response to both good and bad news about the company. To prevent people with inside information about the company's activities taking advantage of that knowledge, there are various prohibitions in place to prevent 'insiders' using information for their own benefit which is not freely available.

32.3.3 THE ADMISSION AND LISTING PARTICULARS REQUIREMENTS

When a company wishes to seek a listing, it must firstly satisfy the admission requirements and secondly provide information which satisfies the listing particulars or prospectus requirements which are governed by the rules laid down in the Financial Services Authority (acting as the UKLA) publication, *The Listing Rules*. Provided the company satisfies these requirements, and for those having their shares admitted to trading by the London Stock Exchange, it can be admitted to the Senior Equity Market in London which is known as the Official List.

There is a secondary market, open to smaller companies, called the Alternative Investment Market. We shall not look further at the rules relating to companies quoted on this market.

To be admitted to listing, the company must be registered as a public company and it must intend to place on the market shares which are expected to have a market value of £700,000 or more. The company will not be admitted (save in exceptional circumstances) if it has not published or filed accounts covering the three years preceding the application for listing, and the company must have arranged for a report prepared by independent accountants covering the three preceding years to be produced.

The directors must obviously consider that the company is financially viable and therefore a further condition for admission is that they must be satisfied that the company's working capital is sufficient. This admission requirement is satisfied by the 'approved sponsor' to the issue (usually a merchant bank or stockbroker with overall responsibility for arranging the issue) sending a letter to the UKLA stating that the directors have made careful enquiries to satisfy themselves and the sponsor that the working capital is indeed adequate. The final principal admission requirement is that it must be intended that at least 25% of any class of shares will be in the hands of the public as defined by the *The Listing Rules*.

If the company can satisfy the admission requirements, it must then also satisfy the listing particulars requirements. This obligation involves the company publishing listing particulars or a prospectus which complies with Chapters 5 and 6 of *The Listing Rules*. The range of information which must be published includes information on the shares which are to be listed, on the company and its share or loan capital, on the company's principal activities, place of business and employees, on the company's finances (in the form of balance sheet and profit and loss accounts for the last three years) and management and on trends in the company's business. The prospectus needs to include a statement that the annual accounts of the company have been audited for the last three financial years, and the people responsible for the prospectus need to make a declaration to the effect that 'to the best of their knowledge, the information given in that part of the prospectus for which they are responsible is in accordance with the facts and contains no admissions likely to affect the import of the prospectus'. There are a variety of additional detailed rules (relating to such information as changes in the auditors in the previous three years, details of options, tax clearances, and the terms of the directors' service contracts) which are beyond the scope of this book.

Should information in the prospectus prove to be misleading, false or deceptive, both civil and criminal liability can arise under the Financial Services Act 1986. The detail of this liability is beyond the scope of this book.

32.3.4 METHODS OF LISTING

All applicants for listings must be represented by an 'approved sponsor' (see **32.3.4**) who must satisfy certain conditions. The 'approved sponsor' must:

(a) be either an approved person under the Financial Services Act 1986 or an authorised credit institution;

(b) satisfy the UKLA that it has sufficient experience and standing to discharge the responsibilities of a sponsor;

(c) undertake to the UKLA to discharge the responsibilities of a sponsor as contained in the listing rules; and

(d) be entered on the UKLA's register of sponsors.

If the securities do not need to be marketed, the company can become listed by way of an 'introduction'. However, if the shares need to be marketed, admission can be achieved by any of the following methods:

(a) An offer for sale under which securities already in issue or allotted are offered to the public at large. This will entail making application forms available to the public who will complete and return them, paying the specified fixed price for the shares. It is, however, possible for the offer merely to fix a minimum price and require the applicants of the shares to tender a higher price, with the shares going to the highest bidder.

(b) An offer for subscription under which securities not yet in issue or allotted are offered to the public at large. The same procedures as in (a) will be followed.

(c) A placing. In this case, the company's shares will not be offered to the public generally, rather they will be offered to clients of the sponsor.

(d) An intermediaries offer. This involves securities being allocated to 'intermediaries' (for example, Stock Exchange member firms) who will in turn allocate the securities to their own clients.

32.3.5 CONTINUING OBLIGATIONS AFTER A LISTING HAS BEEN ACHIEVED

Chapter 9 of *The Listing Rules* sets out a variety of continuing obligations to which listed companies are subject. These include obligations to avoid a false market in the company's shares; to give notice of the date of a board meeting at which the directors will decide on payment of dividends (and details of their decision); to announce preliminary profits and losses for the year once the board has given approval for the figures; to publish information about certain acquisitions and realisations of assets (including the purchase by the company of its own shares); to comply with the detailed provisions of the *The Listing Rules* as to the content of the company's annual report and accounts (which includes the obligation to prepare half yearly accounts) and to give details of any change in the board of directors, as well as adopting rules on dealings by the directors in the companies' shares which are no less strict than those contained in the Model Code on directors' share dealings as set out in *The Listing Rules*.

THIRTY THREE

BUSINESS CONTRACTS — AGENCY OR DISTRIBUTORSHIP AGREEMENTS

This chapter covers the following topics:

33.1 Introduction
33.2 An agent or a distributor?
33.3 Agency agreements
33.4 Distributorship agreements
33.5 The Competition Act 1998.

33.1 Introduction

It is in the very nature of running a trade or business, whether it is run as a partnership or through a company, that the proprietors of the business will deal with 'outsiders'. The most important group of 'outsiders' are the customers of the business who buy its goods or services. They are not, however, the only 'outsiders' with whom the business must deal.

While many businesses will deal direct with their customers (particularly businesses which involve supplying services directly to the customers), some businesses enter into contracts with intermediaries to whom they supply goods which the intermediaries sell on to the ultimate purchasers.

Of all the wide range of contracts businesses can enter into, the ones which we will look at in this chapter are the contracts with such intermediaries. Depending on the nature of the arrangement with the intermediary, the contract may be either an agency or a distributorship (or marketing) agreement.

Before we look at these agreements in more detail, it is worth considering why a business might enter into such arrangements. At first sight, it might appear to make more financial sense for the supplying business to deal directly with its ultimate customers rather than through an intermediary who will, obviously, be looking to make a profit on the transaction. The reasons why it would in fact make commercial sense to use the intermediary will depend on the nature of the supplier's business and its reasons for considering using an intermediary. For example, a manufacturer of goods may not have the finance to support, or the expertise to run the retail outlets it needs to sell its goods to the general public. Alternatively, a supplier may have decided that there is a wider market for its goods, but that it lacks the necessary knowledge of the new market to be able to exploit the opportunity. In these types of

BUSINESS CONTRACTS — AGENCY OR DISTRIBUTORSHIP AGREEMENTS

circumstances the most sensible way for the supplier to reach its ultimate customer, or to expand its business, is to use an intermediary with the necessary facilities or expertise.

33.2 An Agent or a Distributor?

When setting up the relationship with the intermediary, the supplier will need to decide whether he wishes to appoint an agent or a distributor. So what is the difference between an agent and a distributor?

In brief, the agent will represent the supplier when seeking, negotiating and concluding contracts with the ultimate purchaser of the goods. Even though the ultimate purchaser may deal principally (or even exclusively) with the agent, the contract created will be between the supplier and the ultimate purchaser (assuming that the supplier is fully disclosed as the principal of the agent). In this circumstance, the agent will usually take a fee for each contract concluded and the risks, financial and commercial, will be borne by the supplier.

Conversely, a distributor will buy the goods from the supplier and then re-sell them to the distributor's own customers, with the return the distributor seeks from the arrangement represented by whatever profit he can make on the re-sale. Given that the distributor will be bearing the financial and commercial risk involved in finding the ultimate purchaser, the profit margin the distributor adds when re-selling the goods may be greater than the commission which an agent would charge. This will have the effect of increasing the ultimate sale price of the supplier's goods. This in turn may have an adverse affect on the marketability of those goods if a supplier's principal rivals in the particular market are able to sell at lower prices (because, for example, they have the necessary resources or expertise to be able to sell directly to the ultimate purchaser). Where a distributor is involved, the supplier will have no direct contractual relationship with the purchaser (since the contractual relationship will be between the distributor and the ultimate purchaser), but this will not necessarily protect the supplier from liability for defective goods.

Whichever type of intermediary arrangement the supplier decides to opt for, it is sensible to set out the terms of the arrangement in a written agreement. The written agency agreement will define the authority and duties of the agent and set out the agent's rights as against the supplier. The structure of a distribution agreement will be different to reflect the fact that the distributor buys the goods outright from the supplier. Perhaps the key provisions in a distributorship agreement relate to the restrictions on competition which each party to the agreement wishes to impose on the other.

Once the supplier has taken the decision to use an intermediary, the supplier's business objectives will determine which of an agency or distributorship arrangement is most appropriate. An agency arrangement will be appropriate where the supplier wants to retain control of the terms of sale of his products, where direct contact with the customer is important (for example, where only the supplier can provide specialist after-sales service) or where the supplier wants to retain control over the purchasers of his products or services. Conversely, a distributorship arrangement will be attractive where the supplier is selling products which require little or no direct contact with the ultimate purchaser or where the supplier is trying to break into a new market. In the latter case, a distributorship arrangement could be especially attractive as the agreement can impose an obligation on the distributor to make an agreed volume of purchases thus, in effect, guaranteeing the supplier a market. In return, the distributor will be given rights to resell the supplier's goods. Whether those rights are exclusive or not will depend on the nature of the distributorship agreement but, obviously, an exclusive right to resell a highly valued product could be extremely valuable to the distributor.

BUSINESS CONTRACTS — AGENCY OR DISTRIBUTORSHIP AGREEMENTS

One problem with both agency and distributorship arrangements is that by their very nature they can restrict competition. The national and EC competition rules, therefore, may have an impact on the terms of the arrangement into which the principal or supplier and the agent or distributor can enter.

In the rest of this chapter, we will look at the provisions relating to agency and distributorship arrangements dealing with each arrangement separately. We will look firstly at the different types of arrangements which can be created under agency or distributorship agreements, then at the legal rules (including competition rules) which can have an impact on such agreements and finally at some common provisions to be found in agency and distributorship agreements.

33.3 Agency Agreements

33.3.1 TYPES OF AGENCY AGREEMENT

The key aspect of an agency agreement is that the agent is merely an intermediary between the supplier (his principal) and the supplier's customer, the agent's acts being regarded as those of the supplier (his principal). While the agent may be closely involved in concluding the contract, he will not usually be a party to the contract, nor will he acquire rights or obligations under it. Having said that, there are a number of different types of agency agreement into which the principal and agent can enter. The agent's powers can be limited merely to seeking 'contracts' for the supplier (the agent in those circumstances is commonly called a 'marketing agent'). It is perhaps more common for the agent to be appointed as a 'sales agent' in which case the agent will have power to enter into contracts on behalf of his principal. The powers of a 'sales agent' can be determined by the agreement between the two parties and the most common types of arrangements are:

(a) *An exclusive agency agreement*

   As the title implies, the agent has exclusive rights to represent the principal and the principal cannot appoint other agents to represent him. The exclusivity may apply worldwide or be limited to particular territories.

(b) *The sole agency arrangement*

   The principal is barred from appointing other agents (again on a worldwide or territorial basis) but is free to seek customers directly himself.

(c) *The non-exclusive agency agreement*

   Under this form of agreement, the principal can appoint other agents and seek customers himself.

33.3.2 THE REGULATION OF AGENCY AGREEMENTS

33.3.2.1 The general rules

Prior to 1 January 1994, the regulation of the principal-agent relationship was largely a matter of agreement between the parties as the common law imposed limited rights and obligations on either side. The Commercial Agents (Council Directive) Regulations 1993 (SI 1993 No. 3053) (which came into effect on 1 January 1994) made radical changes to the old position (see **33.3.2.2** below).

Under the common law, the duties owed by an agent to his principal included the duties:

BUSINESS CONTRACTS — AGENCY OR DISTRIBUTORSHIP AGREEMENTS

(a) to obey the principal's lawful instructions;

(b) to act within the limits of the authority given to the agent by the principal;

(c) to use reasonable diligence and care;

(d) to avoid conflicts between the agent's interests and those of his principal;

(e) to disclose all material facts to the principal and not to reveal confidential information; and

(f) to account to the principal for any property or money belonging to the principal under the agent's control.

The common law duties imposed on the principal include the obligation to pay the agent remuneration and/or commission and the agent's expenses as well as giving the agent an indemnity against losses incurred while acting within the scope of the agent's authority.

The agent's responsibilities in relation to contracts which he helps to conclude on behalf of his principal will depend on whether the customer, the third party, was aware that the agent was acting as such. If the customer knows the agent is acting as such for a 'disclosed principal', the contract will be between the principal and the third party *provided* the agent was acting within the scope of his actual or ostensible authority. If the agent was acting within the scope of his authority, he would not be liable in respect of the contract; only the principal can sue or be sued on it. If the agent was acting outside the scope of his authority the agent will be liable unless the principal has ratified the contract.

In circumstances where the agent is acting for an 'undisclosed principal' (that is to say the third party is unaware of the agency arrangement), both the agent and his principal can sue or be sued under the contract (provided the agent was acting within the scope of his authority). If the 'undisclosed principal' informs the third party of the agency arrangement, the third party will have a choice of either continuing to regard the agent as the other party to the contract or regard the contract as being with the agent's principal (which has the effect of relieving the agent of any liability).

33.3.2.2 The Commercial Agents (Council Directive) Regulations 1993 (SI 1993 No. 3053)

General

These Regulations (which came into effect on 1 January 1994) regulate most comercial agency arrangements where the agent is required to perform any part of his duties anywhere in the EC. The freedom of principals and agents to agree the terms of their relationship have been severely curtailed by the Regulations since many of the Regulations are mandatory and cannot be overriden by contrary agreement. Not only do the Regulations apply to agency arrangements (called 'agency contracts' in the Regulations) entered into on or after 1 January 1994, they also apply to arrangements in existence on 1 January 1994.

As their title suggests, the Regulations implemented EEC Council Directive 86/653 on the co-ordination of laws of member States relating to agents. As such, this Directive may be of relevance when interpreting the Regulations. Also, all other member States, therefore, have their own similar implementing legislation. This may be relevant when considering the issues raised in the next paragraph.

Jurisdiction and territorial application

The Regulations apply to the activities of commercial agents in Great Britain (not to Northern Ireland where separate, but identical, Regulations apply) unless the parties have agreed that

BUSINESS CONTRACTS — AGENCY OR DISTRIBUTORSHIP AGREEMENTS

the agency contract should be covered by the law of another EC country. Therefore, an agency contract under which the agent is based in Great Britain and will perform his duties in Great Britain will be governed by the Regulations unless the agency contract provides that the law of another EC country is to govern the agreement. That situation could arise where the principal is from an EC country other than Great Britain and in those circumstances the relevant legislation from the other EC country will apply to the agreement. If the commercial agent is to perform his duties in a country outside the EC, the Regulations will be irrelevant. The position is somewhat complicated where a British principal appoints a commercial agent to act in another EC country and the governing law of the contract is that of England. The Regulations would seem not to apply because the agent is not performing his duties in Great Britain. In addition, it would appear that the regulations of no other country can apply because of the governing law clause.

Until quite recently, there was no solution to this unsatisfactory problem. However, it has now been remedied by the introduction of the Commercial Agents (Council Directive) (Amendment) Regulations 1998 which bring about a change to the 1993 Regulations. The effect of the change is twofold:

(a) It is possible for parties to choose a governing law from another member State, in which case, an English court is obliged to apply that chosen law. (This assumes, of course, that the English court has jurisdiction to hear the matter.)

(b) Where the governing law is that of England and Wales, but the agent is to perform his or her duties outside Great Britain in another member State, a court must still apply the Regulations, so long as the relevant regulations of that member State allow the contract to be governed by law from a jurisdiction other than that in which the agent is to perform his or her duties.

Commercial agents

The Regulations apply to 'commercial agents' and the term is defined as 'a self-employed intermediary who has continuing authority to negotiate the sale or purchase of the goods on behalf of the principal or to negotiate and conclude the sale and purchase of goods on behalf of and in the name of that principal'. There were differing views among the commentators on the Regulations as to whether this definition of a 'commercial agent' was intended to mean that the Regulations only apply to individuals. Probably, the better argument is that the Regulations are applicable to a 'commercial agent' whether an individual, a partnership or a company.

In *AMB Imballaggi Plastici* v *Pacflex* [1999] 2 All ER (Comm) 249, the defendant, Pacflex, attempted to construe itself as an agent, in order to substantiate a claim for compensation on termination of its contract with the claimant. At no stage in the proceedings was the argument put forward that the defendant did not qualify as an agent, because it was a company. In fact, the defendant failed in its argument on other grounds, namely that it was not acting 'on behalf of' the claimant, but, rather, was buying and selling for itself only.

Application of the Regulations

The Regulations apply to any agency contract whether oral or written. However, the Regulations provide that a number of 'agents' should be excluded from the coverage of the Regulations, including:

(a) an officer of a company or an association (not just company directors) acting as an 'agent' of the company or association;

(b) a partner authorised to enter into binding commitments on behalf of his partners or his fellow partners;

(c) any insolvency practitioner acting as such;

(d) a commercial agent whose activities are unpaid; and

(e) commercial agents whose activities as such are considered to be secondary (the criteria for determining whether the activities are 'secondary' are very wide and are contained in the Schedule to the Regulations).

Duties of the principal and agent

Regulation 3 sets out the duties of the commercial agent to his principal and cannot be contracted out of. The agent is required to look after the interests of his principal and to act dutifully and in good faith. In particular, the agent must make proper efforts to negotiate and, where appropriate, conclude the transactions he is instructed to take care of, to communicate to his principal all necessary information available to him and to comply with reasonable instructions given by his principal.

The duties of a principal to his commercial agent are set out in Regulation 4 and cannot be contracted out of. The Regulation imposes an obligation on the principal to act dutifully and in good faith in his relations with his commercial agent. Furthermore, the principal must provide his commercial agent with necessary documentation relating to the goods concerned, obtain for his commercial agent the information necessary for the performance of the agency contract and notify the agent (within a reasonable period) once he anticipates that the volume of commercial transactions will be significantly lower than that which the commercial agent could normally have expected. Finally, the principal is required to inform his commercial agent (within a reasonable period) of his acceptance or refusal of, and of any non-execution by him of, a commercial transaction which the commercial agent has procured for him.

Remuneration and commission

If the parties to the agency contract have not agreed a level of remuneration or commission, the Regulations provide that the agent will receive the amount which it is customary to pay to agents marketing the types of goods or services concerned in the same geographical area. In the absence of any such custom and practice, the agent will receive 'reasonable remuneration taking into account all aspects of the transaction'. The Regulations contain detailed provisions determining how commission is to be calculated and when it is to be paid. However, these do not apply if the agent is not remunerated, whether wholly or in part, through 'commission'. 'Commission' is defined as 'any part of the remuneration of the commercial agent which varies with the number or value of business transactions'.

Under Regulation 7 (which can be contracted out of), the agent is entitled to receive commission transactions concluded during the period covered by the agency agreement where the transaction has been concluded as a result of his actions or where the transaction is concluded with a third party who he previously acquired as a customer for transactions of the same kind. The agent will also be entitled to commission on transactions concluded during the period covered by the agency contract where he has an exclusive right to a specific geographical area or to a specific group of customers where the transactions have been entered into with the customer belonging to that area or group. It is normal to deal with the situation covered by Regulation 7 in the agency agreement and so the provisions of this Regulation are likely to come into play only when the parties have, for whatever reason, omitted to deal expressly with this issue. (See *Kontogeorgas v Kartonpak* [1997] 1 CMLR 1083 where the scope of Article 7 was crucial as the agreement was silent on the point.)

It is perhaps more likely that the parties may have failed to agree on the agent's entitlement to commission on transactions concluded **after** the agency contract is terminated. Regulation 8 (which can be contracted out of) covers this situation and provides that the commercial agent will be entitled to commission. In the circumstances if the transaction is mainly attributable to his efforts during the period covered by the agency contract and if the transaction was entered into within a reasonable period after that contract terminated or (provided commission would have been payable under Regulation 7 if the contract had been entered into during the agency contract) the order of the third party reached the principal or the commercial agent before the agency contract terminated.

Under Regulation 10, 'commission' becomes due as soon as, and to the extent that, either the principal has executed the transaction, or the principal should, according to his agreement with the third party, have executed the transaction or the third party has executed the transaction.

Provision of information

Regulation 12 requires the principal to supply the agent, each quarter, with a statement of the commission due and the 'main components used in calculating the amount'. The agent will be entitled to demand that he be provided with all the information and records which are available to the principal which he needs in order to be able to check the amount of commission due to him.

While the Directive does not require agency agreements caught by the Regulations to be in writing, Regulation 13 gives both sides the right, on request, to a signed document from the other party setting out the terms of the agency contract, including any variations made subsequent to their original entry into the agency contract.

Termination

Arguably, the most important provisions of the Regulations relate to terminating agency contracts, in particular the provisions introducing minimum notice periods and compensation for termination of agency contracts.

The Regulations make no provision for notice where an agency contract for a fixed term is terminated on the originally agreed date. However, if the fixed term agreement continues to be performed by both parties after the fixed term has expired, the agreement is converted into an agency contract for an indefinite period and the minimum notice period set out in Regulation 15 will apply.

If Regulation 15 applies, either party can terminate it on giving notice which will be at least one month during the first year of the contract, two months during the second and three months during the third and each subsequent year. Regulation 15 is mandatory and so it is not open to the parties to agree shorter periods of notice but they may agree longer periods of notice (although Regulation 15(3) provides that, in those circumstances, the period of notice to be observed by the principal must not be shorter than that to be observed by the agent). Where a fixed term agency agreement is converted into an indefinite term one under Regulation 14, the notice period set out above will apply. The original fixed period must be taken into account in the calculation of the period of notice.

As we have explained, agency agreements in existence before 1 January 1994 (when the Regulations came into effect) are covered by the Regulations. Commentators on the Regulations have taken the view that the duration of the agreement prior to that date should be taken into account in calculating the minimum notice period.

Post-termination indemnity or compensation

Regulation 17 sets out the rules relevant when determining if the commercial agent is entitled to any compensation on the termination of the agency contract. The EC Directive which the

Regulations implement gave member States two alternatives with regard to compensation when implementing the Directive in the national legislation. The member States could either provide for an 'indemnity' for the agent (of a maximum of one year's commission, calculated by reference to an historic average) to which the agent would be entitled if he had substantially enhanced the good will of the principal's business or for 'compensation' for the agent for damage suffered as a result of the ending of the agency relationship.

Regulation 17 permits the principal and agent to choose whichever of 'indemnity' or 'compensation' they prefer (although if the agency agreement is silent on the point, the agent will receive 'compensation' rather than 'indemnity').

Regulation 17(3) provides that the commercial agent should be entitled to an indemnity if and to the extent that:

(a) he has brought the principal new customers or has significantly increased the volume of business with the existing customers and the principal continues to derive substantial benefits from the business with such customers; and

(b) the payment of this indemnity is equitable having regard to all the circumstances and, in particular, the commission lost by the commercial agent on business transacted with such customers.

If these things had not happened, no 'indemnity' is payable. Some commentators on the Regulations have surmised that the effect of this provision is for the principal and agent to be regarded as if they are the joint owners of that part of the goodwill of the principal's business and the agent is being paid to surrender his interest. At this early stage in the 'life' of the Regulations, it is difficult to say precisely how these provisions will be interpreted. As time goes on, the position will become clearer.

Assuming that the commercial agent is entitled to an indemnity, the amount of the indemnity shall not exceed a figure equivalent to an indemnity for one year calculated from the commercial agent's average annual remuneration over the preceding five years. If the contract goes back less than five years, the indemnity should be calculated on the average for the period in question. (The fact that the commercial agent is entitled to an 'indemnity' does not prevent him from seeking damages for breach of contract.)

So far as the 'compensation' alternative is concerned, Regulation 17(6) provides the commercial agent should be entitled to compensation for the damage he suffers as a result of the termination of his relations with the principal. Such damage shall be deemed to occur particularly when the termination takes place in either or both of the following circumstances, namely circumstances which:

(a) deprive the commercial agent of the commission which proper performance of the agency contract would have procured for him whilst providing his principal with substantial benefits linked to the activities of the commercial agent; or

(b) have not enabled the commercial agent to amortise the cost and expenses that he had incurred in the performance of the agency agreement on the advice of his principal.

The commercial agent loses his entitlement to indemnity or compensation if, within one year following the termination of his agency contract, he has not notified his principal that he intends pursuing his entitlement.

These rights to indemnity of compensation can also arise where the agency agreement is terminated as a result of the death of the commercial agent.

The rights to payment of indemnity or compensation are, however, excluded where:

(a) the principal has terminated the agency contract because of the commercial agent's default which would justify immediate termination of the agency contract because of the commercial agent's failure to carry out all or part of his obligations under the contract or where exceptional circumstances arise; or

(b) the commercial agent has himself terminated the agency contract, unless the termination is justified by circumstances attributable to the principal or on the grounds of age, infirmity or illness of the commercial agent in conseqeunce of which he cannot reasonably require to continue his activities; or

(c) the commercial agent, with the agreement of his principal, assigns his rights and duties under the agency contract to another person.

The grounds for excluding these payments are set out in Regulation 18.

The parties to the agency contract have to agree at the start of the contract whether 'indemnity' or 'compensation' within Regulation 17 would be paid at the end.

Therefore, they will have to take a view on this important issue on the basis perhaps of little or no information. 'Indemnity' is subject to a maximum of one year's commission calculated on an averaging basis while there is no maximum for compensation payments. Presumably, this clear limit on the amount of indemnity they will have to pay will lead to many principals favouring that option. From the agent's point of view, compensation may be the more attractive option, given that the right to indemnity only arises if the agent has brought in new customers or 'significantly increased' the volume of the principal's business. (Also, the Court of Appeal has confirmed that the right to compensation under the Regulations does not exclude the right to 'normal' contractual damages as well, although there may be shared similarities between the two. See *Duffen* v *FRA BO SpA* [1998] TLR 379.) Therefore, the agent has to have grown the principal's business to get indemnity whereas the right to compensation would be available if the agent has merely maintained that business. It is obviously simplistic to suggest that there is a general rule of thumb which can be applied. The principal and agent will have to take into account all the surrounding circumstances which may justify reaching a different conclusion.

Further incentive for the principal to adopt the indemnity route comes from the decision of the Court of Appeal in *Page* v *Combined Shipping & Trading* [1997] 3 All ER 565. Here the agent was deprived of further performance of his agency because the principal chose to close its business down. The amount of compensation potentially due to the agent depended on what he would have expected to earn had the contract been 'properly performed'. The principal argued that it was not obliged to put business the way of the agent, and so the agreement could have been properly performed by the agent never earning any commission. As a consequence the agent had suffered no damage from the early termination and, consequently, no compensation was payable. This view was rejected by the Court. The word 'proper' was equated with the word 'normal' and so an entitlement to compensation could be based on what would have happened had the contract been performed in the normal course of events. (It should be understood, however, that, as this involved an application for a Mareva injunction, the Court's main task was to establish whether or not the plaintiff had a good arguable case. As such, the decision does not provide a definitive interpretation of the Regulations, but the Court's approach gives an indication of a willingness to interpret them in favour of an agent.)

What is still missing, however, is clear guidance on the specific formulae to be adopted when calculating compensation or an indemnity. Some guidance can be taken from the case of *Moore* v *Piretta PTA* [1998] TLR 379. The case was concerned primarily with the calculation of an indemnity, so does not provide precedent for compensation calculations. Two interesting points should be taken from the case:

(a) The judge felt that, when looking at compensation, the laws of France should be considered, as the concept is an established one in that jurisdiction; when looking at indemnity, the laws of Germany should be considered for the same reason.

(b) The indemnity calculation produced a figure of £92,000. However, the cap imposed by Regulation 17(4) meant that the actual award was just under £65,000.

As such, compensation looks an unattractive option to a principal and an indemnity, with its more specific delineation, is, it is submitted, preferable, particularly if the agency is to be for any considerable period of time. Of course, there will be numerous agreements in existence drafted prior to the Regulations and, hence, with no regard to this issue. As such, compensation will be payable by default.

Settlement of disputes

The parties may not derogate from the compensation and indemnity provisions to the detriment of the commercial agent before the agency contract expired (Regulation 19).

Restraint of trade clauses

Any restraint of trade clause in any agency contract will be valid only if and to the extent that:

(a) it is concluded in writing;

(b) it relates to the geographical area or group of customers and the geographical area entrusted to the commercial agent and to the kind of goods covered by his agency under the contract; and

(c) it is for not more than two years after the termination of the agency contract.

The Regulation which deals with the restraint of trade clauses (Regulation 20) goes on to provide that 'nothing in this Regulation shall affect any enactment or rule of law which imposes other restrictions on the validity or enforceability of restraint of trade clauses or which enables the court to reduce the obligations on the parties resulting from such clauses'. Therefore, the existing common law rules on restraint of trade (which require that any such clause must be reasonable as between the parties and not against the public interest) will still apply to such clauses in agency contracts.

33.3.2.3 The competition issues

The UK rules

Agency agreements tend not to present the parties with any UK competition law difficulties. Price-fixing is not an issue in most agency agreements, as the sale is made directly by the principal. See **33.4.2** for a more detailed explanation of the law.

The EC rules

Article 81 of the Treaty of Rome (with Article 82) governs the competition policy of the European Community (see **Chapter 21**). It will be remembered that Article 81 prohibits agreements which restrict or distort competition and which affect trade between EC member States. The nature of terms commonly found in agency agreements (for example, provisions relating to customers, trading terms, limitations on the agent's ability to handle competing products etc.) are such that agency agreements can fall foul of Article 81. If they do, the EC Commission can impose substantial fines but the precise extent of the application of Article 81 to agency agreements is currently in a state of some uncertainty.

The general position is that Article 81 will not apply if the agent's relationship with the principal is so close that the agent does not act as an independent player in the market (that it, the agent's activities are 'integrated' with those of the principal). Conversely, subject to any exemption being available, Article 81 will apply where the agent enjoys a degree of independence from the principal.

However, the uncertain state of the existing EC rules means that it can be difficult to ascertain whether or not Article 81 applies to the particular circumstances of an agency agreement. The position used to be reasonably clear but now there is a need for further guidance to be issued by the EC Commission. There is no indication that new guidance will be issued imminently.

It is necessary to look at the background to the EC rules to understand why new guidance is needed. The Commission published its Notice on exclusive agency agreements with commercial agents in 1962. The Notice stated that the 'decisive criterion' of an agent's independence was whether the agent 'accepted a financial risk' from the sale contract. Only if the agent accepted a 'financial risk' did the exclusive agency agreement fall within Article 81. The 1962 notice also said (as a secondary point) that a true commercial agent 'performed an auxiliary function in the market for goods'. Thus, he would act on the instructions of and in the interests of the principal rather than independently. Any agreement to appoint an agent on these terms would be outside the scope of Article 81. (Commentators on these Rules have said that it was not clear how this latter point fitted together with the 'decisive criterion' of financial risk.)

As time went on, the Commission began to depart from regarding financial risk as the 'decisive criterion' for determining the independent status of an agent. Instead, it began emphasising the 'auxiliary function' concept and looked at a wider range of factors to establish that. In recent years it has become evident that the 1962 Notice needed to be revised. In 1990, the Commission published a preliminary draft of a new Notice on Agency agreements. However, that draft has proved unpopular and the Commission appears to have abandoned it.

What, therefore, is the current position? The 1962 Notice is still in force (in that it has not yet been formally withdrawn) but it is out of line with the case law. It should not, therefore, be relied upon for help in determining whether the agent is 'integrated' in the principal's business (with the result, generally speaking, that Article 81 will not apply).

The lack of clear rules means that it is not possible to give definitive guidance as to when an agent is 'integrated' in its principal's business. However, the agent clearly will be 'integrated' if the agent has no business activity at all other than acting as an agent for this principal. When the circumstances do not fall within such a simple factual situation, regard should be had to:

(a) whether the latest De Minimis Notice issued in 1987 might be relevant. Under this notice, Article 81(1) does not apply where both parties' combined market shares for the relevant products do not represent more than 5% (in the case of 'horizontal' agreements) or 10% (in the case of 'vertical' agreements) of the total market for the relevant product in the affected area of the EC. (A horizontal agreement will be between undertakings operating at the same level of production or marketing; a vertical agreement will be between undertakings operating at different marketing and production levels. As regards an agency agreement, therefore, it will be regarded as being of a vertical nature.) The Notice also exempts from the impact of Article 81 agreements between parties whose annual turnover is less than 40 million Euros (formerly ECU) or whose total balance sheet worth is less than 27 million Euros (formerly ECU) and which employ not more than 250 people, regardless of the market share thresholds enjoyed by the parties. (It should be noted, however, that agreements the purpose of which is price fixing or market sharing will not benefit from the exemption, irrespective of the size of the parties or their market shares.)

(b) the wording of the agency agreement itself. If the agreement permits the agent to choose the customers and determine the terms of the sale without the need to refer these issues back to the principal, the agent may be 'unintegrated'.

(c) the extent of the agent's other commercial activities and the importance for the agent of those other activities in relation to the agency activities.

For an agent with activities other than those covered by the agency agreement with the principal, to be regarded as 'integrated', the other activities will have to be small in comparison with the agency business or in a non-competing or unrelated product or in a geographical market which had little trade with the territories in which the agency product is marketed. It is probably unlikely that that covers the other activities of most commercial agents. Therefore, most agency agreements will probably be 'unintegrated' and (potentially at least) within Article 81. This will certainly be the case if no restrictions on the agent's activities are imposed by the agency agreement and if the agent also acts for a principal's competitors.

While on the face of it Article 81 should have no relevance to the agency agreement between a principal and an 'integrated' agent, the Commission nevertheless regard that certain terms of such an agency agreement may be within Article 81. These include any attempt to prevent the agent being able to sell to customers outside his territory who approach him to make purchases on their own initiative, any restriction on the agent's ability to pass on part of his commission to the customers or any non-competition undertakings given by the agent for a period extending after the agreement has terminated.

On the assumption that the agent is 'unintegrated', in principle Article 81 will apply. However, the Commission will issue a 'comfort letter' confirming that the Article does not apply if the arrangements are not, in fact, regarded as anti-competitive. Provisions which are within Article 81 but for which the Commission may issue a comfort letter include provisions which appoint any one agent for an area and for the principal to agree not to supply direct to the customers in the territory, prevent the agent carrying the products of competitors, prevent the agent seeking business outside his exclusive territory, restrict the agent's choice of customer, or impose confidentiality obligations.

33.3.2.4 The provisions of agency agreements

In this section we will look, in outline, at the key provisions which could be included in such agreements. It should be remembered that the Commercial Agents (Council Directive) Regulations 1993 (SI 1993 No. 3053) give each party the right to a written statement of terms (Regulation 13) and render void any post-termination restrictive covenant which is not in writing (Regulation 18).

Appointment and authority

When appointing the agent, the agreement should set out the extent of the agent's authority. Is the agent to have authority to sell the products covered by the agreement with all powers necessary to market the products, negotiate terms and enter into contracts on behalf of the principal? (In other words, is the agent to be a 'sale agent'?) Alternatively, is the agent to be a 'marketing agent' and so only have power to promote the products and solicit orders which have to be passed back to the principal?

The subject matter of the agreement: goods or services

The 'products' which are the subject matter of the agency agreement, whether they be goods or services, need to be clearly defined. What is to happen if circumstances merit a change in those goods and services? Can the principal change them unilaterally or does the agent have to agree to such changes?

Customers, territory and exclusivity

It is usual to restrict the agent's appointment to finding customers in a defined territory or to a specified type of customer.

The agency agreement can give exclusive or non-exclusive rights to the agent for the defined territory. If the agency is to be exclusive, the principal will agree not to appoint another agent in the teritory but may wish to reserve the right to supply existing (specified) customers in the territory. The agent will usually agree not to seek orders for the products from the customers outside the specified territory.

Duration

The agreement can be either for an indefinite term or for a fixed period. If it is for an indefinite term, the 1993 Regulations impose minimum notice periods (or up to three months). If the agreement is for a fixed term but continues beyond the agreed termination date, it will be regarded as being for an indefinite period and the Regulations' provisions relating to minimum notice periods will apply.

The duties of the agent

Irrespective of the duties imposed on agents by common law and by the 1993 Regulations, the agent's duties will usually be set out in full in the agreement. This will normally include an obligation on the agent to use its best endeavours to promote a market product in the territory, and to seek and (if the agency is a sole agency) accept orders, on the principal's standard terms and conditions. Although the common law will imply obligations to act in good faith and obey all the principal's reasonable lawful instructions, they should be expressly stated. A variety of more specific obligations can be imposed including the obligation on the agent to make its status clear to all potential customers, a prohibition on the agent incurring liability for representations or warranties on the principal's behalf, save as authorised and a prohibition on making secret profits.

The rights and duties of the principal

As with the agent, the common law and the 1993 Regulations impose a number of duties on the principal (including the obligation to act towards the agent in good faith). The agreement will give or impose a number of additional rights and duties on the principal. The principal will normally want the ability to change the goods or services (and their price) which are the subject of the agreement. The principal will also want the right to approve any expenses incurred by the agent which are to be reimbursed by the principal as well as the right to inspect the agent's books. The agent will want the reassurance that the principal has taken all the necessary steps to ensure the quality of the goods or services being provided, that the principal maintains appropriate product liability insurance and can perform its contracts with third parties.

Commission

Should the parties fail to agree on the amount of commission paid under the agency agreement, the 1993 Regulations give the agent the right to the remuneration customarily paid to agents dealing with the same goods and services in the same geographical area. The Regulations do not, however, specifically provide what is the amount of the commission to be paid. Having said that, it is usual for agency agreements to cover the question of commission and it is usually in the form of a percentage of the net invoice price of the goods sold through the agent or of cash received by the principal from those sales. The commission provisions should determine when commission becomes due (usually once a principal has been paid by the customer) and for the date on which the commission should be paid. If the agent is a sales agent, the agent may reserve the right to retain the commission from the payments in which case the agreement will contain strict provisions dealing with how the payments should be accounted for.

Termination

In addition to providing minimum notice periods for indefinite term agreements, if the Regulations apply to a particular case, they provide for agents to receive compensation or indemnity on termination, irrespective of whether or not the principal is in breach. In any event, the principal will want to reserve the right to terminate early (either summarily or on notice) if the agent is in breach of contract, is declared bankrupt or insolvent, purports to assign the agreement or is likely to become unable to perform the contract.

Restrictive covenants

The principal may want to protect his business interests by imposing such a covenant on the agent. Under English law, the covenant will be enforceable if the principal has an interest worthy of protection and the restrictions (as to time, subject matter, geographical area etc.) are considered to be reasonable as between the parties at the date the restriction is imposed and not against the public interest.

Other provisions

Agency agreements commonly also include a variety of other provisions including those relating to:

(a) intellectual property

(b) confidentiality

(c) assignment

(d) force majeure

(e) notices

(f) governing law and jurisdiction.

33.4 Distributorship Agreements

33.4.1 TYPES OF DISTRIBUTORSHIP AGREEMENT

33.4.1.1 Exclusive distributorship agreements

The distinguishing feature of such agreements is that they give the distributor the exclusive right to sell the product in the territory covered by the distributorship agreement. The supplier will be prevented from selling the goods in the relevant area either on his own account or through agents or other distributors.

The Office of Fair Trading in the UK and the European Commission favour this form of distributorship agreement for a variety of reasons. Exclusive distributorship arrangements are considered to encourage competition between different brands of the same type of goods. This is because knowing that he is the only source of a particular brand of goods within his territory will encourage the distributor to market those goods heavily and the supplier's wish to establish itself within that area will encourage it to maintain the continuity of supply. Furthermore, appointing an exclusive distributor means that the supplier of each brand of goods only has to deal with one entity in the region and thus avoid the necessity for maintaining a potentially expensive network of dealers. Exclusive distributorship arrangements will usually mean that there are a number of brands of the same product competing vigorously against each other. The effect of this will be to benefit members of the public who will have access to a wider choice of goods at more competitive prices.

33.4.1.2 Sole distributorship agreements

The key difference between a sole distributorship agreement (although the term 'sole' is not a term of art here) and an exclusive one is that while the distributor under a sole distributorship agreement will be the only distributor with whom the supplier will deal in a particular territory, the supplier is *not* prevented from continuing to sell its products in the territory on its own account. In return, the distributor will commonly agree to regard the supplier as his sole supplier of the type of goods which are the subject of the agreement.

The economic benefits of an exclusive distributorship agreement do not apply to a sole distributorship agreement and so these types of agreements are not so favourably treated by the Office of Fair Trading and the European Commission.

33.4.1.3 Non-exclusive distributorship agreements

Under such an arrangement, the distributor merely takes the supplier's products. The distributor has no exclusive rights to those products, so that the supplier can appoint other distributors in the same territory, nor is the supplier prohibited from selling its own products on its own accounts in the territory.

Again, the economic benefits of exclusive distributorship agreements do not apply to non-exclusive ones, and so the Office of Fair Trading and the EC Commission do not look upon them as favourably as exclusive arrangements.

33.4.1.4 Selective distributorship agreements

The distinguishing feature of such an arrangement is that the supplier limits the number of distributors he will appoint in a particular territory so that the distributors who enter into such an agreement will not be given exclusive rights to deal with the supplier's goods.

A selective distributorship arrangement may not encourage as much inter-brand competition as an exclusive distributorship arrangement, and so they are less favourably treated by the UK and EC competition authorities than are exclusive arrangements. Nevertheless, they will be permitted, subject to satisfying certain conditions which are set out in **33.4.2.2** below.

In **33.4.2** below we will look at the competition issues, both from the UK and European perspectives in relation to exclusive and selective distribution agreements.

33.4.2 THE COMPETITION ISSUES

33.4.2.1 The UK rules

The introduction of the Competition Act 1998 substantially reformed the regulation of competition in the UK. Until 1 March 2000, the legislation was somewhat piecemeal. Now, with a few notable exceptions, for example, merger control, the Competition Act is the main source of legislative control of competition. Full details are given at **33.5**.

BUSINESS CONTRACTS — AGENCY OR DISTRIBUTORSHIP AGREEMENTS

33.4.2.2 The EC rules

General

In **Chapter 21** we looked at Article 81 of the Treaty of Rome which (with Article 82) governs the competition policy of the European Community.

It will be remembered from that chapter that Article 81(1) prohibits 'all agreements between undertakings, decisions by associations of undertakings and concerted practices which may affect trade between member States which have as their object or effect the prevention, restriction or distortion of competition within the common market'. The controls imposed by reason of Article 81 have direct effect in the UK and so that article must be borne in mind when considering distributorship agreements (even where both parties to it are based in the UK) in addition to the national rules.

If a distributorship agreement falls within Article 81(1) it is automatically void and the parties to it can be subject to substantial fines. However, there are various ways of ensuring that Article 81 does not apply to particular distributorship agreements and these are considered in this section.

Article 82 of the Treaty of Rome is intended to prevent companies with a dominant market position from abusing that position. This was covered in **21.3** and the provisions of that article are not considered further in this chapter.

Notification of the agreement for negative clearance

Parties to the agreement can apply to the European Commission for a certificate to the effect that the Commission has no grounds for action under either Article 81 or 82. Obviously, this will depend on the facts of a particular case.

Notification of the agreement for exemption

Parties can apply to the European Commission for a decision that the arrangement is suitable for exemption under Article 81(3), even though the agreement does in fact fall within the scope of Article 81(1). (See **21.2.3** for the details of Article 81(3).)

Informal clearance by a comfort letter

The parties to the distributorship agreement can provide the European Commission with details of the arrangement which they are entering into and ask the Commission to confirm that Article 81 does not apply. This approach avoids the parties going to the time and expense of seeking a formal decision from the Commission. However, all they will get in return is a 'comfort letter' recording an administrative decision from the Commission confirming that the arrangements, as described to the Commission, are not within Article 81. This 'comfort letter' will not prevent the national courts of the parties reaching the conclusion that the agreement is anti-competitive (and so void) but with most distributorship agreements it is considered to be protection enough.

Commission Notice on agreements of minor importance

Details of this notice are given in **33.3.2.3**.

The EC block exemptions

Certain specified types of agreements have been declared by the European Commission to be outside the scope of Article 81. One of these 'block exemptions' applies to exclusive distributorship agreements, allowing certain approved clauses (the 'white list clauses') to be included and excluding disapproved clauses (the 'black list clauses') (Regulation (EEC) No. 1983/83).

This block exemption expired on 31 May 2000, but agreements which benefited from it at that date will continue to do so until 31 December 2001. Because of this and because many agreements drafted on the basis of the exemption will continue to be operative for some time to come, details of the Regulation are set out below. (See **21.2.4.3** for further details of the Regulation which has replaced the block exemption.)

To be within the scope of the block exemption, the exclusive distributorship agreement must impose a restriction on the supplier not to supply goods to other distributors in the territory. However, no other restrictions on competition can be imposed on the supplier. If they are, the exemption will not apply.

The block exemption allows certain restrictions on competition to be imposed on the distributor and also allows the agreement to impose on the distributor certain obligations. These restrictions and obligations are as follows:

(a) *Restrictions*

   The distributor can have imposed on him obligations not to:

   (i) manufacture or distribute competing goods;

   (ii) obtain the goods which are the subject matter of the agreement from anyone other than the supplier; and

   (iii) seek customers, establish a branch or maintain a distribution depot in relation to the goods which are the subject matter of the agreement outside the territory covered by the distribution agreement.

(b) *Obligations*

   The block exemption permits the distributor to accept obligations to:

   (i) buy complete ranges of products or buy minimum quantities of them;

   (ii) sell goods under trademarks or in packaging determined by the supplier; and

   (iii) promote sales for the goods by taking steps to advertise, maintain stocks, provide backup services and so on.

These conditions relating to restrictions and obligations from the 'white list clauses'. The 'black list clauses' which must not be present if the block exemption is to apply are aimed at preventing a variety of potential abuses. The exemption will not apply to reciprocal exclusive distributorship agreements entered into by manufacturers of goods which can be regarded as being identical or at least equivalent. This is designed to prevent the situation where manufacturers of competing goods, in effect, agree that each shall have exclusive rights to market the product in particular territories. (Even if the agreement is not reciprocal, the block exemption will still not apply unless the total annual turn-over of one or more of the manufacturers does not exceed 100 million Euros (formerly ECU).) Given that this area of regulation is aimed at ensuring there is proper competition, hardly surprisingly the block exemption will not apply if the effect of entering into the exclusive distributorship agreement means that there is a single supplier of the products which are the subject matter of the agreement in the territory in question. It should be emphasised that the block exemption only

BUSINESS CONTRACTS — AGENCY OR DISTRIBUTORSHIP AGREEMENTS

applies to *exclusive* distributorship agreements. Therefore, if the distributorship agreement which the parties enter into is either a 'sole' or a 'non-exclusive' agreement, the block exemption will not apply, and if the agreement is caught by Article 81 the parties will have to decide whether they can use the points described above to give them protection from Article 81.

33.4.2.3 Selective distribution agreements and competition issues

As we explained in **33.4.1.4** above, a selective distribution agreement will limit the number of distributors of a supplier's goods in a particular territory. The anti-competition rules of both the EC and the UK can apply where the supplier uses the selective distributorship arrangements to maintain prices (by, for example, terminating a distribution agreement with a distributor who wishes to reduce the sale price of the goods which are the subject matter of the arrangement).

A supplier wishing to enter into selective distribution arrangements will not fall foul of the anti-competition rules if he uses objective criteria for deciding with which entities to enter into the selective distribution arrangements. The objective criteria can relate to the distributor's technical and financial resources, but the supplier must take care to ensure that the criteria are applied in the same way to all the potential distributors and that there is no discrimination against one or more of the potential distributors.

Apart from making sure that there are no provisions which offend the general UK or EC competition rules, the supplier must be sure that the goods which would be the subject matter of the selective distributive arrangements are suitable for that kind of distributorship scheme. High value consumer goods are suitable, while food is probably not. The criteria which the supplier applies must not be more rigorous than is necessary to ensure the distributorship scheme works efficiently. This means that requiring the distributor to provide repair facilities at central locations within each region of the territory covered by the arrangement is probably acceptable, whereas a provision requiring repair facilities to be available at each retail outlet of the distributor probably is not.

33.4.3 THE PROVISIONS OF EXCLUSIVE DISTRIBUTION AGREEMENTS

In this section we will look, in outline, at the key provisions which could be included in such agreements.

33.4.3.1 Exclusivity

The very nature of such agreements are that they should grant exclusive rights to the products to the distributor, and the rights and obligations imposed on both sides of the agreement must be clearly stated. Care should be taken when drafting these provisions to ensure that the block exemption for exclusive distributive agreements applies (see above).

33.4.3.2 Term

If a supplier is using the exclusive distributorship agreement as a way of establishing its products in a new territory, it will obviously want to ensure that the distributor he chooses is encouraged to put in the necessary marketing effort to achieve the supplier's aim. Accordingly, the supplier will probably want to offer the distributor a long term contract while reserving for himself the right to terminate the agreement if, for example, there is a major structural or financial change to the distributor adversely affecting the promotion of the supplier's goods. The distributor will probably also be keen to enter into a long term arrangement with the supplier as it will ensure continuity of supply of the goods. However, from the distributor's viewpoint, such long term arrangements can have their problems, for example if the supplier tries to impose an obligation of a heavy 'minimum purchase commitment' on the distributor.

Furthermore, should the agreement be for a fixed term the distributor will probably want to include a provision giving him the right to extend the term provided the arrangements specified by the agreement are working satisfactorily. He will want to do this as a way of protecting his investment if he has spent time and money promoting the supplier's goods. The distributor will not want to face the risk of the supplier switching the distributorship arrangement to another, cheaper distributor after the initial effort of establishing the product in the territory has been made.

33.4.3.3 Minimum purchase commitment

A distributorship agreement can be a way of guaranteeing a market for some at least of the supplier's products and many exclusive distributorship agreements contain a provision to this effect (whether setting a minimum purchase requirement for each year of the agreement or over the whole term of the agreement). Such a requirement can be unattractive to a distributor who will not only have to lay out funds to promote the goods, but may also have to lay out funds to buy stocks before the market in the goods has been properly established.

33.4.3.4 Territory

The area which the agreement will cover should be specified and obviously should be realistic given the resources and expertise of the distributor.

33.4.3.5 Price, payment, title and delivery

Most agreements will provide for an agreed price for the goods to be supplied at the start of the term of the agreement but the supplier will usually reserve the right to increase the price subsequently to cover increased manufacturing costs and the like. If this right to increase the price is entirely at the discretion of the supplier, the distributor can find himself in an extremely difficult financial position, especially where he is subject to a minimum purchase commitment. Therefore, distributors try to limit the rights of the supplier to increase prices to inflation-linked rises, or increases in the cost of production, as well as trying to ensure that the prices can only be increased at fixed intervals (say, annually).

Whatever the price agreed may be, the supplier will want to ensure he receives payment before he loses control of the goods. One device which is often incorporated into these agreements is a provision permitting the supplier to retain title of the goods until full payment has been received.

From the distributor's point of view, he will need to ensure that the goods are delivered on time to mesh in with his own distribution schedules. The distributor will usually try to include in the agreement a provision enabling him to claim damages from the supplier for late delivery.

33.4.3.6 Trade mark and patents

The agreement should include provisions dealing with whether the distributor must sell on the goods using the supplier's trade mark or whether the distributor can re-brand them. Similarly, there must be protections built into the agreement to cover the situation where there is any allegation of an intellectual property right infringement (usually in the form of an indemnity given by the supplier to the distributor in such circumstances).

33.4.3.7 Restrictive covenants, warranties and exclusion clauses

The supplier will often want to protect himself from the distributor taking advantage of any knowledge acquired in the course of the distributorship agreement. The nature of the restrictive covenants which the supplier will want to impose will depend on the

BUSINESS CONTRACTS — AGENCY OR DISTRIBUTORSHIP AGREEMENTS

circumstances, but might include preventing the distributor acting as a distributor for competing goods produced by a rival supplier (but whether such a provision will be enforceable will depend on the nature of the restriction).

The distributor may be willing to rely on the warranties given by the Sale of Goods Act 1979 but the supplier will usually give express warranties (subject to exclusion clauses usually limiting or excluding altogether a supplier's liability for any loss of profits the distributor suffers).

33.4.3.8 Other clauses

There may be a variety of other clauses which the parties will want to consider, such as obligations imposed on the distributor in relation to marketing, reporting, providing adequate technical backup, taking out appropriate insurance, seeking any necessary approvals, dealing with assignment of the benefit of the contract and disputes.

33.4.3.9 Other types of distributorship agreements

The terms of the other types of distributorship agreements (see **33.4.1** above) will often be broadly similar to those found in exclusive distributorship agreements, save that the terms creating the exclusive nature of the arrangement will, obviously, not apply.

33.5 The Competition Act 1998

33.5.1 INTRODUCTION

The Competition Act 1998 received Royal Assent on 9 November 1998. Agreements entered into both before and after that date are affected. The Act came fully into force on 1 March 2000 at which date the Resale Prices Act 1976, the Restrictive Trade Practices Act 1976 and the bulk of the Competition Act 1980 were repealed. Most agreements entered into prior to 1 March 2000, benefited from a twelve month exclusion from that date from the effect of the Act. This was to allow businesses time to make arrangements to deal with any changes which may have been required to their contractual arrangements to comply with the Act.

33.5.2 THE PROHIBITIONS

33.5.2.1 General

The prohibitions are known as Chapter I and Chapter II prohibitions. Chapter I of the Act is concerned with anti-competitive agreements and Chapter II is concerned with abuse of a dominant position within the market. Put simply, Articles 81 and 82 of the Treaty of Rome have been transposed into UK legislation. However, the Act does not replace them, rather, its prohibitions run in parallel with those of the EU. As such, only agreements which affect trade within the UK and the behaviour of undertakings dominant in the UK will be governed by the Act. There is, however, an obligation on the courts to interpret the Act in accordance with principles of EC competition law.

The effect of an agreement does not have to extend across the whole of the UK. If an agreement is only intended to operate in part of the UK, that will be sufficient.

33.5.2.2 Chapter 1 prohibition

Agreements between undertakings which may affect trade within the UK and have as their object or effect the prevention, restriction or distortion of competition within the UK are caught by this prohibition. Any such agreement will be void, or, if the offending terms are severable from the rest of the agreement in question, those terms. In addition, the parties concerned may face fines of up to 10% of their UK turnover.

It is proposed that only agreements which have an *appreciable* effect on competition will be prohibited. It is thought that only if the market share of the parties to the agreement in question exceeds 25% will an agreement have an appreciable effect. It is anticipated that this will take many agreements outside the prohibition. However, if the purpose of any agreement is price-fixing, resale price maintenance or market sharing, the issue of appreciability is irrelevant. A further exception is a category of agreements identified in the Act as 'small agreements'. If an agreement is 'small', no fine will be imposed in respect of it. Regulations defining these agreements have yet to be published. However, all price-fixing agreements fail to qualify.

It is important to note that for the purposes of the Act, if an agreement is intended only to operate in a part of the UK, that part will constitute the UK. It is unnecessary for an agreement to be shown to have an appreciable effect on competition across the whole of the UK. Similarly, in this instance, market share presumably need not be assessed on a UK-wide basis, so it may be a mistake to assume that agreements between small local undertakings are not caught by the Act.

33.5.2.3 Chapter 2 prohibition

Conduct by one or more undertakings which amounts to the abuse of a dominant position in a market which may affect trade within the UK or part of it is caught by this prohibition. Taking a lead from EC law, a forty per cent market share can be viewed as dominance.

Parties which infringe the Chapter 2 prohibition may be requested by the Director General of Fair Trading to modify or cease such conduct. They may also be fined in the same way as for a breach of the Chapter 1 prohibition. There is an exception to this second sanction if the conduct is of 'minor significance'. This is to be determined by reference to the turnover of the person involved and the size of the market affected by the conduct in question. As yet, the specifics of this have not been finalised.

33.5.2.4 Chapter 1 exemptions

As well as the possible exclusion due to lack of appreciability discussed above, there are four main exemptions to this prohibition:

(a) Individual exemption granted by the Director General of Fair Trading — must be applied for. This may take two forms: either the agreement does offend the prohibition, but will be exempted because of some perceived greater benefit (akin to art. 81(3) exemption) or confirmation that the agreement does not, in fact, offend against the Act;

(b) Under any block exemption pursuant to the Act — none have yet been confirmed, but any that are will appear in the guise of a statutory instrument;

(c) If an agreement qualifies for the benefit of any EC block exemption. This is the case even if the agreement has no effect on inter-state trade within the EU. As such, it is possible to draft an agreement, the effect of which will be limited to the UK, to comply with a block exemption and gain exemption from the Act. The Act does, however, reserve the right to withdraw the benefit of this exemption if the OFT sees fit;

(d) If the agreement constitutes a vertical agreement. At the time of writing, a draft of The Competition Act 1998 (Land and Vertical Agreements Exclusion) Order 2000 is available as part of a formal consultation draft issued by the Office of Fair Trading. The draft Order contains a definition of vertical agreement virtually identical to that

BUSINESS CONTRACTS — AGENCY OR DISTRIBUTORSHIP AGREEMENTS

contained in Commission Regulation (EC) No. 2790/1999 (see **21.2.4.3**). However, the major difference was that no 30% market share threshold featured in the Order. Also, no vertical agreement which contained a price-fixing arrangement was intended to benefit from the exclusion. It is anticipated that this will become law in substantially the same form as the draft, but the reader should confirm this.

33.5.2.5 Chapter 2 exemptions

The main exemptions to Chapter 2 are contained in Schedules 1 and 3 of the Competition Act. The Act also reserves the right for the Secretary of State to make amendments to these Schedules. The reader is recommended to consult these for the full picture.

It is also possible to apply to the Director General of Fair Trading for guidance as to whether or not the Chapter 2 prohibition is infringed.

33.5.2.6 Enforcement

The Director General of Fair Trading (through the Office of Fair Trading) will enforce competition matters. The Act grants the Director powers to search premises and seize documents etc. as part of the conduct of any investigation into breaches of the Act. In addition, failure to produce documents when requested, the destruction of documentation during an investigation and providing false or misleading information are criminal offences. If such offences are committed by a body corporate, but with the consent or connivance of, or through the neglect of, any director, secretary of manager of that body corporate, that person also commits a criminal offence.

33.5.2.7 Civil liability

Whilst the Act is not explicit on this point, it is understood that third parties affected by breaches of either the Chapter 1 or Chapter 2 prohibitions will have a claim in damages. This is presumably by analogy with the concept of breach of Article 81 entitling a third party to bring a claim, because of its direct effect. Although it is equally possible that a claim can be based on the more 'traditional' ground of breach of statutory duty.

33.5.2.8 Agency and distribution agreements

When considering the impact of the Competition Act on agency and distribution agreements, the first consideration must be jurisdictional. The effect and purpose of the agreement must be to distort competition within the UK or part of it. If the effects of the agreement will be felt solely outside the UK, the Act is irrelevant. In any event, even if the impact or possible impact is limited to the UK only, this may still amount to an agreement which affects inter-state trade within the EU. (See, for example, *Re Vacuum Interrupters Ltd* [1977] 1 CMLR D67.) If this is the case, the agreement should be considered first under Article 81.

Does this mean that the Competition Act can be effectively ignored? This will depend upon whether or not the agreement also raises appreciable issues of competition in the UK. However, if an EC block exemption applies or would apply, but for the fact that the agreement does not affect inter-state trade, this will result in any agreements being automatically exempted from the effect of the Act. The appropriate exemption will be that on vertical agreements. There can be little doubt that a distributorship agreement is 'vertical', but the status of an agency agreement is less certain. Similarly, if a distributorship agreement is neither subject to Article 81(1) nor would it benefit from the EC block exemption, it may well benefit from the exemption under UK law for vertical agreements. Again, there must be doubt as to the status of an agency agreement. However, because 'true' agency agreements are less 'offensive' to the principles of competition law in general, that is, arrangements where the agent is merely an extension of the principal, it is conceivable that neither Article 81(1) nor the Competition Act will be of major concern in relation to such agreements.

33.5.2.9 Conclusion

As is becoming increasingly the case, the Competition Act is legislation which is being introduced piecemeal so at the time of going to press the detail is still to be worked out. Also, as it represents a sea-change in the way competition is regulated in the UK and because of its complex inter-relationship with EC law, it is difficult to predict how both lawyers and the new Competition Commission will react.

Certainly, its rationale is that there should be firmer regulation of competition. Therefore, one would expect greater scrutiny and policing of commercial arrangements. This needs to be contrasted with the apparent freedom proposed to be granted to vertical agreements both under the UK and EC regimes. As such, whether or not agency and distributorship agreements will be afforded lenient treatment remains to be seen.

THIRTY FOUR

LIMITED LIABILITY PARTNERSHIPS

This chapter covers the following topics:

34.1 Introduction
34.2 Key elements of LLPs
34.3 Factors influencing choice
34.4 The prospects for LLPs.

It is recommended that the concepts governing both partnerships and companies have been studied and understood before reading this chapter.

34.1 Introduction

The popularity of private limited companies as business media can be attributed to one thing: the availability of limited liability for the owners and managers. However, the trade-off is public disclosure of much of what the company does, together with a complex regulatory regime. For this reason, the medium of a partnership can still be an attractive choice in certain circumstances, particularly for professional firms.

Of course, one of the major disincentives to setting up in business through the medium of a partnership is the exposure which each partner faces to liabilities of the partnership. Not only is each partner personally liable for all liabilities (either contractual or tortious) of the partnership, there is also no limit on such liability. This has been a source of considerable concern to large professional partnerships, where the work undertaken can be advising on matters running into millions of pounds. With clients becoming increasingly litigious in relation to their advisers, the threat of a massive (and potentially ruinous) claim is ever present.

It is against this background that the concept of limited liability partnerships ('LLPs') has been introduced by the Limited Liability Partnerships Act (LLPA) 2000, which received Royal Assent on 20 July 2000. However, the LLPA 2000 actually came into force on 6 April 2001. It is important to note that the Act merely provides a framework and that the detail is to be introduced by regulations made by the Secretary of State (ss. 14–17 LLPA 2000). Therefore, it is crucial that reference is made to such regulations. At the time of writing, the only regulations in existence are the Limited Liability Partnerships Regulations 2001.

It should be noted at the outset that the LLPA 2000 does not replace the existing regime for partnerships under the PA 1890. It is still possible, therefore, to operate a business as a 'traditional' partnership. In addition, LLPs will be available to any type of business and not limited to professional partnerships.

The key rationale for the creation of LLPs is to allow entrepreneurs the protection of limited liability, while preserving the flexibility of the partnership structure. As such, LLPs can best be described as a hybrid of both companies and partnerships. However, as will become apparent, they owe much more to the former than the latter. (This is reinforced by the fact that s. 1(5) of the LLPA 2000 categorically states that the law of partnerships does not apply to LLPs.)

34.2 Key Elements of LLPs

34.2.1 LIMITED LIABILITY

Third parties who deal with LLPs will contract and deal with the LLP as a distinct legal entity (s. 1(2) LLPA 2000). This is in contrast to partnerships, where the partners and the partnership are one and the same. This means that any recourse the third party has will be against the LLP entity and its assets rather than the partners themselves. That much is straightforward. What is more difficult is just how partners will limit their liability. Section 1(4) LLPA 2000 states that members of an LLP shall contribute to the assets of the LLP in the event of its being wound up as is provided for by the Act. Unfortunately, the Act makes no further provision in this regard and it is anticipated that further regulation will be necessary to clarify this issue. However, the expectation is that partners will guarantee to contribute a fixed sum in the event of insolvency, as do members of a company limited by guarantee. Therefore, it is feasible that partners' liability could be limited to as little as £1.

However, it is perhaps an over-simplification to imagine that those involved in LLPs will never incur any form of personal liability. Although the issue is not clear-cut, the belief is that liability for negligent misstatement will still attach to the errors of a partner. This is particularly germane in the instance of a professional LLP, such as a law or accountancy firm. As such, whilst the partnership as a whole may not bear the liability for negligent advice, the individual who gave that advice may be liable.

34.2.2 CREATION

An LLP is very much like a company in that it will have to be registered with the Registrar of Companies and a certificate of incorporation will be issued as proof of this fact (ss. 2 and 3 LLPA 2000). To achieve incorporation, details of the LLP must be entered on form LLP2 and submitted to the Registrar of Companies with a fee of £95. The basic contents are of the form are:

(a) the signatures of two or more persons associated with the business;

(b) name of the LLP (which must end with the words 'Limited Liability Partnership' or 'LLP');

(c) a statement about the intended location of the registered office and the actual address of the same;

(d) the names and addresses of those persons who are to be involved with the business.

This shares similarities with the procedure for registration of a company. However, one major difference is that s. 1(3) of the Act imbues LLPs with unlimited capacity to act. As such, there will be no need to consider the issue of objects and powers and submit a memorandum of association.

LIMITED LIABILITY PARTNERSHIPS

34.2.3 MEMBERS AND DESIGNATED MEMBERS

In the preceding paragraphs reference has been made to 'partners' in LLPs. Strictly speaking, this is incorrect. The persons involved in an LLP will be classed as 'members', thus drawing another parallel with companies.

The initial members of the LLP are those who signed the incorporation document. Further members can join the LLP with the consent of the then current members.

There must be a minimum of two members in an LLP. Should the number fall to one and remain so for at least six months, the benefit of limited liability will cease and the remaining member will be liable together with the LLP for all debts and liabilities incurred during that period. This requirement excludes the availability of LLPs for sole traders. It also puts LLPs at a disadvantage as compared to private limited companies which can allow their membership to fall to one, should the situation ever arise.

There is a special class of members known as 'designated members', as specified by s. 8 LLPA 2000. The incorporation document will have to contain details of such members. Their key responsibility is in relation to ensuring that the LLP's accounts are signed off and filed with the Registrar of Companies.

34.2.4 DISCLOSURE REQUIREMENTS

As with companies, the *quid pro quo* for limited liability is public disclosure. The key filing responsibilities of an LLP are:

- The filing of accounts.

- The filing of an annual return.

- The notification of changes to the membership.

- The notification of changes in designated members.

- The notification of a change to the registered office.

34.2.5 RELATIONSHIP OF MEMBERS WITH THE LLP, EACH OTHER AND THIRD PARTIES

34.2.5.1 LLP

Every member is an agent of the LLP (s. 6(1) LLPA 2000). This presumably means that members acting with either actual or apparent authority have the power to bind the firm, although the Act does not make this point explicitly. What the Act does do, however, is provide an exception to this basic rule, which is akin to the 'unless' exception in s. 5 of the PA 1890. Thus, if any member is acting without authority and the person he is dealing with either knows that he has no authority or does not know or believe him to be a member, the LLP will not be bound by the acts of the member.

Persons ceasing to be members of LLPs can still operate as its agents until either the third party is notified of the fact or notice is sent to the Registrar of Companies.

LLPs are also liable for the wrongful acts or omissions of individual members, when acting in the course of the LLP's business (s. 6(4)) to the same extent as the member. The LLPA 2000 is silent on the meaning of 'wrongful acts or omissions'. Presumably it includes tortious acts, but does it also include criminal acts?

More difficult still is the issue of ownership by the members of a stake in the LLP. Shareholders in a company can point to an asset which represents their holding in the company. Similarly, partners in a 'traditional' partnership have a direct proprietorial stake in the assets used by the partnership or at least a claim in their proceeds of sale (see *Popat v Schonchhatra* [1997] 3 All ER 800). However, with LLPs, the separation between the legal entity and its owners exists, without any legal mechanism being in place to record ownership. Therefore, if an LLP uses its funds to buy an asset, that asset is owned by the LLP. However, in substance, the members will be of the view that it is their money which has been used and, therefore, the property is theirs. Furthermore, profits made by the LLP will be profits of that entity, but must be available to the members.

The LLPA 2000 is silent on this issue, presumably on the basis that LLPs should be free to govern their internal affairs as they see fit. Therefore, to ensure certainty, members will have to enter into arrangements with their LLPs (contractual or otherwise) to provide for these issues. The exact nature of such a relationship will have to be determined carefully. However, if no such formal arrangement exists, reg. 7, para. (1) of the Limited Liability Partnerships Regulations 2001 provides that members are entitled to share equally in the capital and profits of the LLP.

Regulation 7, para. (1) borrows heavily from s. 24(1) PA 1890. Underpinning that section is the basic premise that partners have a legal or equitable right to the assets and profits of a partnership. Therefore, s. 24(1) merely operates to apportion such ownership. Regulation 7, para. (1) has no such legal underpinning and moreover is only to apply if not displaced by any specific agreement. As such, it is arguable that in neither the LLPA 2000 nor the Limited Liability Partnerships Regulations 2001 is there an absolute statement about the rights of ownership which members enjoy in an LLP. Also, because of the effect of s. 1(5) LLPA 2000 it is not possible to treat members of an LLP as equivalent to partners in terms of their legal status.

Such a situation is unsatisfactory. For example, if members of an LLP enter into an agreement amongst themselves (but not with the LLP itself) which states that they are to share profits unequally, this presumably displaces reg. 7. If so, upon what basis can they claim that the LLP's money is theirs, other than by implication? Alternatively, if members and LLPs are free to organise their affairs as they see fit, would it be possible for the LLP to hold assets on trust for the members as beneficiaries? If so, how would this be represented in the accounts which must follow a specific format? It is clearly a serious shortcoming in the new law that one of the most fundamental issues has been left to an unhappy alliance of implication and circumstance.

34.2.5.2 Each other

As stated above, members of LLPs are free to organise their internal affairs as they wish. This is the flexibility of the existing partnership regime which the Government has wished to preserve. Doubtless the basis for any such agreement will be pre-existing partnership deeds, although these obviously cannot be left unamended. Should such an agreement not be in place, the default provisions in the Limited Liability Partnership Regulations 2001 can be relied upon. However, many of these will not be satisfactory for all but the simplest of LLP arrangements.

34.2.5.3 Third parties

Essentially there is no relationship between members of LLPs and third parties. Therefore, unlike in a partnership, issues of liabilities of a business following a member after retirement do not arise. However, as has been mentioned already, it is possible that, in certain circumstances, individual members may find themselves liable in tort to third parties, particularly when giving professional advice.

Also, there may be instances where due to the principal/agent relationship between an LLP and its members, a member may be held liable for breach of warranty of authority to an outsider.

34.2.6 TAXATION

The principle of separate legal personality is not maintained as far as taxation is concerned, so an LLP is not a taxable person. Instead, as with partnerships, it is the members who are taxed as profit centres.

34.2.7 IMPACT OF OTHER ACTS

Sections 14–16 LLPA 2000 allow for the Secretary of State to make provision for company and insolvency law to apply to LLPs. This has been done through the Limited Liability Partnership Regulations 2001. As such, large tracts of the Companies Act 1985, the Directors Disqualification Act 1986 and the Insolvency Act 1986 apply to LLPs. For example:

- LLPs' accounts have to be audited in accordance with the Companies Act 1985 to give a true and fair view of the business.

- Charges granted by LLPs over their assets have to be registered at Companies House.

Members of LLPs can face disqualification orders, such that they can be neither members of other LLPs nor company directors.

Insolvent LLPs are subject to the same insolvency regime as companies.

34.3 Factors Influencing Choice

There will be two instances where the question of choosing an LLP arises: as part of a business start-up or existing partnerships considering conversion. When considering LLPs, it should always be remembered that their resemblance to traditional partnerships is an exception rather than a rule and that it is better to think of them as corporate structures.

The authors consider that there is very little likelihood of the members of an existing company wishing to alter its status to that of an LLP, as this will alter fundamentally their relationship with each other and their business medium, with no corresponding benefit.

34.3.1 BUSINESS START-UP

One easy decision can be made at the outset, when advising on the appropriate business medium. If only one person is to be involved in the venture, neither a partnership nor an LLP is possible. Thereafter the basic rules about choice of business medium (as set out in **Chapter 31**) apply and, whilst there are three possible formats to choose from, the basic choice is between a corporate entity (company or LLP) or a partnership. In turn, this means a choice between limited liability, public disclosure, substantial regulations and compliance and unlimited liability, absolute secrecy and very limited compliance. This distinction is, however, blurred when taxation is considered, because LLPs do share the taxation regime of partnerships rather than companies.

If a decision is made in favour of a corporate entity, then some of the distinctions to be drawn are as follows:

(a) The decision-making regime within an LLP can be as simple or as complex as the members wish. There is no such choice with companies. However, the two-tier

LIMITED LIABILITY PARTNERSHIPS

decision-making process within companies (that is, directors and shareholders) may allow for greater flexibility in power-sharing.

(b) Raising capital is still likely to be easier through a company, because of the flexibility inherent in shares as an investment mechanism. If, however, the business is likely to remain close-knit and to rely primarily upon its initial members for finance, this may not be a disincentive to choosing an LLP.

(c) Within the framework of a company there is more scope for leaving profits within the company or paying them out. Within an LLP, profits earned are taxed in the hands of the members, irrespective of whether or not they are drawn out.

(d) The regime for companies is relatively clear and well-understood, whereas the regime governing LLPs may throw up unforeseen problems as it matures.

(e) It is relatively inexpensive to set up a company and considerable precedents exist for many permutations of memoranda and articles. Whilst an LLP members' agreement is not a requirement of law, clients would be ill-advised not to have one. At present the length and complexity of such documents is an unknown quantity and may result in a considerable initial cost burden.

34.3.2 CONVERSION FROM PARTNERSHIP TO LLP

Much of what has just been discussed will be relevant in this situation also. However, a number of other issues may have to be considered, such as:

(a) The cost of conversion. The re-draft of any existing partnership deed may be a lengthy and costly process. In addition, there is the practical issue that every existing partner should sign the incorporation document and it should contain their addresses. In a professional partnership of, say, more than 100 partners worldwide, this would pose logistical problems.

(b) The cost/management of disclosure. Notification must be made every time a member either joins or leaves and every time a member's address changes. Again in large partnerships this is an extra burden of bureaucracy. Moreover, having such details on the public register may be regarded as undesirable by some.

(c) Disclosure of financial information. For professional partnerships, the disclosure of accounts is seen by many to be a major disincentive to adopting LLP status. Also, the accounts of a partnership are prepared for the purposes of internal consumption and those of the Inland Revenue, whereas the accounts of an LLP will have to conform to the standards and requirements set out in the Companies Act 1985.

(d) Borrowing. When a bank lends to a partnership, it can take comfort from the fact that the individual estates of the partners will be available to meet any shortcomings in the assets of the firm. Such comfort would be removed if conversion to an LLP took place. To overcome this, banks may ask individual partners to act as guarantors of the LLP, thus partially eroding the benefits of limited liability. Furthermore, individuals cannot grant floating charges; LLPs can. As such, whereas a partnership is free from the threat of the appointment of an administrative receiver, an LLP may not be.

(e) Leasehold property. Many of the same issues for banks arise in relation to any leases the partnership may hold.

(f) Novation of key contracts. Contracts with the existing firm will have to become contracts with the LLP.

(g) Ownership of assets. As mentioned in **34.2.5.1** it would appear that members of an LLP will own part of the LLP, rather than the LLP's assets direct. Conversion will, therefore, require the transfer of the business of the firm into the hands of the LLP. However, the LLP cannot offer shares in return, as would happen if a partnership were to convert to a company. It makes no sense for the LLP to pay the partners cash for the assets, as this would involve the LLP borrowing money effectively to return every partner's capital contribution. Instead the price of the assets could be left outstanding, in which case every partners' capital account is converted into a members' loan account, which may have accounting implications as it is likely that they will contain different figures. An alternative approach may be to make the consideration for the assets the entering into an agreement by the LLP with the prospective members, which sets out the rights of ownership the members have in the LLP. Whichever method is chosen will be a tax-neutral event, as the sale to the LLP will not be treated as a disposal for capital gains tax purposes. Moreover, in most circumstances, no stamp duty will be payable.

34.4 The Prospects for LLPs

The introduction of the LLP may have a profound impact upon the way people carry on business in the United Kingdom and it may be chosen in preference to starting up a new company. Certainly, when faced with a client who wishes to operate a small, closely-held business, the option of forming an LLP has considerable attractions.

However, the governing law is an unhappy amalgam of two regimes which are based on diametrically opposed premises. In fact, it may not be an over-statement to say that Parliament has put together the front end of a sports car with the back end of an estate car in order to produce a saloon car!

Therefore, it is anticipated that in the immediate future, choosing to run an enterprise through the medium of an LLP is a somewhat 'speculative' act, as there are a number of fundamental problems which have yet to be overcome.

INDEX

Accounting bases
  bills delivered basis 135
  cash basis 135
  earnings basis 135, 140–1
Accounting period 136
Accounting reference date 60
  alteration
    method 60
    reasons 60
Accounts *see* Company accounts
Acid test 299
Administration orders 241
  administrative receivership and 246, 249–50
  administrator 243
    powers and duties 244–5
  'balance sheet test' 243–4
  consequences of order 244
  consequences of petition 243
  discharge of order 246
  discretion by court 243–4
  grounds for petition 242–3
  moratorium 246
    continuation 244
    creation 243
  partnerships 257
  petitioners 242
  property
    fixed charge 245
    floating charge 244–5
  proposals 245
  statement of affairs 245
  voluntary arrangements and 247
  winding up and 246
  stay on 243
Administrative receivers 243
  administration and 246, 249–50
  definition 248
  powers and duties
    disposal of property subject to prior charge 249
    general powers 248–9
    investigation and report into affairs 249
    legal position 249
    preferential creditor payment 249
Advance corporation tax
  abolition 177
  surplus 177
Agency 332–3
  agency by estoppel 75–6
  appointment of agent 342

Agency — *continued*
  authority 342
    actual 75
    apparent 19–20, 75–6
    express actual 18
    implied actual authority 18
    partner 18
    usual 75–6
  commercial agents 335
  Commercial Agents Regulations 333, 334–40
  commission 336–7, 343–4
  company and 45, 75–6
  compensation 337–40
  competition issues
    Competition Act 1998 352
    EC rules 340–2
    UK rules 340
  disclosed and undisclosed principal 334
  disputes 340
  duration 343
  duties of agents and principals 336, 343
  exclusive 333
  general rules 333–4
  liability of agent to third party 76
  non-exclusive 333
  partnerships and 18–20
    persons held out as partner 19, 21
  post-termination indemnity 337–40
  provision of information 337
  provisions of agreement 342–4
  ratification 76
  regulation 333–44
  remuneration 336
  restraint of trade 340
  restriction on customers, territory and exclusivity 343
  restrictive covenants 344
  sole agency 333
  subject matter of agreement 342–3
  termination 337, 344
Agenda 128
Agricultural forestry buildings 195
Agricultural property relief 158
Alternate directors 72
Alternative Investment Market 159, 161, 328
Annual general meeting 123
  default in holding 126
Annuities, partnership retirements 202
'Approved sponsor' 328, 329

INDEX

Arbitration 286
  between partners 24
Articles of association 56
  address of first registered office 54
  alteration 88, 274, 314
    benefit of company 276–7
    class rights 277
    decision of shareholders 276
    discrimination 276–7
    power to alter 275, 286
    registration 275
  amendment 54
  choice of form 53–4
  directors 54, 274–5
  dividends 89
  enforcement 284
  first directors and secretary 54
  Form 10 54
  Form 12 54
  meetings 274
  membership 44
  private companies 271–7
  registration fee 54
  share capital 272
  share issue 44, 272
  share transfer 44, 272–4
    variation of articles 274
  source of company law 40
  statutory declaration of compliance with registration requirements 54
  Table A 53–4, 271–5
  written resolutions 129
Auditors, notification of resolutions 129
Authorised minimum capital 42, 322
Authorised share capital 53

Balance sheet 295–7
Bankruptcy 227–39
  assets in estate
    avoidance of dispositions 233
    distribution *see* distribution of assets
    family home 235
    property not available to trustee 233
    transactions defrauding creditors 233–4
    undervalue transactions 234
    vesting in trustee 233
    voidable preferences 234–5
  committee of creditors appointment 231
  companies *see* Insolvency procedures
  consequences of petition
    restrictions on dispositions 230
    restrictions on proceedings 230
  creditor's petition
    court dismissal grounds 229
    grounds 228–9
    prerequisites for presentation 228
    proving inability to pay debts 229
  debtor's petition 229
  discharge of bankrupt 237
  distribution of assets
    priority order 236
    procedure 235
  DPP petition 230
  official receiver 230
  order
    effect on bankrupt person 232–3
    making of 230

Bankruptcy — *continued*
  procedure following 230–1
  partner 28
  petitioners 228
  procedure 228–31
  public examination 230
  statement of affairs 230
  supervisor's petition 229–30
  trustee in bankruptcy
    appointment
      by court 231
      by creditors 231
      by Secretary of State 231
    functions 231
    powers 231–2
    property not available to 233
    removal 232
    resignation 232
    vesting of assets 233
  undischarged bankrupt 232
  voluntary arrangements *see* Voluntary arrangements (individuals)
  voluntary scheme 229–30
Benefits in kind 173, 182–4
Bills delivered basis 135
Board meetings 123
  decisions 66
Bonus shares, taxation 176
Book debts 306
Books of the company *see* Statutory books
Business property relief 158–60, 161–2, 203, 204, 318
  anti-avoidance 160
  'business' 159
  period of ownership 159
  potentially exempt transfers 160

Capital
  companies *see* Share capital
  partnerships 267
    interest on 12–13
    partners' 10–11
    sharing 12
  risk of 311–13
Capital allowances 191–5
  agricultural forestry buildings 195
  cemeteries 195
  companies 166
  crematoria 195
  dredging 195
  hotels 195
  industrial buildings
    balancing charge 194
    definition 194
    'residue of expenditure' 194
    sale 194–5
    writing down allowance 194
  know-how 195
  mines and mineral rights 195
  patents 195
  plant and machinery
    balancing charge allowance 192
    definition 191–2
    leasing 193–4
    motor cars 194
    pooling 193
    qualifying expenditure 192
    unrelieved expenditure 192

INDEX

Capital allowances — *continued*
    use of allowances 193–4
    pooling 193
    sale of business to company 302
    scientific research 195
Capital gains tax
    allowable deductions 144
    allowable expenditure
        creation of losses 145
        part disposals 144
    'business assets', roll over relief 148, 150
    business assets owned by investor 155
        retirement relief 156
        roll-over relief 156
    business property relief *see* Business property relief
    charged tax 143–4
    choice of business medium 317
    companies 166
        purchase of own share 162–3
        re-investment relief 151–2
        retirement relief 154–5
        undervalue sales 149
    death of taxpayer 152
    deferment of liability 151–2
    'disposal' 143–4
    EIS deferral of chargeable gains 151–2, 201
    hold over relief 149, 156
        gifts 148
    indexation allowance 144–5
        creation of losses 145
        replacement by tapering relief 146
    losses creation 145
    part disposal 144
    partnerships 153–4
        admission of new partner 205–6
        assessment 153
        asset surplus ratio 153
        death of partner 203
        dissolution 198
        reliefs 154
        retirement 198–202
            disposals amongst partners 199–201
            entitlement to relief 201
            goodwill 201
            payment of annuities 202
            personally owned assets 202
            relief 154
    rate of tax 152
    re-investment relief 151–2
    reliefs
        general 147–8
        see also individual reliefs eg tapering relief
    retirement relief 148–9, 305
        business assets owned by investor 156
        companies 154–5
        partnerships 154, 201
    roll over relief 150, 154
        business assets 150
            owned by investor 156
    sale of business to company
        assets transferred 303
        disposal 302–4
        gifts of business assets 304
        hold over relief 304
        payment methods 304
        reliefs 303–4
        retention of assets 304–5

Capital gains tax — *continued*
    retirement relief 305
    roll over relief 305
    shares 154–5, 162–3
    taper relief 305, 317
        'business assets' 146
            partly 147
        operation 147
    taxable person 143–4
    transfers between spouses 147, 149
Cash basis 135
Cassis principle 215–16
Cemeteries, capital allowance 195
Certificate of incorporation 55, 323
Charges
    avoidance 111
    fixed 105, 106–7, 110–11
        creditors with 254–5
        debenture document 281
    floating 105, 107–8, 111
        creditors with 256
        debenture document 281–2
        insolvency and 261
    instruments creating 57
    mortgages 106–7
    over land 110
    priority 110–11
    registration
        CA 1985 requirement 108
        CA 1989 system 110
        certificate 109
        extension of time limit 109
        method 108
        non-registration 109–10
        register of charges 56, 57, 108–9, 110
Class rights, alteration 277
Close companies 43
    corporation tax 172–3
    inheritance tax 318
Close investment holding companies 173
Comfort letters 342, 346
Commercial Agents Regulations 333
    application of 335–6
    commercial agents 335
    commission 336–7
    compensation 337–40
    competition issues 340–2
    dispute settlement 340
    duties 336
    information provision 337
    jurisdiction 334–5
    post-termination indemnity 337–40
    remuneration 336
    restraint of trade 340
    termination 337
    territorial application 334–5
Companies
    agency and *see* Agency
    articles *see* Articles of association
    authorised minimum share capital 42, 322
    books *see* Statutory books
    borrowing powers
        exercise of 105
        express and implied 105
        'ultra vires' borrowing 105
    capital *see* Share capital
    capital gains tax

INDEX

Companies — *continued*
    business assets owned by investor   155–6
    choice of business medium   317
    EIS deferral of chargeable gains   151–2, 201
    purchase of own shares   162–3
    re-investment relief   151–2
    retirement relief   156
    undervalue sales   149
  certificate of incorporation   55, 323
  certificate to commence business   323
  charges
    avoidance   111
    fixed   105, 106–7, 110–11
    floating   105, 107–8, 111
    priority   110–11
    registration
      CA 1985 requirement   108
      CA 1989 system   110
      certificate   109
      extension of time limit   109
      methods   108
      non-registration   109–10
      register of charges   108–9, 110
  close   43, 172–3
  corporations   39
  differences between public and private   322–3
  directors *see* Directors
  disclosure of information   316
  disputes
    just and equitable winding up   88
    powers of court   87–8
  dissolution   256
  dividends *see* Dividends
  EIS deferral of chargeable gains   151–2, 201
  elective regime company   43
  finance
    assistance for purchase of shares   104
    borrowing   105
    capital *see* Share capital
    charges *see* charges
    debenture-holders remedies *see* Debenture-holders
    lending to company   112–13
    loans, *see also* Debenture-holders
    purchase of own shares   99–104, 119–21, 162–3
    receivers   112
    secured loans   105–8
    share capital *see* Share capital
    shares *see* Shares
    taxation *see individual taxes*
  formation of limited company *see* Formation of company
  income tax, purchase of own shares   162
  inheritance tax   160–1, 173
    choice of business medium   318
  inspection of books   57
  internal disputes   82–8
  internal flexibility   314
  legal status   44, 315
  liability clause   52–3
  lifting the veil   44–6
  limited
    by guarantee   41, 321
    by shares   41, 321
    formation *see* Formation of company
  listing *see* Stock Exchange listing
  loans
    fixed charges   105, 106–7

Companies — *continued*
    floating charges   105, 107–8
    types of security   105–6
  management   314–15
  medium-sized   43, 293
  members *see* Shareholders
  memorandum of association *see* Memorandum of association
  name   42
    change   51, 59
    choice   50–1, 59
    letters and order forms   56
    liability of officers   55
    notification of change   59
    passing-off   51
    PLC   322
    publication   55–6
    stationery   56
  objects   51–2, 60
  'off the peg' company   47–9, 313
    advantages and disadvantages   59
    articles of association   58
    documentation   58
    name   57–8
  partnership company   43
  private
    differences between public and   42–3
    see also Private company
  profits   88–9
  public
    differences between private and   42–3
    see also Public company
  quoted   43
  registered office   51, 54
  registration   40–1, 323
  retirement relief   156
  sale of business to *see* Partnerships: Sole traders
  seal   55
  secretary   54, 76, 314, 322
  separate legal personality   44
  shareholders *see* Shareholders
  shares
    issuing *see* Issue of shares
    payment for   42
  'shelf' company *see* 'off the peg' company
  small   43, 293
  sources of company law
    articles of association   40
    general law   40
    judicial decisions   40
    legislation   39–40
    tax legislation   40
  statutory books *see* Statutory books *and individual registers*
  succession to business   315
  'tailor made' company   57
  taxation
    interest relief   317
    legislation   46
    profits   316
    see also capital gains tax: Corporation tax; inheritance tax
  ultra vires doctrine   51–2
  unlimited   41, 321
Companies House Direct   292

INDEX

Company accounts 324
  balance sheet 295–7
  duty to submit accounts 292–3
  efficiency ratios 300
  format 297
  group accounts 45, 46
  interpretation 297–8
  investment 300
  limits inherent in 298–9
  profit and loss accounts 294–5
  profitability 299
  small and medium sized companies 293
  solvency 299
  sources of information 298
  see also Accounting bases; Accounting period; Accounting reference date
Company cars 183–4
Company meetings see Meetings
Company searches 289, 290
  Companies House Direct 292
  failure to file returns 292
  information available for inspection 291–2
  methods 292
  official notification 290
  personal search 292
  post 292
  procedure for making 292
  telephone 292
Company secretary 314, 322
  appointment 76
  first 54, 76
  register of secretaries 79
  responsibilities and powers 76–7
Competition
  agency relationships 340–2
  comfort letters 342, 346
  distributorship agreements 344–50
    selective distribution agreements 348
  EC see European Community competition issues
  UK Act 1998 see Competition Act 1998
  UK rules 340, 345
Competition Act 1998
  agency agreement 352
  civil liability 352
  enforcement 352
  European Community competition issues and 223
  exemptions
    block 351
    individual 351
    vertical agreement 352
  prohibitions 350–1
    anti-competitive agreements 351
    dominant position abuse 351
Compulsory winding up
  discretion of court to refuse order 251
  grounds 250
  liquidators 252
  locus standi 251
  see also Winding up
Concerted practice 220
Connected persons 74
Contracts 331–53
  agency see Agency
  directors' interests in 70
  distributors see Distributorship agreements
  novation 309, 360
Copyright 216, 217

Corporation tax
  ACT
    abolition 177
    shadow 178
    surplus 177
  assessment basis 166–7
  capital allowances 166
  capital gains 166
  charges on income 166
  close companies 172–3
    'benefits in kind' 173
  income 165
  loss relief
    capital losses 172
    carry forward 170–1
    group relief 172
    tactical considerations 171
    use within same accounting period 171
  profits
    calculation 165–6
    in form of dividends 169–70
  rates
    main rate 167–8
    new starting rates 169
    small company rate 168
  retained profits 175, 176
  self assessment 167
  surplus ACT 177
Corporations 39
Costs, winding up 255
Creditors
  fixed charges 254–5
  floating charges 256
  meeting, voluntary arrangements 238–9
  order of entitlement 254–5
  ordinary 256
  petition see Bankruptcy
  preferential 249, 255
  transactions defrauding 233–4, 261
  winding up 251
Crematoria 195
CREST 116
'Current ratio' 299
Current year basis 136, 137, 141–2

'Dassonville' formula 215
Death of partner 28, 36, 268
  debt liability 36
  obtaining amounts due 36
  partnership agreement treatment 36
  share in profits 36
  tax consequences 203–4
  treatment as is retired 36
Death of taxpayer, capital gains tax 152
Debenture documents 279–82
  fixed charges 281
  floating charges 281–2
  interest 280
  personal guarantees 282
  receiver appointment 282
  repayment terms 280
  security 280
Debenture-holders
  position 112
  remedies
    application to court 111–12
    express and implied powers 111

INDEX

Debenture-holders — *continued*
    receiver appointment 112
Debenture stock 106
Debentures 105-6
    public and private companies 322-3
    taxation 186-7
        deduction of tax 187
        loan relationships 186
        paying company taxation 186-7
        recipient taxation 187-8
Debt
    composition 246
    for equity swap 247
    interest on 256
    partnerships 33, 34-5, 36
    preference debts 236
    priority 236
    proving inability to pay debts 229
Debtor's petition *see* Bankruptcy
Defrauding creditors, transactions 233-4, 261
Directors 314, 322
    ages 325
    alternate 72
    appointment 61-2, 275, 284
        defective 74
        managing directors 72
    articles provisions
        appointment 275
        voting restrictions 274-5
    authority to issue shares 97
    board meeting decisions 66
    compensation for loss of position 64
    connected persons 74
    disclosure of information 69-70
    disqualification
        1986 Act 64-5
        articles 65
        fast track 65
    division of powers 61
    duties 286
        care and skill 68-9
        fiduciary duties 67-8, 98
        interests of employees 69
        powers exercised in interests of company 68
        ratification of breach 68
        statutory 68-9
        to third parties 69
    fees *see* Directors' fees, taxation
    first 54
    interests in contracts 70
    loans to 71, 172
    managing 72
    model code on share dealings 329
    names 55, 69, 70
    numbers 42
    powers
        decision by written resolution 66
        definition 65-6
        exercise 66
            in interests of company 68
            managing directors 72
            when interest in resolution 66
    property transactions 71
    protection of outsiders
        agency 75-6
        dealing in good faith 74
        defect in appointment or qualification 74

Directors — *continued*
        statutory protection 73-4
        Turquand rule 75
    register of directors 56, 69-70
    register of directors' interests 56, 70
    removal 275, 314
        by ordinary resolution 63, 64
        compensation right 64
        disqualification 64-5
        retirement 63, 274
    retirement
        by notice 63
        by rotation 63, 274
    secret profits 67-8
    service contracts 57, 62, 70, 72, 284
    shadow 72-3
    voting restrictions 274-5
Directors' fees, taxation
    benefits 180
    benefits in kind 182-4
    compensation for loss of office 180
    'emolument' 181
    employing company's perspective 179-81
    'employment' 181
    fees or interest 188
    limitation on deductibility 180
    national insurance payments 180-1, 189
    'office' 181
    schedule E charge 181
    social security contributions 180-1, 186
    taxable receipts 182
    terminal payments 184-5
Disclosure of information
    agency information 337
    company information 291-2, 316
    directors' information 69-70
    limited liability partnerships 357, 360
    partnership information 9, 316
Disqualification of director 64-5
    fast track 65
    partnerships 257
Dissolution of company 256
Dissolution of partnership 27-33
    application of property 31
    automatic 28-9
    by agreement 28
    by court 29-30
        breach of agreement 24, 29
        conduct prejudicial to business 23-4
        incapable of performance 29
        just and equitable 24, 30
    by notice 28
    insufficiency to meet liabilities 32-3
    legal consequences 30-1
    notification 31-2
    realisation of property 30-1
    tax consequences 198-9
Distributions
    definition 90-1
    public companies 324
    taxation
        ACT 177
            shadow ACT 178
        definition of distribution 176-7
        recipient taxation 178-9
        surplus ACT 177
    unlawful 93

INDEX

Distributions — *continued*
  see also Dividends
Distributorship agreements 332–3
  black list clauses 347
  competition issues
    EC rules 346–8
    UK Act 1998 352
    UK rules 345
  exclusive 344–5
    exclusion clauses 349–50
    exclusivity 348
    minimum purchase commitment 349
    price, payment, title and delivery 349
    restrictive covenant 349–50
    term 348–9
    territory 349
    trade mark and patents 349
    warranties 349–50
  non-exclusive 345
  selective 345, 348
  sole 345
  white list clauses 221, 347
Dividends
  articles of association 89
  classes of shares 90
  interim 89
  legal entitlement to 90
  payments 286
  procedure 89–90
  'profits available'
    calculation of profits and loss 91–2
    definition 90–1
    unrealised losses 92
  'relevant accounts' 92
  restrictions on payment in articles 92
  restrictions on sources 90–3
  Table A provisions 89
  taxation 188–9
  unlawful distributions 93
  see also Distributions
Dominant position abuse 222
Dredging, capital allowance 195
Due diligence investigations 105

Earnings basis 135, 140–1
Efficiency ratios 300
Elective regime company 43
Employees
  directors regard for interests of 69
  transfer of undertakings 307–8
Enterprise Investment Scheme 151–2, 201
European Community
  competition policy *see* European Community competition issues
  establishment right 213–15
  free movement of goods
    Cassis principle 215–16
    'Dassonville' formula 215
    derogation 216–17
    measures of equivalent effect 215–16
    restriction on imports 215
  language requirements 214
  legal aptitude tests 215
  limitations on rights 214–15
  qualification recognition 214–15
  services provision right 213–15

European Community competition issues
  agency relationships 340–2
  Article 81 219–22
  beneficial agreements 221
  black list 221, 347
  block exemptions 221–2, 346–8
  comfort letter clearance 342, 346
  Competition Act 1998 and 223
  concerted practice 220
  direct effect 223
  distributorship agreements 346–8
    negative clearance 346
    notification for exemption 346
  dominant position abuse 222
  enforcement 223
  exemptions 221–2
  horizontal agreements 220
  minor importance agreements 221, 346
  price fixing 220
  vertical agreements 220, 221
  white list 221, 347
Expulsion of partner 204
  content of clause 25
  exercise of clause 25
  partnership agreement 25
Extraordinary general meeting 124

Family home, bankruptcy and 235
Fee (registration) 54
Finance raising, business medium and 318–19
Fixed charges 105, 106–7, 110–11
  creditors with 254–5
  debenture document 281
Floating charges 105, 107–8, 111
  advantages and disadvantages 108
  creditors with 256
  debenture document 281–2
  insolvency and 261
Formation of company
  articles *see* Articles of association
  books *see* Statutory books
  certificate of incorporation 55
  expenses of formation 313–14
  limited company 47–59
  memorandum of association 49–53
  'off the peg' *see* 'off the peg' company
  pre-incorporation contracts 48–9
  promoters 48
  provision of company for client 49
  steps after incorporation 55–7
  'tailor made' company 57
  see also Incorporation
Foss v *Harbottle*
  exceptions 84–5
  majority rule 84
Fraud on the minority 68
Fraudulent trading 45
Free movement of goods
  Cassis principle 215–16
  'Dassonville' formula 215
  derogation 216–17
  intellectual property 216–17
  measures of equivalent effect 215–16
  restriction on imports 215
Funding 318–19

INDEX

Gardening leave 184
General meetings
   annual 123
      default in holding 126
   calling 125–6
   extraordinary 124
   minutes 57
   requisitioning 125–6
Gifts
   business assets 304
   capital gains tax 148, 149, 304
   inheritance tax 158
Golden handshakes 184–5
Goodwill 306
   capital gains tax 30–1, 201
   inheritance tax 202
Group accounts 45, 46
Guarantees, personal 282

Hold over relief 149, 156, 304
   gifts 148
Hotels, capital allowances 195

Income tax
   benefits in kind 182–4
      company cars 183–4
      living accommodation 182–3
      loan arrangements 184
      vouchers 183
   'cash equivalent' 183
   companies, purchase of own shares 162
   directors' fees
      benefits in kind 182–4
      schedule E charge 181
   expense accounts 183
   expenses 186
   golden handshakes 184–5
   higher-paid employees 183–4
   interest relief 317
   living accommodation 182–3
   loan arrangements 184
   loss relief 302
   partnerships 140–2
      admission of new partner 205
      current year basis 141–2
      death of partner 203
      deemed cessation 198–9
      dissolution of partnership 198
      earnings basis 140–1
      interest 141
      losses 142
      no deemed discontinuance 199
      rent 141
      retirement 198–9
      salary 141
      see also sole traders
   purchase of own shares 162
   rent 141
   restrictive covenants payments 186
   sale of business to company
      closing year rules 301
      loss relief 302
   sole traders
      accounting bases 135
      accounting period 136
      charges on income 134
      closing year rules 137, 138

Income tax — *continued*
      current year basis 136, 137
      deductible expenditure 134–5
      early years of trade, losses 140
      future income 139–40
      income definition 134
      losses 138–40
         double relief prevention 140
         early years of trade 140
         set-off against future income 139–40
         set-off against same year income 138–9
      opening year rules 137–8
      preceding year basis 137
      sale of business to company 301–2
      same year income 138–9
      self-assessment 136–7
      stock valuation 135–6
      tax schedules 133–4
      work in hand 135–6
      see also partnerships
   terminal payments 184–5
   vouchers 183
Incorporation
   certificate of 55, 323
   lifting the veil 44–6
   steps leading to 49
   see also Formation of company
Indemnity
   partners 9
   pre-incorporation contracts 48
Index of members 56
Indexation allowance 144–5
   creation of losses 145
   replacement by taper relief 146
Industrial buildings capital allowance
   balancing charge 194
   definition 194
   'residue of expenditure' 194
   sale 194
   writing down allowance 194
Inheritance tax
   agricultural property relief 158
   annual exemption 158, 162, 203
   business property relief 158–60, 161–2, 318
      anti-avoidance 160
      'business' 159
      period of ownership 159
      potentially exempt transfers 160
   chargeable transfer 156, 158
   choice of business medium 318
   companies 160–1, 173, 318
   cumulation 157
   death within seven years 160
   exempt transfers 157, 158
   gifts 158
   instalment payments 160–1
   inter vivos transfer 157, 158, 203
   partnerships 161
      admission of new partner 206
      business property relief 203, 204
      choice of business medium 318
      death of partner 204
      dissolution 198
      goodwill 202
      gratuitous benefit 202
      instalment option 204
      retirement 202–3

INDEX

Inheritance tax — *continued*
    potentially exempt transfer   157, 160
    quick succession relief   158
    related property rules   159
    shareholdings   160–2
    spouse exemption   158, 162
    valuation rules   157–8
Insolvency procedures
    administration order *see* Administration orders
    administrative receivership *see* Administrative receivers
    choice of remedy   249–50
    floating charges   261
    liquidation *see* Winding up
    partnerships   256–7
    personal bankruptcy *see* Bankruptcy
    undervalue transactions   234, 260
    voluntary arrangements *see* Voluntary arrangements
    wrongful trading   259–60
Intellectual property   216–17
Intermediaries offer   329
Introductions   329
Investment   300
Investors, partners compared with   11
Issue of shares   42, 285
    articles and   44, 272
    differences between public and private   322–3
    payment for shares   42, 98
    power to issue   96–8
    return of allotment   98
    to public   98

Just and equitable winding up   88

'Know-how'
    capital allowance   195
    stamp duty   306

Land, charges over   110
Legal entity status   44, 315
    agency and trusts   45
    avoiding legal obligations   45
    company   44
    lifting veil   44–6
Letter of renunciation   58
Lifting veil   44–6
Limited companies *see* Companies
Limited liability partnerships   28, 355–6
    borrowing   360
    business start-up   359–60
    choice   359–61
    conversion from partnership to   360–1
    creation   356
    designated members   357
    disclosure   357, 360
    future prospects   361
    key elements   356–9
    legislation   355, 359
    liability   356
    members   357
    novation   360
    ownership of assets   361
    relationships of members
        with each other   358
        with partnership   357–8
        with third parties   358–9
    taxation   359

Liquidators
    compulsory liquidation   252
    functions   252–3
    official receiver   252
    powers   252–3
    voluntary liquidation   252
Liquidity ratio   299
Listing Rules, The   328
Loans
    fixed charges   105, 106–7
    floating charges   105, 107–8
    income tax on arrangements   184
    partnerships, interest on   13
    to directors   71
    types of security   105–6
London Gazette   32, 35, 290
Losses
    capital losses   172
    corporation tax relief   170–2
    double relief prevention   140
    early years   140
    group relief   172
    income tax relief   302
    partnerships   142
    set-off against future income   139–40
    set-off against same year income   138–9
    sole trader   138–40
    terminal, carry back of   140

Machinery *see* Plant and machinery
Maintenance of share capital   98–9, 114, 324
Managing directors
    appointment   72
    powers   72
    service contract   72
Medium-sized companies   43, 293
Meetings
    agenda   128
    board meetings   66, 123
    creditors', voluntary arrangements   238–9
    dispensing with   128–9
    general meetings
        annual general meeting   123, 126
        calling   125–6
        extraordinary general meeting   124
        minutes   57
        requisitioning   125–6
    minutes   57, 129
    notice
        content   127–8
        length   127
        service   126–7
    quorum   128
    resolutions
        elective   125
        extraordinary   124–5
        ordinary   124
        special   124
        written   325
    returns   129
    Table A   274
    voting   128
Members *see* Shareholders
Memorandum of association   56
    alteration   88
    capital clause   53
    compulsory clauses   49–50

INDEX

Memorandum of association — *continued*
   differences between public and private 322
   formation of company and 49–53
   liability clause 52–3
   name of company *see* Names
   objects 51–2
      alteration 52, 60
   registered office 51
   ultra vires doctrine 51–2
Mines and mineral rights 195
Minutes of meetings 57, 129
Moratorium
   administration orders 243, 244, 246
   voluntary arrangement procedure 247–8
Mortgages 106–7
Motor cars
   benefits in kind 183–4
   capital allowances 194

Names
   companies 42
      change 51, 59
      choice 50–1, 59
      letters and order forms 56
      liability of officers 55
      notification of change 59
      passing-of 51
      plc 322
      publication 55–6
      stationery 56
   'off the peg' company 57–8
   partnerships 266
      approval 6
      automatically permitted 5–6
      disclosure 6
      retirement of partner 35
National insurance contributions
   choice of business medium and 318
   directors' fees
      employee perspective 189
      employing company 180–1
   partnerships 142
   priority debt 236
Novation 309, 360

Occupational pension schemes 318
'Off the peg' company 47–9, 313
   advantages and disadvantages 59
   articles of association 58
   documentation 58
   letter of renunciation 58
   name 57–8
Off-the-shelf *see* 'Off the peg' company
Offer for sale 329
Offering of securities *see* Stock Exchange listing
Official notification 290
Official receiver, as liquidator 252

Partners
   admission 268
   authority
      apparent 19–20
      express actual 18
      implied actual 18
      for winding up 30
   bankruptcy 28
   capital 10–11

Partners — *continued*
   conduct prejudicial to business 29
   death 28, 36, 268
      debt liability 36
      obtaining amounts due 36
      partnership agreement treatment 36
      share in profits 36
      tax consequences 203–4
   decisions of 8
   differences between 8
   disqualification 257
   drawings 14
   duty of good faith
      equitable provisions 9
      statutory provisions 9–10
   duty to account
      for competing business profits 10
      for secret profits 9–10
   duty to disclose information 9
   expulsion 25, 204
   incapable of performance 29
   incoming partners 268–9
   indemnities 9
   insufficiency to meet liabilities 32
   legal relationship between 7
   lenders compared with 11
   liability *see* Partnerships, liability to outsiders
   majority rule 8–9
   new
      liability to outsiders 21
      tax consequences 204–6
   non-competing businesses 10
   number 5
   removal 315
   remuneration 13–14, 141–2
   restrictions on majority 8–9
   retirement 268
      Business Names Act compliance 35
      capital gains tax 198–202
      circumstances when occurs 33
      debts incurred after 33–5
      debts incurred before 33
      finance 35
      income tax 198–9
      inheritance tax 202–3
      legal consequences 33–5
      Partnership Act 1890 33
      section 14 35
      section 36 34–5
      taxation consequences 198–203
   security of tenure 314–15
Partnership agreement
   admission of partners 268
   breach causing dissolution 24, 29
   capital 267
   clauses 266–8
   commencement date 266
   disputes 268
   dissolution 268
   drafting 265–6
   income 266–7
   incoming partner issues 268–9
   management 267
   name 266
   nature of business 266
   necessity for 265–6
   parties 266

INDEX

Partnership agreement — *continued*
   prolonged absence 267
   property 267
   restrictions 267–8
   retirement 268
   term 266
   written 265–6
Partnership company 43
Partnerships
   accounts 141
   administration 257
   agency and 18–20
     apparent authority 19–20
     authority of partner 18
     express actual authority 18
     implied actual authority 18
     person held out as partner 19, 21
   agreement *see* Partnership agreement
   'at will' 5
   automatic dissolution 28–9
   capacity to form 5
   capital
     interest on 12–13
     partners' 10–11
     sharing 12
   capital gains tax 153–4
     admission of new partner 205–6
     assessment 153
     asset surplus ratio 153
     choice of business medium 317
     death of partner 203
     dissolution 198
     relief 154
     retirement 198–202
       disposals amongst partners 199–201
       entitlement to relief 201
       goodwill 201
       payment of annuities 202
       personally owned assets 202
     retirement relief 148–9, 154
   capital risk 311–13
   carried on at loss 29–30
   companies compared 41
   definition 4
   disclosure of information 9, 316
   disputes
     arbitration 24
     dissolution *see* dissolution
     expulsion of partner 25
     receiver appointment 24
   dissolution 27–33
     application of property 31
     automatic 28–9
     by agreement 28
     by court 29–30
       breach of agreement 24, 29
       conduct prejudicial to business 23–4
       incapable of performance 29
       just and equitable 24, 30
     by notice 28
     insufficiency to meet liabilities 32–3
     legal consequences 30–1
     notification 31–2
     realisation of property 30–1
     tax consequences 198–9
   duration 5
   duties *see* Partners

Partnerships — *continued*
   expenses of formation 313–14
   expiration 28
   expulsion from 204
   finance
     division of profits 11–14
     drawings 14
     interest on capital 12–13
     interest on loans 13
     interest payments 14
     partners' capital 10–11
     remuneration 13–14, 141–2
     retirement of partner 35
     sharing capital 12
     sharing losses 12
     sharing profits 12
     sources 10
   funding 318–19
   goodwill 30–1
   illegal activity 28
   income tax 140–2
     admission of new partner 205
     current year basis 141–2
     death of partner 203
     deemed discontinuance 198–9
     dissolution 198
     earnings basis 141
     interest 141
     losses 142
     no deemed discontinuance 199
     rent 141
     retirement 198–9
     salary 141
   inheritance tax 161
     admission of new partner 206
     business property relief 203, 204
     death of partner 204
     dissolution 198
     goodwill 202
     gratuitous benefit 202
     instalment option 204
     retirement 202–3
   insolvency 257
     administration 257
     disqualification 257
     voluntary arrangements 257
     winding up 257
   internal flexibility 314
   law relating to 4
   legal entity status 21–2, 315
   liability to outsiders
     agency and partnerships *see* agency and
     nature of liability 17–18
     new partners 21
     suing or being sued 21–2
     tort 21
   limited liability *see* Limited liability partnerships
   management 8, 314
   name
     in agreement 266
     approval 6
     automatically permitted 5–6
     disclosure 6
     retirement of partner 35
   national insurance contributions 142
   nature of 4
   partners *see* Partners

INDEX

Partnerships — *continued*
  property
    definition 14
    realisation 30–1
    test for 15
  receiver appointment 24
  retirement of partner *see* Partners
  sale of business to company
    capital gains tax 302–4
    capital tax relief 304
    company law 308
    employment law 307–8
    income tax 301–2
    novation 309
    retained assets 304–5
    stamp duty 305–7
    value added tax 305, 308
  secret profits 9–10
  sources of finance 10
  succession 315
  suing or being sued 21–2
  taxation 316–17
    see also capital gains tax: income tax: inheritance tax
  voluntary arrangements 257
  winding up
    priority of creditors 257
    as unregistered company 257
Passing-off 51
Patents
  capital allowance 195
  exclusive distributorship agreements 349
  stamp duty 306
Pensions
  occupational pension schemes 318
  personal pensions 318
  see also Retirement provision
Perpetual succession 44
Personal guarantees 282
Personal pensions 318
Personal representatives 119
Personality *see* Legal entity status
Placing 329
Plant and machinery
  capital allowance
    balancing charge allowance 192
    definition 191–2
    leasing 193–4
    motor cars 194
    pooling 193
    qualifying expenditure 192
    unrelieved expenditure 192
    use of allowances 193–4
  stamp duty 306
Poll 128
Pooling 193
Pre-emption rights 97–8, 118–19, 285, 286, 324
Pre-incorporation contracts 48–9
Preceding year basis 137
Preference debts 236
Preferences 260
  voidable
    'associate' 235
    grounds 234–5
    time limits 235

Private company
  dispensing with meetings 128–9
  public distinguished 322–3
  purchase of own shares 120–1
  reregistration as public company 325–6
  reregistration of public company as 326–7
Profit and loss accounts 294–5
Profitability 299
Profits, retained 189
  corporation tax 176
  future taxation 176
Promoters 48
Public company 321–9
  private distinguished 322–3
  reregistration as private company 326–7
  reregistration of private company as 325–6
  see also Companies, limited by shares; limited by guarantee *or* unlimited
Purchase of own shares 99–104, 119–21, 324
  CGT 162–3
  financial assistance 324

Qualifications, recognition across EC 214–15
Quick succession relief 158
Quorum 128
Quoted company 43

Ratification
  agency 76
  of director's breach 68
Ratios 299–300
Re-investment relief 151–2
Receivers
  appointment 282
    by debenture-holder 112
  partnerships 24
Receivership 242
  administrative receivers
    definition 248
    powers and duties 248–9
  nature of 248
Register of charges 56, 57, 108–9, 110
Register of directors 56, 69–70
Register of directors' interests 56, 70
Register of members 56
  contents 80–1
  rectification 81
Register of secretaries 56, 79
Registered office 51, 54
Registrar of Companies
  official notification 290
  returns 69
    of allotment 98
    failure to file 292
    of meetings 129
Registration
  limited companies 40–1
  public and private companies 323
  statutory declaration of compliance 54
  see also Reregistration
Registration fee 54
Remuneration, partners 13–14, 141–2
Representative actions 85
Reregistration
  private company as public 325–6
  public company as private 326–7

Resolutions
  article provisions 129
  documentation 129
  elective 125
  extraordinary 124–5
  notification of auditors 129
  ordinary 124
  recording 129
  special 124
  written 325
Restraint of trade 340
Restrictive covenants 286
  exclusive distributorship agreement 349–50
  income tax on payments 186
Retained profits 189
  corporation tax 176
  future taxation 176
Retirement provision
  choice of business medium 318
  partnerships 198–203
    capital gains tax 198–202
    income tax 198–9
    inheritance tax 202–3
    see also Partners, retirement
  personal pensions 318
Retirement relief 148–9, 154
  business assets owned by investor 156
  conditions 154–5
  partnership 154
  sale of business to company 305
Return of allotment 98
Roll over relief 154
  business assets 150
  business assets owned by investor 156
  sale of business to company 305
Royal British Bank v Turquand rule 75

Sale of business to company
  capital allowances 302
  capital tax relief 304
  disposal 302–3
  retirement relief 305
  roll over relief 305
  stamp duty 305–7
  value added tax 305, 308
Scientific research allowance 195
Seal 55
Searches see Company searches
Secondary market 159, 161, 328
Secret profits
  directors 67–8
  partnerships 9–10
Secretary 314, 322
  appointment 76
  first 54, 76
  register of secretaries 79
  responsibilities and powers 76–7
Self-assessment
  partnership capital gains 153
  sole traders 136–7
Separate legal personality 44
  agency and trusts 45
  avoiding legal obligations 45
  lifting veil 44–6
Service contracts
  directors 57, 62, 70, 72, 284
  managing directors 72

Shadow directors 72–3
Share capital
  in articles 272
  authorised minimum 42, 322
  authorised share capital 53
  capital clause 53, 113
    increase 113–14
    reduction 114
  differences between public and private 322
  increase 113–14
  issued capital 53
  maintenance 98–9, 114, 324
  nominal capital increase 113–14
  nominal value 322
  paid up capital 53
  pre-emption rights on allotment 324
  public companies, payment for 323–4
  purchase of own shares 99–104, 119–21, 162–3, 324
  reduction 114
  risk 311–13
  share premium account 99
Share issue see Issue of shares
Share premium account 99
Shareholders 79–93
  agreements see Shareholders agreement
  contract between members 82–3
  contract between members and company 81–2
  derivative actions 86
  dividends see Dividends
  duties 82
  Foss v Harbottle
    exceptions 84–5
    majority rule 84
  implied contracts 84
  index of members 56
  internal disputes 82–8
  membership in articles 44
  membership rights 79–80, 83
  numbers 322
  powers
    powers of control 81–2
    sources 81
  powers of court
    alteration of memorandum or articles 88
    civil proceedings authorisation 87
    orders 87
    purchase of petitioner's shares 87–8
  profits of company 88–9
  protection 80
  register of members 56, 80–1
    rectification 81
  representative actions 85
  trusts 81
  unfair prejudice 86–7
  voting 285
  winding up entitlement 256
  withdrawal from company 285–6
Shareholders agreement 84
  advantages 283–4
  approval of policy decisions 284–5
  arbitration clause 286
  directors appointment and service contracts 284
  directors' duties 286
  drafting 284–6
  enforcement 287
  enforcement of articles 284
  legal limits 286–7

375

INDEX

Shareholders agreement — *continued*
  payment of dividends 286
  power to alter articles 286
  protection of interests 283–4
  restrictive covenants 286
  secrecy 283
  share issue 285
  veto 284
  voting rights 285
  withdrawal from company 285–6
Shares
  bonus shares 176
  buy-back 99–100, 120, 162–3, 324
  capital gains tax 154–5, 162–3
  classes 104
    dividends 90
    rights alteration 277
  disposal *see* Transfer of shares
  financial assistance for purchase 104, 120–1, 324
  inheritance tax on 160–2
  issue *see* Issue of shares
  legal nature 96
  listing *see* Stock Exchange listing
  nominal value 96
  par value 96
  payment for
    consideration 98
    premium 98
  pre-emption rights 118–19
  purchase of own shares 99–104, 119–21, 162–3, 324
  redeemable 99, 100, 119
  rights attached to 96
  transfer *see* Transfer of shares
  transmission 119
  value 96
'Shelf' company *see* 'Off the peg' company
Show of hands 128
Small companies 43, 293
Social security payments
  choice of medium and 318
  directors 180–1, 186
  see also National insurance contributions
Sole traders
  capital risk 311–13
  expenses of formation 313–14
  flexibility 314
  income tax *see* Income tax, sole traders
  management 314
  sale of business to company
    capital gains tax 302–4
    capital tax relief 304
    company law 308
    employment law 307–8
    income tax 301–2
    novation 309
    retained assets 304–5
    stamp duty 305–7
    value added tax 305, 308
Solvency ratios 299
Sponsor, approved 328, 329
Stamp duty
  charge to tax and 306
  items outside charge to tax 306–7
  rates 307
  sale of business to company 305–7
  savings 307
  transfer of shares 116–17

Stationery 56
Statutory books
  articles of association *see* Articles of association
  directors' service contracts 57, 62
  index of members 56
  inspection 57
  instruments creating charges 57
  memorandum of association *see* Memorandum of association
  minutes of meetings 57, 129
  register of charges 56, 57
  register of directors 56, 69–70
  register of directors' interests 56, 70
  register of members 56, 80–1
  register of secretaries 56
Stock Exchange listing
  admission requirements 328
  advantages and disadvantages 327–8
  'approved sponsor' 328, 329
  continuing obligation 329
  EC harmonisation 328
  initial public offering 329
  intermediaries offer 329
  introduction 329
  offer for sale 329
  placing 329
  subscription offer 329
Stock in trade 306
Stock transfer form 116
Stock valuation 135–6
Subscription offer 329

'Tailor made' company 49, 57
  see also 'Off the peg' company
Taxation
  CGT *see* Capital gains tax
  corporation tax *see* Corporation tax
  death of taxpayer 152
  debentures 186–7
    deduction of tax 187
    loan relationships 186
    paying company taxation 186–7
    recipient taxation 187–8
  directors' fees
    benefits 180
    benefits in kind 182–4
    compensation for loss of office 180
    'emolument' 181
    employee perspective 181–6
    employing company's perspective 179–81
    'employment' 181
    fees or interest 188
    limitation on deductibility 180
    national insurance payments 180–1
    'office' 181
    schedule E charge 181
    social security contributions 180–1, 186
    taxable receipts 182
    terminal payments 184–5
  distributions
    ACT 177
    definition 176–7
    recipient taxation 178–9
    shadow ACT 178
    surplus ACT 177
  dividends 188–9
  income *see* Income tax

INDEX

Taxation — *continued*
  interest on loans to invest   188
  legislation   46
  limited liability partnerships   359
  retained profits   189
    corporation tax   176
    future taxation   176
  VAT *see* Value added tax
Terminal payments
  expenses   186
  gardening leave   184
  golden handshake   184–5
  restrictive covenant payments   186
Trade marks   349
Trading
  fraudulent   45
  wrongful   45, 227, 259–60
Transactions at undervalue   234, 260
  relevant time   260–1
Transactions defrauding creditors   233–4, 261
Transfer of shares   115–19, 315
  in articles   272–4
  contract for sale   116
  CREST   116
  financial involvement by company   120
  instrument of transfer   116
  offer to existing members   273–4
  power to refuse to register   273
  pre-emption rights   118–19
  procedure   116
  purchase of shares   274
  restrictions   117–18
  stamp duty   116–17
  stock transfer form   116
  transmission by operation of law   119
Transfer of undertakings
  employees   307–8
  see also Sale of business to company
Trustee in bankruptcy
  appointment
    by court   231
    by creditors   231
    by Secretary of State   231
  functions   231
  powers   231–2
  property not available to   233
  removal   232
  resignation   232
  vesting of assets   233
Trusts   81
Turquand rule   75

Ultra vires doctrine   51–2
Undervalue transactions   234, 260
  relevant time   260–1
  transfer to associate   235
Unfair prejudice
  grounds   86
  rights prejudiced   86–7
  tests for   86

Value added tax
  accounting for   209–10
  amount payable   209–10
  calculation   210
  charging to customers   209
  de-registration   208

Value added tax — *continued*
  fraction   210
  invoice to customers   209
  registration
    de-registration   208
    documentation   208
    effect   208
    'person'   208
    turnover limits   207–8
  return   209
  sale of business to company   305, 308
  taxable supplies   208
  rates of tax on   208
Veto, in shareholders agreement   284
Voluntary arrangements (companies)   241
  administration and   250
  debt
    composition   246
    for equity swap   247
  implementation of scheme by supervisor   247
  meetings of members and creditors   247
  moratorium   247–8
  nominee's report   246
  proposals   246–7
Voluntary arrangements (individuals)
  creditors' meeting
    acceptance of proposal   238
    challenging decision   238–9
    debtor's proposal consideration   238
  debtor's proposals
    consideration   238
    effect of accepting   238
  deeds of arrangement   237
  interim order
    application by debtor   237
    debtors to provide statements to nominee   238
    discharge   238
    effect   237
    failure of nominee to deliver report   238
    period   237
    procedure after making   238
  nominee's report to court   238
Voluntary arrangements (partnerships)   257
Voluntary winding up
  commencement   251
  conversion from members' to creditors'   252
  creditors'   251–2
  liquidator   252
  members'   251
Voting   128, 285
  restrictions on directors   274–5

Winding up   242
  administration order and   243, 246
  assets
    company property   254
    distribution and collection   254
    in hands of company   254
    held on trust   254
    power to disclaim   254
    power to sell or charge   254
    priority *see* order of entitlement
    subject to retention of title   254
  compulsory
    discretion of court to refuse order   251
    grounds   250
    liquidators   252

INDEX

Winding up — *continued*
    locus standi 251
  costs 255
  dissolution at end of 256
  just and equitable 88
  liquidators
    compulsory liquidation 252
    functions 252–3
    powers 252–3
    voluntary liquidation 252
  order of entitlement
    creditors with fixed charges 254–5
    creditors with floating charge 256
    interest on debts 256
    ordinary creditors 256
    preferential creditors 255

Winding up — *continued*
    shareholders 256
    winding up costs 255
  partnerships 256–7
  proceedings against company 253
  voluntary
    commencement 251
    conversion from members' to creditors' 252
    creditors' 251–2
    liquidators 252
    members' 251
Work in hand 135–6
Wrongful trading 45, 227
  defence 259–60
  grounds 259